# Accounting
## Studies in Global Business

*Edited by*

Shurveer S. Bhanawat

ATLANTIC

PUBLISHERS & DISTRIBUTORS (P) LTD

Published by

**ATLANTIC**

**PUBLISHERS & DISTRIBUTORS (P) LTD**

7/22, Ansari Road, Darya Ganj,
New Delhi-110002
Phones : +91-11-40775252, 23273880, 23275880, 23280451
Fax : +91-11-23285873
Web : www.atlanticbooks.com
E-mail : orders@atlanticbooks.com

Branch Office
5, Nallathambi Street, Wallajah Road,
Chennai-600002
Phones : +91-44-64611085, 32413319
E-mail : chennai@atlanticbooks.com



ISBN: 978-81-269-1932-1



Printed in India at Nice Printing Press, A-33/3A, Site-IV,
Industrial Area, Sahibabad, Ghaziabad, U.P.

# Preface

It gives me great pleasure to present the book entitled *Accounting Studies in Global Business* which is an outcome of International Conference on Global Business Research (special Reference to Human Resource, Banking and Accounting) held during 20-22 September 2012 under the joint auspices of Master of Human Resource Management and Master of Banking and Insurance programme of Mohanlal Sukhadia University, Udaipur, Rajasthan.

Every conference is a mirror of academic activities and events which opens many avenues of learning about research problems and deliberations. The main objective of the international conference was to develop an understanding about the changes that took place in the field of accounting at global level. Major changes in this field are: Introduction of International Financial Reporting Standard (IFRS), Carbon Credit Accounting, shifting of Government Cash Accounting system to Accrual Accounting system, Activity-Based Accounting, introduction of Extensible Business Reporting Language (XBRL), Financial Reporting, and Audit Agent with Net Knowledge (FRAANK), etc. All these issues were discussed elaboratively in the conference.

The book contains research papers relating to the performance measurement techniques, stock market related issues, financial reporting, carbon credit accounting related issues, and human resource accounting, investment options, activity-based costing, just-in-time production system, and direct tax code.

The first paper by Dr. Shurveer S. Bhanawat and Amitha Singhvi is "Global Business Research in the Field of Performance Measurement of a Firm". Over the past two decades, many pharmaceutical companies have started using the modern performance measures like Economic Value Added, Market Value Added and cash flow ratios in order to evaluate their financial performance. But the study clearly indicates that in Indian pharmaceutical industry, there is no strong relationship between MVA/IC and differential financial variables including traditional as well as modern.

The second paper, "New Firm's Measures at the Initial Performance of Indian IPOs: A Binary Probit Analysis", by Rohit Bansal and Ashu Khanna is based on analysing various ex-ante uncertainty determinants which affect the level of underpricing of Initial Public Offerings (IPOs). They have tested the relationship between new firms and all ex-ante uncertainty by using probit regression approach. The results show that ex-ante information has a significant positive impact on the initial returns, while the ownership structure has a significant negative effect on short-run underpricing.

Organizations all over the world have witnessed business growth by following mergers and acquisitions in the banking industry. Nidhi Nalwaya and Rahul Vyas in the third paper, "Mergers and Acquisitions: A Pre-Post Analysis of Financial Performance from the Banking Industry", make a comparative analysis of the impact of mergers on financial performance of the ICICI Bank with Bank of Rajasthan. They conclude that profitability, earning growth and dividend growth of the sample bank attained better results in the post-merger period. All these financial parameters are tested through student 't' test.

The fourth paper by B.L. Heda and Gaurav Mandot, "Impact of Disinvestment on Financial Performance of Public Enterprises", studies the impact of disinvestment in MUL and NTPC in terms of profitability. It shows that the sample companies reported worsening position of liquidity and solvency in post-disinvestment period, while activity rations show good position in post-disinvestment period.

The fifth paper, "Return on Equity Decomposition in Banking Sector: A Case Study of Selected Public Sector Banks in India", by Dr. Hanuman Prasad and Varsha Maheshwari highlights Return on Equity (ROE) as performance measurement of banking industry. Their study is based on the performance of five public sector banks over the period of eight years which seems sufficient to establish the trend. Earnings, efficiency, risk taking and leverage are important financial parameters to analyse the banks' profitability. All these parameters are covered in the paper.

G. Soral and Shilpa Lodha have developed a regression model by adopting a dummy variable to predict the effect of season on BSE sensex returns. Before developing the model they tested the stationary prices of BSE sensex. Graphical method, correlation test and unit root test were used to check the stationary data in series. These issues are discussed in sixth paper, "Seasonality in Indian Stock Market: An Application of Dummy Variable Regression Model."

Seventh paper, "Foreign Direct Investment, Economic Growth and Stock Market Relationship: Empirical Evidence from India", written by Kamlesh Pritwani and Naveen Kumar Sharma examines the relationship of FDI with GDP, BSE sensex and NSE–CNX Nifty by applying the descriptive statistics as well as regression model. They find that FDI inflows contribute to increase of GDP, BSE and NSE sensex, and suggest to implement the FDI Policy in India.

How gold prices are correlated with inflation, crude oil and US dollar is the focus of eighth paper, "Commodity ETF as an Alternative Investment Option", written by Anil Kothari and Pallavi Kudal who have studied the proper reasoning of the movement of gold prices in past years linking it with political events, wars and emergencies. The gold prices from the years 2005-2009 are analyzed with the help of multivariate analysis. They find that gold is well correlated with crude oil and Nifty, and not with dollar. Gold ETF does provide an ease in investment, and trading in gold as holding physical gold is not that safe but one needs to have in-depth analysis of the market for indulging in gold ETFs.

The relationship between the dividend payout and the market price of shares is the focus of ninth paper, "A study on Impact of Dividend Policy on Market Price of Shares". O.P. Jain and Renu Choudhary study the final dividend declared from 2003-2012 and yearly closing market price of the shares of ten companies listed at Bombay Stock Exchange. With the help of Karl Pearson method, they conclude in the paper that there exists a direct relation between dividend declared and the market price of shares. When the dividend declared by the companies is increasing, market price of the shares also increases.

Dr. Shurveer S. Bhanawat and Nidhi Bhanawat, the authors of tenth paper, "Recent Trends in Reporting of Intangible Assets in Selected Indian Companies", study the recent practices adopted in reporting and disclosure of intangible assets in selected sample Indian companies and analyze the item-wise and frequency-wise reporting practices of selected sample companies through content analysis. Data from 35 leading BSE Indian companies from the years 2007-2011 were collected. They find that some companies accept intangible assets as useful part of assets, while other selected companies follow skipping policies in reporting of intangible assets (IA). They suggest a standardized approach for reporting IA with end goal of creating a comprehensive IA accounting system that addresses all types of intangible assets whether developed or acquired by the organization.

In eleventh paper, "Fair Value Accounting: The Controversial Issue in IFRS With Special Reference to Property, Plant and Equipment", Neha Varyani and G. Soral study the fair value measurement about valuation of assets as per the valuation done as against the historical cost concept that goes on the same value in the balance sheet. Fair value measurement gives relevant and reliable information to the decision makers. They have identified two broad areas where fair value and IFRS intersect—the preparation of opening balance sheet—and the adoption of optional valuation models for ongoing accounting under IFRS. There are many factors to consider before making these decisions. They state that one must be aware of positives, negatives and the unknown. Twelfth paper, "Financial Irregularities in Cooperative Banks in Maharashtra", by S.H. Indurwade focuses on financial irregularities in Cooperative Banks of Maharashtra.

The next paper, "Disclosure of Valuation Principle of Work-in-Progress Inventory in Indian Corporate Sector", by Dr. Shurveer S. Bhanawat and Abhay Jaroli, analyzes 53 sample units of different sectors of Indian manufacturing industry. Only capital goods and electrical equipment sector has followed the AS-2 strictly. A very poor disclosure has been identified in automobile sector relating to valuation principle of raw material, work-in-progress and finished goods. All ten sectors of manufacturing industry do not have same disclosure pattern regarding valuation principle of work in progress.

Dharmendra Kumar gives a detailed information on the emerging concept of International Financial Reporting Standards (IFRS) in his paper, "New Issues in Accounting—IFRS". He explains the importance of IFRS like better transparency, better quality of financial reporting, substitution of historic value with fair value, global acceptance of Indian Chartered accountants, accurate risk evaluation, better international investors, etc. He also highlights the major challenges for Indian companies in adopting IFRS which include adjustment in policy and data analyzing, training and development, cost involved, supervision and project planning. He concludes that the challenges can be overcome and acceptance of IFRS will be done with ease.

In fifteenth paper, "Corporate Governance Practices in Information Technology Industry in India", Swati Patel studies the adherence of government norms by major IT companies of

India. Analysis of four major IT companies (Infosys, TCS, Wipro and Tech Mahindra) has been done. The research shows that Infosys got the excellent corporate governance performance followed by Tech Mahindra, Wipro and TCS, respectively.

Different type of accounting and business information to different interest groups can be provided through a common electronic language known as Extensible Business Reporting Language (XBRL). In their paper, "XBRL: Exploring Adoption in India", Vivek Sharma and G. Soral present an overview of XBRL in the context of financial reporting through an opinion survey from professionals in India (Chartered Accountants, Cost Accountants, and Company Secretaries). The findings reveal automatic checking, validation of data, high speed in handling of data, accuracy, and no chance of manual error as major advantages of XBRL. The authors also identify major challenges in adopting XBRL in India.

O.P. Jain and Ravi Mandot, authors of "Accounting Issues of Carbon Credit trading", explain the concept of carbon trading and the accounting issues in relation to disclosure of carbon credit. To resolve the accounting issues, International Accounting Standards Board (IASB) had issued an interpretation IFRIC-3 on Emission Rights but later withdrew it, continuing the debate on inappropriate treatments of carbon credit. The authors in this paper discuss two possible accounting value methods for initial recognition of carbon credits, i.e. "cost, and fair value."

In eighteenth paper, "Carbon Credit in India", Veerta Tantia and Kavitha Jayakumara explain the market of selling and purchasing carbon credit. Carbon credits (CERs) are generated by the companies by lowering down the emission of carbon dioxide in environment by adopting green technology known as Clean Development Mechanism (CDM), or switching on to the renewable sources of energy. Many companies in India are generating revenues through the sale of CERs. In India, ICAI has formulated a guidance note on Accounting for Self Generated CERs. But accounting treatment and the disclosure of CERs in financial accounts still need proper guidelines and format.

In nineteenth paper, "Carbon Credit Trading (Special Reference to Sale of Carbon Credit)", the authors Ravi Mandot and Gaurav Mandot highlight the carbon trading mechanism. The three mechanisms are available to reduce carbon emission: Joint Implementation (JI), Clean Development Mechanism (CDM), and International Emission Trading (IET). They study the impact of share of sale of CERs to total revenue of organization. Four companies: Rajasthan State Mines and Minerals, Shree Cement Limited, Jaiprakash Power Venture Limited, and Sesa Goa Limited have been considered for research study. Their findings conclude that RSMML generated significant revenue from the sale of CERs as compared to other units of selected samples.

In twentieth paper, "Human Resources Accounting—Evolving Concepts and Measuring Value of Employees", the authors Bharti Pandya and N.K. Pandya study how the employees add value to the company's net worth (in terms of turnover). They have undertaken the study of four heavy-industries (BHEL, CCI, SAIL and HCL) and studied five-year data from 2006-2011. Their study shows that BHEL has the highest levels of value per employee, followed by SAIL, CCI and HCL, respectively. Value addition by employees leads to higher turnover, and better growth of the organization.

Alka Swami in the research paper, "Investment Options during Recession in Bikaner City", finds that majority of the respondents (out of 100 respondents) in Bikaner have significant amount of saving which results in low impact of recession on them. Return on investment came out to be the major reason for making any investment, followed by saving for future, tax benefit, and risk covering.

In the twenty-second research paper, "Activity-Based Costing: Reloaded", Vineet Chouhan, G. Soral and Shagufta Khan give a detailed conceptual idea about the activity-based costing (ABC) and activity-based management (ABM) and their prominent role in organization. They conclude that with the use of Life Cycle Coting, Integrated Target Costing, Resource Consumption Accounting and Time-driven ABC, the current system should be reloaded for excellent information.

The authors of twenty-third paper, "Just-in-Time Production System (JIPTS) in Developing Countries: The Indian Experience", Bhupesh Lohar and G. Soral highlight the benefits of JITPS in companies currently adopting the techniques in India and also the factors that hinder the adoption of techniques among companies not applying it. Their findings show that on an average, 54% of all incoming materials is purchased using JIT. Significant reduction of inventory, higher supplier reliability, improved quality and reduction of scrap costs are identified as major advantages of JIT.

In the last research paper, "Direct Tax Code: Boon or Bane for Non-Profit Organizations", Priyabrata Pandam, Sovan Mishra and Kishore Kumar Das analyze the impact of Direct Tax Code on NPO's and Trusts. Their objectives include to diagnose the provisions of the code for NPO's and trusts to find out the pains and gains for the concerned organizations, to study basic taxation structure, to compare the provision of IT Act, 1961 and DTC, and to know about the probable and expected effects of DTC on NPOs and Trusts. Personal interview has been used as a method of collecting data from professionals and NPO proprietors. They conclude that DTC has greater impact on NPOs.

Prominent among the dignitaries who contributed to the deliberations were Gajendra Singh Shaktawat, Parliamentary Secretary, Government of Rajasthan; Prof. Som Deo, Dean, Faculty of Commerce, Rajasthan University, Jaipur; B.P. Singh, former Dean, Delhi School of Economics, New Delhi; Vice Chancellor, Mohanlal Sukhadia University, and I.V. Trivedi. I am highly obliged to these dignitaries for their valuable suggestions and comments.

I express my sincere thanks to our learned contributors who have enriched the purpose, and satisfied the objective of the conference. I also express my thanks to the persons who helped and assisted the work of editing the volume directly and indirectly.

I cannot forget to extend our thanks to Atlantic Publishers & Distributors Pvt. Ltd., New Delhi for publishing the book.

**Shurveer S. Bhanawat**

# Contents

# 1

# GLOBAL BUSINESS RESEARCH IN THE FIELD OF PERFORMANCE MEASUREMENT OF A FIRM (A STUDY OF RELATIONSHIP OF MVA WITH DIFFERENT PERFORMANCE MEASURES)

–*Shurveer S. Bhanawat* and *Amitha Singhvi*

## Introduction

Everyone knows that performance pays but question is that how to measure the performance. Since a long period global business research is being carried out in the field of performance measure to identify a particular measure which can be used in business. No social study has ever been static. It has always evolved. Global business research shows that there are two specific categories of performance measures, viz., traditional performance measures and modern performance measures. Here an attempt has been made to study the relationship between MVA and different performance measures. The present literature includes MVA as modern performance measure.

Both measuring and analysing an organization's performance are necessary and vital. It is a true saying that "what can be measured can be managed". The purpose of measuring performance is not only to know how a business is performing but also to enable it to perform better. The ultimate aim of implementing a performance measurement system is to improve the performance of an organization so that it may better serve its customers, employees, owners and various other stakeholders. If the performance measurement can be done in a proper manner, it becomes very clear how the business is going on and what will be the future of the organization. Thus analysis of financial statements is an important aid to financial performance analysis. Financial performance analysis includes analysis and interpretation of financial statements in such a way that it undertakes full diagnosis of the profitability and financial soundness of the business. There are a number of performance measures available to analyse the financial statements. All these financial measures can be grouped into two categories, viz., (i) traditional performance measures and (ii) modern performance measures. Traditional performance measures include all financial ratios belonging to profitability, activity, solvency and ratios for prospective investors. Modern performance measures include cash flow ratios, Economic Value Added (EVA) and Market Value Added (MVA). In present research paper these types of performance measures including cash flow ratios are analysed in terms of mutual relationship with special reference to the Indian pharmaceutical industry.

### Objectives

1. To compute traditional performance measures as well as the modern performance measures including cash flow ratios of selected units of Indian pharmaceutical industry.
2. To examine the relationship of coefficient of market value added to invested capital (MVA/IC) with different performance measures.

### Major Hypothesis

1. There is no significant relationship between MVA/IC and different financial performance measures.

### Source of Data

This research study is based on secondary data. Secondary data has been collected through annual reports of the respective sample units, Bombay Stock Exchange official directory, electronic data base 'PROWESS' of CMIE (Centre for Monitoring Indian Economy), government publications, etc. The present research work required a variety of data. Websites like www.rbi.org.in, http://www.bseindia.com/, http://www.indiabulls.com/securities/, http://www.moneycontrol.com/stocksmarketsindia/, etc. have also been used. The risk free rates are taken from the website of RBI (www.rbi.org.in.). Data has also been collected from research papers and research reports published in various journals and websites.

### Sample Design

A sample of eight companies (out of sixteen) has been randomly drawn from all the pharmaceutical units that were listed at Bombay Stock Exchange and covered under "BSE 'A' Group" and published in *The Economic Times* on 31 July, 2007.

### Period of Study

A study of five financial years, i.e. 2002-03 to 2006-07 has been conducted for the purpose of present research work. A study of five years seems to be appropriate for establishing a trend.

### Statistical Tools and Techniques

Under the present research study statistical techniques like mean, standard deviation, coefficient of correlation, coefficient of variation, 't'-test, probable error based test of significance, etc. have been used.

### Analysis and Discussion

#### Objective No. 1

The first objective of the present research paper is to compute the traditional performance measures, i.e. financial ratios as well as the modern performance measures, i.e. EVA, MVA and cash flow ratios of the sample units. All these have been calculated by using the financial data available in the annual reports of the sample companies as well as with the help of websites of

BSE and India Bulls Securities. The financial measures that have been computed for this study are explained in the following paragraphs:

(a) **Traditional Performance Measures (Financial Ratios).** Twenty-two traditional financial ratios of the sample units under study have been calculated. These are ratios of the balance sheet and the income statement relating to profitability, liquidity, solvency, turnover, etc. The financial ratios of the eight sample units for a period of five years from 2002-03 to 2006-07 have been computed and the average for the five years is shown in Table 1.

**Table 1:** Traditional Ratios of the Pharmaceutical Industry at a Glance (in %)

| S.No. | Ratio/Year | 2002-03 | 2003-04 | 2004-05 | 2005-06 | 2006-07 | Average |
|---|---|---|---|---|---|---|---|
| | **Profitability Ratios** | | | | | | |
| 1. | Gross Profit Ratio | 35.70 | 23.89 | 20.54 | 23.18 | 27.53 | **26.17** |
| 2. | Net Profit Ratio | 20.19 | 16.27 | 13.82 | 16.25 | 20.74 | **17.45** |
| 3. | Operating Profit Ratio | 19.51 | 23.11 | 19.09 | 21.88 | 25.67 | **21.85** |
| 4. | Operating Ratio | 80.49 | 76.89 | 80.91 | 78.12 | 74.33 | **78.15** |
| | **Solvency Ratios** | | | | | | |
| 5. | Current Ratio | 3.21 | 3.29 | 3.05 | 3.63 | 4.27 | **3.49** |
| 6. | Quick Ratio | 1.81 | 2.03 | 1.93 | 2.51 | 3.04 | **2.26** |
| 7. | Debt Equity Ratio | 0.26 | 0.32 | 0.40 | 0.41 | 0.47 | **0.37** |
| 8. | Interest Coverage Ratio | 70.90 | 224.20 | 793.82 | 1450.85 | 1417.52 | **791.46** |
| | **Activity Ratios** | | | | | | |
| 9. | Inventory Turnover Ratio | 5.54 | 6.03 | 5.28 | 5.84 | 6.65 | **5.89** |
| 10. | Fixed Assets Turnover Ratio | 6.41 | 5.92 | 6.03 | 5.98 | 6.16 | **6.1** |
| 11. | Debtors Turnover Ratio | 8.42 | 8.57 | 8.15 | 9.20 | 10.21 | **8.91** |
| | **Ratios for Prospective Investors** | | | | | | |
| 12. | Earnings per Share | 31.92 | 37.37 | 23.26 | 25.95 | 36.10 | **30.92** |
| 13. | Dividend Payout Ratio | 29.65 | 33.02 | 50.40 | 44.42 | 40.05 | **39.51** |
| 14. | Return on Capital Employed | 29.43 | 29.69 | 22.19 | 23.42 | 26.71 | **26.29** |
| 15. | Return on Net Worth | 26.96 | 25.44 | 22.00 | 22.70 | 23.76 | **24.17** |
| 16. | Return on Long-Term Funds | 29.97 | 30.79 | 23.81 | 24.47 | 27.67 | **27.34** |
| 17. | Return on Investment | 25.83 | 26.44 | 19.15 | 19.65 | 22.29 | **22.67** |
| 18. | Return on Equity | 21.90 | 24.53 | 20.25 | 22.96 | 25.55 | **23.04** |
| 19. | Dividend Yield Ratio | 8.34 | 8.57 | 8.15 | 9.20 | 10.21 | **8.9** |

| | | | | | | |
|---|---|---|---|---|---|---|
| 20. Net Income Return on Equity | 170.21 | 160.75 | 155.21 | 136.92 | 136.47 | **151.91** |
| 21. Net Income Return on Assets | 134.06 | 125.67 | 111.36 | 101.20 | 99.67 | **114.39** |
| 22. Net Income Return on Sales | 103.83 | 103.24 | 105.49 | 104.58 | 104.67 | **104.36** |

*Source*: Computed from Annual Reports of the Sample Units.

**(b) New Performance Measures (MVA, EVA and Cash Flow Ratios)**

**(i) MVA and EVA:** In this section the new performance measures MVA, EVA and cash flow ratios have been calculated. MVA and EVA, both being absolute figures, a computation of the coefficient of MVA and EVA with invested capital, i.e. MVA/IC and EVA/IC has also been done to make comparison more realistic. An average of these measures for the five years period of study is summarised in Table 2.

**Table 2:** Modern Financial Performance Measures of the Pharmaceutical Industry at a Glance (₹ in Crores)

| S.No. | Variable/Year | 2002-03 | 2003-04 | 2004-05 | 2005-06 | 2006-07 | Average |
|---|---|---|---|---|---|---|---|
| 1. | MVA | 1830.85 | 1808.82 | 3456.81 | 4466.28 | 8140.10 | **3941** |
| 2. | MVA/IC (in times) | 1.83 | 1.64 | 3.53 | 3.36 | 3.76 | **2.82** |
| 3. | EVA | 61.67 | 61.18 | 51.64 | 83.99 | 154.00 | **82.50** |
| 4. | EVA/IC (in times) | 0.09 | 0.11 | 0.08 | 0.10 | 0.06 | **0.09** |

*Source*: Computed from Annual Reports of the Sample Units.

**(ii) Cash Flow Ratios:** Cash flow ratios have been considered as modern financial performance measure, as suggested by various authors. Raymond E. Figlewicz and Thomas L. Zeller have identified eleven cash flow ratios. These ratios are calculated mainly from the cash flow statement of the companies. In the present study five ratios out of these eleven ratios have been computed. Due to difficulty in identifying the figures and the limitation of the present study the rest of the six ratios could not be computed. The average of these five cash flow ratios for the five years under study is shown in Table 3.

**Table 3:** Cash Flow Ratios of the Pharmaceutical Industry at a Glance (in %)

| S.No. | Ratio/Year | 2002-03 | 2003-04 | 2004-05 | 2005-06 | 2006-07 | Average |
|---|---|---|---|---|---|---|---|
| 1. | Operating Cash Return on Sales Ratio | 14.30 | 16.54 | 12.69 | 12.15 | 14.41 | **14.02** |
| 2. | Operating Cash Return on Assets Ratio | 18.18 | 20.51 | 14.48 | 12.94 | 14.19 | **16.06** |
| 3. | Operating Cash Return on Equity Ratio | 21.94 | 25.59 | 20.11 | 15.10 | 16.67 | **19.88** |
| 4. | Cash Flow Liquidity Ratio | 96.44 | 117.27 | 74.94 | 89.97 | 107.08 | **97.14** |

| | | | | | | |
|---|---|---|---|---|---|---|
| 5. | Cash Flow from Operations to Net Income | 13.85 | 16.00 | 12.35 | 11.49 | 13.56 | 13.45 |

*Source*: Computed from Annual Reports of the Sample Units.

### Objective No. 2

The second objective of this study is to examine the relationship of coefficient of market value added with invested capital (MVA/IC) with different traditional performance measures and modern performance measures. To attain this objective correlation among MVA/IC and different financial variables has been established.

**(i) Correlation among MVA/IC and Traditional Variables:** Here an attempt has been made to find out the correlation between MVA/IC and the traditional financial ratios. The ratio of MVA to invested capital of each company has been calculated and the correlation with the traditional financial ratios is established.

**Table 4:** Correlation Matrix (MVA/IC and Traditional Financial Variables)

| Variables/Year | 02-03 | 03-04 | 04-05 | 05-06 | 06-07 | Mean 'r' (a) | Pe | 6*pe (b) | Significant if a > b |
|---|---|---|---|---|---|---|---|---|---|
| MVA/IC & G/P Ratio | 0.18 | 0.32 | 0.78 | 0.78 | 0.43 | 0.50 | 0.23 | 1.38 | No |
| MVA/IC & N/P Ratio | 0.76 | 0.58 | 0.58 | 0.89 | 0.48 | 0.66 | 0.17 | 1.02 | No |
| MVA/IC & Operating Profit Ratio | 0.40 | 0.24 | 0.78 | 0.82 | 0.44 | 0.54 | 0.21 | 1.26 | No |
| MVA/IC & Current Ratio | 0.07 | –0.21 | 0.20 | –0.13 | 0.05 | 0.00 | 0.30 | 1.80 | No |
| MVA/IC & Quick Ratio | 0.13 | –0.24 | 0.31 | –0.13 | –0.15 | –0.02 | 0.30 | 1.80 | No |
| MVA/IC & Debt Equity Ratio | –0.46 | –0.77 | –0.82 | –0.64 | –0.57 | –0.65 | 0.17 | 1.02 | No |
| MVA/IC & Interest Coverage Ratio | 0.33 | 0.00 | 0.90 | 0.10 | –0.06 | 0.25 | 0.28 | 1.68 | No |
| MVA/IC & Inventory Turnover Ratio | –0.19 | –0.36 | 0.91 | 0.11 | –0.20 | 0.05 | 0.30 | 1.80 | No |
| MVA/IC & Fixed Assets Turnover Ratio | 0.19 | 0.44 | 0.66 | 0.72 | 0.38 | 0.48 | 0.23 | 1.38 | No |
| MVA/IC & EPS | 0.44 | 0.39 | 0.70 | 0.72 | 0.02 | 0.45 | 0.24 | 1.44 | No |
| MVA/IC & Dividend Payout Ratio | –0.11 | 0.56 | 0.12 | 0.42 | 0.24 | 0.25 | 0.28 | 1.68 | No |
| MVA/IC & Debtors Turnover Ratio | –0.05 | 0.28 | 0.32 | 0.76 | 0.40 | 0.34 | 0.26 | 1.56 | No |
| MVA/IC & Return on Capital Employed (%) | 0.00 | 0.14 | 0.75 | 0.85 | 0.51 | 0.45 | 0.24 | 1.44 | No |
| MVA/IC & Return on Net Worth (%) | 0.04 | 0.17 | 0.43 | 0.90 | 0.46 | 0.40 | 0.25 | 1.50 | No |
| MVA/IC & Operating Ratio | –0.40 | –0.24 | –0.78 | –0.82 | –0.44 | –0.53 | 0.21 | 1.26 | No |
| MVA/IC & Return on Investment | –0.02 | 0.10 | 0.75 | 0.88 | 0.56 | 0.45 | 0.24 | 1.44 | No |
| MVA/IC & Return on Equity | 0.28 | 0.20 | 0.51 | 0.88 | 0.32 | 0.44 | 0.24 | 1.44 | No |
| MVA/IC & Dividend Yield Ratio | –0.10 | 0.28 | 0.32 | 0.76 | 0.40 | 0.33 | 0.26 | 1.56 | No |
| MVA/IC & Net Income Return on Equity | –0.47 | –0.24 | 0.41 | 0.05 | –0.49 | –0.15 | 0.25 | 1.50 | No |
| MVA/IC & Net Income Return on Assets | –0.26 | –0.03 | 0.62 | 0.72 | 0.47 | 0.30 | 0.23 | 1.38 | No |
| MVA/IC & Net Income Return on Sales | 0.19 | 0.55 | 0.21 | 0.34 | 0.10 | 0.28 | 0.24 | 1.44 | No |

*Source*: Computed.

Table 4 shows the correlation between MVA/IC and traditional financial ratios. An analysis of the Table 4 clearly shows that the mean value 'r' in all the cases is less than 6 pe. This clearly indicates that there is no significant relationship of MVA/IC with the traditional financial ratios. However certain studies suggest that where the value of mean is greater than 0.5, even though less than 6 pe some significance can be established between the variables.

MVA/IC with net profit ratio, operating ratio, debt equity ratio and operating ratio indicate 'r' greater than 0.5. Hence, it can be concluded that these four ratios may have a slightly significant correlation with MVA/IC.

**(ii) Correlation among MVA/IC and modern financial variables:**

Table 5: Correlation Matrix (MVA/IC and Modern Financial Variables)

| Variables/Year | 02-03 | 03-04 | 04-05 | 05-06 | 06-07 | Mean 'r' (a) | Pe | 6*pe (b) | Significant if a > b |
|---|---|---|---|---|---|---|---|---|---|
| MVA/IC & Operating Cash Return on Sales Ratio | -0.08 | 0.23 | 0.52 | 0.67 | 0.22 | 0.31 | 0.23 | 1.38 | No |
| MVA/IC & Operating Cash Return on Assets Ratio | -0.34 | 0.04 | 0.60 | 0.75 | 0.29 | 0.27 | 0.24 | 1.44 | No |
| MVA/IC & Operating Cash Return on Equity Ratio | -0.57 | -0.05 | 0.48 | 0.76 | 0.09 | 0.14 | 0.25 | 1.50 | No |
| MVA/IC & Cash Flow Liquidity Ratio | -0.17 | -0.06 | 0.82 | 0.44 | 0.15 | 0.24 | 0.24 | 1.44 | No |
| MVA/IC & Cash Flow from Operations to Net Income | -0.09 | 0.21 | 0.46 | 0.68 | 0.22 | 0.30 | 0.23 | 1.38 | No |
| MVA/IC & EVA/IC | 0.42 | 0.20 | 0.72 | 0.82 | 0.42 | 0.52 | 0.17 | 1.04 | No |

*Source*: Computed.

Table 5 indicates the correlation between MVA/IC with different cash flow ratios and EVA/IC. It is clearly evident from the above table that the value of 'r' (mean) is less than 6 pe of the correlation. This means that there is no significant relationship between MVA/IC and cash flow ratios. Not a single cash flow ratio shows any significant relationship with MVA/IC. EVA/IC also does not indicate any significant relationship with MVA/IC.

### Testing the Hypothesis

The major hypothesis of the study is that there is no significant relationship between MVA/IC and different financial variables. To test this hypothesis correlation between MVA/IC and twenty-eight financial variables and was established for the period of five years from 2002-03 to 2006-07. The financial variables for the study include traditional ratios, cash flow ratios and EVA/IC. After finding the correlation between MVA/IC and the different financial variables for the five years under study their mean values have been computed. Probable Error based test of significance (actual mean of r is > 6 pe) has been applied to test the hypothesis. The mean value computed has been compared with the value of 6 pe. The correlation is significant if the value of mean is greater than 6 pe.

Table 4 shows the correlation between MVA/IC and traditional financial variables which consist of traditional financial ratios. An analysis of the Table 4 shows that the mean value 'r' in all the cases is less than 6 pe. This clearly indicates that there is no significant relationship of MVA/IC with the traditional financial ratios.

Table 5 indicates the correlation between MVA/IC and the new financial variables which include cash flow ratios and EVA/IC. It is clearly evident from the Table 5 that the value of 'r' (mean) is less than 6 pe of the correlation. This means that there is no significant relationship between MVA/IC and cash flow ratios. Not a single cash flow ratio shows any significant relationship with MVA/IC. EVA/IC also does not indicate any significant relationship with MVA/IC.

Therefore, the hypothesis that there is no significant relationship between MVA/IC and different financial variables is accepted. It can be concluded that there is no strong relationship between MVA/IC and different financial variables.

## Conclusion

Over the past two decades many companies have started using the modern performance measures in order to evaluate their financial performance. EVA, MVA and cash flow ratios are becoming very important apart from the traditional ratios in the financial evaluation of the companies. Many companies have also started publishing the same in their annual reports. But our study clearly indicates that with regard to the pharmaceutical industry in India that there is no strong relationship between MVA/IC and different Financial variables.

## REFERENCES

### Research Papers and Articles

Annual Reports of the eight sample companies for the period from 2002-03 to 2006-07.

Ali M. Ghanbari and V.S. More, (2007), "The Relationship between Economic Value Added and Market Value Added: An Empirical Analysis in Indian Automobile Industry". *The Icfai Journal of Accounting Research*, Vol. VI, No. 3.

Bhanawat, Shurveer S. (2013), "In Search of Prediction Model for Determination of Shareholders' Wealth", *Indian Journal of Accounting*, Vol. XLIV (2) June, pp. 53-67.

Carslaw, Charles A., and Mills, John R. (1991), "Developing Ratios for Effective Cash Flow Statement Analysis". *Journal of Accountancy*. New York: Nov. Vol. 172, Iss. 5; p. 63, 6 p.

Ferguson, Robert, and Dean Leistikow, (1998), "Search for the Best Financial Performance Measure: Basics are Better". *Financial Analysts Journal*, Vol. 54, No. 1, pp. 81-86.

Giacomino, Don E. and Mielkeand, David E. (1993), "Cash flows: Another approach to Ratio Analysis". *Journal of Accountancy*. New York: Mar. Vol. 175, Iss. 3; p. 55, 4 p.

Karen, Spinner (1997), "A New Tool to Measure Performance, Global Finance". New York: Nov. Vol. 11, Iss. 11; p. 24, 1 p.

Malik, Madhu (2004), "EVA and Traditional Performance Measures: Some Empirical Evidence". *The Indian Journal of Commerce*, Vol. 57, No. 2, April-June 2004, pp. 32-37.

Ramachandra Reddy, B. and Yuvaraja Reddy, B. (2007), "Financial Performance through Market Value Added (MVA) Approach". *The Management Accountant*, January 2007, pp. 56-59.

Thomas, L. Zeller and Raymond, E. Figlewich, "New Investing and Financing Activity Ratios from the Statement of Cash Flows Enhance Traditional Ratio Analysis in Assessing Future Cash Flows". *Mid-Atlantic Journal of Business*, Winter 1990, 26, 2, ABI/INFORM Global.

### Websites

http://www.bizwiz.ca/cash_flow_ratio_calculation_formulas/cash_flow_ratios

http://www.bseindia.com/

http://www.indiabulls.com/securities/

http://www.moneycontrol.com/stocksmarketsindia/

2

# NEW FIRM'S MEASURES AT THE INITIAL PERFORMANCE OF INDIAN IPOs: A BINARY PROBIT ANALYSIS

–*Rohit Bansal* and *Ashu Khanna*

## Introduction

In both the empirical and theoretic paradigms, one of the most examined phenomena in the finance literature is the pricing of Initial Public Offerings (IPOs). Arguably, the primary attraction of this subject to researchers is the empirically identified first trading day return (underpricing) which on average exceeds 18 per cent (Ibbotson, Sindelar and Ritter, 1994). Under the standard financial theory of efficient markets, such a predictable one-day return should not exist. Numerous theoretical models treat this observed initial return as an equilibrium return. For example, book-building theories such as (Benveniste and Spindt, 1989) argue that issuer conditions its final offer price and share quantity on information acquired through its underwriter's book-building effort, and that initial returns are compensations to informed investors for revealing their private information about the value of the IPO firm.

An alternative explanation is that some portion of the initial return reflects a supra-equilibrium return and that the efficient market hypothesis is violated. However, access to these undervalued securities is rationed. Some evidence documents that this market is inefficient is provided by Loughran and Ritter (2002) who demonstrate the initial returns are correlated with market returns before the offering, suggesting that public information is not fully incorporated into the offer price.

New firm's age is a variable of Ex-ante uncertainty, while the calculated level of underpricing. In this paper, we examine the association between firm firms with another Ex-ante uncertainty and to evaluate the probability however, older firms are less underpricing or less affected the degree of Ex-ante variables. We test binary probit regression using new issuing IPO firm's (dummy variable) as 1 other 0. In new issuing IPO firm's, we embody those firms which are incorporated their business according to Indian company Act, 1956 and started their business since 1 to 5 years. We distribute 1 to those firms which is started their business since 1 to 5 years otherwise 0. Probit regression discloses the relationship between new firms and other Ex-ante uncertainty variables. We tested QML (Huber/White) standard errors and covariance and Convergence achieved after 6 iterations and the Mc fredmann R square.

The remainder of the paper is organized as follows: Section 1 surveys the main reasons of why companies go public, and the ensuing preference for issuing firms age. Section 2 describes the sample of 82 Indian IPOs over the period Oct. 2008 to Dec. 2011. Section 3 analyzes the determinants of the Ex-ante uncertainty and investigates the nature of trade-off between Firm's age and Ex-ante uncertainty. Section 4 furnishes a Methodology and Probit regression. Sections 5 and 6 elaborates about Result and discussion respectively. Section 7 concludes the paper.

**Pricing Mechanism**

In a fixed-price offering (Fixed), the offer price is published in the prospectus without information gathering from potential investors. An increase in asymmetric information would lead to a winner's curse phenomenon, decreasing the participation of uninformed investors (Rock, 1986). Firms would accordingly be forced to underprice their shares in order to induce the first bids and create positive price cascades among investors (Welch, 1992). The need for a new procedure that reduces asymmetric information justifies the use of auction-like procedures.

Book-building efforts can either be aimed entirely at investors whose indications of interests are sought, or they can require some participation by retail investors, i.e., hybrid offerings. In this framework, underwriters may propose a retail tranche with an offer price that is either fixed (a fixed-price offer), or non-fixed (an open-price offer). In a hybrid offering where a book-building mechanism is combined with a fixed-price offer issuers and underwriters the offer price at the end of the pre-market period. Retail investors are less subject to the adverse selection problem observed in a pure fixed-price offer. Nevertheless, as retail investors can condition their demand based upon revealed interests in the book, hybrid mechanisms can cause cascades and thus higher underpricing. This explains the increased use of hybrid book-building procedures combined with an open-price offer. In this system, both open-price and book-building offerings are run simultaneously, and retail investors submit their orders in parallel to institutional investors.

***Theories and models of underpricing***

Therefore, a number of competing theoretical models have been developed to explain the initial underpricing of stocks. The main theories found in the IPO literature are the winner's curse hypothesis, book-building theories, and the principal-agent hypothesis, signaling theories, the law-suit avoidance hypothesis, the ownership and control hypothesis and the investor sentiment theory.

One of the most important models of underpricing is the one developed by (Rock, 1986) based on the winner's curse hypothesis. Rock distinguishes between informed and uninformed investors. If the issues are underpriced, IPOs will be oversubscribed by informed investors, resulting in a limited number of shares being available to uninformed investors. If the issues are overpriced, IPOs will be sold exclusively to uninformed investors who will earn negative initial returns. Thus, uninformed investors will be winning the entire issue but at an unfavorable price, creating a situation termed the winner's curse. In order to keep uninformed investors in the IPO market, securities are offered at a discount from their expected after market prices. Thus, according to the winner's curse theory, IPO underpricing should decrease if the information asymmetry between informed and uninformed investors is reduced.

Empirical studies have found evidence that the underpricing for IPOs of financial institutions is related to proxies for asymmetric information. Signaling (Allen and Faulhaber, 1989), Asymmetric information (Ibbotson, 1975), Offer size (W.L. Megginson and K.A. Weiss, 1991), Age of the firm (Muscarella and Vetsuypens, 1989), Market capitalization, (McDonald and Fisher, 1972), (Baker and Wurgler, 2007), Pricing mechanism (Bansal and Khanna, 2012), Determinants of ipo underpricing at NSE (Kumar, 2010), and Ownership structure at BSE (Bansal and Khanna, 2012a).

**Objectives**

To measures, the IPOs initial performance on first trading day. The aim of our study is to determine and analysis the various Ex-ante uncertainty determinants that affecting the level of underpricing. To testing the relationship between new firm's and with all Ex-ante uncertainty.

**Research Methodology**

***Sample selection***

Comprehensive lists of IPOs and listings were obtained direct from the Bombay Stock Exchange for the period Oct. 2008 to Dec. 2011. These were cross checked with national stock exchange websites, and from similar lists obtained from major brokerage houses to ensure accuracy in the case of India. It resulted in a list of 100 listings having taken place across the region during the period 2008 to 2011. We removed 18 IPO due to the unavailability of their firm-related data. Final sample size is 82 IPOs that were listed at Bombay Stock Exchange.

***Measure of underpricing***

Firstly, we calculate the return on i security, where we used Ri = (P1 – P0)/P0 in which, Ri = return on i security, P1 = Price of i security on first listing day, P0 = offer price of i security.

Equation Ri = (P1 – P0)/P0....................................(1)

Secondly, we calculate index return on corresponding days, where we used Mi = (Ii – I0)/I0 in which, Mi = market return on ith day, Ii = closing index at listing day, I0 = closing index at offer day.

Equation Mi = (Ii – I0)/I0....................................(2)

where P i0 is the offer price of the firm i, P i1 is the first day closing prices of the shares in firm i, and Ri1 is the total first day return on the stock. If markets are highly volatile such that there is a major change in the price of most stocks during the IPO period, then initial returns should be market adjusted. To compute the first day market adjusted return, the return of the market index is initially calculated as is the closing value of the market index on the issue date corresponding to the offering by firm i and P m0 is the value of the market index corresponding to the offering price of the firm i. The market adjusted return abnormal return for each IPO on the first trading day is therefore computed as: MAARO.

Finally, we calculate market adjusted return on security, where we taken Ri from equation (1) and Mi from equation (2).

Equation Maaro = {100* [(1 + Ri)/1 + Mi) – 1]}.............(3)

### Hypothesis modeling

On the based on our research problem, research objectives and empirical evidence about Ex-ante uncertainty and IPO underpricing, we formulated several hypotheses to check and test the validity and robustness of our results. We procure one-tailed t statistics and test it at 5% significance level.

### Null Hypothesis

**H0:** *There is no significant difference between several independent variables with the level of uderpricing.*

*Measure of pricing mechanism*

For the pricing mechanism again a dummy variable is used to indicate the presence of book build in ipo underpricing. The presence is shown with value equal to 1 and 0 otherwise.

**H1:** *There is negative link between book build pricing mechanism and level of underpricing*

*Offer timing (Difference between in days from offer date and listing date)*

Offer timing is a difference in days between the offer date and the first day listing date of IPOs. We transformed it into natural logarithm to make it as standard practice.

**H2:** *There is positive association between book build pricing mechanism and level of underpricing*

*Measures of ownership structure*

The ownership structure of a company comprises of a distribution of the size of investor shareholdings. Applying a single measure in the form of a proportion is to be sufficient to delineate distributions with varying shapes. Numbers of shares are holding by promoters and non-promoters. We have also taken the total percentage of their shares holding in the ownership structure. Afterwards we have converted it into the natural logarithms to make standardized value and to remove the hetroscadisticity.

**H3:** *There is positive significant relationship between Indian promoters and degree of underpricing.*

**H4:** *There is positive relationship between intuitional non promoters and level of underpricing.*

**H5:** *There is positive link between non intuitional non promoters and level of underpricing.*

*Measure of issue size (total amount to be raised)*

The issue size is measured as the total number of shares offered multiplied by the offer price. Again, the natural logarithm of this value is used as a standard practice and to remove hetroscadisticity.

**H6:** *There is negative significant connection between issue size and level of underpricing.*

*Measure of market capitalization*

The market capitalization is measured as the total number of shares multiplied by the market price per share. Again, the natural logarithm of this value is used as a standard practice and to remove hetroscadisticity.

**H7:** *There is optimistic significant relationship between market capitalizations and less underpricing.*

*Measure of subscription*

The subscription is measured as the total number of shares acquired by several investors on the day of offering. Again, the natural logarithm of this value is used as a standard practice and to remove hetroscadisticity.

**H8:** *There is negative relationship between subscription and level of underpricing.*

*Measure of number of share offered*

Number of share offered is measured by the total quantity of shares that issuing firm has offered to their investors. Afterwards we have converted it into the natural logarithms to make standardized value and to remove the hetroscadisticity.

**H9:** *There is positive relationship between number of share offered and degree of underpricing.*

**Results**

***ANOVA & WELCH Test result***

**Test for Equality of Means Between Series**

Sample: 1 82

Included observations: 82

| Method | df | Value | Probability |
|---|---|---|---|
| Anova F-test | (9, 810) | 1335.188 | 0.0000 |
| Welch F-test* | (9, 318.702) | 1729.189 | 0.0000 |

*Test allows for unequal cell variances.

**Analysis of Variance**

| Source of Variation | df | Sum of Sq. | Mean Sq. |
|---|---|---|---|
| Between | 9 | 17961.65 | 1995.739 |
| Within | 810 | 1210.728 | 1.494726 |
| Total | 819 | 19172.38 | 23.40950 |

**Category Statistics**

Table 1: ANOVA and WELCH result

| Variable | Count | Mean | Std. Dev. | Std. Err. of Mean |
|---|---|---|---|---|
| DEPVAR | 82 | 0.109756 | 0.314509 | 0.034732 |
| BB | 82 | 0.975610 | 0.155207 | 0.017140 |
| LOG_DIF_IN_AG | 82 | 2.970073 | 0.215914 | 0.023844 |
| LGNOOFSHARE | 82 | 16.55044 | 1.507279 | 0.166451 |
| LOGMKTCAP | 82 | 7.095889 | 1.935683 | 0.213760 |

| | | | | |
|---|---|---|---|---|
| LOGISSUESIZE | 82 | 5.416361 | 1.619507 | 0.178845 |
| LOGFORGP | 82 | 0.328417 | 1.033727 | 0.114156 |
| LOGFORNONP | 82 | 1.782401 | 1.284191 | 0.141815 |
| LOGINDNONP | 82 | 2.572124 | 1.334836 | 0.147408 |
| LOGSUBSC | 82 | 1.958564 | 1.279276 | 0.141272 |
| All | 820 | 3.975963 | 4.838336 | 0.168962 |

On the based of the above Table 1, it displaying the ANOVA value is 1335.18 and the probability approx. (0.00) at the degree of freedom 819 reveals the validity of ANOVA about the mean variance between new firm' age and Ex-ante uncertainty variables. Nevertheless, Welch 'F' test discloses the value of 1729.18 with probability approx. (0.00), verified the assumption of Welch's test about robustness of the model for Firm's age and all Ex-ante uncertainty.

***Descriptive statistics***

On the based of the descriptive statistics Table 2, it reveals that the mean value for all variables (0.10, 0.97, 16.55, 2.97, 0.32, 1.78, 2.57, 7.09, 1.95, 5.41). It indicates the highest mean value is 7.09 for market capitalization and low is 0.10 for new firm's age. Accordingly, Standard deviation value is describes the features for all Ex-ante variables.

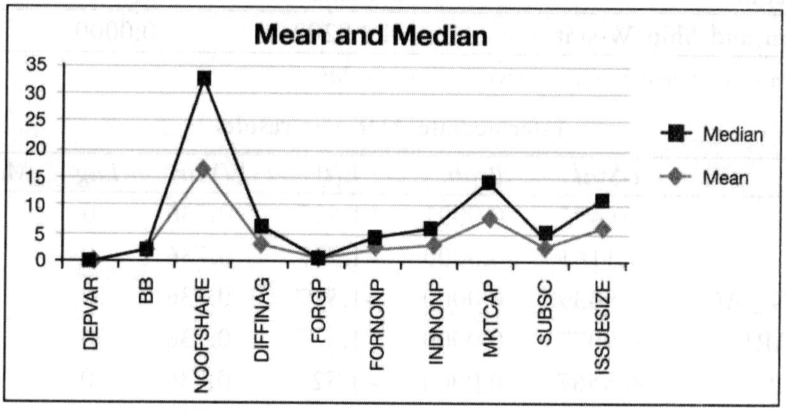


**Fig. 1:** Mean and median value for Ex-ante uncertainty variables.

Table 2: Descriptive results including Ex-ante uncertainty

| Name | DEPVAR | BB | NOOFSHARE | DIFFINAG | FORGP | FORNONP | INDNONP | MKTCAP | SUBSC | ISSUESIZE |
|---|---|---|---|---|---|---|---|---|---|---|
| Mean | 0.10 | 0.97 | 16.55 | 2.97 | 0.32 | 1.78 | 2.57 | 7.09 | 1.95 | 5.41 |
| Median | 0.00 | 1.00 | 15.96 | 2.94 | 0.00 | 2.13 | 2.85 | 6.72 | 1.79 | 4.98 |
| Maximum | 1.00 | 1.00 | 21.24 | 3.80 | 4.31 | 3.74 | 4.20 | 12.28 | 4.53 | 9.64 |
| Minimum | 0.00 | 0.00 | 14.64 | 2.63 | 0.00 | –2.99 | –4.44 | 4.17 | 0.00 | 3.14 |
| Std. Dev. | 0.31 | 0.15 | 1.50 | 0.21 | 1.03 | 1.28 | 1.33 | 1.93 | 1.27 | 1.61 |
| Skewness | 2.49 | –6.16 | 1.25 | 1.11 | 2.96 | –0.88 | –2.19 | 0.81 | 0.17 | 0.84 |
| Kurtosis | 7.23 | 39.02 | 3.76 | 4.93 | 10.2 | 3.65 | 10.92 | 2.87 | 1.73 | 2.81 |

| | | | | | | | | | | |
|---|---|---|---|---|---|---|---|---|---|---|
| Jarque-Bera | 146.46 | 4953.82 | 23.54 | 29.89 | 297.60 | 12.14 | 280.52 | 9.16 | 5.93 | 9.97 |
| Probability | 0.00 | 0.00 | 0.00 | 0.00 | 0.00 | 0.00 | 0.00 | 0.01 | 0.05 | 0.00 |
| Sum | 9.00 | 80.00 | 1357.13 | 243.54 | 26.93 | 146.15 | 210.91 | 581.86 | 160.60 | 444.14 |
| Sum Sq. Dev. | 8.01 | 1.95 | 184.02 | 3.77 | 86.55 | 133.58 | 144.32 | 303.49 | 132.56 | 212.44 |
| Observations | 82 | 82 | 82 | 82 | 82 | 82 | 82 | 82 | 82 | 82 |

### *Unit root test for stationarity*

**Null Hypothesis: Unit root (individual unit root process)**

Series: DEPVAR, BB, LOG_DIFF_IN__AG_, LGNOOFSHARE, LOGMKTCAP, LOGISSUESIZE, LOGFORGP, LOGFORNONP, LOGINDNONP, LOGSUBSC

Exogenous variables: Individual effects

Automatic selection of maximum lags

Automatic lag length selection based on HQC: 0 to 1

Total number of observations: 809

Cross-sections included: 10

**Table 3:** Unit root testing for stationarity of dependent variable

| Method | Statistic | Prob.** |
|---|---|---|
| **Im, Pesaran and Shin W-stat** | –24.8202 | 0.0000 |

** Probabilities are computed assuming asympotic normality.

**Intermediate ADF test results**

| *Series* | *t-Stat* | *Prob.* | *E(t)* | *E(Var)* | *Lag* | *Max Lag* | *Obs* |
|---|---|---|---|---|---|---|---|
| DEPVAR | –10.475 | 0.0001 | –1.527 | 0.736 | 0 | 11 | 81 |
| BB | -9.1161 | 0.0000 | –1.527 | 0.736 | 0 | 11 | 81 |
| LOG_DIFF_IN__AG_ | -6.9439 | 0.0000 | –1.527 | 0.736 | 0 | 11 | 81 |
| LGNOOFSHARE | -6.9077 | 0.0000 | –1.527 | 0.736 | 0 | 11 | 81 |
| LOGMKTCAP | -6.8567 | 0.0000 | –1.527 | 0.736 | 0 | 11 | 81 |
| LOGISSUESIZE | –6.8023 | 0.0000 | –1.527 | 0.736 | 0 | 11 | 81 |
| LOGFORGP | –9.4394 | 0.0000 | –1.527 | 0.736 | 0 | 11 | 81 |
| LOGFORNONP | –9.5012 | 0.0000 | –1.527 | 0.736 | 0 | 11 | 81 |
| LOGINDNONP | –8.9226 | 0.0000 | –1.527 | 0.736 | 0 | 11 | 81 |
| LOGSUBSC | -7.6882 | 0.0000 | –1.525 | 0.750 | 1 | 11 | 80 |
| **Average** | **–8.2653** | | **–1.527** | **0.737** | | | |

On the based upon the Table 4, exhibits that the unit root testing to check the stationarity of data. We execute Im, Pesaran and Shin test to validate the unit root problem about the firm's age and other Ex-ante uncertainty. At the results, test statistics acquired the value of –24.82, which reject the null hypothesis that contains that, Series is having a unit root problems. As the result, we reveal that there is no unit root problem exists in the model.

***Probit regression by (QML & Huber/White)***

Dependent Variable: DEPVAR

Method: ML - Binary Probit (Quadratic hill climbing)

Sample: 1 82

Included observations: 82

Convergence achieved after 6 iterations

QML (Huber/White) standard errors & covariance

**Table 4:** Probit regression for Ex-ante uncertainty

| Variable | Coefficient | Std. Error | z-Statistic | Prob. |
|---|---|---|---|---|
| C | –2.831376 | 6.759811 | –0.418854 | 0.6753 |
| BB | –0.834349 | 0.746090 | –1.118295 | 0.2634 |
| LOG_DIFF_IN_AG_ | –0.398312 | 1.065988 | –0.373656 | 0.7087 |
| LOGFORGP | 0.222662 | 0.194927 | 1.142282 | 0.2533 |
| LOGNONISNONP | 0.486436 | 0.234585 | 2.073604 | 0.0381* |
| LOGINSTNONP | –0.062617 | 0.164374 | –0.380943 | 0.7032 |
| LOGISSUESIZE | –1.618349 | 0.785756 | –2.059608 | 0.0394* |
| LOGMKTCAP | 0.892966 | 0.533238 | 1.674610 | 0.0940** |
| LOGSUBSC | –0.338674 | 0.172518 | –1.963123 | 0.0496* |
| LGNOOFSHARE | 0.333195 | 0.330481 | 1.008212 | 0.3134 |
| McFadden R-squared | 0.262492 | Mean dependent var | | 0.109756 |
| S.D. dependent var | 0.314509 | S.E. of regression | | 0.277957 |
| Akaike info criterion | 0.754266 | Sum squared resid | | 5.562709 |
| Schwarz criterion | 1.047768 | Log likelihood | | –20.92489 |
| Hannan-Quinn criter. | 0.872102 | Deviance | | 41.84979 |
| Restr. deviance | 56.74484 | Restr. log likelihood | | –28.37242 |
| LR statistic | 14.89505 | Avg. log likelihood | | –0.255182 |
| Prob (LR statistic) | 0.093859 | | | |
| Obs with Dep = 0 | 73 | | Total obs | 82 |
| Obs with Dep = 1 | 9 | | | |

**Estimation Equation**

I_DEPVAR = C(1) + C(2)*BB + C(3)*LOG_DIFF_IN__AG_ + C(4)*LOGFORGP + C(5)*LOGFORNONP + C(6)*LOGINDNONP + C(7)*LOGISSUESIZE + C(8)*LOGMKTCAP + C(9)*LOGSUBSC + C(10)*LGNOOFSHARE

**Substituted Coefficients**

DEPVAR = 1-@CNORM (-(-2.83137641426 – 0.83434904126*BB – 0.398312271571*LOG_DIFFIN_AG + 0.222661553064* LOGFORGP + 0.486435625654*LOGFORNONP – 0.0626172297357* LOGINDNONP – 1.6183493561*LOGISSUESIZE + 0.892966445683* LOGMKTCAP – 0.338673777398* LOGSUBSC + 0.333195239581* LGNOOFSHARE))

## Results and Discussions

Derived on the binary probit regression results, it was constructed that the entire variables were regressed against the level of underpricing. There is no significant association between book build pricing mechanism, and the new firms age at 5% significance level ( z = –1.11). Therefore, the null hypothesis is accepted. A result reveals that there is no weighty relationship between offer timing, and the new firms age at 5% significance level (z = –.37). As the results, the null hypothesis is acknowledged. It reveals that there is no significant link between foreign promoters and degree of underpricing @ 5% significance level (z = 1.147). In addition to, the null hypothesis is accepted. It examines for no consequential association between institutional non promoters and level of underpricing @ 5% significance level (z = –.381). There is no significant link between institutional non promoters and underpricing. For this reason, a null hypothesis is accepted.

There is a relevant association between non institutional non promoters with a degree of underpricing at 5% significant level (z = 2.7075). It indicates that, there is a positive significant relationship between non institutional non promoters and firm's age. Nevertheless, the null hypothesis is rejected. It founded for significant relation of issue size at the level of underpricing at 5% significance level (z = –2.05). It expresses the negative link between numbers of share offered with the firm's age. Therefore, the null hypothesis is rejected. There is a weighty association between market capitalization with firm's age at 5% significant level (z = 1.6775). It indicates that, there is a positive significant relationship between market capitalization and firm's age. At the same time, the null hypothesis is rejected. Results disclose the significant association between subscription with the firm's age at 5% significance level (z = –1.96). It obtains the negative association between subscription rate and the firm's age. At consequences, the null hypothesis is rejected. It founded for no significant relation of the number of share offered at the level of underpricing at 5% significance level (z = –1.005). It expresses no link between numbers of share offered with the firm's age. Therefore, the null hypothesis is accepted.

## Conclusions

Taking into account all firms which contain finished public on the official market of the Stock Exchange of Bombay for the period 2009 until 2011, this study examines the evidence on the short-run underpricing of IPOs. In particular, an average underpricing level within the range 50% is found based on first day. Using a probit regression approach, the degree of underpricing in terms of new firm's age is explained by the ex-ante uncertainty hypothesis and the ownership structure hypothesis. However, there is limited support for the signaling hypothesis. In particular, the results show that the ex-ante information and have a significant positive impact on the initial returns while the ownership structure has a significant negative effect on short-run underpricing. The results obtained from this study show that new issues on the BSE are subject to underpricing, consistent with developed and other emerging markets. In this respect, prospective investors should pursue the strategy of buying the new issues at the offer and selling them immediately on the first day of trading. However, the study also reveals that investors should not hold new issues very long as the highest component of the initial returns is establish on the first day of trading.

## REFERENCES

Allen, F. and Faulhaber, G. (1989), "Signaling by underpricing in the IPO market", *Journal of Financial Economics*, Vol. 23, pp. 303-23.

Bansal, R. and Khanna, A. (2012), "Pricing mechanism and explaining underpricing of ipos, evidence from Bombay stock exchange India", *International Journal of Research in Finance and Marketing*, Vol. 2, No. 2, pp. 205-16.

Bansal, R. and Khanna, A. (2012a), "Does ownership structure affecting IPO underpricing: A case of Indian stock market". *International Journal of Business Economics and Management Research*, Vol. 3, No. 5, 39-51.

Benveniste, L.M. and Spindt, P.A. (1989), "How investment bankers determine the offer price and allocation of new issues, *Journal of Financial Economics*, Vol. 24, pp. 343-61.

Dolvin, S.D. and Jordan, B.D. (2008), "Underpricing, overhang, and the cost of going public to pre-exiting shareholders", *Journal of Business Finance and Accounting*, Vol. 35, pp. 434-58.

Ibbotson, R.G. (1975), "Price performance of common stock new issues", *Journal of Financial Economics*, Vol. 2, pp. 235-72.

Loughran, T. and Ritter, J.R. (1994), "Initial Pubic Offerings: International Insights", *Pacific Basin Finance Journal*, Vol. 2, pp. 165-99.

Rock, K. (1986), "Why new issues are underpriced?", *Journal of Financial Economics*, Vol. 15, pp. 187-212.

Ritter, J.R. (1991), "The Long Run Performance of Initial Public Offerings", *The Journal of Finance*, Vol. 46, pp. 3-27.

Saito, Richard and Paulo Maciel, Luiz (2006), "Underpricing of Brazilian IPOs, Empirical Evidence from 1999 to 2005", *Global Finance Conference Proceeding*, Rio de Janeiro, Brazil.

Sherman, A.E. (2000), "IPOs and long term relationships, an advantage of book building", *Review of Financial Studies*, Vol. 13, pp. 697-714.

Welch, I. (1989), "Seasoned offerings, imitation costs and the underpricing of initial public offerings", *Journal of Finance*, Vol. 47, pp. 695-732.

# 3

# MERGERS AND ACQUISITIONS: A PRE-POST ANALYSIS OF FINANCIAL PERFORMANCE FROM THE BANKING INDUSTRY

–*Nidhi Nalwaya* and *Rahul Vyas*

## Introduction

Mergers result in the combination of two or more companies into one, wherein merging entities lose their identities. No fresh investment is made through this process. However, an exchange of shares takes place between the entities involved in such process. Generally, the company that survives is the buyer which retains its identity and the seller company is extinguished.

An acquisition, alternately, is aimed at gaining a controlling interest in the share capital of the acquired company. It can be enforced through an agreement with the persons holding majority interest in the company's management or through purchasing shares in the open market or purchasing new shares by private treaty or by making a takeover offer to the general body of shareholders.

Although they are often uttered in the same breath and used as though they were synonymous, the terms merger and acquisition mean slightly different things.

When one company takes over another and clearly established itself as the new owner, the purchase is called an acquisition. In practice actual mergers of equals don't happen very often. Usually, one company will buy another and, as part of the deal's terms, simply allow the acquired firm to proclaim that the action is a merger of equals, even if it is technically an acquisition. Being bought out often carries negative connotations, therefore, by describing the deal euphemistically as a merger, deal makers and top managers try to make the takeover more palatable.

Whether a purchase is considered a merger or an acquisition really depends on whether the purchase is friendly or hostile and how it is announced. In other words, the real difference lies in how the purchase is communicated to and received by the target company's board of directors, employees and shareholders.

A takeover, which is essentially an acquisition, differs from a merger in its approach to business combinations. In the process of takeover, the acquiring company decides the maximum price that is to be offered to the acquired and hence takes lesser time in completing a transaction than in mergers, provided the top management of the acquired company is co-operative. In merger transactions, the consideration is paid for in shares whereas in a takeover, the consideration is in the form of cash. However, mergers and takeovers can be treated as similar processes, since both cases at least one set of shareholders looses executive control over a corporation which they otherwise held.

### Mergers and Acquisition in India during post Liberalization Era

A recent KPMG study found that only 30 per cent of cases of M&A in India created shareholder's value. In 39 per cent of such deals, there was no discernible difference, while in 31 per cent of cases the shareholder's value was diluted. The finding though shocking to most, stems from imperfections, which exist in most economies and more distinctly in India.

The Indian banking sector, which far too many loss making units, could have possibly benefit from mergers but M&As have failed to perform. The efficient operation of the takeover mechanism requires that vast quantities of information to be widely available, which is not the case in India. Besides, there is a huge transaction costs involved in takeovers, which hamper the efficiency of the mechanism. If a firm's operation is or is perceived to be a symmetric, it may pay rational managers even in rational markets to be narrow-minded. This would lead to short-term measures and to lower rates of investment than would otherwise be the case. The first to be hit in the circumstance is the shareholder's value.

### Research Methodology

### Objectives of the Study

The study has been undertaken to contribute towards the following broad objectives:

1. To gain perspective on Mergers and Acquisitions in Indian Banking Sector during the last decade.
2. To make a comparative analysis of the impact of mergers on financial performance of the selected entity of BFSI industry in India.

### Literature Review

A firm can achieve growth both internally and externally. Internal growth may be achieved if a firm expands its operations or up scales its capacities by establishing new units or by entering new markets.

- Tambi (2005) attempts to evaluate the impact of such mergers on the performance of a corporation. Though the theoretical assumption says that mergers improve the overall performance of the company due to increased market power, Tambi uses his paper to evaluate the same in the scenario of Indian economy. He has tested three parameters—PBITDA, PAT and ROCE—for any change in their before and after values by comparison of means using t-test.
- Ravichandran, Nor and Said (2010), in their paper, have tried to evaluate the efficiency and performance for selected public and private banks before and after the merger, as a results of market forces. After doing a factor analysis, they narrow down the variables for their study to Profit Margin, Current Ratio, Ratio of Advances to

Total Assets, Cost Efficiency (ratio of cost to total assets) and Interest Cover and thereafter a regression is run to identify the relationship between these factors and return on shareholders funds.

- Anand and Singh (2008) study the effect of five specific mergers in the Indian banking sector on the shareholders wealth. These are mergers of the Times Bank with the HDFC Bank, the Bank of Madura with the ICICI Bank, the ICICI Ltd. with the ICICI Bank, the Global Trust Bank with the Oriental Bank of Commerce, and the Bank of Punjab with the Centurion Bank.
- Eckbo (1983) tests the hypothesis that horizontal mergers generate positive abnormal returns to stockholders of the bidder and target firms because they increase the probability of successful collusion among rival producers. Under this hypothesis, rivals of the merging firms benefit from the merger since successful collusion limits the output and raises product prices and/or lower factor prices.
- Mantravadi and Reddy (2008) have studied the impact of mergers on the operating performance of acquiring corporates in different industries, by examining some premerger and post-merger financial ratios, with the sample of firms chosen as all mergers involving public limited and traded companies in India between 1991 and 2003. Their results suggest that there are minor variations in terms of impact on operating performance following mergers, in different industries in India. In particular, mergers seem to have had a slightly positive impact on profitability of firms in the banking and finance industry, the pharmaceuticals, textiles and electrical equipment sectors saw a marginal negative impact on operating performance. In more than 5,763 mergers and acquisitions between 2002 and 2011, acquiring institutions purchased more than $6 trillion in assets globally.

## Hypothesis of the Study

The following hypotheses have been formulated and tested to draw the conclusions:

- There is a considerable difference between pre- and post-merger financial performance.
- Mergers in Indian Banking Sector in general resulted in value addition to shareholders.

## Sample Size and Sample Selection

The researcher has selected a convenient sample of 01 company merged in the Banking sector.

| Acquirer Company | Targeted Company | Year | Deal Value |
|---|---|---|---|
| ICICI Bank | Bank of Rajasthan | 2009-10 | 667 Mn USD |

## Highlight

The sample company from Indian banking sector was merged with 100 per cent stake.

### Period of Study

The researchers have made an attempt to study the impact of Mergers on financial performance of the sample company by using the available information for the period 2006-07 to 2010-11.

### Data Collection

After defining the objectives & hypothesis we need to look at the type and sources of data and other specific information needed to attain the said objectives. The present study is mainly based on secondary data which have been collected through annual reports of the companies, books & journals, newspapers & magazines and websites, etc. The data of just preceding years of the year the merger took place has been considered for pre-merger study and the data for the year 2010-11 has been used for post-merger study.

### Tools and Techniques

To analyze the available financial information to study the company, various techniques of applied research and accounting tools like comparative ratios have been employed. The following 6 major financial ratios and their means were calculated for analyzing the financial performance of the sample case:

- Operating Profit Ratio (OPR)
- Earnings Per Share (EPS)
- Return on Investment (ROI)
- Net Profit Ratio (NPR)
- Debt-Equity Ratio
- Dividend Payout Ratio (DPR)

These average ratios were compared using Paired Sample 't' test. A confidence interval of 95 per cent has been set for difference in means.

### Pre-Post Merger Financial Sample Performance of Sample Merger Case

ICICI BANK AND BANK OF RAJASTHAN LTD. (YEAR OF MERGER: 2009-10)

Table showing the financial results of ICICI Bank and Bank of Rajasthan Ltd. during pre- and post-merger period.

| Ratios | Pre-Merger Period | | | | | | | | Post-Merger Period | |
|---|---|---|---|---|---|---|---|---|---|---|
| | Acquirer or Parent Company (ICICI Bank) | | | | Acquired or Target Company (Bank of Rajasthan Ltd.) | | | | | |
| | 2006-07 | 2007-08 | 2008-09 | Avg. | 2006-07 | 2007-08 | 2008-09 | Avg. | 2010-11 | Avg. |
| Operating Profit Ratio (%) | 28.87 | 26.00 | 26.22 | 27.03 | 28.84 | 21.18 | 21.12 | 23.71 | 24.81 | 24.81 |
| Net Profit Ratio (%) | 10.81 | 10.51 | 9.74 | 10.35 | 12.56 | 9.75 | 7.81 | 10.04 | 15.91 | 15.91 |
| Return on Investment (%) | 82.46 | 62.34 | 56.72 | 67.17 | 140.81 | 173.00 | 185.2 | 166.44 | 42.97 | 42.97 |
| Earnings per Share (₹) | 34.59 | 37.37 | 33.76 | 35.24 | 10.28 | 8.57 | 7.30 | 8.72 | 44.73 | 44.73 |
| Dividend Payout Ratio (%) | 28.91 | 29.43 | 32.58 | 30.31 | 19.45 | 5.83 | 2.74 | 9.34 | 31.29 | 31.29 |
| Debt-Equity Ratio | 9.50 | 5.27 | 4.42 | 6.39 | 25.37 | 26.15 | 23.60 | 25.04 | 4.10 | 4.10 |

*Source*: Published Financial Statements of the Company.

## ANALYSIS OF THE FINANCIAL RESULTS

The above table shows the position of ICICI Bank and Bank of Rajasthan Ltd. during pre- and post-merger period. ICICI Bank acquired Bank of Rajasthan Ltd., raising the share value of ICICI Bank to new heights and making the former a stronger bank with a stronger balance sheet.

- When we start comparing the ratios of both the banks pre- and post-merger, one very important ratio which indirectly tells the strength of the companies operation is operating ratio which was 27.03 per cent for ICICI Bank pre-merger while it was 23.71 per cent for Bank of Rajasthan. Post-merger the ratio changed to 24.81 per cent indicating a decline. This clearly indicates that the company has realized some losses which might be due to the high costs incurred during the merger period.
- Talking about the Net ratio for the acquirer company before merger was 10.35 per cent while the net profit ratio for the acquired company was 10.04 per cent. During post-merger the average Net profit ratio was 15.91 per cent which shows a significant increase from 10.35 per cent to 15.91 per cent and a clear communication that the company has made profits after merger. It can be suggested that the company has gained monopoly and the advantages of goodwill are helping the company gain some substantial profit.
- The pre-merger average for ROI for the acquirer company was 67.17 per cent while the return on investment for the acquired company was 166.44 per cent. Post-merger the average return on investment declined to 42.97. Also the average of Net worth before merger for the acquiring company was 9.89 per cent while the return on net worth for the target company was 22.96 per cent. After merger the average on return on net worth slightly declined to 9.35 per cent for the acquired company. This indicates that less was incurred at the time of merger.
- Taking the financial condition of the bank in consideration average earnings per share during pre-merger for ICICI Bank was (35.24) while that of the target company was (8.72). Post-merger the average earnings per share increased to (44.73). This might be attributed that the shareholders had retained some profits or dividends to make the company a stronger financial organization.
- The operating ratio, return on investment has indicated a slight decline in their performance. The company has shown potential in attaining high profits as the main parameter, i.e. net profit ratio, earning per share have shown significant increase in their performance.
- Further the table shows that dividends payout ratio average was 30.31 per cent for the acquirer company while of the target company it was 9.34 per cent. After merger the payout ratio changed to 31.29 per cent. This indicates a very slight increase in the post-merger period for the acquirer company from 30.31 per cent to 31.29 per cent. The average of debt-equity ratio before merger for the acquirer company was 6.39 and that of the target company was 25.04. Post-merger the ratio had declined to 4.10.

**Financial Indicator-wise-Analysis**

- **Operating Profit Ratio of ICICI Bank**

| Period | N | Mean | SD | t | df | Result |
|---|---|---|---|---|---|---|
| Pre-Merger | 3 | 27.030 | 1.597 | 1.204 | 2 | NS |
| Post-Merger | 1 | 24.810 | 0.000 | | | |

The operating profit ratio for ICICI bank before merger was 27.030. After merging the Bank of Rajasthan Ltd. into it this ratio was decreased to 24.810. The test for difference of mean was found to be non-significant (t = 1.204 < tab = 2.920 at 5% level of significance).

Hence the hypothesis taken 'There is a considerable difference between pre- and post-merger financial performance' is proved to be rejected.

The above position has graphically been presented as below:

**Pre- and Post-merger Operating Profit Ratio position of ICICI Bank**

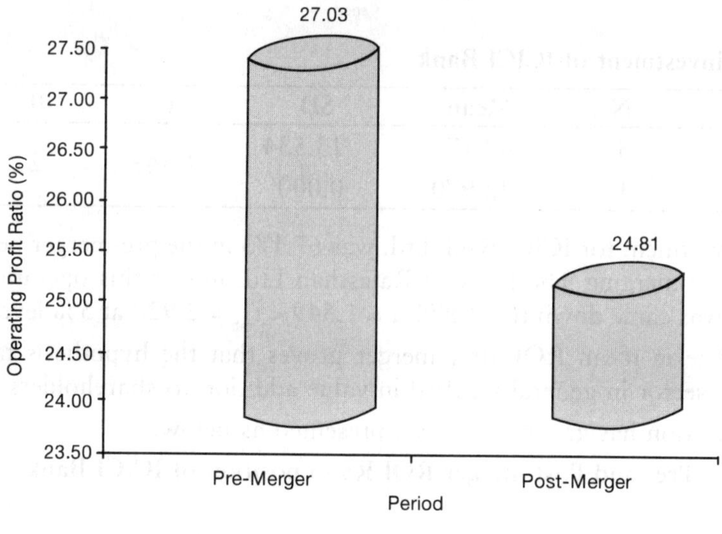


- **Net Profit Ratio of ICICI Bank**

| Period | N | Mean | SD | t | df | Result |
|---|---|---|---|---|---|---|
| Pre-Merger | 3 | 10.353 | 0.552 | –8.719 | 2 | * |
| Post-Merger | 1 | 15.910 | 0.000 | | | |

The Net Profit Ratio for ICICI Bank Ltd. was 10.353 in the pre-merger period which was slightly increased to 15.910 in the post-merger period. The difference in the net profit ratio between pre-merger and post-merger period was found to be significant ($t = 8.719 > t_{tab} = 2.920$ at 5% level of significance).

Hence the hypothesis taken 'There is a considerable difference between pre- and post-merger financial performance' is proved to be accepted.

The above position has graphically been presented as below:

**Pre- and Post-merger Net Profit Ratio position of ICICI Bank**

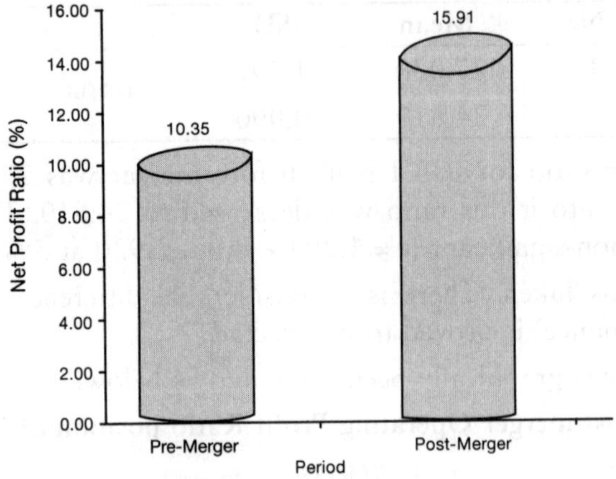


- **Return on Investment of ICICI Bank**

| Period | N | Mean | SD | t | df | Result |
|---|---|---|---|---|---|---|
| Pre-Merger | 3 | 67.173 | 13.534 | 1.549 | 2 | NS |
| Post-Merger | 1 | 42.970 | 0.000 | | | |

Return on Investment for ICICI Bank Ltd. was 67.173 in the pre-merger period. In the post-merger period after merging The Bank of Rajasthan Ltd. into it this operating profit ratio of ICICI Bank Ltd. was came down to 42.970 ($t = 1.549 < t_{tab} = 2.920$ at 5% level of significance).

A sharp decline in mean ROI after merger proves that the hypothesis taken 'Mergers in Indian Corporate sector in general resulted in value addition to shareholders' is rejected.

The above position has graphically been presented as below:

**Pre- and Post-merger ROI Ratio position of ICICI Bank**

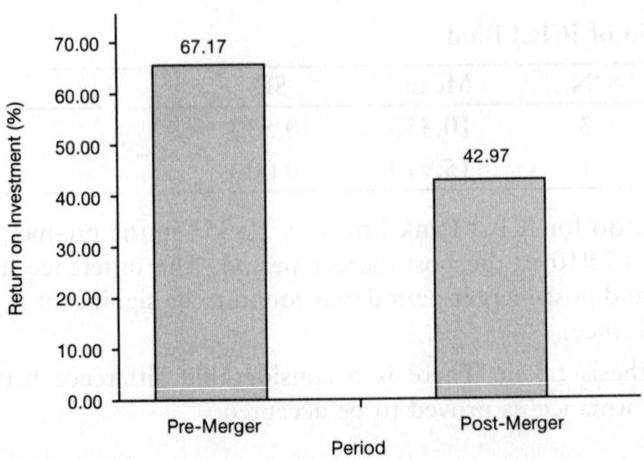

- **Earning Per Share of ICICI Bank**

| Period | N | Mean | SD | t | df | Result |
|---|---|---|---|---|---|---|
| Pre-Merger | 3 | 35.240 | 1.891 | –4.347 | 2 | * |
| Post-Merger | 1 | 44.730 | 0.000 | | | |

Earnings per share for ICICI Bank Ltd. was 35.240 in the pre-merger period. After merger this figure was increased to 44.730. The test for difference of means was applied between pre-merger and post-merger situation. The test results show that the difference is significant ($t = 4.347 > t_{tab} = 2.920$ at 5% level of significance).

Hence the hypothesis taken 'Mergers in Indian Corporate sector in general resulted in value addition to shareholders' is accepted.

The above position has graphically been presented as below:

**Pre- and Post-merger EPS Ratio position of ICICI Bank**

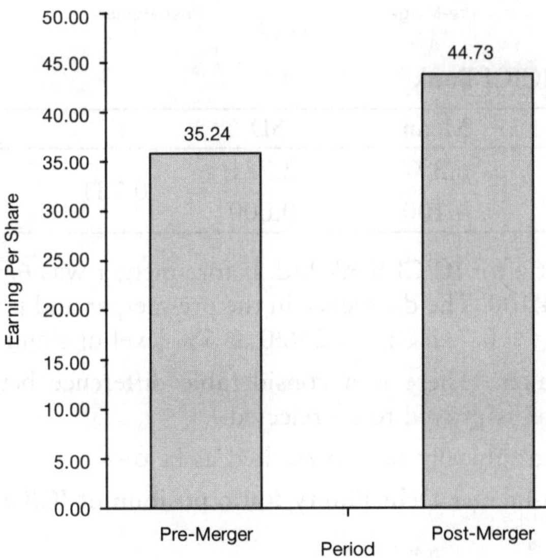


- **Dividend Payout Ratio of ICICI Bank**

| Period | N | Mean | SD | t | df | Result |
|---|---|---|---|---|---|---|
| Pre-Merger | 3 | 30.307 | 1.986 | –0.429 | 2 | NS |
| Post-Merger | 1 | 31.290 | 0.000 | | | |

Dividend payout ratio for ICICI Bank Ltd. in the pre-merger situation was 30.307 which is slightly increased to 31.290 in the post-merger period. The test for difference of means was found to be non-significant ($t = 0.429 < t_{tab} = 2.920$ at 5% level of significance).

Hence the hypothesis taken 'Mergers in Indian Corporate sector in general resulted in value addition to shareholders' is rejected.

The above position has graphically been presented as below:

**Pre- and Post-merger Dividend Payout Ratio position of ICICI Bank**

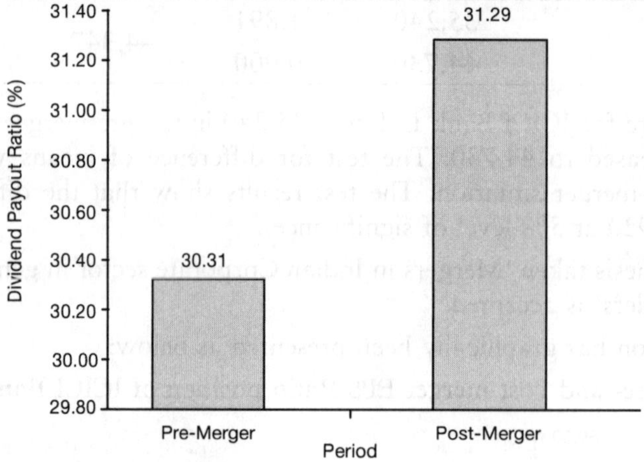


- **Debt Equity Ratio of ICICI Bank**

| Period | N | Mean | SD | t | df | Result |
|---|---|---|---|---|---|---|
| Pre-Merger | 3 | 6.397 | 2.721 | 0.731 | 2 | NS |
| Post-Merger | 1 | 4.100 | 0.000 | | | |

The mean debt equity ratio for ICICI Bank Ltd. before merger was 6.397. After merger this ratio was came to figure of 4.100. The difference in the pre-merger and post-merger period was found to be non-significant ($t = 0.731 < t_{tab} = 2.920$ at 5% level of significance).

Hence the hypothesis taken 'There is a considerable difference between pre- and post-merger financial performance' is proved to be rejected.

The above position has graphically been presented as below:

**Pre- and Post-merger Debt Equity Ratio position of ICICI Bank**

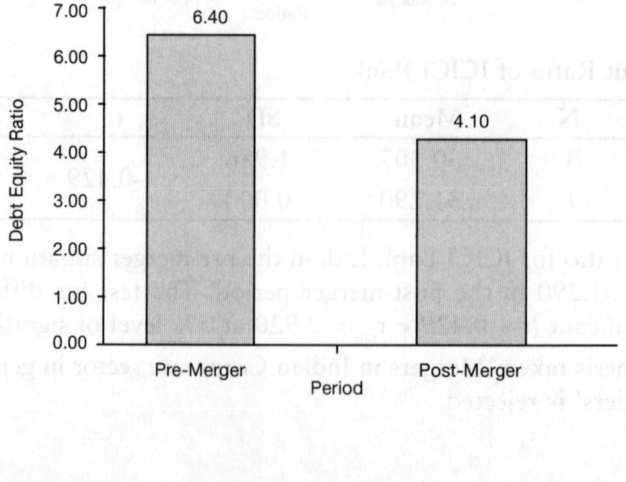

## Limitations of the Study

Though researchers have made a humble attempt to encompass the pre- and post-merger performance of the selected sample merger case, it is difficult to narrate all incidents and changes brought up due to mergers and acquisitions and therefore necessary inferences are inserted wherever required.

Secondly, the study is based purely on secondary data which are taken from the financial statements of the case through Internet only and therefore can't be denied for any ambiguity in data used for the analysis.

## Conclusions

To analyze the financial performance of sample case during pre- and post-merger period, 6 major financial ratios were used as financial indicators. The average of these ratios for pre- and post-merger period was used for comparative analysis. To test the significance level in difference between pre- and post-merger period, statistical test 't' test at 5 per cent level of significance has been applied. In other words, a confidence interval of 95 per cent has been set for difference in means.

On the basis of analytical study of sample case completed, the following conclusions have been drawn which are perfectly in the line of objectives predetermined:

- From the shareholders point of view of Profitability the sample company attained positive results in the post-merger period.
- The earnings growth after merger was found at the much higher rate resulted in value addition to shareholders.
- A substantial dividend growth was observed after merger in Sample Company.
- Significant difference was found between pre- and post-merger financial performance of the sample case.

## Suggestions

After concluding the results of this study, it is found appropriate to put the following suggestions:

1. It is observed on the basis sample study that the small and medium sized banking entities are working under threats from economic environment which is full of problems like inadequacy of resources, outdated technology, non-systematized management pattern, faltering marketing efforts and weak financial structure, etc. It is therefore advised to re-organize such industries through merger/acquisitions so that they could offer succor to re-establish them in viable industries of optimal size with global presence.
2. It is also suggested that corporate mergers/acquisitions should be bound to change drastically and rapidly the economy in size and quality performance through re-organized undertakings, combined resources and united efforts of experienced executives and skilled workforce.

## REFERENCES


Amihud, Y. and Lev, B. (1981), "Risk Reduction as a Managerial Motive for Conglomerate Merger," *Bell Journal of Economics*, 12(2), 605-07.

Anand, M. and Singh, J. (2008), "Impact of Merger Announcements on Shareholders Wealth: Evidence from Indian Private Sector Banks". Vikalpa: *Journal for Decision Makers*, 33(1), 35-54.

Bhaumik, S. and Selarka, E. (2008), Impact of M&A on firm performance in India: Implications for concentration of ownership and insider entrenchment. William Davidson Institute Working Paper Number 907.

Belton, Timothy D., The Venture Industries Credit Bid: A Template for Effective "Loan to Own" Acquisitions. *Journal of Private Equity*, Spring 2006, Vol. 9, Issue 2, pp. 115-18, 4p.

Estanol, A.B. and Ottaviani, M. (2007), "Bank Mergers and Diversification: Implications for Competition Policy". *European Financial Management*, Volume 13, Issue (2), 578-90.

Kalimeris, D. (2010), *An Event Analysis of Asymmetric Information on Merger and Acquisition.* Announcements in the SE European Region: The Case of Greek Early Mover Companies. *International Research Journal of Finance and Economics*, Issue (39).

Kwan, S.H. and Eisenbeis, R.A. (1999), "Mergers of publicly traded banking organizations revisited". *Economic Review*, Issue q4, pp. 26-37.

Mandelkar, G. (1972), "The Microeconomic Consequences of Corporate Mergers". *Journal of Business*, 45(1), 85-104.

Mitchell, Mark L. and J. Harold Mulherin, "The Impact of Industry Shocks on Takeover and Restructuring Activity." *Journal of Financial Economics* 41 (1996), 193-229.

Mitchell, Mark L. and Kenneth Lehn, "Do Bad Bidders Become Good Targets?" *Journal of Political Economy* 98:2 (April 1990), 372-98.

Mylonakis, J. (2006), The Impact of Banks? Mergers & Acquisitions on their Staff Employment & Effectiveness. *International Research Journal of Finance and Economics*, Issue (3).

Olson, Gerard T. and Pagano, Michael S. "A New Application of Sustainable Growth: A Multi-Dimensional Framework for Evaluating the Long Run Performance of Bank Mergers". *Journal of Business Finance & Accounting*, Nov./Dec. 2005, Vol. 32 Issue 9/10, pp. 1995-2036, 42p, 5 charts.

Travlos, N.G. (1987), "Corporate takeover bids, methods of payment, and bidding firms' stock returns", *Journal of Finance*, Vol. 42, No. 4, pp. 943-63.

Weston, J. Fred, K.S. Chung, and S.E. Hoag, *Mergers, Restructuring, & Corporate Control*, Prentice Hall, 1990.

Weston, J. Fred, and Piotr S. Jawien, "Perspectives on Mergers and Restructuring," *Business Economics* (January 1999), 29-33.

Weston, J.F., Mitchell, M., and Mulherin, L. (2004), Takeovers, Restructuring, and Corporate Governance, 4th ed., Prentice-Hall, Englewood Cliffs, NJ.


### Websites


www.google.com; www.moneycontrol.com

www.thehindubusinessline.com

www.vodafone.com; www.investegate.co.uk; www.hotstocked.com

http://wiki.answers.com/q/advantage of a merger

http://www.economicshelp.org/microessays/competition/benefits-merger.html

http://www.economywatch.com/merger-acquisition/history.html

http://en.wikipedia.org/wiki/merger and acquisition/motives behind M.26A

http://www.investopedia.com/ask/answers/05/mergervstakeover.asp

http://www.associatedcontent.com/article/1189676/the advantages and disadvantages of mergers pg2.html?cat=3

# 4

# IMPACT OF DISINVESTMENT ON FINANCIAL PERFORMANCE OF PUBLIC ENTERPRISES: A CASE STUDY OF MUL AND NTPC

–*B.L. Heda* and *Gaurav Mandot*

## Introduction

Disinvestment is common parlance refers to sale of shares of enterprises by the government to the private entrepreneur with view to minimize economic burden of the government and to direct the way for free flow of economic development. In other words, disinvestment from public sector is a drive to move a more market friendly regime in India. It is move towards privatization of public sector undertakings (PSUs) so that challenges of globalization may be faced.

There are two approaches to explain the disinvestment programme. According to first approach, whenever government sell its equity holding in PEs to public or private parties, financial institutions, mutual funds, etc., it is called as disinvestment. According to second approach, when PEs are generally directed by the government to issue their equity shares to the public, private parties, financial institutions and mutual funds with a view to reduce its control, that is also taken as disinvestment.

The idea of disinvestment was brought from U.K., where Prime Minister Margaret Thatcher realized that is the only way to uplift economy at fastest rate. She took decision to sale government's share from public enterprises and consequently several positive results were discovered. Indian public sector companies were also facing the problems like low productivity, high cost of production, lack of professional management, very low rate of return, excessive interference of politicians, etc. For getting the advantage of experience of U.K., the Government of India decided to follow the same path.

## Disinvestment of PSUs

Public enterprises in India have become a drain on the public exchequer due to their mounting losses in spite of all kinds of required resources of best quality made available to them. The government are neither in the position to improve their performance nor able to liquidate these white elephant. Since the losses of these enterprises are mounting year after year, the government is in a dilemma of finding solution. It is regarded by many countries that privatization of public enterprises as a solution for easening their administrative and financial burden.

The question of whether or not to privatize the public unit is not a simple one to be answered straight, particularly in a country like India. Many issues are to be considered, before taking final decision of privatization of any public sector unit, such as the character of the economy, stage of economic development, industrial policy, labour problems and social objectives, etc.

Considering the precarious financial position, can the center and state government's afford to bear every the huge losses from public units?

Certainly, they cannot hold any longer the luxury of running public enterprises with their massive losses. The respective governments are finding it difficult to raise resources for meeting various welfare programmes. It would be better for the governments either to close such units or transfer to the private sector, the later would always the better proposal from the economic point of view.

The disinvestment on Indian public sector was initiated, only in the union budget 1991-92 presented by Dr. Manmohan Singh in the Lok Sabha and before that in the industrial policy statement on 24th July 1991.

In this first budget speech, he stated that he regretted the need for partial disinvestment of government equity in the public sector enterprises.

The industrial policy statement of July 1991, mentioned that the government did not want to continue with all the sundry enterprises it owned. It promised that portfolio of public sector investment will be reviewed with a view to focus the public sector strategic, high-tech and essential infrastructure. Six categories mention for disinvestment were:

(i) PEs based on low technology
(ii) Small scale PEs
(iii) Non-strategic PEs
(iv) Inefficient and unproductive PEs
(v) PEs having low or nil social consideration or public purpose, and
(vi) Areas where the private sector has developed sufficient expertise and resources.
(vii) A large number of PEs producing consumer goods and most of these which were sick, met these criteria.

**Review of Literature**

Early research on this topic was conducted by Prajapati Trivedi (1993) was found disinvestment would not be pruning and restructuring of the public sector but would contribute towards increased in accountability of existing public enterprises.

G. Ganesh (1998) was found that the success and failure of privatization programme has to large extent depends on political commitment. Pakistan, Sri Lanka, Malaysia, have all demonstrated that success could be achieved with political commitment.

G.S. Batra and B.S. Bhatia (1999) was found that privatization produce some ill-effects which is not harmful and painful to the economy in long-run and in short-term it was very harmful.

Pradip Baijal (2002) was found that the option of disinvestment/privatization has compulsion for loss making units for mobilizing resources.

Ranu Sarupriya (2003) was found that all sample units (MFIL, LJMCL, and BALCO) have shown decline in most of ratios relative to the operating performance based on sales.

B.N. Puri (2003) was found that the government should be formulating new policies, offering more attractive incentives packages and developing mechanism to ensure greater participation of the private sector.

Sudhir Naib (2004) was found that disinvestment improve the financial and organizational performance.

P. Periasamy and J. Venkatash (2005) was found that privatization improved the sales, growth and earning.

Hemant Kothari (2007) was found that HZL considerably improved after its disinvestment.

G.L. Dave (2007) was found that privatization has improved performance as comparison made in sample units.

Bala Y. (2010) was suggested that it would be better to spend the disinvestment proceeds on infrastructure like roads, social sector schemes including education, health, as well as for environment protection.

## Objective

The present research entitled "Impact of Disinvestment on Financial Performance of Business Unit: A Case Study of MUL and NTPC", covers the analysis of financial performance of MUL and NTPC in pre and post disinvestment periods.

## Data and Methodology

For the purpose of the study we used secondary data which collected from published annual report and for analysis we used ratio analysis and t test for hypothesis testing.

## Hypothesis

For the purpose of the above study the null hypothesis were taken as:

$H_0$ = There is no effect of disinvestment on financial performance of the company.

## Maruti Udyog Limited (MUL)

MUL was incorporated in February 1981 after taking over of the assets of the erstwhile Maruti Limited, which was nationalized by an act of parliament in the year 1980. The objective of the company was envisaged to employ modern manufacturing technology entered into collaboration agreement with Suzuki Motor Corporation of Japan in October 1982 for transfer of technology relating to passenger cars and light vehicles. The production commenced in November 1983.

The government was decided to disinvested 20 per cent equity of MUL in March 2003 and in June 2003 the equity was disinvested towards domestic and foreign investors.

**Table 1:** Analysis of Maruti Udyog Limited

| S. No. | Name of Ratios | Average in Pre Disinvestment Period | Average in Post Disinvestment Period | Calculated Value of t Test | Critical Value of t Test | Hypothesis Accepted/Rejected |
|---|---|---|---|---|---|---|
| 1. | Current Ratio | 1.7 | 1.54 | 0.712 | 2.45 | Accepted |
| 2. | Quick Ratio | 1.203 | 1.76 | 0.124 | 2.45 | Accepted |
| 3. | Debt Equity Ratio | 0.27 | 0.074 | 3.144 | 2.45 | Rejected |
| 4. | Proprietary Ratio | 0.57 | 0.678 | 4.93 | 2.45 | Rejected |
| 5. | Fixed Assets to Net Worth | 0.88 | 0.44 | 6.11 | 2.45 | Rejected |
| 6. | Fixed Assets Turnover Ratio | 2.86 | 5.332 | 4.44 | 2.45 | Rejected |
| 7. | Working Capital Turnover Ratio | 7.78 | 10.908 | 0.76 | 2.45 | Accepted |
| 8. | Debtors Turnover Ratio | 10.01 | 19.57 | 3.08 | 2.45 | Rejected |
| 9. | Average Collection Period | 29.46 | 16.574 | 4.46 | 2.45 | Rejected |
| 10. | Net Profit Ratio | –0.166 | 8.818 | 4.97 | 2.45 | Rejected |
| 11. | Operating Ratio | 1.53 | 16.844 | 8.71 | 2.45 | Rejected |
| 12. | Return on Capital Employed | 3.24 | 34.816 | 9.19 | 2.45 | Rejected |
| 13. | Return on Equity | -1.67 | 20.042 | 5.36 | 2.45 | Rejected |
| 14. | Return on Total Assets | -0.123 | 20.042 | 6.18 | 2.45 | Rejected |

- Liquidity ratio is the company's ability to covert non cash assets into cash. According to liquidity ratios of MUL, it has found that the liquid position decreased in post disinvestment period because of current liabilities have more increased as compared to current assets.
- Solvency is the ability of a company to meet its long-term debt payment. According to solvency ratios of MUL, it has found that the solvency position has not well in post disinvestment period as compared to pre disinvestment period. Fixed assets to net worth ratio has more in pre disinvestment it indicate the MUL invested more amounts in fixed assets. In 2005-06 Debt Equity ratio has lowest throughout the study period because of very low amount of debt in that particular year.
- Activity ratios are accounting ratios that measures a firm's ability to convert different accounts within their balance sheet into cash or sales. All the activity ratios of MUL shown good activity position in post disinvestment period. According to debtors turnover ratio which has 10.01 in pre disinvestment period increased up to 19.57 in post disinvestment period, it shows effective collection mechanism in post disinvestment period. According to working capital turnover ratio, it was highest in 2003-04 (22.31) throughout the study period because of decrease in working capital.
- Profitability ratios measure the success of the firm's management in earning a net return from the resources entrusted to them. All the ratios related to profitability shown good returns in post disinvestment period. In 2001-02 the ratio was negative because of loss and the net profit ratio has highest in 2006-07 (10.70) because of increase in profit and sales.

- The null hypothesis related to all the ratios has rejected except liquidity ratios (current ratio and quick ratio). So it may be said that the difference between pre disinvestment and post disinvestment has found to be significant.

## National Thermal Power Corporation Limited (NTPC)

NTPC Limited is the largest power generating company in India both in terms of installed capacity and generation output. The company contributed 28.6 per cent of total power generation on india. In October 2004 the company launched their IPO consisting of 5.25 per cent as fresh issue 5.25 per cent as offer for sale by Government of India. Thus the company became a listed in November 2004 with the government holding 89.5 per cent of the equity share capital. In June 2010 the government disinvested 5 per cent equity through FPO.

**Table 2: Analysis of NTPC**

| S. No. | Name of Ratios | Average in Pre Disinvestment Period | Average in Post Disinvestment Period | Calculated Value of t Test | Critical Value of t Test | Hypothesis Accepted/Rejected |
|---|---|---|---|---|---|---|
| 1. | Current Ratio | 3.13 | 2.748 | 0.596 | 2.45 | Accepted |
| 2. | Quick Ratio | 2.79 | 2.43 | 0.615 | 2.45 | Accepted |
| 3. | Debt Equity Ratio | 0.417 | 0.496 | 1.82 | 2.45 | Accepted |
| 4. | Proprietary Ratio | 0.627 | 0.6 | 1.21 | 2.45 | Accepted |
| 5. | Fixed Assets to Net Worth | 0.83 | 0.882 | 0.86 | 2.45 | Accepted |
| 6. | Fixed Assets Turnover Ratio | 0.71 | 0.73 | 0.75 | 2.45 | Accepted |
| 7. | Working Capital Turnover Ratio | 2.077 | 2.54 | 0.71 | 2.45 | Accepted |
| 8. | Debtors Turnover Ratio | 2.017 | 21.744 | 4.8 | 2.45 | Rejected |
| 9. | Average Collection Period | 161.033 | 21.796 | 2.5 | 2.45 | Rejected |
| 10. | Net Profit Ratio | 22.24 | 21.736 | 0.2 | 2.45 | Accepted |
| 11. | Operating Ratio | 33.453 | 31.778 | 0.28 | 2.45 | Accepted |
| 12. | Return on Capital Employed | 13.38 | 13.444 | 0.034 | 2.45 | Accepted |
| 13. | Return on Equity | 12.867 | 18.954 | 0.89 | 2.45 | Accepted |
| 14. | Return on Total Assets | 11.313 | 12.222 | 0.49 | 2.45 | Accepted |

- The short-term and long-term solvency has decreased in post disinvestment period as compared to pre disinvestment period according to liquidity and solvency ratios.
- According to activity ratios good activity position in post disinvestment period. Debtors turnover ratio shows improvement in post disinvestment period and it was highest in 2006-07 (30.75) because of decrease in debtors.
- Profitability has well in both pre and post disinvestment period. The net profit ratio was highest in 2003-04 (27.91) because of increase in profit and decrease in sales.
- The null hypothesis related to all the ratios has accepted except debtors turnover ratio and average colletion period. So it may be said that the difference between pre disinvestment and post disinvestment has found to be insignificant.

## REFERENCES

Baijal Prajapati (2002). "Privatization: Compulsions and options for economic reform", *Economic and Political Weekly*, Vol. 37, No. 41, Oct. pp. 4189-91 & 4193, quoted in www.jstor.org, visited on 26th Oct. 2010.

Batra, G.S. and Bhatia, B.S. "Privatization of a Public Sector Unit (A Case Study)", quoted in Batra, G.S. and Dangwal, R.C. (1999). *Commerce and Business*. Deep & Deep Publications Pvt. Ltd., New Delhi, pp. 65-71.

Dave, G.L. (2007). *Disinvestment in Indian Public Enterprises*. Renuka Publishers, Jaipur, p. 260.

Ganesh, G. (1998). *Privatization Experience Around the World*, Mittal Publications Pvt. Ltd., New Delhi, p. 369.

Gupta, Nandini (2005). "Partial privatization and firm performance", *The Journal of Finance*, Vol. LX, No. 2, April, pp. 987-1015, quoted in www.bus.indiana.edu, visited on 26th Oct. 2010.

Kothari, Hemant (2007). *Implication of Disinvestment on Organizational Efficiency and Effectiveness*. An unpublished Thesis for Ph.D. Degree submitted to MLSU, Udaipur, p. 42.

Naib, Sudhir (2004). *Disinvestment in India Policies, Procedure, Practices*. Sage Publications, New Delhi, p. 478.

Periasamy, P. and Venkatash, J. (2005). "Necessity and Effects of Privatization". *ICFAI Reader*, May, pp. 45-49.

Puri, B.N. (2003). "Private sector participation in the transport sector in India". *Transport and Communications Bulletin for Asia and the Pacific*, No. 73, quoted in www.unescap.org, visited on 26th Oct. 2010.

Sarupriya, Ranu (2003). *Disinvestment and Corporate Performance*. An Unpublished Thesis for Ph.D. Degree, Submitted to MLSU, Udaipur, p. 404.

Trivedi, Prajapati (1993). "What is India's privatization policy?" *Economic and Political Weekly*, Vol. 28, No. 22, May, pp. M71-M76, quoted in www.jstor.org, visited on 26th Oct. 2010.

www.ntpc.co.in, Visited on August 15, 2012.

www.indiainfoline.com, Visited on August 15, 2012.

www.marutisuzuki.com, Visited on August 15, 2012.

5

# RETURN ON EQUITY DECOMPOSITION IN BANKING SECTOR: A STUDY OF SELECTED PUBLIC SECTOR BANKS IN INDIA

–*Hanuman Prasad* and *Varsha Maheshwari*

## Introduction

Banks and other financial institutions are a unique set of business firms whose assets and liabilities, regulatory restrictions, economic functions and operating make them an important subject of research, particularly in the conditions of the emerging financial sectors. Banks' performance monitoring, analysis and control needs special analysis in respect to their operation and performance results from the viewpoint of different audiences, like investors/ owners, regulators, customers/clients, and management themselves. In measuring the performance of an organization, there are several tools that can be used, one of which is financial ratio analysis. Ratios provide a concise and systematic way to organize the enormous quantity of data contained in financial statements into a framework that creates meaningful information. Financial managers use ratios to benchmark their firm's performance against that of their competitors and set goals for future performance. Different financial ratios provide different answers in relation to organizational performance, and no single ratio provides an adequate indication of a bank's performance (Halkos & Dimitrios, 2004). Therefore, the components of the DuPont analysis, which combine several financial ratios in three profitability ratios, are used since this analysis measures profit relative to the sales, assets and equity of each bank (Brigham & Ehrhardt, 2006). The DuPont (or ROE) model of profitability is a progressive decomposition model that permits identification of strengths and weaknesses in firms' operations, expense controls, asset revenues, and financial leverage. This analysis generally prompts other questions that delineate further where the strengths or weaknesses may exist within the corporation.

## Decomposition of Return on Equity: A Model for Profitability Analysis

Return on Equity (ROE) decomposition (DuPont Analysis) allows financial statement users to examine what is the difference between companies who gain competitive advantage shown up in accounting performance measures (Purohit & Mazumder, 2006). Return on equity analysis provides a system for planning as well as analyzing financial institution performance. The profit margin allows the analyst to develop a pro forma income statement. That is, net income is equal to revenues less expenses. Thus, the financial planner can determine the revenue level necessary to achieve the net income target. The total asset turnover ratio allows the analyst to project the total asset level necessary to generate the projected revenue level. The total asset requirement can be used to project the pro forma levels of all of the asset accounts. The fundamental equation of accounting is that assets equal liabilities plus owners equity. Thus, the equity multiplier ratio can be used to project the financial needs and the financial structure of the financial institution. Return on equity, ROE, is first decomposed into return on asset, ROA, and the equity multiplier, EM. Return on Equity is decomposed into net profit margin and total asset turnover:

*ROE* = (*Net Income/Sales*) × (*Sales/Average Assets*) × (*Average Assets/Average Equity*).

The DuPont Formula disaggregates earnings into their basic components. Those components are:

| Component | | Formula |
|---|---|---|
| Return on Sales | Net Income/Net Sales | |
| × | Asset Turnover Ratio | Net Sales/Total Assets |
| = | Return on Assets | Net Income/Total Assets |
| × | Financial Leverage | Total Assets/Total Equity |
| = | Return on Equity (ROE) | Net Income/Total Equity |

Following figure provides a summary of the breakdown of the return on equity (ROE) framework. A decomposition provides a convenient and systematic method for identifying the strengths and weaknesses of an FI's performance. Identification of strengths and weaknesses and the reasons for them provide a useful tool for FI managers as they look for ways to improve performance.

**Decomposition of 'Return on Equity'**

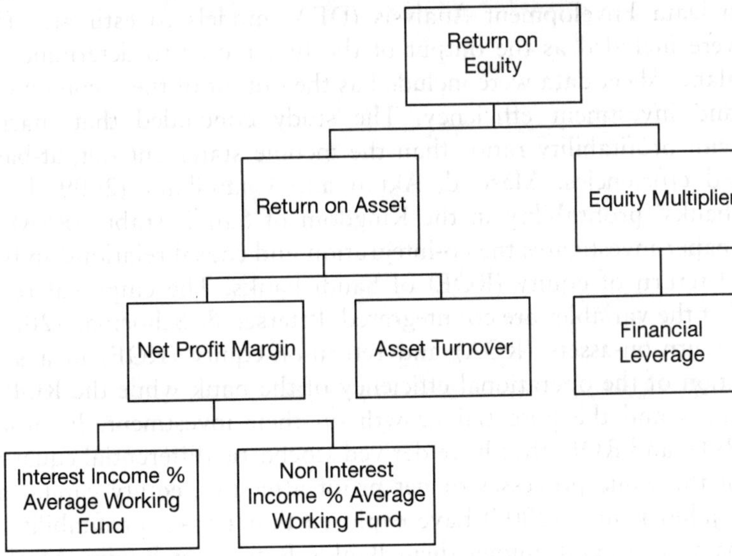

## Literature Review

Generally, the financial performance of banks and other financial institutions has been measured using a combination of financial ratios analysis, benchmarking, measuring performance against budget or a mix of these methodologies (Avkiran, 1995). McGowan & Stambaugh (2012) have explored an expanded version of the DuPont system of financial analysis to perform a financial analysis of a bank using disaggregated data to compute return on assets. The DuPont system of financial analysis is based on return on equity which is based on net profit margin, total asset turnover, and the equity multiplier. Almazari (2012) has measured the financial performance of the Jordanian Arab commercial bank for the period 2000-09 by using the DuPont system of financial analysis which is based on analysis of return on equity model. The return on equity model disaggregates performance into three components: net profit margin, total asset turnover, and the equity multiplier. Khrawish (2011) has identified two major factors that have effects on commercial banks performance, viz. internal determinants of statement variables and non-financial statement variables and external factors that are considered to be beyond the control of the management of a bank. This study comes to examine and analyse the factors that might affect on the Jordanian commercial banks performance during the period from 2000 through 2010. Gul, Irshad & Zaman (2011) have examined the relationship between bank-specific and macroeconomic characteristics over bank profitability by using the Pooled Ordinary Least Square (POLS) method to investigate the impact of assets, loans, equity, deposits, economic growth, inflation and market capitalization on major profitability indicators, i.e., return on asset (ROA), return on equity (ROE), return on capital employed (ROCE) and net interest margin (NIM) separately. The empirical results have found strong evidence that both internal and external factors have a strong influence on the profitability. Oberholzer, Westhuizen & Rooyen (2010) have determined the degree to which banks' market performance, as measured by market value ratios, is affected by their internal performance. The internal performance measures used are the profitability ratios in the DuPont analysis and two Data Envelopment Analysis (DEA) models to estimate efficiency. Income statement data were included as the output of the first model to determine banks' operating efficiency, and balance sheet data were included as the output of the second model to determine banks' finance and investment efficiency. The study concluded that market value ratios correlate better with profitability ratios than the income statement output-based and balance sheet output-based efficiencies. Masood, Aktan and Chaudhary (2009) have analyzed the determinants of banks' profitability in the Kingdom of Saudi Arabia (KSA) over the period 1999-2007. This paper investigates the co-integration and causal relationship between return of assets (ROA) and return of equity (ROE) of Saudi banks. The empirical results have found strong evidence that the variables are co-integrated. Petersen & Schoeman (2008) modeled bank profitability via return-on-assets (ROA) and return-on-equity (ROE) in a stochastic setting. ROA is an indication of the operational efficiency of the bank while the ROE is a measure of equity holder returns and the potential growth on their investment. In order to model the dynamics of the ROA and ROE, they have derived stochastic differential equations that contain information about the value processes of net profit after tax, equity capital and total assets. Jahangir, Shill & Jahid Haque (2007) have explored that Banks 'profitability depends on the results of some parameters and among them Bank's Return on Equity, Market Size, Market

Concentration Index, and Bank Risk measure are widely used and the same are investigated in the Bangladesh Banking Industry in this study for a period of the last six years. Tarawneh (2006) has classified the commercial banks in Oman in cohesive categories on the basis of their financial characteristics revealed by the financial ratios. A total of five Omani commercial banks with more than 260 branches were financially analyzed, and simple regression was used to estimate the impact of asset management, operational efficiency, and bank size on the financial performance of these banks. The study found that the bank with higher total capital, deposits, credits, or total assets does not always mean that has better profitability performance.

## Objectives

The objectives of this study are as follows:

- To study Return on Equity (ROE) and its determinants in order to measure the performance of the banking institutions.
- Identify regions which affects profitability of the company and need improvement in terms of both financially and operationally.
- Comparison of the performance of the selected public sectors banks on the basis of Return on Equity and its determinants.

**Study Period and Area:** The study covers the period from 2003-04 to 2010-11. All those public sector banks which were found on top five positions on the basis of size of total asset during the study period form the subject matter of this study, these are State Bank of India, Punjab National Bank, Bank of Baroda, Canara Bank, Bank of India. Data were collected from publications of the Reserve Bank of India and annual reports of the banks.

**Analysis Tools:** For the purpose of analysis ratio technique, trend analysis, rate of Growth have been used. Financial ratios like PBIDT/Sales (%), PAT/PBIDT (%), Net Profit Margin (%), Interest Income % Average Working Fund, Non Interest Income % Average Working Fund, Return on Asset, Net Assets/Net Worth (Equity Multiplier), Return on Equity have been calculated for the purpose of analysis. To catch the bird eye view graphical presentations also has been used.

### *Data Analysis and Interpretation*

A comprehensive financial statement analysis will provide insights as to a firm's performance and/or standing in the areas of liquidity, leverage, operating efficiency and profitability. A complete analysis will involve both time series and cross-sectional perspectives. Time series analysis will examine trends using the firm's own performance as a benchmark. Cross-sectional analysis will augment the process by using external performance benchmarks for comparison purposes. Every meaningful analysis will begin with a qualitative inquiry as to the strategy and policies of the subject company, creating a context for the investigation. Next, goals and objectives of the analysis will be established, providing a basis for interpreting the results. The DuPont ratio can be used as a compass in this process by directing the analyst toward significant areas of strength and weakness evident in the financial statements. The comprehensive data analysis of banks on these perspectives are as follows:

## 1. State Bank of India

**Table 1: State Bank of India**

| Analysis Points | 11-Mar | 10-Mar | 9-Mar | 8-Mar | 7-Mar | 6-Mar | 5-Mar | 4-Mar | Rate of Growth |
|---|---|---|---|---|---|---|---|---|---|
| Net Profit Margin (%) | 8.50 | 10.66 | 11.93 | 11.53 | 10.17 | 10.14 | 10.88 | 9.67 | –12.06 |
| Interest Income % Average Working Fund | 6.96 | 6.8 | 7.29 | 7.32 | 7.34 | 7.19 | 7.7 | 7.99 | –12.89 |
| Non-Interest Income % Average Working Fund | 1.35 | 1.43 | 1.45 | 1.3 | 1.07 | 1.48 | 1.69 | 1.99 | –32.16 |
| Sales/Net Assets (Asset Utilization) | 0.32 | 0.29 | 0.27 | 0.3 | 0.29 | 0.26 | 0.2 | 0.2 | 60.00 |
| Return on Asset | 2.72 | 3.09 | 3.22 | 3.46 | 2.95 | 2.64 | 2.18 | 1.93 | 40.70 |
| Net Assets/Net Worth (Equity Multiplier) | 4.62 | 4.55 | 4.83 | 3.93 | 4.86 | 5.98 | 8.3 | 9.31 | –50.38 |
| Return on Equity | 12.57 | 14.07 | 15.55 | 13.60 | 14.33 | 15.77 | 18.07 | 18.01 | –30.18 |

### Interpretation

In case of State Bank of India, the three main ratios of profitability analysis show relatively same pattern of behavior, these are return on asset, net profit margin and equity multiplier. The points of change in 'equity multiplier', i.e. change in the degree of financial leverage shows positively correlated shift in all profitability ratios, viz. net profit, return of asset and return on equity.

**Graphical Representation**

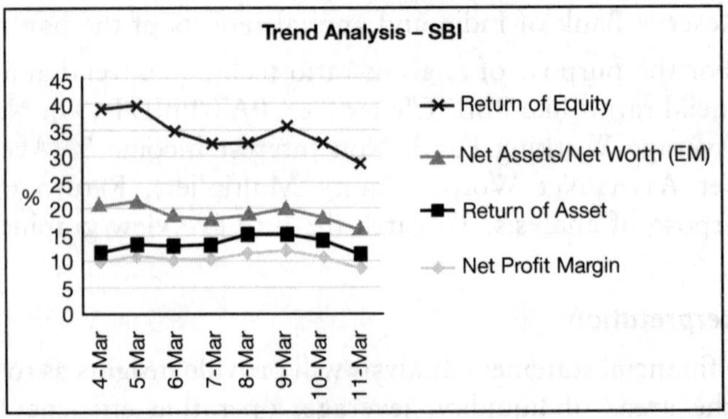


## 2. Punjab National Bank

**Table 2: Punjab National Bank**

| Analysis Points | 11-Mar | 10-Mar | 9-Mar | 8-Mar | 7-Mar | 6-Mar | 5-Mar | 4-Mar | Rate of Growth |
|---|---|---|---|---|---|---|---|---|---|
| Net Profit Margin (%) | 14.49 | 15.60 | 13.89 | 12.60 | 12.24 | 13.26 | 13.24 | 11.27 | 28.61 |
| Interest Income % Average Working Fund | 8.11 | 7.87 | 8.47 | 8.01 | 7.49 | 7.28 | 7.04 | 8.12 | –0.12 |
| Non-Interest Income % Average Working Fund | 1.09 | 1.33 | 1.36 | 1.12 | 1.15 | 0.94 | 1.39 | 1.95 | –44.10 |
| Sales/Net Assets (Asset Utilization) | 0.31 | 0.31 | 0.34 | 0.29 | 0.27 | 0.26 | 0.21 | 0.23 | 34.78 |

| | | | | | | | | | |
|---|---|---|---|---|---|---|---|---|---|
| Return on Asset | 4.49 | 4.84 | 4.72 | 3.65 | 3.30 | 3.45 | 2.78 | 2.59 | 73.34 |
| Net Assets/Net Worth (Equity Multiplier) | 4.9 | 4.94 | 5.01 | 5.22 | 4.56 | 4.64 | 6.58 | 9.17 | –46.56 |
| Return on Equity | 22.01 | 23.89 | 23.67 | 19.07 | 15.07 | 15.99 | 18.30 | 23.77 | –7.38 |

**Graphical Representation**

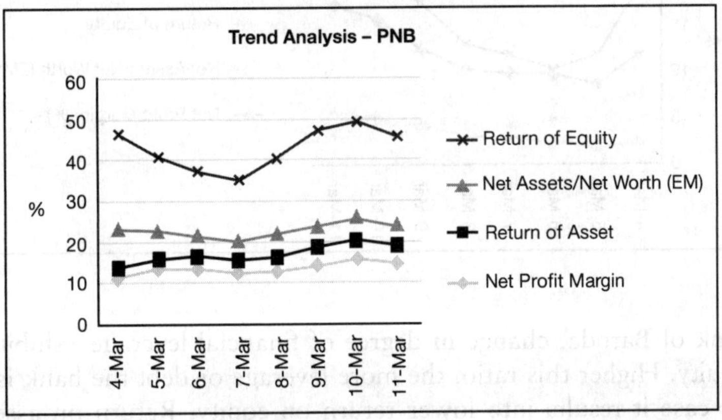


## Interpretation

In case of Punjab National Bank, increasing level of asset utilization relatively contributes more to drive return on asset as the rate of growth of Sales/Net asset is high than Net Profit Margin. Non-interest income shows relatively greater variability in contrast of interest income as % of average working fund. In this case also change in net asset/net worth exhibits change in the profitability patterns.

## 3. Bank of Baroda

Table 3: Bank of Baroda

| Analysis Points | 11-Mar | 10-Mar | 9-Mar | 8-Mar | 7-Mar | 6-Mar | 5-Mar | 4-Mar | Rate of Growth |
|---|---|---|---|---|---|---|---|---|---|
| Net Profit Margin (%) | 17.18 | 15.68 | 12.46 | 10.33 | 9.84 | 9.80 | 8.70 | 11.98 | 43.39 |
| Interest Income % Average Working Fund | 6.97 | 6.86 | 7.78 | 7.63 | 7.22 | 6.69 | 6.86 | 7.43 | –6.19 |
| Non-Interest Income % Average Working Fund | 0.89 | 1.15 | 1.42 | 1.32 | 1.11 | 1.12 | 1.39 | 2.08 | –57.21 |
| Sales/Net Assets (Asset Utilization) | 0.34 | 0.31 | 0.33 | 0.3 | 0.29 | 0.23 | 0.2 | 0.21 | 61.90 |
| Return on Asset | 5.84 | 4.86 | 4.11 | 3.10 | 2.85 | 2.25 | 1.74 | 2.52 | 132.16 |
| Net Assets/Net Worth (Equity Multiplier) | 3.5 | 4.2 | 4.25 | 4.19 | 4.17 | 4.59 | 6.74 | 7.57 | –53.76 |
| Return on Equity | 20.44 | 20.411 | 17.47 | 12.99 | 11.89 | 10.34 | 11.73 | 19.04 | 7.34 |

**Graphical Representation**

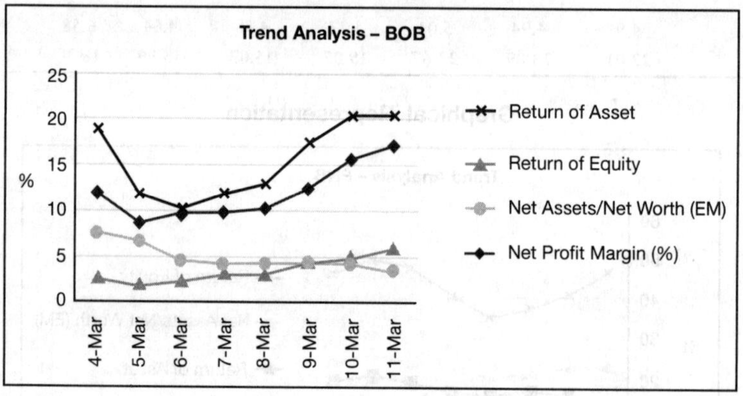


### Interpretation

In case of Bank of Baroda, change in degree of financial leverage exhibits inverse relation with return on equity. Higher this ratio, the more leverage or debt the bank is using to fund its assets and in this case it results into lower return on equity. Return on asset shows variable pattern of behavior with the contribution of net profit margin and asset utilization.

### 4. Canara Bank

Table 4: Canara Bank

| Analysis Points | 11-Mar | 10-Mar | 9-Mar | 8-Mar | 7-Mar | 6-Mar | 5-Mar | 4-Mar | Rate of Growth |
|---|---|---|---|---|---|---|---|---|---|
| Net Profit Margin (%) | 15.63 | 13.98 | 10.60 | 9.48 | 11.03 | 13.20 | 11.88 | 14.63 | 6.82 |
| Interest Income % Average Working Fund | 8.13 | 8.1 | 8.73 | 8.31 | 7.85 | 7.32 | 7.28 | 7.92 | 2.65 |
| Non-Interest Income % Average Working Fund | 0.95 | 1.23 | 1.18 | 1.3 | 1 | 1.16 | 1.48 | 2.34 | –59.40 |
| Sales/Net Assets (Asset Utilization) | 0.3 | 0.3 | 0.32 | 0.31 | 0.27 | 0.27 | 0.24 | 0.25 | 20.00 |
| Return on Asset | 4.69 | 4.16 | 3.39 | 2.94 | 2.98 | 3.56 | 2.85 | 3.66 | 28.18 |
| Net Assets/Net Worth (Equity Multiplier) | 4.82 | 5.78 | 6.05 | 6.36 | 5.93 | 5.37 | 6.46 | 7.11 | –32.21 |
| Return on Equity | 22.60 | 24.24 | 20.53 | 18.69 | 17.66 | 19.14 | 18.42 | 26.00 | –13.10 |

**Graphical Representation**

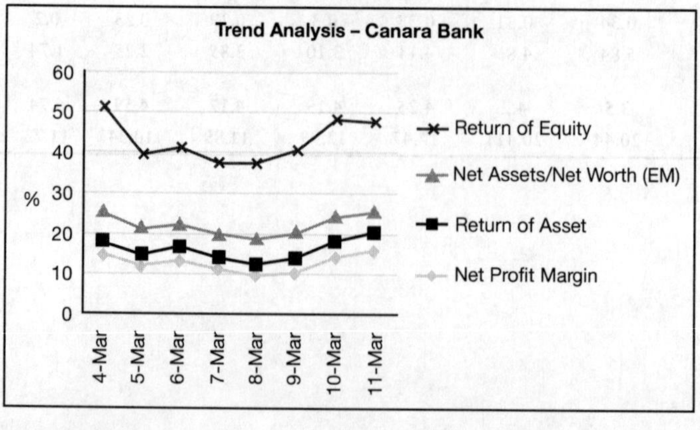

### Interpretation

In this case, all the critical ratios relatively exhibits similar behavior in charts. In the constituent parts of net profit margin, non-interest income shows greater variability in comparison with a very little change in interest income as per cent of average working fund. The financial position of Canara bank shows relatively consistent behavior in terms of profitability measures.

### 5. Bank of India

Table 5: Bank of India

| Analysis Points | 11-Mar | 10-Mar | 9-Mar | 8-Mar | 7-Mar | 6-Mar | 5-Mar | 4-Mar | Rate of Growth |
|---|---|---|---|---|---|---|---|---|---|
| Net Profit Margin (%) | 10.20 | 8.50 | 15.50 | 13.89 | 10.70 | 8.54 | 47.29 | 13.29 | -23.21 |
| Interest Income % Average Working Fund | 6.95 | 7.14 | 8.09 | 7.71 | 7.03 | 6.78 | 6.71 | 7.19 | -3.34 |
| Non-Interest Income % Average Working Fund | 0.84 | 1.05 | 1.51 | 1.32 | 1.23 | 1.14 | 1.29 | 2.22 | -62.16 |
| Sales/Net Assets (Asset Utilization) | 0.28 | 0.3 | 0.35 | 0.33 | 0.29 | 0.25 | 0.24 | 0.27 | 3.70 |
| Return on Asset | 2.86 | 2.55 | 5.42 | 4.58 | 3.10 | 2.14 | 11.35 | 3.59 | -20.37 |
| Net Assets/Net Worth (Equity Multiplier) | 5.53 | 5.42 | 4.68 | 5.01 | 6.31 | 6.75 | 6.86 | 7.29 | -24.14 |
| Return on Equity | 15.80 | 13.81 | 25.39 | 22.96 | 19.58 | 14.41 | 77.86 | 26.16 | -39.60 |

### Graphical Representation

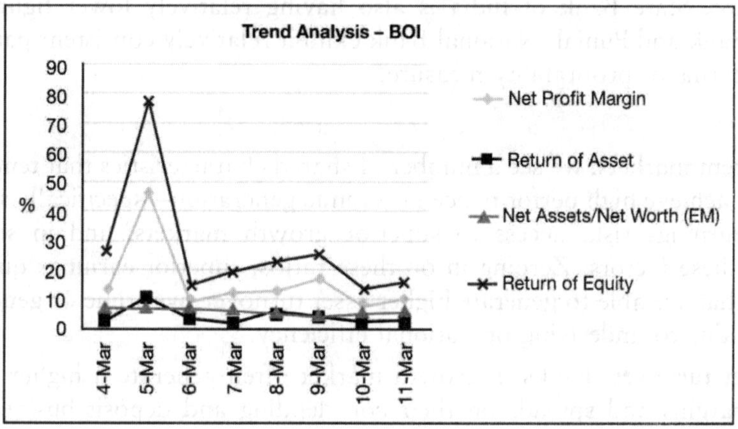


### Interpretation

In case of Bank of India, there is a sharp rise in the profitability of the bank in the financial year of 2004-05 as depicted by net profit margin, return on asset and return on equity. Asset utilization efficiency measure has not significant change as a contributing element of return on asset. As the figures shows that change in the degree of financial leverage contributes in the change in the return on equity.

**Peer Comparison Metrics: Comparative Study of Selected Public Sector Banks**

Rate of Growth (%)

| Analysis Point | State Bank of India | Punjab National Bank | Bank of Baroda | Canara Bank | Bank of India |
|---|---|---|---|---|---|
| Net Profit Margin | –12.06 | 28.60 | 43.39 | 6.82 | –23.21 |
| Asset Utilization | 60.00 | 34.78 | 61.9 | 20.00 | 3.70 |
| Return on Asset | 40.71 | 73.34 | 132.16 | 28.18 | –20.37 |
| Equity Multiplier | –50.37 | –46.56 | –53.76 | –32.20 | –24.14 |
| Return of Equity | –30.18 | –7.37 | 7.34 | –13.10 | –39.60 |

## Data Interpretation

In the study period of 8 years (ranging from 2003-04 to 2010-11), with the help of decomposition analysis of Return on equity the further study of relative competitive position of 5 major public sector banks can be done. For this purpose, Rate of growth has been used. On the basis of main profitability ratio, i.e. Return on equity, Bank of Baroda is having positive ratio in comparison of other public sector banks as the contributing force of net profit margin and asset utilization measure, it results into magnified return on assets hence increasing return on equity and Bank of India is behind on this step. The analysis of figures exhibits that change in degree of financial leverage, i.e. use of debt as financing of assets have significant effect on Return on equity. Asset utilization measure and degree of financial leverage are the major forces that drive the return on equity. Bank of India is relatively at a weak position in regards of profitability ratios. State Bank of India is also having relatively lower figures of return on equity. Canara Bank and Punjab National Bank exhibit relatively consistent pattern in financial performance in terms of profitability measure.

## Major Findings

Across different markets, we see a number of shared characteristics that tend to differentiate those banks that achieve high performance in revenue generation—specifically superior earnings quality, lower earnings risk, access to superior growth markets, and in some instances a combination of these factors. Zeroing in on these ratios, superior earnings quality is typically found in banks that are able to generate higher asset turnover over time or generate earnings at a higher margin due to underlying operational efficiency.

**1. High asset turnover.** Banks in growth market often generate a higher return on assets through wide margins and spreads on their core lending and deposit businesses, or through holdings of high-yielding domestic bonds. However, their earning potential is frequently impacted by poor asset quality and low levels of leverage required to operate in less stable financial markets. Banks such as Bank of Baroda have been able to expand their return on equity with the contribution of efficient asset utilization than most of their domestic peers.

**2. Operational efficiency.** Bank and banking markets outperform their peers in terms of efficient generation of income.

**3. Low earnings risk.** In addition to high quality sustainable earnings, banks that have a focus towards lower risk businesses or markets also benefit from a higher market premium. Banks that have a higher weighting towards non lending business activities and solid long-term customer relationships tend to outperform the market in terms of asset quality and suffer less impact from a market downturn. Bank of Baroda demonstrated more stable earning than their peers through their resilient asset and wealth management businesses.

**4. Degree of financial leverage.** A higher value of equity multiplier indicates that the banks is financed more by debt. Higher this ratios, the more leverage or debt the bank is using to fund its assets. This degree of financial leverage have significant impact on return on equity.

In nutshell, the decomposition of return on equity presents an analytical picture of the relative position of the institution in terms of profitability analysis.

## Limitations

The analysis points to an initial limitation of RoE, namely that it is not risk-sensitive. A decomposition of RoE shows that a risk component represented by leverage can boost RoE in a substantial manner. Other risk elements, on the other hand, are missing in the RoE figure (e.g. the proportion of risky assets and the solvency situation). RoE is therefore not a stand-alone performance measure, in order to come up with a more "informed" assessment of banks' performance, RoE must be refined. In particular, desirable features of banks' performance measures may cover comparability, stability over time and the capacity to be forward-looking as well. In that context, complementary measures to RoE, such as risk returns, funding capacity, assets and own funds quality, cost of equity and capital allocation across business lines may be of some help. RoE is a short-term indicator and must be interpreted as a snapshot of the current health of institutions (Helfert, 2008). It does not take into account either institution's long-term strategy or the long-term damages caused by the crisis. Its weaknesses are even more obvious in times of stress, when there is a climate of uncertainty surrounding the medium-term profitability of institutions. In challenging times, extraordinary elements may become very significant, but fail to appear in reported RoE measures. As a matter of fact, RoE does not reflect the sustainable performance of the bank, if the change comes from a one-shot element that cannot be reproduced in the future. RoE from continuing operations proves to be more relevant for comparing institutions and assessing operating performance accurately (Horne, 2009).

## Synthesis

This study investigated the performance of five public sector banks over eight-year period. The performance is measured by means of decomposition of profitability ratio, i.e. Return on equity. The main drivers of banks' profitability remain earnings, efficiency, risk-taking and leverage. For the purpose of more crisp results various issues like risk adjusted measures, asset quality, quality of banks' capital in relation to its assets, liquidity and funding capacity, composition and sustainability of earnings should be addressed.

## REFERENCES

Almazari, A.A. (2012), "Performance Analysis of the Jordanian Arab Bank by Using the DuPont System of Financial Analysis", *International Journal of Economics and Finance,* Vol. 4, No. 4.

Avkiran, N.K. (1995), "Developing an instrument to measure customer service quality in branch banking", *International Journal of Banks Marketing*, Vol. 12, No. 6, pp. 10-18.

Brigham, E.F. and Ehrhardt, M.C. (2006), *Financial Management*. Mason, OH: Thomson.

Gul, S., Irshad, F. and Zaman, K. (2011), "Factors Affecting Bank Profitability in Pakistan", *The Romanian Economic Journal*, Year XIV, No. 39, March 2011.

Halkos, G.E. and Dimitrios, S. (2004), "Efficiency measurement of the Greek commercial banks with the use of financial ratios: a data envelopment analysis approach", *Management Accounting Research*, 15(2): 201-24.

Helfert, E.A. (2008), *Techniques of Financial Analysis: A practical guide to applied managerial finance*. Jaico Publishing House, New Delhi.

Horne, James C. Van (2009), *Financial Management & Policy*, Twelfth Edition, Pearson Prentice Hall.

Jahangir, N., Shill, S., Haque, A.J. (2007), "Examination of profitability in the context of Bangladesh banking industry", *ABAC Journal*, Vol. 27, No. 2 (May-August, 2007, pp. 36-46).

Khrawish, H.A. (2011), "Determinants of Commercial Banks Performance: Evidence from Jordan". *International Research Journal of Finance and Economics*, Euro Journals Publishing, Inc.

McGowan, C.B., Stambaugh, A.R. (2012),"Using Disaggregated Return on Assets to Conduct a Financial Analysis of a Commercial Bank Using an Extension of the DuPont System of Financial Analysis", *Accounting and Finance Research*, Vol. 1, No. 1; May 2012, URL: http://dx.doi.org/10.5430/afr.v1n1p152

Oberholzer, M., Westhuizen, G.V., Rooyen, S.V. (2010), "The influence of banks' internal performance on market performance: a non-parametric approach", *Southern African Business Review*, Volume 14 Number 2, 2010, pp. 65-88.

Omar Masood, O., Aktan, B., Chaudhary, S. (2009), "An empirical study on Banks profitability in the KSA: A co-integration approach", *African Journal of Business Management*, Vol. 3 (8), pp. 374-82.

Petersen, M.A., Schoeman, I. (2008), "Modeling of Banking Profit via Return-on-Assets and Return-on Equity", *Proceedings of the World Congress on Engineering*, Vol. II, July 2-4, 2008, London, U.K.

Purohit, K.K. and Mazumder, B.C. (2006), "Performance Measurement of Banks: An Application of Balanced Scorecard", *The Cost and Management*, Vol. 34, No. 6, November-December, 2006, pp. 21-30.

Saunders, Anthony (2000), *Management of Financial Institutions*, Third Edition, McGraw Hill, 2000.

Tarawneh, M. (2006), "A Comparison of Financial Performance in the Banking Sector: Some Evidence from Omani Commercial Banks", *International Research Journal of Finance and Economics*, Euro Journals Publishing, Inc.

www.bankofbaroda.com

www.bankofindia.com

www.canarabank.in

www.pnbindia.in

www.sbi.co.in

# 6

# SEASONALITY IN INDIAN STOCK MARKET: AN APPLICATION OF DUMMY VARIABLE REGRESSION MODEL

–*G. Soral* and *Shilpa Lodha*

## Introduction

Financial markets always remain in news as they are the life blood of any nation and barometer of the economy. Stock markets are also attaining much public attraction these days. In India after Industrial Policy of 1991, globalization and liberalization has increased the integration of Indian stock markets with global stock markets. Two decades thereafter, several features of stock markets have been changed. Introduction of NSE, online trading system, several sectoral and other indices, introduction of futures and options, international capital market instruments, exchange market developments, etc. have changed the point of view of financial managers, financial analysts and individual investors. They are now watching the stock prices attentively, analyzing them and taking appropriate actions to maximize their returns.

A generation back, stock market returns were assumed to be in accordance with Efficient Market Hypothesis, as proposed by Fama (1969). It was generally believed that stock markets are as much efficient as necessary to incorporate all the information available to be reflected in stock prices immediately. But due to its impractical assumptions like: All investors have free access to same information, Markets absorb information quickly, Investors behave in a rational manner, etc., market cannot be perfectly efficient and it may show some pricing regularities and predictable patterns over time.

Seasonality implies some regular and repetitive variations in time series of data which occurs periodically. For instance, during summer season, demand for air conditioners and coolers increases. Likewise in stock market also, security prices show some regular and repetitive trend at definite times like day-of-the-week, time-of-the-day, month-of-the-year, turn-of-the-year or month, holiday effects, etc. At these instances, markets behave in a particular manner which could be analyzed by past prices, popularly known as calendar effects. Thus calendar effects are those anomalies in return, which occur periodically based on calendar.

Researchers have offered a number of hypotheses to explain this phenomenon. Amongst them the tax-loss selling hypothesis and the window dressing hypothesis are the most popularly evidenced. The tax-loss selling hypothesis states that individual investors tend to sell their stocks just before the end of the year, whose prices have fallen, to book their losses and thus, to lower their capital gain tax liability. This selling reduces the stock return by having a downward pressure on stock prices. As soon as the year ends, investors start buying stocks and prices escalate back, which in turn leads to higher return in January.

The window dressing hypothesis states that portfolio managers tend to replace their poor performing stocks by top performing stocks. The reason behind this tendency is to make their portfolio attractive in order to increase cash inflows.

The random walk model suggests that returns are not easily predictable but research studies evidenced the occurrence of short-run regularities in the stock market and that realization of excess stock returns cannot be the results of chance and are thus useful for making predictions. Several research studies have been conducted to analyze seasonal effects in U.S. or other developed stock markets and a few have been conducted on emerging/developing stock markets. So, it would be interesting to know the seasonal effects on stock markets in an emerging economy like India.

**Review of Literature**

Seasonal anomalies of stock prices are one of the most actively researched areas in Financial Economics. Seasonality Effect suggests that the share prices tend to behave differently depending on the day of the week, month of the year and following holidays. The majority of the research was confined to the developed capital markets with some research conducted on Asian stock markets.

Watchel (1942) was the first to found that the average rate of return on stocks in January is higher than in other months. Rozeff & Kinney (1976) evidenced statistically significant differences in mean returns among months due to large January returns. Kulkarni (1978) also rejected Random Walk Hypothesis and confirmed the seasonality in monthly prices. Keim et al. (1983) evidenced that daily abnormal return distributions in January have larger means relative to the remaining eleven months, and that the relation between abnormal returns and size is always negative. Further, more than 50 per cent of the January premium is attributable to large abnormal returns during first week of trading in the year, particularly on the first trading day. Roll (1983) revealed that stock returns for small and large firms show a pattern in that average returns are high in general and the average returns of small firms are invariably greater than the average returns of large firms.

Glutekin and Glutekin (1983) examined empirically stock market seasonality in 17 major industrialized countries. Evidence is provided that there is strong seasonality in the stock market return distributions in most of the capital markets around the world. The seasonality, when it exists, appears to be caused by the disproportionately large January returns in most countries and April returns in the U.K. With the exception of Australia, these months also coincide with the turn of the tax year.

Lakonishok and Smidt (1984) confirmed the existence of a year-end seasonal pattern in rates of return for small companies and suggest that there may be a seasonal pattern for large companies as well. Reinganum and Shapiro (1987) showed that after the introduction of capital gain tax, the British stock return data exhibit apparent monthly effects in both January and April. Boudreaux (1995) found strong evidence of a week end effect and January effect in foreign stock markets. Agarwal and Tondon (1994) examined five seasonal patterns in stock markets of eighteen countries: the weekend, turn-of-the-month, end-of-December, monthly and Friday effects and found a daily seasonality in nearly all the countries, but a weekend effect in only nine countries. The last trading day of the month has large returns and low variance in most countries. Many countries have large December pre-holiday and inter-holiday returns. The January returns are large in most countries and a significant monthly seasonal exists in ten countries.

Huffman, Stephen (1997) explained the presence of the January and October seasonality in defaulted bond return, the abnormal positive return in January and abnormal negative return in October follow the pattern of seasonality in small company stocks. Ignatius (1998) evidenced the December effect. Rajen Mookerjee (1999) investigated seasonal patterns in stock returns on the Shanghai and Shenzhen stock markets and found highest daily returns on Thursday rather than Friday.

Chan, Khanthavit and Thomas (1996) found strong day of the week effect on four Asian stock markets—Kuala Lumpur Stock Exchange (KLSE), Bombay Stock Exchange (BSE), Singapore Stock Exchange (SES) and Thailand Stock Exchange (SET). In general, they also found a strong effect of cultural holidays than state holidays. Zhiwu Chen and Jan Jindra (2001) found that from January to December, the undervalued fraction of stocks follows a U-shaped pattern, with December and January at the high ends and May-June at the bottom. Hamori and Tokihisa (2002) analyzed monthly data for the stock price indices of G7 countries and revealed that observed seasonality in stock prices was deterministic and thus it is possible to forecast seasonal patterns. Lucey and Whelan (2002) reported that the abnormally high returns (frequently in January and April and occasionally in February and other months) are perhaps more accurately ascribed to the half-year effect captured in the Irish Stock Market. Pinnuck and Gallagher (2003) reported evidenced that investment manager performance is greater than normal in December, possibly due to both window dressing and the Christmas holiday effect.

I.M. Pandey (2002) used monthly returns of BSE's SENSEX from 1991 to 2002, i.e. the post reform period. The analysis showed that the Indian market may not informational efficient. The results confirmed the existence of monthly effect (maximum return in February and lowest return in March) and also supported the tax-loss-selling hypothesis. Sharma (2004) examined 1667 observations of BSE200, SENSEX, and NATEX during 1996 to 2002 and his findings suggested that Monday-Friday set for all the indices had the highest positive deviation thereby indicating the opportunity to make abnormal returns through a trading strategy of buying on Mondays and selling on Fridays.

Worthington (2006) examined the calendar effects in Australian daily stock returns from 1958 to 2005. His results indicated that the Australian market is characterized by seasonality of all three forms with Tuesday (day of the Week), September (month of the year) and second trading day of the month most significant. Lazar, Priya and Jeyapaul (2006) studied the monthly return data of the BSE SENSEX for the period from 1991 to 2005 and confirmed the existence of seasonality in stock returns in India and also in conformity with the tax-loss selling hypothesis. Saez (2006) analyzed the effect of seasonality on mutual fund performance and found strong seasonality effects at year end, month end and at the beginning of July.

On going through the available literature, it was found that several research studies has been carried out for developed stock markets like in U.S., U.K., Australia, etc., but a very few has taken place for an emerging stock market like India.

## Scope

The scope of the study is restricted to find out the month of the year effect in stock returns of BSE SENSEX over the period from 1991 to 2011.

## Objective

The objective of the study is to find out the monthly effects in BSE SENSEX returns.

## Hypothesis

The null hypothesis taken is that returns for all the months are equal.

## Data and Sources

For the purpose of analysis, BSE SENSEX has been chosen as a representative index of India, since it is the oldest and most prominent stock index of not only India but of Asia also. Daily closing prices of BSE SENSEX from January 1991 to December 2011 have been collected.

## Data Analysis

A key concept underlying time series processes is that of stationarity. A time series is said to be stationary only when it possesses the following three features:

1. It has a constant mean over time, i.e. it exhibits mean reversion.
2. It has a time invariant constant variance.
3. It has a theoretical Correlogram that dies out quickly as the lag length increases.

When a data series does not have the above mentioned three characteristics it is said to be non-stationary. Yule discovered the phenomenon of spurious or non-sense regression. Regression of one-time series variable on one or more time series variables often can give nonsensical or spurious results. Therefore, it is necessary to find out whether the series is stationary or not and if not, how to make it stationary. A time series is said to be stationary if its mean, variance and covariance are constant over time and they remain the same no matter at what point we measure them; i.e. they are time invariant. Such a time series will tend to return to its mean.

For testing the stationarity of closing prices of BSE SENSEX, three methods are discussed namely: Graphical method, Correlogram Test and Unit Root (ADF) Test.

## Graphical Analysis

Before any formal test is pursued, the time-series is first plotted under study because such a plot gives an initial clue about the likely nature of the time series. Figure 1 is showing an upward trend in SENSEX, suggesting that the mean of the series is changing and that perhaps the series is not stationary.

**Daily Closing Prices of SENSEX from 1991 to 2011**

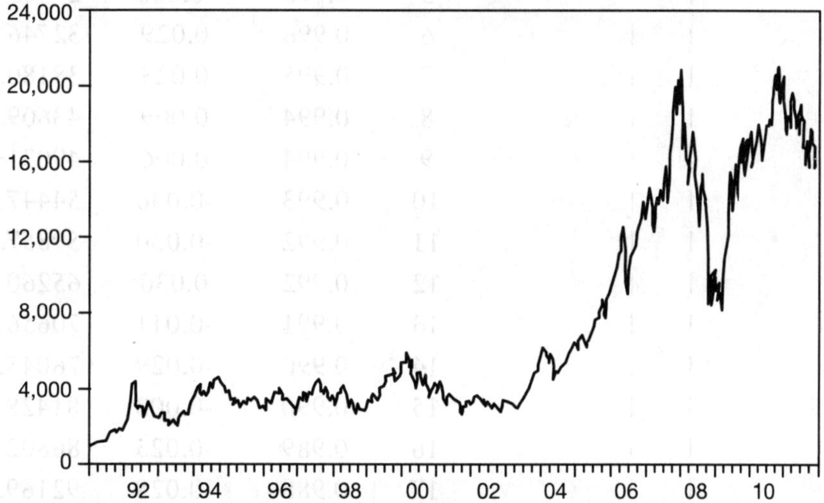


**Fig. 1**

Figure 1 is clearly depicting the trend existing in the stock series. The stock prices over time are showing an upward trend, suggesting perhaps that the mean of the series has been changing. This perhaps gives a clue that the series is not stationary.

### ACF and Correlogram

Autocorrelation means covariance between members of series of observations ordered in time. In the regression context, the classical regression model assumes that such autocorrelation does not exist in the distribution, i.e. the disruption of one period's value does not affect next period's value. But if the correlation exists, one period's disturbances are correlated with its prior period disturbances. One simple test of stationarity is based on the so-called autocorrelation function (ACF). The ACF at lag κ, denoted by $\rho_\kappa$ is defined as:

$$\rho_\kappa = \gamma_\kappa / \gamma_0 \text{ (i.e. Covariance at lag } \kappa \text{ / Variance)}$$

Covariance is the covariance between the values of $Y_t$ and $Y_{t+k}$, i.e. between two Y values k periods apart. $\rho_\kappa$ lies between –1 and +1 just like any other correlation coefficient does. If we plot $\rho_\kappa$ against k, the obtained graph is Correlogram. Figure 2 shows Autocorrelation and partial autocorrelation of BSE SENSEX upto 32 lags.

**Correlogram of ACF and PACF of Closing Prices**

Sample: 1/01/1991 12/30/2011
Included observations: 5479

| Autocorrelation | Partial Correlation | | AC | PAC | Q-Stat. | Prob. |
|---|---|---|---|---|---|---|
| \|******* | \|******* | 1 | 0.999 | 0.999 | 5474.7 | 0.000 |
| \|******* | \| \| | 2 | 0.999 | -0.039 | 10943. | 0.000 |
| \|******* | \| \| | 3 | 0.998 | -0.009 | 16404. | 0.000 |

| | | | | | | |
|---|---|---|---|---|---|---|
| \|******* | \| \| | 4 | 0.997 | 0.009 | 21858. | 0.000 |
| \|******* | \| \| | 5 | 0.996 | -0.008 | 27305. | 0.000 |
| \|******* | \| \| | 6 | 0.996 | 0.029 | 32746. | 0.000 |
| \|******* | \| \| | 7 | 0.995 | 0.023 | 38180. | 0.000 |
| \|******* | \| \| | 8 | 0.994 | 0.009 | 43609. | 0.000 |
| \|******* | \| \| | 9 | 0.994 | 0.006 | 49031. | 0.000 |
| \|******* | \| \| | 10 | 0.993 | -0.036 | 54447. | 0.000 |
| \|******* | \| \| | 11 | 0.992 | -0.030 | 59857. | 0.000 |
| \|******* | \| \| | 12 | 0.992 | 0.030 | 65260. | 0.000 |
| \|******* | \| \| | 13 | 0.991 | -0.011 | 70656. | 0.000 |
| \|******* | \| \| | 14 | 0.990 | -0.029 | 76045. | 0.000 |
| \|******* | \| \| | 15 | 0.990 | -0.003 | 81428. | 0.000 |
| \|******* | \| \| | 16 | 0.989 | -0.025 | 86802. | 0.000 |
| \|******* | \| \| | 17 | 0.988 | -0.028 | 92169. | 0.000 |
| \|******* | \| \| | 18 | 0.987 | -0.033 | 97528. | 0.000 |
| \|******* | \| \| | 19 | 0.986 | 0.011 | 102879 | 0.000 |
| \|******* | \| \| | 20 | 0.985 | 0.009 | 108221 | 0.000 |
| \|******* | \| \| | 21 | 0.985 | 0.000 | 113556 | 0.000 |
| \|******* | \| \| | 22 | 0.984 | 0.023 | 118883 | 0.000 |
| \|******* | \| \| | 23 | 0.983 | 0.012 | 124203 | 0.000 |
| \|******* | \| \| | 24 | 0.982 | 0.004 | 129515 | 0.000 |
| \|******* | \| \| | 25 | 0.982 | -0.006 | 134820 | 0.000 |
| \|******* | \| \| | 26 | 0.981 | 0.025 | 140118 | 0.000 |
| \|******* | \| \| | 27 | 0.980 | 0.002 | 145410 | 0.000 |
| \|******* | \| \| | 28 | 0.979 | -0.007 | 150694 | 0.000 |
| \|******* | \| \| | 29 | 0.979 | -0.023 | 155970 | 0.000 |
| \|******* | \| \| | 30 | 0.978 | -0.006 | 161239 | 0.000 |
| \|******* | \| \| | 31 | 0.977 | -0.018 | 166500 | 0.000 |
| \|******* | \| \| | 32 | 0.976 | 0.025 | 171753 | 0.000 |
| \|******* | \| \| | 33 | 0.975 | -0.013 | 176999 | 0.000 |
| \|******* | \| \| | 34 | 0.975 | 0.002 | 182237 | 0.000 |
| \|******* | \| \| | 35 | 0.974 | -0.008 | 187467 | 0.000 |
| \|******* | \| \| | 36 | 0.973 | 0.022 | 192690 | 0.000 |

The above Correlogram shows that the coefficient of AC starts at a very high value at lag 1 (0.999) and declines very slowly. Thus, it appears that the series is non stationary.

**Unit Root (ADF Test)**

Then the formal test of stationarity, i.e. Augmented Dickey Fuller Test was finally applied for finding out whether the series has a unit root. This test includes extra lagged terms of the dependent variable in order to eliminate autocorrelation. The results of the test including an intercept and trend are presented in Table 1.

**Table 1: Unit Root Test of Closing Prices**

Null Hypothesis: CLOSE has a unit root
Exogenous: Constant, Linear Trend
Lag Length: 11 (Automatic—based on SIC, maxlag = 32)

| | | t-Statistic | Prob.* |
|---|---|---|---|
| Augmented Dickey-Fuller test statistic | | −1.851768 | 0.6792 |
| Test critical values: | 1% level | −3.959716 | |
| | 5% level | −3.410626 | |
| | 10% level | −3.127092 | |

*MacKinnon (1996) one-sided p-values.

**Augmented Dickey-Fuller Test Equation**

Dependent Variable: D(CLOSE)
Method: Least Squares
Sample (adjusted): 1/17/1991 12/30/2011
Included observations: 5467 after adjustments

| Variable | Coefficient | Std. Error | t-Statistic | Prob. |
|---|---|---|---|---|
| CLOSE(-1) | −0.001217 | 0.000657 | −1.851768 | 0.0641 |
| D[(CLOSE(-1)] | 0.064813 | 0.013492 | 4.803904 | 0.0000 |
| D[CLOSE(-2)] | 0.007486 | 0.013503 | 0.554418 | 0.5793 |
| D[CLOSE(-3)] | −0.023571 | 0.013492 | −1.747123 | 0.0807 |
| D[CLOSE(-4)] | 0.017631 | 0.013494 | 1.306594 | 0.1914 |
| D[CLOSE(-5)] | −0.039155 | 0.013499 | −2.900555 | 0.0037 |
| D[CLOSE(-6)] | 0.052113 | 0.013492 | −3.862553 | 0.0001 |
| D[CLOSE(-7)] | −0.004490 | 0.013500 | −0.332561 | 0.7395 |
| D[CLOSE(-8)] | 0.019578 | 0.013513 | 1.448859 | 0.1474 |
| D[CLOSE(-9)] | 0.044802 | 0.013515 | 3.314992 | 0.0009 |
| D[CLOSE(-10)] | 0.053342 | 0.013528 | 3.942943 | 0.0001 |
| D[CLOSE(-11)] | −0.084767 | 0.013525 | −6.267259 | 0.0000 |
| C | 0.056260 | 3.971728 | 0.014165 | 0.9887 |
| @TREND(1/01/1991) | 0.004079 | 0.002302 | 1.771996 | 0.0765 |

| | | | |
|---|---|---|---|
| R-squared | 0.022160 | Mean dependent var | 2.640790 |
| Adjusted R-squared | 0.019829 | S.D. dependent var | 145.5756 |
| S.E. of regression | 144.1251 | Akaike info criterion | 12.78180 |
| Sum squared resid | 1.13E+08 | Schwarz criterion | 12.79872 |
| Log likelihood | –34925.04 | Hannan-Quinn criterion | 12.78770 |
| F-statistic | 9.506042 | Durbin-Watson statistic | 1.996099 |
| Prob (F-statistic) | 0.000000 | | |

Output generated by Eviews

The results are also proving the series to be non stationary since the calculated ADF statistic (–1.851768) is higher than the critical value at 1% level and hence the null hypothesis that the series has a unit root is accepted. Therefore it becomes necessary to make the series stationary before we proceed further. A time series can be made stationary by calculating first differences, but many time series e.g. GDP, money supply, stock prices all have an underlying growth rate. Such series are not stationary as the mean is continuously changing but no amount of differencing can make them stationary since they are not integrated. So we have to calculate log of the series because it turns the series into the one which is integrated and follows a linear trend. Then to eliminate the trend, logarithmic differences will be calculated which is called return. Stock returns are calculated by taking log difference of closing prices of two consecutive trading periods as follows:

$$r_t = (\ln P_t - \ln P_{t-1})*100$$

Then again to check out, all the above three tests were conducted with the return series.

**Graphical analysis**

**SENSEX Return Series from 1991 to 2011**

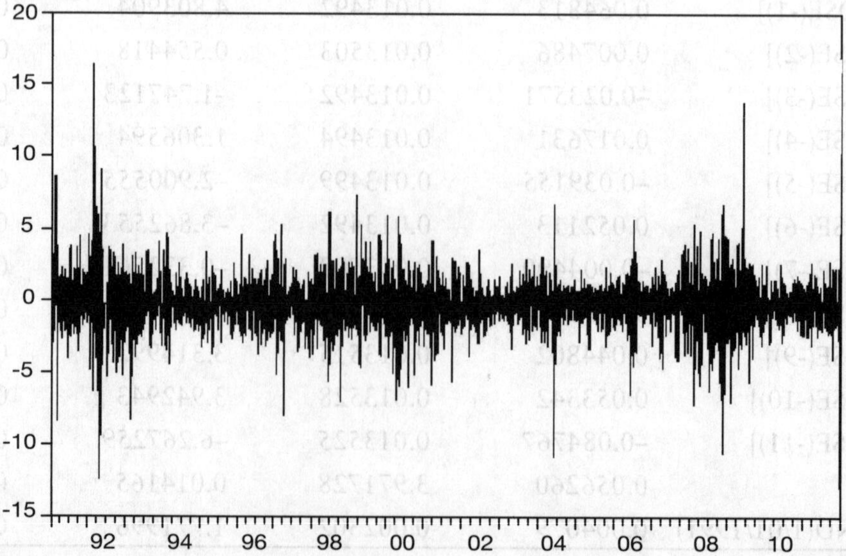


**Fig. 3**

It is quite clear from the above figure that the return series is showing mean reversion, indicating signs of stationarity.

### ACF and Correlogram

A Correlogram of ACF and PACF obtained from the return series was generated which is shown in figure 4. It is apparent from the Correlogram that values of ACF and PACF are very low at a lag length of 1 and as the lag length is increased they falls drastically to zero. Therefore now the series has become stationary.

**Correlogram of ACF and PACF of Closing Prices**

Sample: 1/01/1991 12/30/2011
Included observations: 5456

| Autocorrelation | Partial Correlation | | AC | PAC | Q-Stat. | Prob. |
|---|---|---|---|---|---|---|
| \|* \| | \|* \| | 1 | 0.076 | 0.076 | 31.866 | 0.000 |
| \| \| | \| \| | 2 | –0.016 | –0.022 | 33.261 | 0.000 |
| \| \| | \| \| | 3 | 0.009 | 0.012 | 33.743 | 0.000 |
| \| \| | \| \| | 4 | 0.030 | 0.028 | 38.588 | 0.000 |
| \| \| | \| \| | 5 | –0.008 | –0.012 | 38.905 | 0.000 |
| \| \| | \| \| | 6 | –0.040 | –0.037 | 47.449 | 0.000 |
| \| \| | \| \| | 7 | –0.026 | –0.021 | 51.013 | 0.000 |
| \| \| | \| \| | 8 | 0.002 | 0.003 | 51.027 | 0.000 |
| \| \| | \| \| | 9 | 0.036 | 0.037 | 58.268 | 0.000 |
| \| \| | \| \| | 10 | 0.051 | 0.048 | 72.391 | 0.000 |
| \| \| | \| \| | 11 | –0.032 | –0.038 | 78.069 | 0.000 |
| \| \| | \| \| | 12 | –0.011 | –0.006 | 78.685 | 0.000 |
| \| \| | \| \| | 13 | 0.028 | 0.023 | 82.969 | 0.000 |
| \| \| | \| \| | 14 | 0.007 | 0.001 | 83.262 | 0.000 |
| \| \| | \| \| | 15 | 0.020 | 0.026 | 85.437 | 0.000 |
| \| \| | \| \| | 16 | 0.014 | 0.015 | 86.466 | 0.000 |
| \| \| | \| \| | 17 | 0.035 | 0.031 | 93.110 | 0.000 |
| \| \| | \| \| | 18 | 0.007 | –0.001 | 93.382 | 0.000 |
| \| \| | \| \| | 19 | 0.006 | 0.004 | 93.595 | 0.000 |
| \| \| | \| \| | 20 | –0.002 | –0.003 | 93.627 | 0.000 |
| \| \| | \| \| | 21 | –0.013 | –0.009 | 94.612 | 0.000 |
| \| \| | \| \| | 22 | –0.002 | 0.001 | 94.625 | 0.000 |
| \| \| | \| \| | 23 | 0.018 | 0.017 | 96.308 | 0.000 |
| \| \| | \| \| | 24 | 0.003 | 0.002 | 96.350 | 0.000 |
| \| \| | \| \| | 25 | –0.017 | –0.019 | 98.014 | 0.000 |

| | | | | | | |
|---|---|---|---|---|---|---|
| \| \| | \| \| | 26 | –0.016 | –0.017 | 99.476 | 0.000 |
| \| \| | \| \| | 27 | 0.010 | 0.008 | 100.05 | 0.000 |
| \| \| | \| \| | 28 | 0.001 | –0.000 | 100.06 | 0.000 |
| \| \| | \| \| | 29 | 0.023 | 0.026 | 102.96 | 0.000 |
| \| \| | \| \| | 30 | –0.006 | –0.009 | 103.13 | 0.000 |
| \| \| | \| \| | 31 | –0.031 | –0.032 | 108.55 | 0.000 |
| \| \| | \| \| | 32 | 0.010 | 0.008 | 109.09 | 0.000 |
| \| \| | \| \| | 33 | –0.011 | –0.018 | 109.73 | 0.000 |
| \| \| | \| \| | 34 | –0.013 | –0.007 | 110.64 | 0.000 |
| \| \| | \| \| | 35 | –0.011 | –0.003 | 111.34 | 0.000 |
| \| \| | \| \| | 36 | 0.014 | 0.014 | 112.43 | 0.000 |

**Fig. 4**

**Unit Root (ADF Test)**

Then with the return series we conducted the formal test of stationarity, i.e. the ADF test for finding out if there is a unit root in the series the results are as follows:

**Table 2:** Unit Root Test of Return Series

Null Hypothesis: RETURN has a unit root
Exogenous: Constant, Linear Trend
Lag Length: 0 (Automatic—based on SIC, maxlag = 32)

| | | t-Statistic | Prob.* |
|---|---|---|---|
| Augmented Dickey-Fuller test statistic | | –68.40481 | 0.0000 |
| Test critical values: | 1% level | –3.959715 | |
| | 5% level | –3.410626 | |
| | 10% level | –3.127092 | |

*MacKinnon (1996) one-sided p-values.

Augmented Dickey-Fuller Test Equation
Dependent Variable: D(RETURN)
Method: Least Squares
Date: 08/25/12 Time: 11:09
Sample (adjusted): 1/03/1991 12/30/2011
Included observations: 5468 after adjustments

| Variable | Coefficient | Std. Error | t-Statistic | Prob. |
|---|---|---|---|---|
| RETURN(–1) | –0.921685 | 0.013474 | -68.40481 | 0.0000 |
| C | 0.073605 | 0.046747 | 1.574547 | 0.1154 |
| @TREND(1/01/1991) | –1.08E-05 | 1.48E-05 | -0.729544 | 0.4657 |

| | | | |
|---|---|---|---|
| R-squared | 0.461270 | Mean dependent var | 0.000564 |
| Adjusted R-squared | 0.461073 | S.D. dependent var | 2.354334 |
| S.E. of regression | 1.728356 | Akaike info criterion | 3.932767 |
| Sum squared resid. | 16325.13 | Schwarz criterion | 3.936392 |
| Log likelihood | −10749.19 | Hannan-Quinn criterion | 3.934032 |
| F-statistic | 2339.611 | Durbin-Watson statistic | 1.998299 |
| Prob (F-statistic) | 0.000000 | | |

The calculated ADF statistic is less than the critical value at 1% level, thereby rejecting the null hypothesis of a unit root. The return series does not have a unit root, i.e. it is stationary. Therefore we will conduct the test of seasonality with return series.

**Dummy Variable Regression Model**

In regression analysis the dependent variable is not only affected by continuous variables (e.g. income, output, price, etc.) but also by some qualitative or categorical variables such as gender, color, nationality, geographical regions, religion, etc. Since these variables being qualitative in nature cannot be included in the regression model, we will have to proceed with a technique called dummy variable regression model. This technique quantifies the categorical variables and then we can include them in the regression equation as independent or explanatory variables. Dummy variables, also called binary or categorical or indicator variables, takes only two values: 1 for the presence of attribute and 0 for the absence of attribute. For example 1 may indicate a person to be male and 0 that the person is not male (i.e. female). Such regression model containing dummy variables are also called ANOVA Models.

To examine the monthly effect, one less than the available categories dummy variables are taken. This is because of the fact that if we have dummy variables for all the categories, this is the case of perfect collinearity. Since we have to compare the mean value of other groups with the reference group, the value of reference group is taken as intercept. In our case which month should be selected as the reference or benchmark month it may be decided with the help of descriptive statistics of all the months, which is presented in Table 3.

**Table 3:** Descriptive Statistics for RETURN Series of SENSEX for Jan. 1991 to Dec. 2011

| MONTH | Mean | Median | Max. | Min. | Std. Dev. | Skew. | Kurt. | Obs. |
|---|---|---|---|---|---|---|---|---|
| Jan | 0.007624 | 0.000000 | 7.117780 | −7.695694 | 1.722634 | 0.038318 | 5.649700 | 461 |
| Feb | 0.183620 | 0.061170 | 10.08303 | −5.251809 | 1.761170 | 0.593391 | 6.126059 | 423 |
| Mar | −0.012281 | 0.000000 | 18.89998 | −9.097025 | 2.238012 | 1.327300 | 17.21363 | 466 |
| Apr | 0.040447 | 0.000000 | 7.433645 | −13.66073 | 1.883161 | −0.767150 | 10.94308 | 451 |
| May | −0.018850 | 0.000000 | 15.98998 | −11.80918 | 2.116051 | 0.303777 | 14.95426 | 463 |
| Jun | 0.039585 | 0.035206 | 7.314106 | −6.725771 | 1.642981 | −0.066489 | 5.230383 | 451 |
| Jul | 0.087678 | 0.027396 | 5.772215 | −6.366458 | 1.644857 | −0.160957 | 4.893939 | 465 |
| Aug | 0.107898 | 0.010413 | 4.251637 | −4.378896 | 1.350988 | −0.108883 | 3.774968 | 464 |
| Sep | 0.059144 | 0.071378 | 5.313935 | −6.027435 | 1.491421 | −0.373562 | 5.045795 | 448 |

| | | | | | | | | |
|---|---|---|---|---|---|---|---|---|
| Oct | −0.121644 | 0.000000 | 7.900533 | −11.60444 | 1.816938 | −0.557973 | 9.007081 | 463 |
| Nov | 0.041207 | 0.000000 | 5.580545 | −6.838894 | 1.536221 | −0.003215 | 5.028529 | 450 |
| Dec | 0.157711 | 0.000000 | 5.367202 | −5.590850 | 1.361022 | 0.015321 | 4.967389 | 467 |
| All | 0.046790 | 0.000000 | 18.89998 | −13.66073 | 1.734463 | 0.142341 | 11.40849 | 5472 |

There are wide variations in the return of different months. Returns for February, August and December are higher than returns of other months while October, May and March are providing negative returns. Over all the series is positively skewed and leptokurtic. Since we want to prove tax loss selling hypothesis and in India March is the end of the tax year, March was taken as the benchmark month and the following equation was estimated:

$$Y_t = \alpha_3 + \alpha_1 D_{Jan} + \alpha_2 D_{Feb} + \alpha_4 D_{Apr} + \alpha_5 D_{May} + \alpha_6 D_{Jun} + \alpha_7 D_{Jul} + \alpha_8 D_{Aug} + \alpha_9 D_{Sep} + \alpha_{10} D_{Oct} + \alpha_{11} D_{Nov} + \alpha_{12} D_{Dec} + \varepsilon_1 \quad \text{... Equation 1}$$

The intercept or constant term is the average return for March and coefficients $\alpha_1$ to $\alpha_{12}$ represents the average differences between the return for March and other months. If the value of these coefficients is zero, then the return for each month is same and no seasonal monthly effects are there. $\varepsilon_1$ is the white noise error term. The results of equation 1 are presented in Table 4.

**Table 4: Test for March Effect**

Dependent Variable: RETURN
Method: Least Squares

| Variable | Coefficient | Std. Error | t-Statistic | Prob. |
|---|---|---|---|---|
| C | −0.012281 | 0.080346 | −0.152852 | 0.8785 |
| Jan | 0.019905 | 0.113934 | 0.174710 | 0.8613 |
| Feb | 0.195901 | 0.116478 | 1.681870 | 0.0927 |
| Apr | 0.052728 | 0.114567 | 0.460236 | 0.6454 |
| May | −0.006569 | 0.113810 | −0.057723 | 0.9540 |
| Jun | 0.051866 | 0.114567 | 0.452710 | 0.6508 |
| Jul | 0.099959 | 0.113687 | 0.879248 | 0.3793 |
| Aug | 0.120179 | 0.113748 | 1.056528 | 0.2908 |
| Sep | 0.071425 | 0.114762 | 0.622374 | 0.5337 |
| Oct | −0.109363 | 0.113810 | −0.960925 | 0.3366 |
| Nov | 0.053488 | 0.114632 | 0.466603 | 0.6408 |
| Dec | 0.169992 | 0.113565 | 1.496868 | 0.1345 |
| R-squared | 0.002051 | Mean dependent var | | 0.046790 |
| Adjusted R-squared | 0.000041 | S.D. dependent var | | 1.734463 |
| S.E. of regression | 1.734427 | Akaike info criterion | | 3.941422 |
| Sum squared resid | 16424.98 | Schwarz criterion | | 3.955912 |

| | | | |
|---|---|---|---|
| Log likelihood | –10771.73 | Hannan-Quinn criter. | 3.946478 |
| F-statistic | 1.020311 | Durbin-Watson stat | 1.847033 |
| Prob(F-statistic) | 0.424927 | | |

The results indicate that except for February, none of the coefficients are significant at conventional level of significance indicating February effect in the SENSEX returns over the sample period. $R^2$ is .002 which is very low and F-statistic indicates the poor fit of the overall model. Further, the D-W statistic indicates the autocorrelation in the residuals. Therefore LM test (Breusch-Godfrey Lagrange Multiplier test) with number of lags as 1 was applied to find out general, high order ARMA errors and the results are presented in Table 5.

**Table 5:** Breusch-Godfrey Serial Correlation LM Test

| | | | |
|---|---|---|---|
| F-statistic | 31.69634 | Prob. F (1.5459) | 0.0000 |
| Obs*R-squared | 31.58841 | Prob. Chi-Square(1) | 0.0000 |

The F-Statistic (31.69634) and the LM-statistic both are very high with an insignificant p value, thereby rejecting the null of no serial correlation. Thus there is serial correlation of order one in the residuals. To overcome the problem of serial correlation equation 1 was improved by adding ar(1) term on the right-hand side of the equation.

Therefore a model called ARIMA (Auto Regressive Integrated Moving Average Model) will have to be constructed. The next step is to decide what kind of ARIMA model to use. If the autocorrelation function (ACF) for the residual series dies off smoothly at a geometric rate, and the partial autocorrelations were zero after one lag, then a first-order autoregressive model is appropriate. Alternatively, if the autocorrelations were zero after one lag and the partial autocorrelations declined geometrically, a first-order moving average process would seem appropriate.

## REFERENCES

Agarwal, Anup and Kishore Tandon (1994), "Anomalies or Illusions? Evidence from stock Markets in Eighteen Countries", *Journal of International money and Finance,* Vol. 13, pp. 83-106.

Boudreaux Denis O. (1995), "The Monthly Effect in International Stock Markets: Evidence and Implications", *Journal of Financial and Strategic Decisions,* Vol. 8, No. 1, pp. 15-20.

Chan, M.W.L., Khanthavit, Anya and Thomas, Hugh (1996), "Seasonality & Cultural influences on four Asian Stock Markets", *Asia Pacific Journal of Management*, Vol. 13, No. 2, pp. 1-24.

Chen, Zhiwu and Jindra, Jan (2001), "A Valuation Study of Stock Market Seasonality and Size Effect", *Yale ICF Working Paper* No. 00-37. Taken from http://www.janjindra.com/seasonality_20091030.pdf, visited on 10th June, 2010.

Gultekin, Mustafa N. and Gultekin, N. Bulent (1983), "Stock Market Seasonality: International Evidence", *Journal of Financial Economics*, Volume 12, Issue 4, December 1983, pp. 469-81.

Huffman, Stephen P. (1997), "Seasonality in the returns of defaulted bonds: the January and October effects", *Quarterly Journal of Business and Economics*. Taken from www.allbusiness.com/business-planning/business... /659624-1.html, visited on 7th June, 2010.

Kulkarni, S.N. (1978), "Share Price Behavior in India: A Spectral Analysis of Random Walk Hypothesis", *Sankhya,* Vol. 40, series D. part 2. 135-62.

Lazar, D., Priya Julia and Jeyapaul Joseph (2006), "SENSEX Monthly Return: Is There Seasonality?" *Indian Institute of Capital Markets 9th Capital Markets Conference Paper*. Taken from http://ssrn.com/abstract=876551, visited on 11 June, 2010.

Lakonishok, Josef and Smidt Seymour (1984), "Volume and Turn-of-the-year behavior", *Journal of Financial Economics,* Vol. 13, Issue 3, pp. 435-55.

Marsh, Terry A., Philip, Brown, Keim, Donald B. and Kleidon, Donald B. (1983), "Stock Return Seasonality and the Tax-loss Selling Hypothesis: Analysis of the Arguments and Australian Evidences", Working Paper Alfred P. Sloan School of Management.

Mookerjee, Rajen and Qiao Yu (1999), "Seasonality in returns on the Chinese stock markets: the case of Shanghai and Shenzhen", *Global Finance Journal,* Vol. 10, Issue 1, pp. 93-105.

Pandey, I.M. (2002), "Is There Seasonality in the SENSEX Monthly Returns?", *IIMA Working Paper*, IIM Ahemadabad. Taken from www.iimahd.ernet.in/publications/data/2002-09-08IMPandey.pdf, visited on 8th June, 2010.

Pinnuck, Matt and Gallagher, R. David (2006), "Seasonality in Fund Performance: An Examination of the Portfolio Holdings and Trades of Investment Managers", *Journal of Business, Finance and Accounting*, Vol. 33, 1240-66.

Reinganum, Marc R. (1983), "The anomalous stock market behavior of small firms in January: Empirical tests for tax-loss selling effects", *Journal of Financial Economics*, Vol. 12, Issue 1, pp. 89-104.

Roll, R. (1983), "The turn-ofs-the-year effect and the return premia of small firms", *Journal of Portfolio Management*, Vol. 9, Issue 2, pp. 18-28.

Rozeff, Michael S. and Kinney, William R. Jr. (1976), "Capital market seasonality: The case of stock returns", *Journal of Financial Economics*, Vol. 3, Issue 4, pp. 379-402.

Saez, J.C. Mattalin (2006), "Seasonality, Market Timing and Performance amongst Benchmarks and Mutual Fund Evaluation", *Journal of Business Finance & Accounting,* Vol. 33, No. 9-10, pp. 1484-1507.

Sah, Ash Narayan (2009), "Stock Market Seasonality: A Study of the Indian Stock Market", *University of Petroleum & Energy Studies. NseIndia, Working Paper, No. 228*. Taken from nseindia.com/content/research/res_paper_final228.pdf, visited on 15th June, 2010.

Sarma, S.N. (2004), "Stock Market Seasonality in an Emerging Market", *Vikalpa*, Vol. 29, No. 3, pp. 35-41.

Watchel, S.B. (1942), "Certain Observation on seasonal movement in Stock Prices." *Journal of Business,* Vol. 15, pp. 184-93.

Worthington, A.C. (2008), "The Decline of Calendar Seasonality in the Australian Stock Exchange, 1958-2005", *Accounting & Finance Working Paper 06/12, School of Accounting & Finance, University of Wollongong, 2006,* Paper 28. Taken from http://ssrn.com/abstract=1290905, visited on 11th June, 2010.

# 7

# FOREIGN DIRECT INVESTMENT, ECONOMIC GROWTH AND STOCK MARKET RELATIONSHIP: EMPIRICAL EVIDENCE FROM INDIA

–*Kamlesh Pritwani* and *Naveen Kumar Sharma*

## Introduction

Over the past two decades, many countries around the world have experienced substantial growth in their economies, with even faster growth in international transactions, especially in the form of foreign direct investment (FDI). The share of net FDI in world GDP has grown five-fold through the eighties and the nineties, making the causes and consequences of FDI and economic growth a subject of ever-growing interest. This paper attempts to make a contribution in this context, by analyzing the existence and nature of causalities, if any, between FDI and economic growth. It uses as its focal point the South and Southeast Asian region, where growth of economic activities and FDI has been one of the most pronounced.

The literature on FDI and economic growth generally points to a positive relationship between the two variables, and offers several, standard explanations for it. In principle, economic growth may induce FDI inflow when FDI is seeking consumer markets, or when growth leads to greater economies of scale and, hence, increased cost efficiency. On the other hand, FDI may affect economic growth, through its impact on capital stock, technology transfer, skill acquisition, or market competition. FDI and growth may also exhibit a negative relationship, particularly if the inflow of FDI leads to increased monopolization of local industries, thus compromising efficiency and growth dynamics. Empirically, the positive effect of economic growth on FDI and also the positive and negative effects of FDI on economic growth have been identified in the literature. However, very few studies attempt to directly test for causality between FDI and growth. Two studies that do so include Basu, Chakraborty and Reagle (2003), and Trevino and Upadhyaya (2003). Both find that FDI-to-growth causality is more likely to exist in more open economies. In addition, an earlier study by Ericsson and Irandoust (2000) explores the causal relationship between FDI and total factor productivity growth in Norway and Sweden, and finds the two to be causally related in the long run.

This paper extends the line of work mentioned above, and provides a direct test of causality between FDI and economic growth in one of the most dynamic regions of the world: India. To better understand, the paper extends the analysis using regression techniques, and identifies institutional variables that affect the FDI-growth relationship. The importance of institutions to economic dynamics is now well recognized, and given the widespread but varying institutional reforms across countries through the eighties and the nineties, the inclusion of institutional factors is indispensable for the analysis at hand. To identify their relevance to the FDI-growth relationship, separate from their direct effects on FDI or growth alone, the analysis focuses on interaction effects involving the explanatory variables. The results show that FDI-to-growth causality is reinforced by greater trade openness, more limited rule of law, lower receipts of bilateral aid, and lower income level in the host country. Growth-to-FDI causality, on the other hand, is reinforced by greater political rights and more limited rule of law.

The remainder of the paper is structured as follows: Section II discusses the background literature on the determinants of and relationship between FDI and economic growth. Section III carries out the sample used in the present analysis. Section IV extends the analysis using regression analysis and testing of hypotheses. Finally, Section V concludes. Relevant tables, with descriptive statistics and results of the analyses, are presented in the appendix.

### Foreign Direct Investment and Economic Growth

Standard economic theory points to a direct, causal relationship between economic growth and FDI that can run in either direction. On the one hand, FDI flows can be induced by host country economic growth if the host country offers a sizeable consumer market, in which case FDI serves as a substitute for commodity trade, or if growth leads to greater economies of scale and cost efficiency in the host country. On the other hand, FDI itself may contribute to host country economic growth, by augmenting the country's capital stock, introducing complementary inputs, inducing technology transfer and skill acquisition, or increasing competition in the local industry. Of course, FDI may also inhibit competition and thus hamper growth, especially if the host country government affords extra protection to foreign investors in the process of attracting their capital.

Empirically, the positive effect of host country economic growth on FDI inflow has been confirmed by various studies (see Veugelers, 1991; Barrell and Pain, 1996; Grosse and Trevino, 1996; Taylor and Sarno, 1999; Trevino et al., 2002). The effects of FDI on subsequent economic growth has been shown to be both positive (Dunning, 1993; Borensztein et al., 1998; De Mello, 1999; Ericsson and Irandoust, 2000; Trevino and Upadhyaya, 2003) and negative (Moran, 1998). Generally, the positive growth effects of FDI have been more likely when FDI is drawn into competitive markets, whereas negative effects on growth have been more likely when FDI is drawn into heavily protected industries (Encarnation and Wells, 1986). Overall, though, FDI turns out to be associated with greater domestic investment, not smaller. Moreover, this positive association between FDI and domestic investment tends to be greater than that between foreign portfolio investment and domestic investment (Bosworth and Collins, 1999).

Basu, Chakraborty and Reagle (2003) study a panel of 23 developing countries from Asia, Africa, Europe and Latin America, and find the causal relationship between GDP growth and FDI to run both ways in more open economies, and in only one direction—from GDP growth to FDI—in more closed economies. Trevino and Upadhyaya (2003) find a comparable result, based on their study of five developing countries in Asia, that the positive impact of FDI on economic growth is greater in more open economies. Whether other factors, especially institutional ones that directly affect FDI or economic growth, also influence FDI-growth relationship remains an open question.

Generally speaking, FDI decisions depend on a variety of characteristics of the host economy, in addition to its market size. These include the general wage level, level of education, institutional environment, tax laws, and overall macroeconomic and political environment. The impact of host country wage level or education level on FDI depends on the skill intensity of the particular production process in question and, hence, may vary from case to case. The impact of institutional quality, physical infrastructure, import tariffs, macroeconomic stability, and political stability on FDI inflow is usually positive (see Wei, 1997; Mallampally and Sauvant, 1999; Trevino et al., 2002; Biswas, 2002), whereas that of corporate taxes tends to be negative (see Wei, 1997; Gastanaga et al., 1998; Hsiao, 2001). Turning to economic growth, the standard determinants include the rate of capital accumulation and variables that raise total factor productivity, such as education level, institutional quality, macroeconomic stability, political environment, and, potentially, trade openness. In studying the direct, causal relationship between FDI and economic growth in this paper, we explore the relevance of some of these economic and political economy variables just mentioned. Our study covers the FDI-growth relationship in India.

## Review of Literature

The inflow of FDI increased rapidly during the last two decades in almost every region of the world. A number of empirical studies on the role of FDI in host countries suggest that FDI is an important source of capital, complements domestic private investment, and is usually associated with new job opportunities and enhancement of technology transfer, and boosts overall economic growth in host countries (Chowdhury & Mavrotas, 2006).

The relationship between growing FDI stock and economic growth has motivated a voluminous empirical literature in developed and developing countries. FDI has been acknowledged as most crucial factor in enhancing economic development and the standard of living for emerging economies. Based on references, the consensus seems to be that there is a positive correlation between FDI inflows and economic growth, provided that the receiving countries have reached a minimum level of educational, technological and/or infrastructure development (Hansen & Rand, 2006).

South Korea, Singapore, and Taiwan are examples of nations outside the OECD countries that have greatly benefited from FDI and the integration in the global economy. In recent years, China and India have made remarkable progress in attracting FDI and realizing technological and economic success. A number of studies find that FDI inflows have a strong and positive effect on economic growth in China (Tian, Lin, & Lo, 2004).

In Russia, FDI appears to have been an essential force in supporting the economy during the initial chaos of transition (Brock, 2005). The CEE countries increased their participation in the world economy since the fall of communism; particularly over the last few years. They accepted the challenge of trade openness and attracted significant foreign direct investment (Cernat & Vranceanu, 2002). The CEE countries acknowledge FDI as an essential tool in the development and modernization of their economies (Kornecki & Raghavan, 2008).

Salehizadeh, Asheghian and others confirm the existence of a positive and significant relationship between FDI and the economic growth in the United States (Asheghian, 2004). He examines the determinants of economic growth in the United States over time uses a model based on the postulates of de Mello based on and found a causal relationships between FDI growth and economic growth is uni-directional, running from economic growth to FDI and a causal relationships between FDI growth and total factor productivity growth is uni-directional, running from FDI to total factor productivity.

Mayang Pramadhani, Rakesh Bissondeeal and Nigel Driffield (2007) have examined the causal relationships between inward direct investment, growth and trade in Indonesia for the period 1990-2004. They seek to establish whether there were strong, weak positive or negative associations between the presences of multinational enterprises and Indonesian exports and imports determent the causal links between the variables.

The Foreign Direct Investment (FDI) has contributed significantly to Malaysia's electronics exports as well as the growth and development of the electronics industry [Koi Nyen Wong and Tuck Cheong Tang (2007)].

Frank S.T. Hsiao and Mei-chu W. Hsiao (2006) have examined the Granger causality relations between GDP, Exports and FDI among East and Southeast Asia. In this Paper, the authors estimated the VAR and VECM of the three variables to find various Granger Causal relations for each of the eight Economies and they used the fixed effects and random effects approaches to estimate the panel data VAR equations for Granger Causality tests.

Zhang (2005) examines the role of FDI on Chinese export performance. The investigation is not only the estimates of full sample of industries. The result indicates that FDI has a superior influence on export performance in China at the industrial level.

Pacheco-Lopez (2005) demonstrates the causal relationship between inward FDI and Export performance on Mexico by using the Granger causality test. The result indicates that there is a bi-directional causality between inward FDI and export performance.

Melina Dritsaki, Chaido Dritsaki and Antonios Adamopoulos (2004), investigates the relationship between Trade, Foreign Direct Investment (FDI) and economic growth for Greece over the period 1960-2002. The cointegration analysis suggested that there is a long-run equilibrium relationship among the above variables. The results of Granger causality test showed that there is a causal relationship between the economic growth, trade and FDI.

Metwally (2004) tests the relationship between FDI, exports and economic growth in three European Union (EU) countries, viz., Egypt, Jordan and Omen, during the period from 1981 to 2000 by using a simultaneous equation model. The result suggests that the export of goods and services is strongly influenced by the inward FDI in these three countries.

Baliamoune-Lutz (2004) examines the causal relationship between FDI, Exports and economic growth in Morocco from 1973 to 1999 by using the Granger causality test. The result shows that there is a two-way causal relationship between FDI and exports at a national level.

Alici and Ucal (2003) investigate the causal links among inward FDI, exports and economic growth in Turkish economy during the period of 1987 to 2002 on a quarter bases. The linkage of FDI-led export growth is not found in Turkey.

Alireza Karbasi, Ebrahim Mohamadi and Samane Ghofrani (2002) have analysed the role of FDI and trade in promoting economic growth across selected developing countries and the interaction among FDI, Trade and Economic growth. The authors examined data from forty-two developing countries over the last three decades. The study results suggest that FDI, Trade, human capital and domestic investment are important sources of economic growth for developing countries and FDI stimulates domestic investment.

Liu et al. (2002) investigate the causal relationship between inward FDI, trade and economic growth in China at the aggregate level from 1981 to 1997 on a quarter basis. A two-way causal relationship between inward FDI and exports is found.

Liu et al. (2002) investigate the causal links between GDP, FDI, exports and imports in China with the methods developed by Johansen (1988) and Hall and Milne (1994). They show that each of these variables with the tests proposed by Hall and Milne (1994). They also provide evidence to support the presence of bi-directional short-run causal links between GDP, FDI and exports. But, uni-directional causal link can be found from GDP, FDI and exports to imports.

Liu et al. (2001) examine the causal relationship between inward FDI and foreign trade between China and 19 economies by using the Granger causality test during the period 1984 to 1998. The result reveals that the growth of imports in China leads to the growth of inward FDI in China.

Khan and Leng (1997) examine the interactions among inward FDI, exports and economic growth for Singapore, Taiwan and South Korea, at the aggregate level during the period from 1965 to 1995 by using Granger causality test. They claim that there is no evidence to support the causal relationship between FDI and Exports in Taiwan and South Korea. Moreover, a one-way causal relationship which flows from exports to inward FDI is found in Singapore.

## Objectives

The main objective in this paper, therefore aims:

- To ascertain the relationship between FDI and economic growth (GDP) in India for the period 2001-12.
- To analyze the relationship between FDI and BSE-Sensex.
- To study the relationship between FDI and NSE-CNX Nifty-50.
- To explore the effect of FDI Inflow on Merchandise Exports in India.

## Hypotheses

H01: The growth of FDI inflows does not contribute to the increase of GDP in India.

H02: The growth of FDI inflows does not contribute to the increase of BSE-Sensex indices in India.

H03: The growth of FDI inflows does not contribute to the increase of NSE-CNX-Nifty-50 in India.

H04: The growth of FDI inflows does not contribute to the increase of Merchandise Exports in India.

## Research Methodology

The present study is basically empirical in nature based on secondary data. The goal of this study is to investigative the relationship between FDI and economic growth, and to determine the extent to which foreign capital contributes to India's productivity growth. Over the last two decades, India has attracted handsome inflows of foreign direct investment. This research analyzes the relationship among foreign capital inflows (in the form of foreign direct investment and foreign institutional investment), Capital Market Indicators (in the form of BSE-Sensex and NSE-CNX-Nifty-50) and GDP Growth rate (Annual %) (Table 1). The data for the current study was obtained from secondary sources including the official websites of Indian government, World Investment Reports, as well as other selected databases. We use multiple regression analysis, Descriptive statistics, correlation, t-test and the empirical analysis which is conducted by using annual data on FDI and economy growth in India over the 2001-11 periods. We use annual data from IMF International Financial Statistics tables, published by International Monetary Fund to find out the relationship between FDI and economic growth in India case.

**Table 1:** Year-wise data on Foreign Direct Investment, Foreign Institutional Investment Inflows, BSE Sensex, NSE-CNX Nifty-50, Merchandise Exports and GDP in India

| S. No. | Years | FDI Inflow (Amount US$ million) | FII Inflow (Amount US$ million) | Economic growth factors taken by the researchers in present study | | | | | | |
|---|---|---|---|---|---|---|---|---|---|---|
| | | | | BSE-Sensex Indices | NSE-CNX-Nifty-50 | GDP Growth Rate (Annual %) | Merchandise Exports (In US$ million) | GNI Growth (Annual %) | GNI Per Capita Growth (Annual %) | GDP (In US$ million) |
| 1. | 2001 | 4065 | 1847 | 3262.33 | 1059 | 4.9 | 4336 | 5.15 | 3.43 | 49237.00 |
| 2. | 2002 | 2705 | 1505 | 3377.28 | 1093 | 3.9 | 4925 | 4.12 | 2.46 | 52279.00 |
| 3. | 2003 | 2188 | 377 | 5838.96 | 1879 | 7.9 | 5896 | 7.85 | 6.18 | 61757.00 |
| 4. | 2004 | 3219 | 10918 | 6602.69 | 2080 | 7.8 | 7664 | 7.9 | 6.25 | 72158.00 |
| 5. | 2005 | 5540 | 8686 | 9397.93 | 2836 | 9.3 | 9961 | 9.26 | 7.62 | 83421.00 |
| 6. | 2006 | 12492 | 9926 | 13786.91 | 3966 | 9.3 | 12180 | 9.18 | 7.58 | 94911.00 |
| 7. | 2007 | 24575 | 3225 | 20286.99 | 6138 | 9.8 | 15015 | 10.2 | 8.61 | 123870.00 |
| 8. | 2008 | 31396 | 20328 | 9647.31 | 2959 | 3.9 | 19482 | 3.7 | 2.22 | 122409.00 |
| 9. | 2009 | 25834 | –15017 | 17464.81 | 5201 | 8.2 | 16490 | 8.23 | 6.72 | 136105.00 |
| 10. | 2010 | 19427 | 29048 | 20509.09 | 6134 | 9.6 | 21967 | 9.05 | 7.55 | 168432.00 |
| 11. | 2011 | 28403 | 29422 | 15454.92 | 4624 | 6.9 | 29655 | 6.94 | 5.49 | 184798.00 |

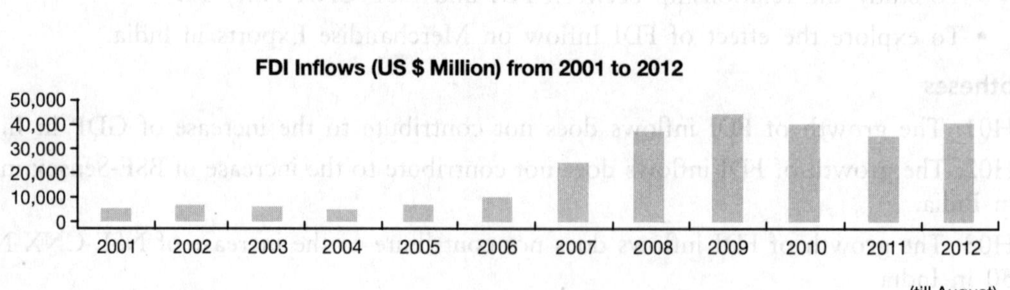


**Fig. 1:** FDI Inflows in US $ Million from 2001 to 2012 (till August)

**Table 2:** Descriptive Statistics

| | FDI Inflow (Amount US$ million) | FII Inflow (Amount US$ million) | BSE-Sensex Indices | NSE-CNX-Nifty-50 | Merchandise Exports (In US$ million) | GDP (In US$ million) |
|---|---|---|---|---|---|---|
| Mean | 14531.27273 | 9115 | 11420.18182 | 3451.727273 | 13415.54545 | 104488.8182 |
| Standard Error | 3495.671604 | 3981.385 | 1936.415723 | 567.090246 | 2418.247785 | 13954.51945 |
| Median | 12492 | 8686 | 9647 | 2959 | 12180 | 94911 |
| Standard Deviation | 11593.8311 | 13204.76 | 6422.36439 | 1880.825568 | 8020.420555 | 46281.90515 |
| Sample Variance | 134416919.6 | 1.74E+08 | 41246764.36 | 3537504.818 | 64327145.87 | 2142014744 |
| Kurtosis | –1.907009934 | 0.030545 | –1.49591514 | –1.4014535 | –0.056259809 | –0.932518381 |
| Skewness | 0.249109368 | 0.104075 | 0.177335741 | 0.222933627 | 0.745107419 | 0.482054819 |
| Range | 29208 | 44439 | 17247 | 5079 | 25319 | 135561 |
| Minimum | 2188 | –15017 | 3262 | 1059 | 4336 | 49237 |
| Maximum | 31396 | 29422 | 20509 | 6138 | 29655 | 184798 |
| Sum | 159844 | 100265 | 125622 | 37969 | 147571 | 1149377 |
| Count | 11 | 11 | 11 | 11 | 11 | 11 |
| Largest (1) | 31396 | 29422 | 20509 | 6138 | 29655 | 184798 |
| Smallest (1) | 2188 | –15017 | 3262 | 1059 | 4336 | 49237 |

**Table 3:** Correlation Matrix

| | FDI Inflow | FII Inflow | BSE-Sensex | NSE-CNX-Nifty-50 | GDP Growth Rate | Merchandise Exports | GNI Growth | GNI Per Capita Growth | GDP |
|---|---|---|---|---|---|---|---|---|---|
| FDI Inflow | 1 | | | | | | | | |
| FII Inflow | 0.321 | 1 | | | | | | | |
| BSE-Sensex | 0.732 | 0.245 | 1 | | | | | | |
| NSE-CNX-Nifty-50 | 0.734 | 0.245 | 0.999 | 1 | | | | | |
| GDP Growth Rate | 0.053 | 0.009 | 0.660 | 0.657 | 1 | | | | |
| Merchandise Exports | 0.868 | 0.633 | 0.740 | 0.739 | 0.185 | 1 | | | |
| GNI Growth | 0.029 | -0.053 | 0.637 | 0.634 | 0.993 | 0.140 | 1 | | |
| GNI Per Capita Growth | 0.066 | -0.032 | 0.665 | 0.662 | 0.994 | 0.178 | 0.999 | 1 | |
| GDP | 0.853 | 0.547 | 0.848 | 0.849 | 0.326 | 0.976 | 0.282 | 0.320 | 1 |

## Regression Results

The dependent variable for the present study were FII Inflow, BSE-Sensex indices, NSE-CNX-Nifty, Merchandise Exports and Gross Domestic Products. Independent variable for the present study was FDI inflow.

**Table 4:** Regression Statistics

| Regression Statistics | |
|---|---|
| Multiple R | 0.954852851 |
| R Square | 0.911743968 |
| Adjusted R Square | 0.823487936 |
| Standard Error | 4870.955544 |
| Observations | 11 |

Table 5: Anova on Regression Model

| ANOVA | | | | | |
|---|---|---|---|---|---|
| | df | SS | MS | F | Significance F |
| Regression | 5 | 1225538157 | 245107631.3 | 10.33067 | 0.011402675 |
| Residual | 5 | 118631039.6 | 23726207.92 | | |
| Total | 10 | 1344169196 | | | |

Table 6: Regression Model Development

| | Coefficients | Standard Error | t Stat | P-value | Lower 95% | Upper 95% | Lower 95.0% | Upper 95.0% |
|---|---|---|---|---|---|---|---|---|
| Intercept | 6748.546893 | 7501.520411 | 0.899623879 | 0.409553 | -12534.72521 | 26031.81899 | -12534.72521 | 26031.81899 |
| X Variable 1 | -0.373802881 | 0.168444464 | -2.219146133 | 0.077211 | -0.806803161 | 0.059197398 | -0.806803161 | 0.059197398 |
| X Variable 2 | -7.321317734 | 6.809590581 | -1.075148006 | 0.33143 | -24.82592758 | 10.18329212 | -24.82592758 | 10.18329212 |
| X Variable 3 | 29.29711247 | 23.92990122 | 1.224288901 | 0.275377 | -32.21665692 | 90.81088185 | -32.21665692 | 90.81088185 |
| X Variable 4 | 4.493367932 | 1.563995856 | 2.873005012 | 0.034872 | 0.472988595 | 8.513747269 | 0.472988595 | 8.513747269 |
| X Variable 5 | -0.637445291 | 0.33174855 | -1.921471218 | 0.112716 | -1.490232088 | 0.215341506 | -1.490232088 | 0.215341506 |

Thus the regression equation is $Y = 6748.54 - 0.3738X_1 - 7.321X_2 + 29.297X_3 + 4.493X_4 - 0.637X_5$

Where:

$Y$ = FDI Inflow (In US$ Million)

$X_1$ = FII Inflows (In US$ Million)

$X_2$ = BSE Sensex

$X_3$ = NSE-CNX-Nifty

$X_4$ = Merchandise Exports (In US$ Million)

$X_5$ = GDP (In US$ Million)

Table 7: Residual Output

| RESIDUAL OUTPUT | | | |
|---|---|---|---|
| Observation | Predicted Y | Residuals | Standard Residuals |
| 1. | 1298.986198 | 2766.013802 | 0.803073277 |
| 2. | 2288.462205 | 416.5377946 | 0.120935901 |
| 3. | 6041.233108 | -3853.233108 | -1.11873214 |
| 4. | 3710.41583 | -491.4158298 | -0.142675688 |
| 5. | 9371.99765 | -3831.99765 | -1.112566723 |
| 6. | 12527.49268 | -35.49268262 | -0.010304802 |
| 7. | 25356.02871 | -781.0287111 | -0.226760722 |
| 8. | 24722.03899 | 6673.961006 | 1.937690887 |
| 9. | 24212.8797 | 1621.120301 | 0.470669522 |
| 10. | 16785.53142 | 2641.468577 | 0.76691332 |
| 11. | 33528.9335 | -5125.933499 | -1.488242832 |

**Table 8: Probability Output**

| PROBABILITY OUTPUT | |
|---|---|
| Percentile | Y |
| 4.545454545 | 2188 |
| 13.63636364 | 2705 |
| 22.72727273 | 3219 |
| 31.81818182 | 4065 |
| 40.90909091 | 5540 |
| 50 | 12492 |
| 59.09090909 | 19427 |
| 68.18181818 | 24575 |
| 77.27272727 | 25834 |
| 86.36363636 | 28403 |
| 95.45454545 | 31396 |

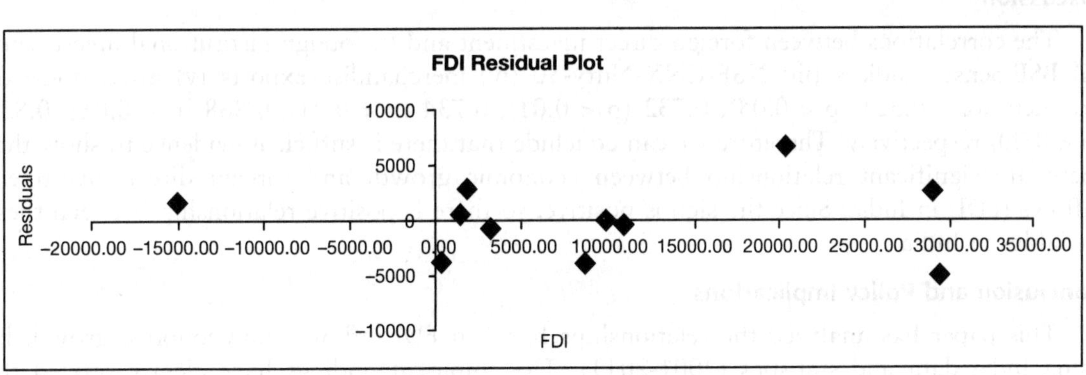


**Fig. 2:** FDI Residual Plot

The result from regression model show that that result from regression equations are reliable, where their computed t-statistics are greater than t-critical value in 5 per cent level, therefore, we can conclude that there is sufficient evidence to show that there are significant relationship between economic growth and foreign direct investment inflows (FDI) in India.

## Hypotheses Testing and Discussion

### *Section-I: Hypothesis Testing*

**Testing of Null Hypothesis $H_{01}$:** To test $H_{01}$ {the growth of FDI inflows does not contribute to the increase of GDP}, the researchers analyzed data using t-test.

For $v = 9$ (11 – 2), $t_{0.05} = 1.645$. The calculated value of $t$ (9.41) is more than the table value. The hypothesis is rejected. Hence the researchers conclude that the growth of FDI inflows contribute to the increase of GDP in India.

**Testing of Null Hypothesis $H_{02}$:** To test $H_{02}$ {the growth of FDI inflows does not contribute to the increase of BSE-Sensex indices in India}, the researchers analyzed data using t-test.

For $v = 9\ (11 - 2)$, $t_{0.05} = 1.645$. The calculated value of $t$ (4.73) is more than the table value. The hypothesis is rejected. Hence the researchers conclude that the growth of FDI inflows contribute to the increase of BSE-Sensex indices in India.

**Testing of Null Hypothesis $H_{03}$:** To test $H_{03}$ {the growth of FDI inflows does not contribute to the increase of NSE-CNX-Nifty-50 in India}, the researchers analyzed data using t-test.

For $v = 9\ (11 - 2)$, $t_{0.05} = 1.645$. The calculated value of $t$ (4.77) is more than the table value. The hypothesis is rejected. Hence the researchers conclude that the growth of FDI inflows contribute to the increase of NSE-CNX-Nifty-50 in India.

**Testing of Null Hypothesis $H_{04}$:** To test $H_{04}$ {the growth of FDI inflows does not contribute to the increase of Merchandise Exports in India}, the researchers analyzed data using t-test.

For $v = 9\ (11 - 2)$, $t_{0.05} = 1.645$. The calculated value of $t$ (5.22) is more than the table value. The hypothesis is rejected. Hence the researchers conclude that the growth of FDI inflows contribute to the increase of Merchandise Exports in India.

## Discussion

The correlations between foreign direct investment and (i) foreign institutional investments (ii) BSE-Sensex indices (iii) NSE-CNX-Nifty-50 (iv) merchandise exports (v) gross domestic products were 0.321 ($p < 0.05$), 0.732 ($p < 0.01$), 0.734 ($p < 0.01$), 0.868 ($p < 0.01$), 0.853 ($p < 0.00$) respectively. Therefore we can conclude that there is sufficient evidence to show that there are significant relationship between economic growth and foreign direct investment inflows (FDI) in India. Since the sign is positive, so there is positive relationship between these variables in India.

## Conclusion and Policy Implications

This paper has analyzed the relationships between FDI inflows and economic growth by using India data and statistics (2001-2011). The empirical findings have clearly proved the afore-formulated hypotheses that Qatar's inward FDI and economic growth are positively correlated. Moreover, the inward FDI is positively affected by the economic growth, but more sensitive to its own performance change than to the economy growth. Thus, it implies that to attract FDI inflows to India, the government should continue its efforts to create promising economic and investment environment; while to promote economic growth, it shall attach more importance onto other original momentum.

Further, foreign direct investment has continued to play a significant role in the India's economy. Through the empirical result, the analysis shows that there is a positive relationship between the FDI and economic growth, which the relationship is found to be significant. These findings have important policy implication where the government has to concern the importance of the FDI contributed to economic growth. Economy development of a country can be achieve by encourage more foreign direct investment, which it can help to create more employment in the country. In addition, advance technology in production will trained more skilled labor; therefore it will enhance the productivity and fulfill the satisfaction and demand from the consumers.

Therefore, government should impose the relevant policies likes joint venture in order to give opportunities to the domestic producer become one of the part and enjoy the profit together with foreign direct investors. This will benefit to local partner as they are expose to higher technology. Besides, government plays an important role in maintaining political stability. Because if a new government come in with highly different policies, foreign direct investors need to adjust their strategies in accordance with those new policies. In some cases, bribery may start and causing higher costs to investors. This will decelerate the growth in a country. Furthermore, economic instability likes higher inflation and fluctuation in exchange rate in a country also one of the important factor to discourage foreign direct investments.

## REFERENCES


Akaike, H. (1969), "Fitting autoregression for prediction", *Annals of the Institute of Statistical Mathematics*, 21, pp. 203-17.

——. (1970), "Statistical predictor identification", *Annals of the Institute of Statistical Mathematics*, 22, pp. 243-47.

Alesina, A. and D. Dollar (2000), "Who gives foreign aid to whom and why?", *Journal of Economic Growth*, 5(1), pp. 33-63.

Alia, A.A. and Ucal, M.S. (2003), "Foreign direct investment, exports and output growth of Turkey: Causality Analysis", Paper presented at the European Trade Study Group (ETSG) fifth annual conference, Madrid, 11-13, Sept.

Baliamoune-Lutz, M.N. (2004), "Doest FDI contributes to economic growth? Knowledge about the effects of FDI improves negotiating positions and reduces risk for firms investing in developing countries", *Business Economics*, 39(2), pp. 49-56.

Barrell, R. and N. Pain (1996), "Domestic institution, agglomeration and foreign direct investment in Europe", *European Economic Review*, 43, pp. 29-45.

Basu, P., C. Chakraborty, and D. Reagle (2003), "Liberalization, FDI, and Growth in Developing Countries: A Panel Cointegration Approach", *Economic Inquiry*, 41, pp. 510-16.

Biswas, R. (2002), "Determinants of foreign direct investment", *Review of Development Economics*, 6 (3), pp. 492-504.

Borensztein, E., J. Gregorio, and J. Lee (1998), "How does foreign direct investment affect economic growth?", *Journal of International Economics*, 45 (1), pp. 115-35.

Bosworth, B.P. and S.M. Collins (1999), "Capital flows to developing economies: Implications for saving and investment", *Brookings Papers on Economic Activity*, no. 1, pp. 143-69.

De Mello, L.R. (1999), "Foreign direct investment in developing countries and growth: A selective survey", *Journal of Development Studies*, 34 (1), pp. 1-34.

Dunning, J.H. (1993), *Multinational Enterprises and the Global Economy*, Wokingham: Addison-Wesley.

Encarnation, D.J. and L.T. Wells, Jr. (1986), "Evaluating foreign investment", in T.H. Moran et al. *Investing in development: new roles for foreign capital*? Washington, DC: Overseas Development Council.

Ericsson, J. and M. Irandoust (2000), "On the causality between foreign direct investment and output: A comparative study", *International Trade Journal*, 15, pp. 1-26.

Gastanaga, V.M., J.B. Nugent, and B. Pashamova (1998), "Host country reforms and FDI inflows: How much difference do they make?" *World Development*, 26, pp. 1299-1314.

Grosse, R. and L.J. Trevino (1996), "Foreign direct investment in the United States: An analysis by country of origin", *Journal of International Business Studies*, 27, pp. 139-55.

Hall, S. and Milne, A. (1994), "The relevance of P-star analysis to UK monetary policy", *The Economic Journal*, 104, pp. 597-604.

Hsiao, C. (1981), "Autoregressive modeling and money income causality detection," *Journal of Monetary Economics*, 7, pp. 85-106.

——. (2001), "Efficient estimation of dynamic panel data models with an application to the analysis of foreign direct investment in developing countries", paper presented at the 2001 Far Eastern Econometric Society Meeting, Kobe, Japan.

Johansen, S. (1988), "Statistical analysis of Cointegration vectors", *Journal of Economic Dynamic and Control*, 12, 231-54.

Johansen, S. and Juselius, K. (1990), "Maximum likelihood estimation and inference on Cointegration with applications to the demand for money", *Oxford Bulletin of Economics and Statistics*, 52, pp. 169-210.

Khan, K. and Leng, K. (1997), "Foreign Direct Investment, exports and Exonomic growth", *Singapore Economic Review*, 42(2), 40-60.

Liu, X., Burridge, P. and Sinclair, P.J.N. (2002), "Relationship between economic growth, foreign direct investment and trade: evidence from China", *Applied Economics*, 34, pp. 1433-40.

Liu, X.M., Wang, C.G. and Wei, Y.Q. (2001), "Causal links between foreign direct investment and trade in China", *China Economic Review*, 12, pp. 190-202.

Mallampally, P. and K.P. Sauvant (1999), "Foreign direct investment in developing countries," *Finance and Development*, 36(1), p. 36.

Mayang Pranadhani, Rakesh Bissoondeeal and Nigel Driffield (2007), "FDI, Trade and growth, a causal link".

Melina Dritsaki, Chaido Dritsaki and Antonios Adamopoulos, "A Causal Relationship between Trade, Foreign Direct Investment and Economic Growth for Greece", *American Journal of Applied Sciences* 1(3): 230-35, 2004.

Metwally, M.M. (2004), "Impact of EU FDI on economic growth in Middle Eastern Countries", *European Business Review*, 16(4), pp. 381-89.

Moran, T.H. (1998), "Foreign direct investment and development: The new policy agenda for developing countries and economies in transition", Washington, DC, Institute for International Economics.

Nelson, C. and C. Plosser (1982), "Trends and random walks in macroeconomic time series: Some evidence and implications", *Journal of Monetary Economics*, 10, pp. 130-62.

Pacheco-Lopez, P. (2005), "Foreign Direct Investment, Exports and Imports in Mexico", *The World Economy*, 28(8), pp. 1157-72.

Phillips, P. and P. Perron (1988), "Testing for a unit root in time series regression", *Biometrika,* 75, pp. 335-46.

Phillips, P. (1987), "Time series regression with unit roots", *Econometrica*, 55 (2), pp. 277-301.

Taylor, M.P. and L. Sarno (1999), "Capital flows to developing countries: Long- and short-term determinants", *World Bank Economic Review,* 11, pp. 451-70.

Trevino, Len J. and K.P. Upadhyaya (2003), "Foreign aid, FDI and economic growth: Evidence from Asian countries", *Transnational Corporations*, 12(2), pp. 119-35.

Trevino, Len, J., J.D. Daniels, H. Arbelaez, and K.P. Upadhyaya (2002), "Market reform and foreign direct investment in Latin America: Evidence from an error correction model", *International Trade Journal*, 16 (4), pp. 367-92.

Veugelers, Reinhilde (1991), "Locational determinants and rankings of host countries: An empirical assessment", Kyklos, 44 (3), pp. 363-82.

Wei, Shang-Jin (1997), "Why is corruption so much more taxing than tax? Arbitrariness kills", NBER Working Paper No. 6255.

World Bank (2003), World Development Indicators on CD-ROM, World Bank: Washington, D.C.

Yongkul Won, Frank S.T. Hsiao, and Doo Yong Yang, "FDI Inflows, Exports and Economic Growth in First and Second Generation ANIEs: Panel Data Causality Analyses", Korea Institute for International Economic Policy, 300-04 Yomgok-Dong, Seocho-Gu, Seoul 137-747, Korea 2008.

Zhang, K.H. (2005), "How does FDI affect a host country's export performance? The case of China", Paper presented to International conference of WTO, China, and the Asian Economics, III Xi'an, China, 25-26, June.

Zhang, K.H. and Song, S. (2000), "Promoting exports: the role of inward FDI in China", *China Economic Review*, 11, pp. 385-96.

Zhang, Q. and Felmingham, B. (2001), "The relationship between inward direct foreign investment and China's provincial export trade", *China Economic Review*, 12, pp. 82-99.

# 8

# COMMODITY ETF AS AN ALTERNATIVE INVESTMENT OPTION

*–Anil Kothari* and *Pallavi Kudal*

## Introduction

There are many savings and investment options available in India. One of the options is gold. Gold is one of the most valuable and universally accepted metals, its price movements are keenly watched in global economics. Even today, after gold has been officially delinked from currencies, it has a huge role to play in the global economy. Gold is widely considered to be an asset whose intrinsic value and purchasing power will not be widely subjected to the fluctuations of inflation. It is widely respected as a store of value. Gold has been popular in India because it acted as a good hedge against inflation. There is so much uncertainty in the world in terms of economic growth and geopolitics, it is no surprise that many investors, big and small have chosen to hedge their investments through gold.

The purpose of the paper is to have in-depth knowledge of hyped topic of Gold and its Exchange Traded Fund (ETF)—an alternate investment options. For these variables like Crude, Dollar, and Nifty are studied. The paper also deals with the much hyped topic of Gold and its Exchange Traded Fund (ETF)—an alternate investment options.

## Objectives

1. To determine the present factors affecting the demand of Gold ETF.
2. To determine the correlation of Gold prices with inflation, crude oil and US dollar.

## Methodology

The methodology followed of the paper is as follows:

- Movement of gold prices in the past years is studied. In depth analysis is done mentioning the proper reasoning of the movement of price in past years linking it with political events, wars and emergencies. For analysis the data is collected from internal Meta stock tool. The data available for this analysis is from 1970 to 2009.
- Multivariate analysis is done on gold prices, crude oil and US dollar. The data is collected on monthly basis from year 2005 to March 2009.

### Exchange Traded Fund

An exchange-traded fund (or ETF) is an investment vehicle traded on stock exchanges, much like stocks. An ETF holds assets such as stocks or bonds and trades at approximately the same price as the net asset value of its underlying assets over the course of the trading day. Most ETFs track an index, such as the Dow Jones Industrial Average or the S&P 500. ETFs may be attractive as investments because of their low costs, tax efficiency, and stock like features. An ETF combines the valuation feature of a mutual fund or unit investment trust, which can be purchased or redeemed at the end of each trading day for its net asset value, with the tradability feature of a closed-end fund, which trades throughout the trading day at prices that may be substantially more or less than its net asset value.

#### History

Exchange Traded Funds came into existence in 1993 when, State Street Global Advisors, together with the American Stock Exchange, developed and launched the ETF market. The name of the product was SPDRs. SPDR, which is benchmarked against the S&P 500 Index, continues to be the most successful product with over $102 billion of Assets under Management. In 1999, AMEX introduced the first ETF in Asia and currently they are doing the same in other major markets around the globe.

#### Features of ETF

- Exchange Traded Funds (ETFs) are open ended mutual funds which means an investors can enter or exit the trade at any time.
- ETFs represent a fractional ownership in the underlying securities in a particular index.
- ETFs can be traded like stock on the major stock exchanges.
- Intraday portfolio values are calculated every fifteen seconds. ETFs range in style, sector, country ranging from value, growth, international equity, commodity, and domestic to equity and fixed income.

#### Creation of ETF

ETFs are different from Mutual funds in the sense that ETF units are not sold to the public for cash. Instead, the Asset Management Company that sponsors the ETF (Fund) takes the shares of companies comprising the index from various categories of investors like authorized participants, large investors and institutions. In turn, it issues them a large block of ETF units. Since dividend may have accumulated for the stocks at any point in time, a cash component to that extent is also taken from such investors. In other words, a large block of ETF units called a "Creation Unit" is exchanged for a "Portfolio Deposit" of stock and "Cash Component".

The number of outstanding ETF units is not limited, as with traditional mutual funds. It may increase if investors deposit shares to create ETF units; or it may reduce on a day if some ETF holders redeem their ETF units for the underlying shares. These transactions are conducted by sending creation/redemption instructions to the Fund. The Portfolio Deposit closely approximates the proportion of the stocks in the index together with a specified amount of Cash

Component. This "in-kind" creation/redemption facility ensures that ETFs trade close to their fair value at any given time.

Some investors may prefer to hold the creation units in their portfolios. While others may break-up the creation units and sell on the exchanges, where individual investors may purchase them just like any other shares.

*Redemption*

ETF units are continuously created and redeemed based on investor demand. Investors may use ETFs for investment, trading or arbitrage. The price of the ETF tracks the value of the underlying index. This provides an opportunity to investors to compare the value of underlying index against the price of the ETF units prevailing on the Exchange. If the value of the underlying index is higher than the price of the ETF, the investors may redeem the units to the Sponsor in exchange for the higher priced securities. Conversely, if the price of the underlying securities is lower than the ETF, the investors may create ETF units by depositing the lower-priced securities. This arbitrage mechanism eliminates the problem associated with closed-end mutual funds, viz. the premium or discount to the NAV.

### *Relationship of Gold ETF with Different Market Factors*

*History*

Gold has played a pivotal role in the Indian social fabric for as far back as man's memory will stretch. In India, gold has a religious significance. Gold was acquired in India in Roman times as part of the silk and spice trade, and the first gold ducats struck by the Venice Mint in 1285 went into the Levant (i.e. the countries bordering the eastern Mediterranean) and into India. In the seventeenth century the Dutch and English East India companies paid for goods with gold and silver and during the American Civil war India received gold from the US in return for the cotton that it supplied to make up for the lost crops in America. Indian people are renowned for saving for the future and the financial savings ratio is strong, with a ratio of financial assets-to-GDP of 93 per cent.

According to World Gold Council, India is world's largest consumer of gold accounting to some 20 per cent of worlds demand. In India gold is historically and culturally tied to the concepts of wealth and prosperity. Consumer demand still remains high as Indians believe gold offers the best protection against inflation. To quote few facts:

- Gold jewellery demand in India, the world's largest gold jewellery market, rose 67 per cent year-on-year to 272 tons in the first half of 2010, despite the higher gold price.
- Over the past decade, gold demand in India has increased at an average rate of 13 per cent per year, outpacing the country's real GDP, inflation and population growth by 6 per cent, 8 per cent and 12 per cent respectively.
- Currently, the country has one of the highest saving rates in the world; estimated at around 30 per cent of total income, of which 10 per cent is invested in gold. Continued rapid economic growth and urbanization will create greater wealth but also inflationary pressures stimulating gold demand.

The World Gold Council reports: "In the longer term, we are confident that India's favorable demographic trends, the growing affluent middle class and declining age profile, should ensure a buoyant consumption growth."

*Gold Prices and Crude Oil*

From 1965 to 1994, the monthly correlation between gold and oil weighed at a very impressive +0.879. From 1995 to 2000, however, this correlation seemingly vanished with a negative 0.133 reading. Since 2000 though, the historical oil and gold correlation has been restored, again running positive at +0.715. It seem that gold may be well correlated with oil in the long-term, but it is not necessarily so in the short-term.

**Y(Gold Prices) = 6660.08 + X (Crude Oil)**

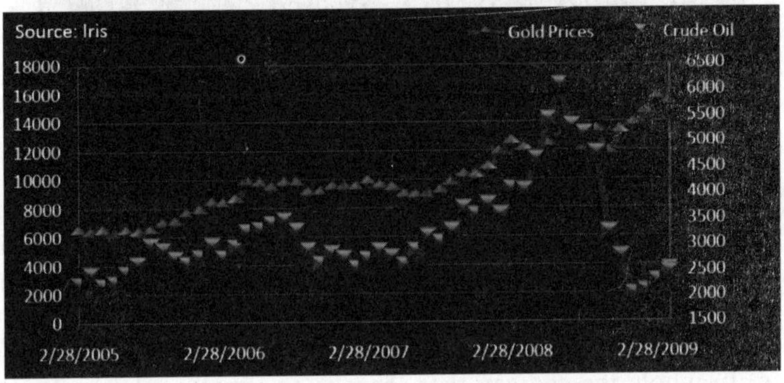


**Fig. 1:** Gold Prices and Crude Oil

*Source*: Spider Iris

*Gold Prices and Dollar*

In 2008 when the dollar depreciated with respect to rupees, we observed an increase in the gold prices mainly because gold is seen as relentless safe haven. To a greater extent, the outlook for gold (in dollar terms) is linked to the outlook for the U.S. dollar. Unfortunately the future for dollar remains bleak this is primarily because of huge amount of debt of US in both government and private sector the world is flooded with dollar and the degree of external financing of debts is unsustainable.

Weakening of dollar could drive more funds into the market and can potentially take the gold prices further up in Indian market. Further to verify the relationship between Gold prices and dollar regression is done between the two, which gives us the coefficient of +300.9, this value signifies that if there is an increase of 1 dollar the gold prices increases by ₹ 300.9. However the R square for this model is very small which signifies that this model is insignificant and does not capture the true relationship between the two.

Y (Gold Prices) = –3481.26 + 300.99 X (US dollar)

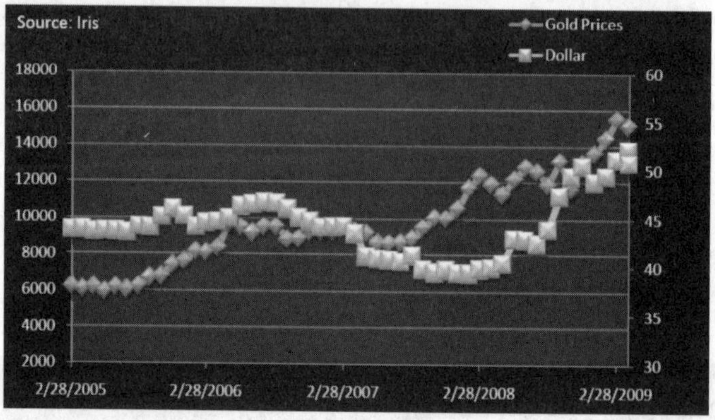


**Fig. 2:** Gold Prices and Dollar

*Source*: Spider Iris.

*Gold Prices and Nifty*

Figure 3 below show the relationship of gold prices and NIFTY index Closing price. In Jan. 2008, when the market was hit by global meltdown we observed an upward trend of gold prices primarily because it was seen as the better option. However this trend was seen in 2009 too, but with sign of recovery in some sectors like reality, automobile we see that the prices of gold shifted a bit down. In whole we can say that there is an inverse relationship between the two primarily because of the following reason:

- Gold is seen as a Safe Haven Asset.
- Gold Hedge against financial risk and credit crises.

The regression between the gold prices and NIFTY closing index also verifies that there is negative correlation between the two with the regression coefficient of –1.13.

Gold Price = 13946.74 – 1.13 (Nifty)

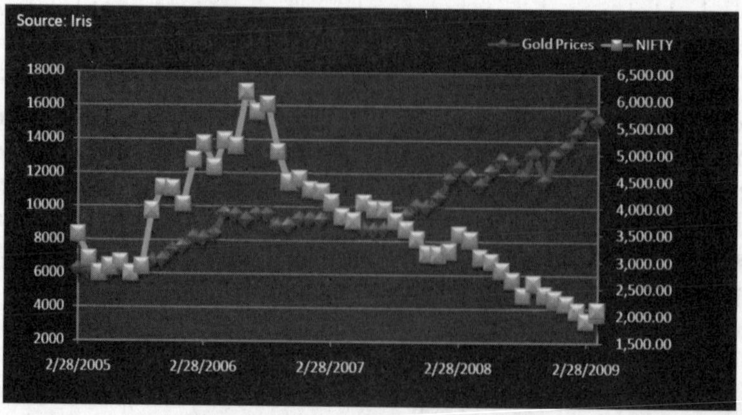


**Fig. 3:** Gold Prices and NIFTY

*Source*: Spider Iris.

The regression between the gold prices and NIFTY closing index also verifies that there is negative correlation between the two with the regression coefficient of –1.13.

## Conclusion

Development of Gold ETF has been very crucial in the stock markets. Ever since they were introduced there has been endless debate that which is a better way of holding gold, physical gold or Gold ETF. However adding Gold Exchange Traded Funds (ETFs) may be a good way to diversify one's portfolio. We have seen that Gold prices do depend upon number of factors like crude oil prices, price of Dollar and Nifty. Gold ETF does provide an ease in investment and trading in Gold as holding physical gold is not that safe but one needs to have an in-depth analysis of the market for indulging in Gold ETFs.

## REFERENCES

Andrew Pole (2008), *Statistical Arbitrage : Algorithmic Trading Insights and Techniques*, John Wiley & Sons, New Jersey. Available from: www.wiley.com/WileyCDA/WileyTitle/productCd-0470138440.html [Accessed 28 April 2009.]

Damodaran (2006), *Investment Valuation: Second Edition*, Tata McGraw Hill Publishing Co. Ltd.

Ganapathy Vidhyamurthy, *Pair Trading: Quantitative Methods and Analysis*, John Wiley & Sons, New Jersey.

J.D. Steinhilder (2009), *Gold ETF More than a Flash in the Pan*. Agile Investment. Available from: www.agileinvesting.com/html/Gold%20ETF.pdf [Accessed on 10 May 2009].

Kumad Das (19th March, 2008), PSBs go slow on credit derivative exposures. *The Financial Express*. Taken from: http://www.financialexpress.com/news/psbs-go-slow-on-creditderivatives exposure/286026/ [Accessed 10 March 2009].

Pat Dorsey (2004), *The five rules for successful stock investing*, John Wiley & Sons, New Jersey.

Praveen, April (2009), *Gold Exchange Traded Funds: Features of Investment in GoldETF*. Aarudhra Financial Services. Available from: www.equitybulls.com/mutualfunds/goldetf.asp

Reserve Bank of India (2008), *A profile of Indian banks 2007-08*, Mumbai, Department Of Statistics And Information Management. Available from: http://rbidocs.rbi.org.in/rdocs/Publications/PDFs/87122.pdf [Accessed 8 April 2009].

Rhona O' Connell (2009), *India: exciting advances in the local gold market*, World Gold Council. Available from: www.thebulliondesk.com/content/reports/temp/india2.pdf [Accessed on 4th May 2009].

Subarao, D. (2008), *The Global Financial Turmoil and Challenges for the Indian Economy*, Kolkata. Available from: http://rbidocs.rbi.org.in/rdocs/Speeches/PDFs/89133.pdf [Accessed 12 April 2009].

Tom Capeland, Tim Koller and Jack Murrin, *Valuation Measuring and managing the values of companies: Third Edition*, McKinney & Company Inc.

9

# A STUDY ON IMPACT OF DIVIDEND POLICY ON MARKET PRICE OF SHARES

–*O.P. Jain* and *Renu Choudhary*

## Introduction

Dividend policy decision is one of the most crucial decisions for a firm. The important aspect of a dividend policy is to determine the amount of earnings to be distributed to shareholders and the amount to be retained in the firm. Dividend policy is important for all stakeholders. For investors it is not only a current source of income but also a way to assess company from investment point of view. For a company, retained earnings are the most significant internal source of financing the growth of the firm. Lenders are also interested in dividend policy as more dividend paid by the company means less amount will be available for retiring their debt.

The objective of a dividend policy is to maximise a shareholder's return. Shareholder's return consists of two components dividends and capital gains. Dividend policy has a direct impact on both the components of return. Dividend Policy is the policy used by a company to decide how much it will pay out to shareholders in dividends. Corporations earn profits—they do not distribute all of it. Part of profit is ploughed back or held back as retained earnings. Part of the profit gets distributed to the shareholders. The part that is distributed is the dividend. The ratio of the actual distribution or dividend, and the total distributable profits, is called dividend payout ratio.

Companies have to frame and work on a definitive policy of dividend payout ratio. Of course, no corporate management can afford to stick to a fixed dividend payout ratio year after year—neither is such fixity of dividend payout ratio required or expected. However, management has to broadly decide its policy on its broad attitude towards distribution—liberal dividend payout ratio, or conservative dividend payout ratio, etc.

## Objective

Whether dividend policy affects the market price of the share or not is always a debatable issue. The objective of this research paper is to unfold the relationship between the dividend payout and the market price of shares and analyse whether the dividend payment affects the market price of the share.

### Research Methodology

For this study the final dividend declared from 2003 to 2012 and the yearly closing market price of the shares of ten companies listed at Bombay Stock Exchange has been taken into account.

Karl Pearson correlation is used to analyse the relationship between dividend declared and market price of the shares.

### Literature Review

Dividend policy affects the market price of the share or not is always a debatable issue. The brief findings of the major studies done in India in this context are as follows:

Reddy Y. Subha and Rath Subhrendu (2005) examined the dividend behavior of Indian corporate firms. Dividend trends for large sample of stocks traded on Indian markets indicated that the percentage of companies paying dividend declined from over 57% in 1991 to 32% in 2001, and that only a few firms paid regular dividends. Even though regular payers consistently paid higher dividends than did other firms, on average. Dividend-paying companies were less likely to be larger and more profitable than non-paying companies, though growth opportunities do not seem to have 30 significantly influenced the dividend policies of Indian firms. Overall for all firms, investment opportunities faced by Indian firms do not show any distinguishing pattern or trend over the years. The rise of the number of firms not paying dividends is not supported by the requirements of cash for investments.

Singhania Monica (2005) studied 590 manufacturing, non-government, non-financial, non-banking companies listed on the Bombay Stock Exchange for a period from 1992 to 2004. The sample companies were categorized into payers and non-payers, in the period understudy. Payers were further classified into regular payers, initiators and current payers. Non-payers companies were further categorized as never paid, former payers and current non-payers.

In a study done by Sharma Dhira (2007), "Are dividends in vogue in India? An empirical study of Sensex companies", the dividend behavior of the Indian firms with the help of signaling and tax effect theory for 1990-2005 was analyzed. It was found that firms paying dividend during this period have followed continuous progressive trend. In the recent years, companies in the growth sector like software firms have paid greater dividends as compared to other sectors firms.

To analyse the relationship between dividend declaration and market price of shares, final dividend declared from 2003 to 2012 and the yearly closing market price of the shares of ten companies listed at Bombay Stock Exchange has been taken into account.

**1. Asian Paints Ltd.** Asian Paints, incorporated in the year 1942, is India's largest paint company and Asia's third largest paint company, with a turnover of ₹ 96.32 billion. The group has an enviable reputation in the corporate world for professionalism, fast track growth, and building shareholder equity. Asian Paints operates in 17 countries and has 24 paint manufacturing facilities in the world servicing consumers in over 65 countries. Besides Asian Paints, the group operates around the world through its subsidiaries Berger International Limited, Apco Coatings, SCIB Paints and Taubmans.

**Table 1:** Movement of closing price and dividend declared during 2003-2012

| Year | Close price | Change in price | (%) Change in price | Dividend (%) | (%) Change in dividend rate |
|---|---|---|---|---|---|
| 2003 | 336.15 | –16 | –4.76 | 65 | –15 |
| 2004 | 320.15 | 257.25 | 80.35 | 50 | 5 |
| 2005 | 577.4 | 156.15 | 27.04 | 55 | 25 |
| 2006 | 733.55 | 369 | 50.30 | 80 | –70 |
| 2007 | 1,102.55 | –207.45 | –18.82 | 10 | 95 |
| 2008 | 895.1 | 901.15 | 100.68 | 105 | 5 |
| 2009 | 1,796.25 | 1078.6 | 60.05 | 110 | 75 |
| 2010 | 2,874.85 | –279.9 | –9.74 | 185 | 50 |
| 2011 | 2,594.95 | 1127.3 | 43.44 | 235 | 70 |
| 2012 | 3,722.25 | –3722.25 | –100 | 305 | –305 |

http://economictimes.indiatimes.com/asian-paints-ltd/infocompanydividends/companyid-14034.cms

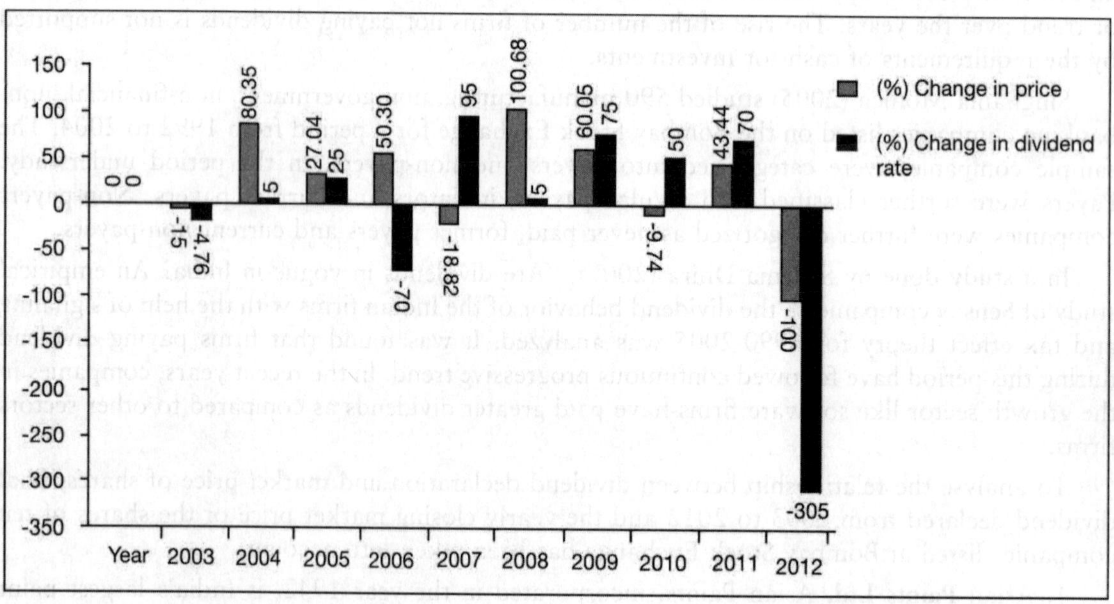


**Fig. 1:** Movement of closing price and dividend declared during 2003-2012.

As per the Table 1 and graph (Fig. 1), it is seen that from years 2003 to 2004, the dividend rates have increased by 20% i.e. earlier in 2003 it was –15% and in the upcoming year it came up to 5% while this highly affected the market price which also increased by 85.11% as earlier it was in negative. While moving further, to years 2004 to 2005, the dividend rate increment is same as above while the market price came down from 80.35% to 27.04% due to the increment in dividend rates of this particular year. Seeing year 2005 to 2006, the dividend rates announced have been decreased by a difference of 95% and which came at a % of –70 that directly shows the change in price where in 2005 it was 27.04% and in 2006 it came up to 50.03%. Moving further to years 2006 to 2007, it can be observed clearly from the table corresponding to it that the dividend rates were –70% which came up to 95% with an increase of 165%. Now, through this observation, price came down from 50.03% to –18.82% with a decrease of 68.85%, this is a complete opposite situation where the rates are fluctuating from upward to downward direction. Putting emphasis on years 2007 to 2008, here, the dividend rate decreased from a huge difference of 90% placing the 5% rate changing the market price to 100.68% from –18.82% in 2007. In 2008 to 2009, dividend rates have increased up to a difference of 70% claiming 75% as the particular rate, hence the price changed with a decrement of 40.63% i.e. value decreased from 100.68% in 2008 to 60.05% in 2009. Further observing back years 2009 to 2010, the dividend rate claimed is 50% with a decrease in difference of 25% which highly affected the price indulging into a decreased rate of –9.74% while the price in 2009 was 60.05%. Finally putting eyes over the current year 2011 to 2012, the maximum variation in dividend rates is particularly through this year wherein it was 70% in 2011 and which decreased by a difference of 375% i.e. –305%, affected the market price changing the values in same manner, i.e. decreasing by a difference of 143.44% and hence, the current market price is –100%.

The correlation is 0.582 which is a positive correlation. This analysis depicts that the change in dividends shows a positive impact on the market price, i.e. there is a direct relationship. This shows when the company declares dividends with fluctuations every year, the market price tends to increase its stability.

**2. Bharat Heavy Electricals Ltd.** Bharat Heavy Electrical Ltd. (BHEL) was incorporated on 13-11-1964 with an objective to have indigenous Heavy Electrical Equipment industry in India. It is an integrated power plant equipment manufacturer and one of the largest engineering and manufacturing companies in India in terms of turnover.

**Table 2:** Movement of closing price and dividend declared during 2003-2012

| Year | Close price | Change in price | (%) Change in price | Dividend (%) | (%) Change in dividend rate |
|---|---|---|---|---|---|
| 2003 | 507.95 | 261.95 | 51.57 | 40 | –10 |
| 2004 | 769.9 | 616.35 | 80.06 | 30 | 15 |
| 2005 | 1,386.25 | 911.9 | 65.78 | 45 | –25 |
| 2006 | 2,298.15 | 286.1 | 12.45 | 20 | 40 |
| 2007 | 2,584.25 | –1221.85 | –47.28 | 60 | 3 |
| 2008 | 1,362.40 | 1043.7 | 76.61 | 63 | 18 |
| 2009 | 2,406.10 | –81.35 | –3.38 | 80 | 43 |

| | | | | | |
|---|---|---|---|---|---|
| 2010 | 2,324.75 | –2085.75 | –89.72 | 123 | 56 |
| 2011 | 239 | –6.35 | –2.66 | 179 | 5 |
| 2012 | 232.65 | –232.65 | –100 | 184 | –184 |

http://economictimes.indiatimes.com/bharat-heavy-electricals/infocompanydividends/companyid-11831.cms

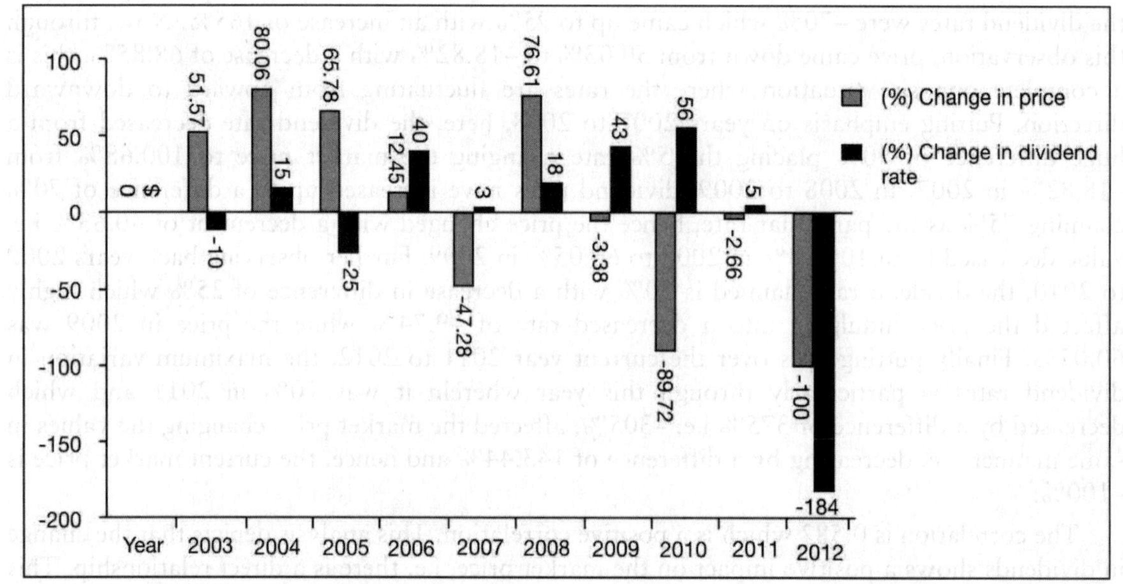


**Fig. 2:** Movement of closing price and dividend declared during 2003-2012.

As per Table 2 and graph (Fig. 2), it is seen that from years 2003 to 2004, the dividend rates have increased by 25% i.e. earlier in 2003 it was –10% and in the upcoming year it came up to 15% while this affected the market price in positive manner by increasing the rate by 28.49% i.e. 80.06% while in 2003 it was 51.57%, a quite range to look upon. While moving further to years 2004 to 2005, the dividend rate decreased by a difference of 40% changing the rates from 15% in 2004 to –25% in 2005, it affected market price in the same manner by decreasing it by a difference of 14.28% which led down the rate to 15.78%. Seeing year 2005 to 2006, the increment in the dividend rate set 40% as 2006 rate through a difference of 65% which directly changed the market price from 65.78% in 2005 to 12.45% in 2006. At a decreasing note, this was a complete opposite reaction to the change in rates in this particular phase. Moving further to years 2006 to 2007, the dividend rates announced have been decreased by a difference of 37% and which came to 3% that directly shows the change in price where in 2006 it was 12.45% and in 2007 it came down to –47.28% showing values downward to x-axis. In 2007 to 2008, it can be observed clearly from the table corresponding to it that the dividend rate was 3% which came up to 18% with an increase of 15%. Now, through this observation, price came up from –47.28% to 76.61% with an increase of 123.89%, here, there is direct relationship between both dividend rate and market price. Putting emphasis on years 2008 to 2009, here, the dividend rate increased by a small difference of 25% placing the 43% rate changing the market price to –3.38% from 76.61% in 2008. Further observing back years 2009 to 2010, the dividend rate claimed is 56% with an increase in difference of 13% which highly affected the price indulging into a decreased rate of –89.72% while the price in 2009 was –3.38%. In years 2010 to 2011, the dividend rate decreased to 5% with a decrease in difference of 51% that affected the price back to its rate known –2.66% with a decrement in difference of 87.06% pushing both the values to downward direction. Finally coming and focusing on current year 2011 to 2012, there's a sudden decrement in the dividend rate which led to –184% with a decreased difference of 189%, side by side letting down the market prices as well—from –2.66% in 2011 to –100% in 2012 as the current market price.

The correlation is 0.349 which is a positive correlation. This analysis depicts that the change in dividends shows a positive impact on the market price, i.e. there is a direct relationship. This shows when the company declares dividends with fluctuations every year, the market price tends to increase in stability.

**3. Hero Motocorp Ltd.** Hero Motocorp Ltd. was incorporated on 19th January 1984, at New Delhi. Formerly known as Hero Honda Motors Ltd., is the world's largest manufacturer of two-wheelers, based in India. In 2001, the company achieved the coveted position of being the largest two-wheeler manufacturing company in India and also, the 'World No. 1' two-wheeler company in terms of unit volume sales in a calendar year. Hero Motocorp Ltd. continues to maintain this position till date. The company was established as a joint venture company between Honda Motor Company of Japan and Hero Group. In the year 1983, they signed a joint collaboration agreement and formed the company.

**Table 3:** Movement of closing price and dividend declared during 2003-2012

| Year | Close price | Change in price | (%) Change in price | Dividend (%) | (%) Change in dividend rate |
|---|---|---|---|---|---|
| 2003 | 448.85 | 122.25 | 27.24 | 900 | –400 |
| 2004 | 571.1 | 288.6 | 50.53 | 500 | 500 |
| 2005 | 859.7 | –97.35 | –11.32 | 1000 | 0 |
| 2006 | 762.35 | –64.7 | –8.49 | 1000 | –150 |
| 2007 | 697.65 | 107.45 | 15.40 | 850 | 100 |
| 2008 | 805.1 | 911.35 | 113.20 | 950 | 50 |
| 2009 | 1,716.45 | 269.65 | 15.71 | 1000 | 3000 |
| 2010 | 1,986.10 | –80.85 | –4.07 | 4000 | –2250 |
| 2011 | 1,905.25 | 135.25 | 7.10 | 1750 | 500 |
| 2012 | 2,040.50 | –2040.5 | –100 | 2250 | –2250 |

http://economictimes.indiatimes.com/hero-motocorp-ltd/infocompanydividends/companyid-13636.cms

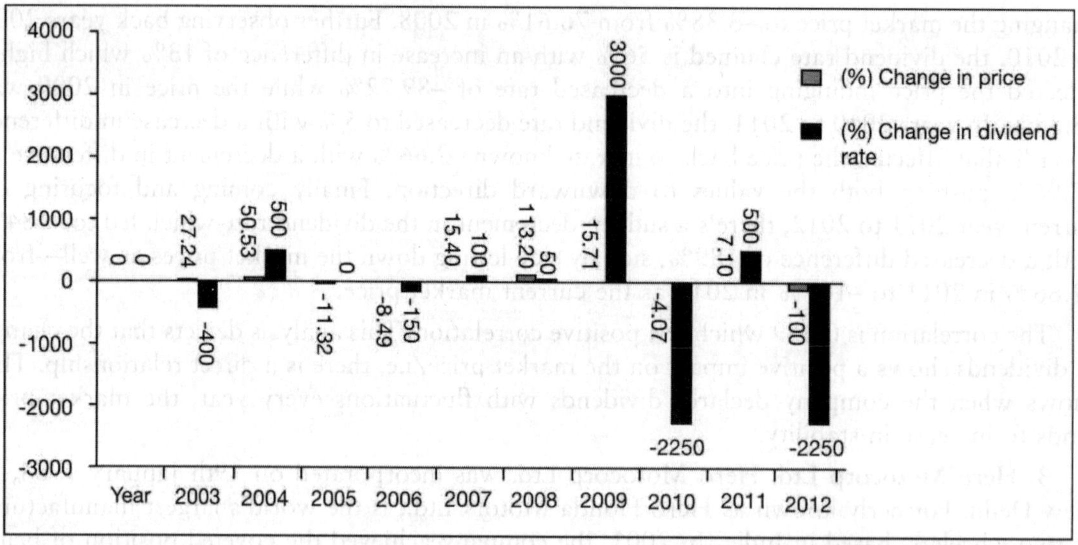


**Fig. 3:** Movement of closing price and dividend declared during 2003-2012.

As per Table 3 and graph (Fig. 3), it is seen that from years 2003 to 2004, the dividend rates have increased by a huge difference of 900% i.e. earlier in 2003 it was –400% and in the upcoming year it came up to 500% while it affected the market price in a manner, that it increased to 50.53% with a difference of just 23.29%. Now, moving further to years 2004 to 2005, the dividend rate came down to zero level i.e. 0% while the market price came down from 50.53% to –11.32% due to 0% rate declared as dividend of this particular year. Seeing year 2005 to 2006, the dividend rates announced have been decreased to lower than zero level placing at –150% that directly shows the change in price where in 2005 it was –11.32% and in 2006 it came down to –8.49%. Moving further to year's 2006 to 2007, it can be observed clearly from the table corresponding to it that the dividend rates were –150% which came up to 100% with an increase of 250%. Now, through this observation, price also rises from –8.49% to 15.4% with an increase of 23.89% which actually depicts a direct relationship as to when dividend rates are set high, ultimately price came up, with respect to only this particular year showing the rates above x-axis. Putting emphasis on year's 2007 to 2008, here, the dividend rate decreased to half a rate from the previous year placing 50% rate at a difference of 50% changing the market price to 113.2% from 15.4% in 2007. In 2008 to 2009, dividend rates have increased up to a difference of 2950% claiming 3000% as the particular rate, hence the price changed with a decrement of 97.49% i.e. value decreased from 113.02% in 2008 to 15.71% in 2009. Further observing back years' 2009 to 2010, the dividend rate announced is –2250% with a huge decrease in difference of 5250% which highly affected the price indulging into a decreased rate of –4.07% while the price in 2009 was 15.71%. Going through year's 2010 to 2011, it is observed that the dividend rate moved to positive note denoting 500% rate with an increase in difference of 2750% highlighting the price which rose up to 7.1% through the previous rate –4.07% in 2010. Finally putting eyes over current year 2011 to 2012, the rate again went into a decreased value of –2250% with a decrease in difference of 2750% showing directly the same change towards market price wherein with a decrease in difference of 107.1%, the price went down from 7.1% to –100% as the current year's price.

The correlation is 0.444 which is a positive correlation. This analysis depicts that the change in dividend shows a positive impact on the market price i.e. there is a direct relationship. This shows when the company declares dividends with fluctuations every year, the market price tends to increase in stability.

**4. Hindustan Unilever Ltd.** Hindustan Unilever Limited (HUL) is India's largest Fast Moving Consumer Goods Company with a heritage of over 75 years in India and touches the lives of two out of three Indians. HUL works to create a better future every day and helps people feel good, look good and get more out of life with brands and services that are good for them and good for others. With over 35 brands spanning 20 distinct categories such as soaps, detergents, shampoos, skin care, toothpastes, deodorants, cosmetics, tea, coffee, packaged foods, ice cream, and water purifiers, the Company is a part of the everyday life of millions of consumers across India.

**Table 4:** Movement of closing price and dividend declared during 2003-2012

| Year | Close price | Change in price | (%) Change in price | Dividend (%) | (%) Change in dividend rate |
|---|---|---|---|---|---|
| 2003 | 204.7 | –61.2 | –29.90 | 300 | 0 |
| 2004 | 143.5 | 53.75 | 37.46 | 300 | –50 |
| 2005 | 197.25 | 19.3 | 9.78 | 250 | 0 |
| 2006 | 216.55 | –2.65 | –1.22 | 250 | 50 |
| 2007 | 213.9 | 36.35 | 16.99 | 300 | 0 |
| 2008 | 250.25 | 14.5 | 5.79 | 300 | 100 |
| 2009 | 264.75 | 47.55 | 17.96 | 400 | –50 |
| 2010 | 312.3 | 95.5 | 30.58 | 350 | 0 |
| 2011 | 407.8 | 33.5 | 8.21 | 350 | 50 |
| 2012 | 441.3 | –441.3 | –100 | 400 | –400 |

http://economictimes.indiatimes.com/hindustan-unilever-infocompanydividends/companyid-13616.cms

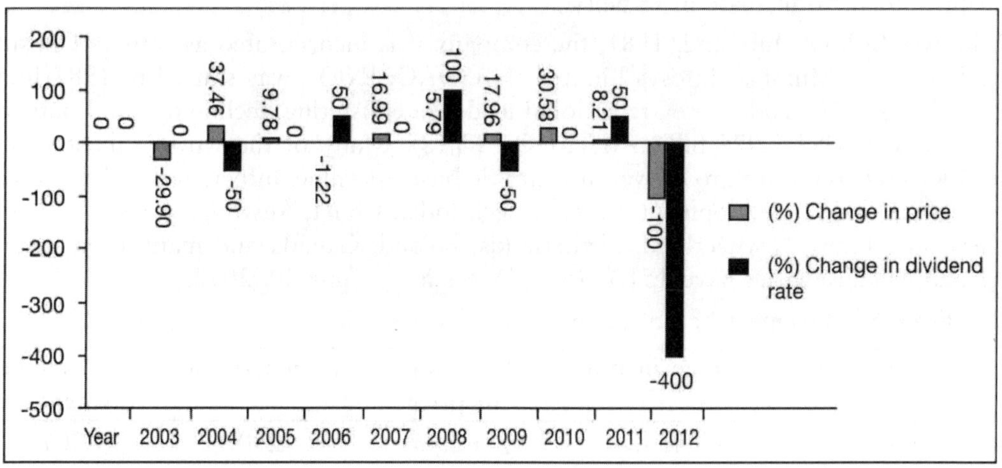


**Fig. 4:** Movement of closing price and dividend declared during 2003-2012.

As per Table 4 and graph (Fig. 4), it is seen that from years 2003 to 2004, the dividend rates have decreased by 50% i.e. earlier in 2003 it was 0% and in the upcoming year it came down to –50% which affected price indirectly as in the price came up to 37.46% from –29.9% in 2003 with an increased difference 67.36%. Now, moving further to years 2004 to 2005, the dividend rate came down to zero level i.e. 0% while the market price came down from 37.46% to 9.78% due to decrement in dividend rate or loss to company. Seeing years 2005 to 2006, the dividend rates announced have been increased by a difference of 50% which came to a particular 50% rate that shows change in price where in 2005 it was 9.78% and in 2006 it came down to –1.22%. Moving further to years 2006 to 2007, it can be observed clearly from the table corresponding to it that the dividend rate once again came down to zero level i.e. 0% rate and hence, affect market price indirectly where through this observation price came up from –1.22% to 16.99% with an increment in difference of 18.21%, an opposite reaction showing rates fluctuating from upward to downward direction in relation to x-axis. Putting emphasis on years 2007 to 2008, here, the dividend rate increased from a huge difference of 100% placing the 100% rate changing the market price to 5.79% from 16.99% in 2007. In 2008 to 2009, the dividend rates have decreased half rate to previous year up to a difference of 150% claiming –50% as the particular rate, hence, the price changed with an increment of 12.17% i.e. value increased from 5.79% in 2008 to 17.96% in 2009. Further observing back years 2009 to 2010, the dividend rate claimed is again switching back to zero level i.e. 0% which affected the price indulging into an increased rate of 30.58% while the price in 2009 was 17.96%. Now, further towards years 2010 to 2011, the dividend rate claimed at 50% changed the price to 8.21% from 30.8% in 2010 due to decrease in the difference of 22.37%. Now, at last moving on to the current year 2011 to 2012, the dividend rate changed to –400% with a maximum variation to 50% in 2011 while affecting market price with a huge decrease in difference of 108.21% and resulting into the current market price i.e. –100%.

The correlation is 0.776 which is highly positive correlation. This analysis depicts that the change in dividend shows a highly positive impact on the market price i.e. there is a direct relationship. This shows when the company declares dividends with fluctuations every year, the market price tends to increase in stability.

**5. Infosys Ltd.** On July 2nd, 1981, the company was incorporated as Infosys Consultants Private Limited at Mumbai. Infosys Limited (NASDAQ: INFY) was started in 1981 by seven people with US$ 250. Today, we are a global leader in consulting, technology and outsourcing with revenues of US$ 7.075 billion (LTM Q1 FY13). Many of the world's most successful organizations rely on Infosys to deliver measurable business value. Infosys has a global footprint with 68 offices and 70 development centers in US, India, China, Australia, Japan, Middle East, UK, Germany, France, Switzerland, Netherlands, Poland, Canada and many other countries. Infosys and its subsidiaries have 151,151 employees as on June 30, 2012.

**Table 5:** Movement of closing price and dividend declared during 2003-2012

| Year | Close price | Change in price | (%) Change in price | Dividend (%) | (%) Change in dividend rate |
|---|---|---|---|---|---|
| 2003 | 5,563.70 | –3,474.70 | –62.45 | 290 | 2010 |
| 2004 | 2,089.00 | 907.75 | 43.45 | 2300 | –2170 |

| | | | | | |
|---|---|---|---|---|---|
| 2005 | 2,996.75 | –756.25 | –25.24 | 130 | 640 |
| 2006 | 2,240.50 | –472.10 | –21.07 | 770 | –640 |
| 2007 | 1,768.40 | –650.55 | –36.79 | 130 | 415 |
| 2008 | 1,117.85 | 1,487.40 | 133.06 | 545 | –275 |
| 2009 | 2,605.25 | 839.75 | 32.23 | 270 | 30 |
| 2010 | 3,445.00 | –679.95 | –19.74 | 300 | 100 |
| 2011 | 2,765.05 | –298.70 | –10.80 | 400 | 240 |
| 2012 | 2,466.35 | –2,466.35 | –100 | 640 | –640 |

http://economictimes.indiatimes.com/infosys-ltd/infocompanydividends/companyid-10960.cms

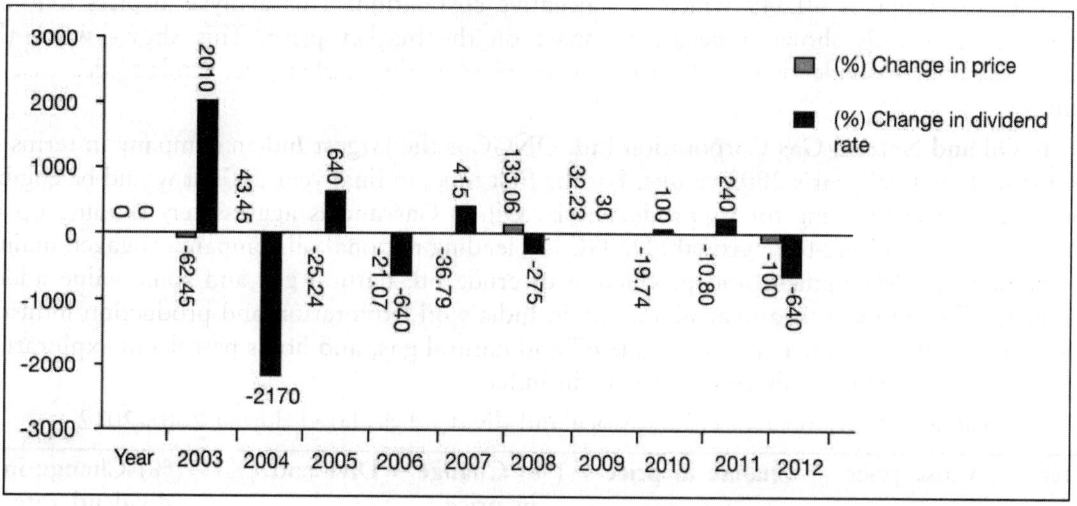


**Fig. 5:** Movement of closing price and dividend declared during 2003-2012.

As per Table 5 and graph (Fig. 5), it is seen that from years 2003 to 2004, the dividend rates have decreased by 4180% i.e. earlier in 2003 it was 2010% and in the upcoming year it came down to 2170% which affected price indirectly as in the price came up to 43.45% from –62.45% in 2003 with an increased difference of 105.9%. Now, moving further to years 2004 to 2005, the dividend rate came up to 640% while the market price came down from 43.45% to –25.24% due to the increment in dividend rates of this particular phase. Seeing years 2005 to 2006, the dividend rates announced have been decreased by a huge difference of 1280% i.e. which came at –640% that directly shows the change in price wherein in 2005 it was –25.24% and in 2006 it came up to –21.07%. Moving further to years 2006 to 2007, it can be observed clearly from the table that the dividend rate was –640% which came up to 415% with an increase of 1055%. Through this explanation, the observation is regarded in change in price wherein the price is decreased by a difference of 15.72% i.e. the price came down from –21.07% in 2006 to –36.79% in 2007. Putting emphasis on years 2007 to 2008, here, the dividend rate decreased from a huge difference of 690% placing the –275% rate changing the market price to 133.06% from –36.79% in 2007. In 2008 to 2009, dividend rates have increased up to a difference of 305% claiming 30% as the particular rate, hence the price changed with a decrement of 100.83% i.e. value decreased from 133.06% in 2008 to 32.23% in 2009. Further observing back years 2009 to 2010, the dividend rate claimed is 100% with an increased difference of 70% which highly affected the price indulging into a decreased rate of –19.74% while the price in 2009 was 32.23%. Going through years 2010 to 2011, the situation says that dividend rates have increased by a difference of 140% i.e. placing 240% as particular rate and in return affecting a decrease in price wherein it came down from –19.74% in 2010 to –10.8% in 2011. Finally focusing over current year 2011 to 2012, the varied difference in dividend rate showing decrease in rate by a difference of 880% i.e. –640% directly showing the decrement in the same manner i.e. the price of the current year is –100% with a difference of 89.2% compared to its previous year showing decrement in the values.

The correlation is –0.349 which is a negative correlation. This analysis depicts that the change in dividends shows a negative impact on the market price. This shows when the company declares dividends with fluctuations every year, the market price tends to decrease in stability.

**6. Oil and Natural Gas Corporation Ltd.** ONGC is the largest Indian company in terms of profits with its final year's 2002 results. For the first time, in final year 2003 it would be eligible for market driven pricing for its products, viz. Oil & Gas and is aggressively shaping up its business model for long-term growth. ONGC is a leading national oil company, engaged mainly in exploration, development and production of crude oil; natural gas and some value added products. The company is a near monopoly in India's oil exploration and production industry and produces 90% of the country's crude oil and natural gas, and holds petroleum exploration licenses for 80% of the sedimentary basins in India.

**Table 6:** Movement of closing price and dividend declared during 2003-2012

| Year | Close price | Change in price | (%) Change in price | Dividend (%) | (%) Change in dividend rate |
|---|---|---|---|---|---|
| 2003 | 799.5 | 20.05 | 2.51 | 130 | –30 |
| 2004 | 819.55 | 355.4 | 43.37 | 100 | 100 |
| 2005 | 1,174.95 | –304.9 | –25.95 | 200 | 0 |
| 2006 | 870.05 | 366.45 | 42.12 | 200 | –70 |
| 2007 | 1,236.50 | –568.85 | –46.00 | 130 | 10 |
| 2008 | 667.65 | 509.9 | 76.37 | 140 | 0 |
| 2009 | 1,177.55 | 115.85 | 9.84 | 140 | 10 |
| 2010 | 1,293.40 | –1036.45 | –80.13 | 150 | –135 |
| 2011 | 256.95 | 21.25 | 8.27 | 15 | 25 |
| 2012 | 278.2 | -278.2 | –100 | 40 | –40 |

http://economictimes.indiatimes.com/oil-and-natural-gas-corporation-ltd/infocompanydividends/companyid-11599.cms

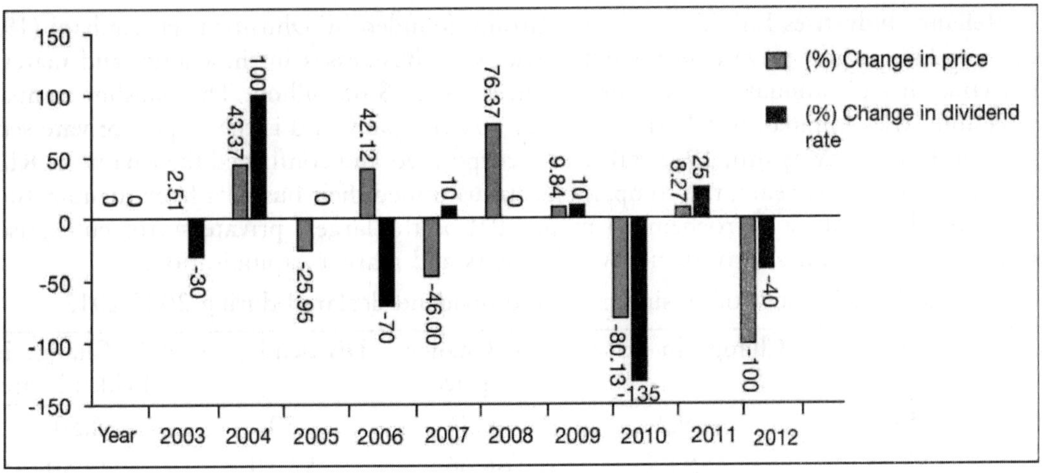


**Fig. 6:** Movement of closing price and dividend declared during 2003-2012.

As per Table 6 and graph (Fig. 6), it is seen that from years 2003 to 2004, the dividend rates have increased by 130% i.e. earlier in 2003 it was –30% and in the upcoming year it came up to 100% while this affected the market price directly which also increased by 40.86% although the rate was in positive. Now, moving further to years 2004 to 2005, the dividend rate came down to zero level i.e. 0% while the market price came down with a high difference from 43.37% to –25.95% due to no dividend rate declared. Seeing years 2005 to 2006, the dividend rates announced have been decreased by a difference of 70% and which came at –70% that shows the change in price where in 2005 it was –25.95% and in 2006 it came up to 42.12%, deliberately focusing on an indirect relationship between the two. Moving further to years 2006 to 2007, clearly it is been observed that the dividend rate was –70% which came up to 10% with an increase of 80%. Now, through this observation, price came down from 42.12% in upward as well as downward direction. Putting emphasis on years 2007 to 2008, here, the dividend rate again came down to zero level i.e. 0% changing the market price to 76.37% from –46% in 2007. In 2008 to 2009, dividend rates have increased up to a difference of 10% claiming 10% as the particular rate, hence the price changed with a decrement of 66.53% i.e. value decreased from 76.37% in 2008 to 9.84% in 2009. Further observing back years 2009 to 2010, the dividend rate claimed is –135% with a decrease in difference of 145% which highly affected the price indulging into a decreased rate of –80.13% while the price in 2009 was 9.84%. Now, further towards years 2010 to 2011, the dividend rate has increased by a huge difference of 160% claiming 25% as rate and this affected the price in same manner wherein it came up from –80.13% in 2010 to 8.27% in 2011. Finally putting eyes over the current year 2011 to 2012, the dividend rate was 25% in 2011 and it decreased by a difference of 65% i.e. –40% affected the market price changing the values in same manner, i.e. decreasing by a difference of 108.27% and hence, the current market price is –100%.

The correlation is 0.479 which is a positive correlation. This analysis depicts that the change in dividends shows a positive impact on the market price i.e. there is a direct relationship. This shows when the company declares dividends with fluctuations every year, the market price tends to increase in stability.

**7. Reliance Industries Ltd.** The Reliance Group, founded by Dhirubhai H. Ambani (1932-2002), is India's largest private sector enterprise, with businesses in the energy and materials value chain. Group's annual revenues are in excess of US$ 66 billion. The flagship company, Reliance Industries Limited, is a Fortune Global 500 company and is the largest private sector company in India. In May 8th, 1973 RIL was incorporated and confirmed their name as RIL in the year 1985. Over the years, the company has transformed their business from manufacturing of textile products into a petrochemical major. RIL is the largest private sector enterprise in India in terms of revenues, profits, net worth, assets and market capitalisation.

**Table 7:** Movement of closing price and dividend declared during 2003-2012

| Year | Close price | Change in price | (%) Change in price | Dividend (%) | (%) Change in dividend rate |
|---|---|---|---|---|---|
| 2003 | 573 | –39.2 | –6.84 | 50 | 2.50 |
| 2004 | 533.8 | 355.85 | 66.66 | 52.50 | 22.50 |
| 2005 | 889.65 | 380.7 | 42.79 | 75 | 25.00 |
| 2006 | 1,270.35 | 1610.7 | 126.79 | 100 | 10.00 |
| 2007 | 2,881.05 | –1650.8 | –57.30 | 110 | 20.00 |
| 2008 | 1,230.25 | –140.85 | –11.45 | 130 | 0.00 |
| 2009 | 1,089.40 | –31.15 | –2.86 | 130 | –60.00 |
| 2010 | 1,058.25 | –365.35 | –34.52 | 70 | 10.00 |
| 2011 | 692.9 | 32.8 | 4.73 | 80 | 5.00 |
| 2012 | 725.7 | –725.7 | –100 | 85 | –85.00 |

http://economictimes.indiatimes.com/reliance-industries-ltd/infocompanydividends/companyid-13215.cms

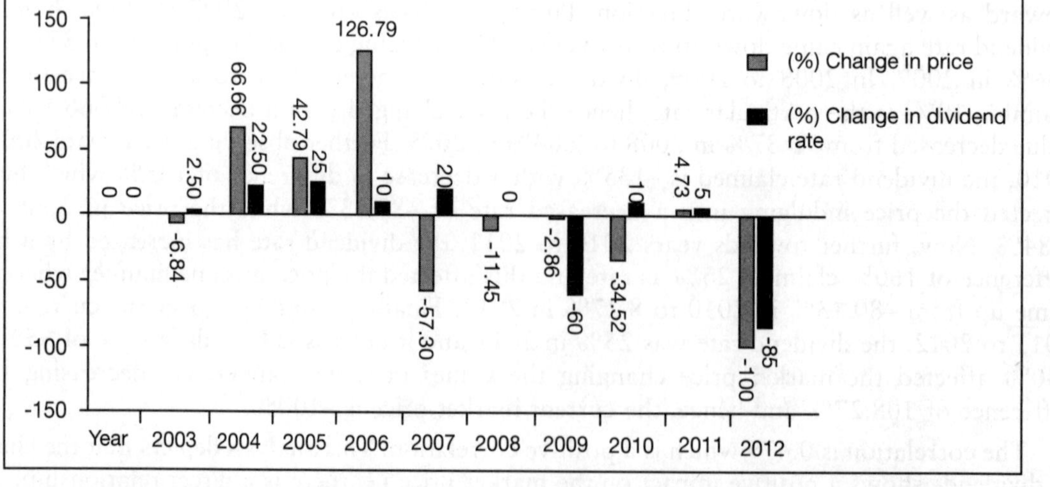


**Fig. 7:** Movement of closing price and dividend declared during 2003-2012.

As per Table 7 and graph (Fig. 7), it is seen that from years 2003 to 2004, the dividend rates have increased by 20% i.e. earlier in 2003 it was 2.5% and in the upcoming year it came up to 22.5% while this highly affected the market price which also increased by 73.5% as earlier it was in negative. Now, moving further to years 2004 to 2005, the dividend rate increment is same as above while the market price came down from 66.66% to 42.79% due to the increment in dividend rates of this particular phase. Seeing years 2005 to 2006, the dividend rates announced have been decreased by a difference of 15% i.e. 10% that directly shows the change in price where in 2005 it was 42.79% and in 2006 it came up to 126.79%. Moving further to years 2006 to 2007, it can be observed clearly from the table corresponding to it that the dividend rates were 10% which came up to 20% with an increase of 10%. By observing this, the price came down from 126.79% to –57.3% with a decrease of 184.09%, depicting an opposite reaction wherein the values will surround upside and downside at x-axis. Putting emphasis on years 2007 to 2008, here, and the dividend rate came down to zero level i.e. 0% changing the market price to –11.45% from –57.3% in 2007. In 2008 to 2009, dividend rates have decreased up to a difference of 60% claiming –60% as the particular rate, hence the price changed with an increment of 8.59% i.e. value increased from –11.45% in 2008 to –2.86% in 2009. Further observing back years 2009 to 2010, the dividend rate claimed is 10% with an increase in difference of 70% which alternately affected the price indulging into a decreased rate of –34.52% while the price in 2009 was –2.86%. Seeing years 2010 to 2011, it is been judged that the dividend rate has decreased from a small amount of 5% i.e. the rate is 5% which affected price indirectly showing increase in the rate from –34.52% in 2010 to 4.73% in 2011. Finally going on to the current years 2011 to 2012, here the dividend rate tends to go negative showing –85% with a decreased difference of 90% while the price seems to move in the same manner, i.e. decreasing by a difference of 104.73% and hence, the current market price is –100%.

The correlation is 0.552 which is a positive correlation. This analysis depicts that the change in dividends shows a positive impact on the market price i.e. there is a direct relationship. This shows when the company declares dividends with fluctuations every year, the market price tends to increase in stability.

**8. State Bank of India.** State Bank of India (SBI) is that country's largest commercial bank. The government-controlled bank the Indian government maintains a stake of nearly 60% in SBI through the central Reserve Bank of India also operates the world's largest branch network, with more than 13,500 branch offices throughout India, staffed by nearly 220,000 employees.

**Table 8:** Movement of closing price and dividend declared during 2003-2012

| Year | Close price | Change in price | (%) Change in price | Dividend (%) | (%) Change in dividend rate |
|---|---|---|---|---|---|
| 2003 | 538.5 | 113.95 | 21.16 | 85 | 25 |
| 2004 | 652.45 | 255 | 39.08 | 110 | 15 |
| 2005 | 907.45 | 338.45 | 37.30 | 125 | 15 |
| 2006 | 1,245.90 | 1,125.1 | 90.30 | 140 | 0 |
| 2007 | 2,371.00 | –1,082.75 | –45.67 | 140 | 75 |
| 2008 | 1,288.25 | 981.2 | 76.17 | 215 | 75 |

| | | | | | |
|---|---|---|---|---|---|
| 2009 | 2,269.45 | 541.6 | 23.86 | 290 | –90 |
| 2010 | 2,811.05 | –1,191.55 | –42.39 | 200 | 100 |
| 2011 | 1,619.50 | 596.5 | 36.83 | 300 | 50 |
| 2012 | 2,216.00 | –2216 | –100 | 350 | –350 |

http://economictimes.indiatimes.com/state-bank-of-india/infocompanydividends/companyid-11984.cms

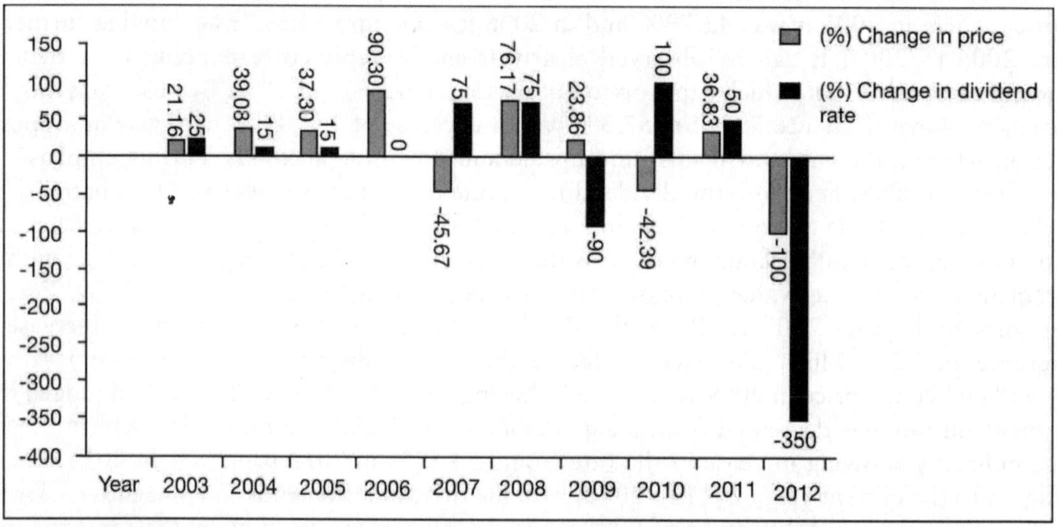


**Fig. 8:** Movement of closing price and dividend declared during 2003-2012.

As per Table 8 and graph (Fig. 8), it is seen that from years 2003 to 2004, the dividend rates have decreased by 10% i.e. earlier in 2003 it was 25% and in the upcoming year it came down to 15% while this affected price indirectly as in the price came up to 30.08% from 21.16% in 2003 with an increased difference of 17.92%. Now, moving further to years 2004 to 2005, the dividend rate is same as the previous year's rate i.e. 15% which led the market price came down from 39.08% to 37.3% due to the constant maintenance of dividend rates. Seeing years 2005 to 2006, the dividend rates announced has came down to zero level i.e. 0% that directly shows the change in price where in 2005 it was 37.3% and in 2006 it came up to 90.3%. As and when there is no share for the shareholders, price ultimately rises in order to maintain the stake in the market. Moving further to years 2006 to 2007, it is clearly observed that the dividend rates were 0% which came up to 75%. With this reference, it further goes on wherein the price came down from 90.3% to –45.67% with a decrease of 135.97%, a high make over in the company shows the growth stability with the opposite relationship between dividend rates and the price. Putting emphasis on years 2007 to 2008, here, the dividend rate remains constant, i.e. 75% changing the market price to 76.17% from –45.67% in 2007. In 2008 to 2009, dividend rates have decreased up to a difference of 165% claiming –90% as the particular rate, hence the price changed with a decrement of 52.31% i.e. value decreased from 76.17% in 2008 to 23.86% in 2009. Further observing back years 2009 to 2010, the dividend rate claimed is 100% with an increased difference of 190% which highly affected the price indulging into a decreased rate of

–42.39% while the price in 2009 was 23.86%. Viewing more years from 2010 to 2011, here, the dividend rate decreased the half amount of previous one, i.e. 50% while the price increased with a difference of 79.22%, hence depicting 36.83% rate. Finally putting eyes over current year 2011 to 2012, the maximum variation in dividend rates is particularly through this year wherein it was 50% in 2011 and which decreased by a difference of 400% i.e. –350%, affected the market price changing the values in same manner, i.e. decreasing by a difference of 136.83% and hence, the current market price is –100%.

The correlation is 0.511 which is a positive correlation. This analysis depicts that the change in dividends shows a positive impact on the market price i.e. there is a direct relationship. This shows when the company declares dividends with fluctuations every year, the market price tends to increase in stability.

**9. Tata Steel Ltd.** Tata Steel was incorporated on 26th August, 1907. Steel is among the top ten global steel companies with an annual crude steel capacity of over 28 million tonnes per annum. It is now one of the world's most geographically-diversified steel producers, with operations in 26 countries and a commercial presence in over 50 countries. The Tata Steel Group, with a turnover of US$ 22.8 billion in FY '10, has over 80,000 employees across five continents and is a Fortune 500 company. Tata Steel was founded in India in 1907. Since 2004 the Company has expanded globally, acquiring Asian steel producers NatSteel and Millennium Steel (now called Tata Steel Thailand) as well as Europe's second largest steel producer Corus (now called Tata Steel Europe Limited). Tata Steel Ltd. is the world's 10th largest steel company and the world's 2nd most geographically diversified steel producer.

**Table 9:** Movement of closing price and dividend declared during 2003-2012

| Year | Close price | Change in price | (%) Change in price | Dividend (%) | (%) Change in dividend rate |
|---|---|---|---|---|---|
| 2003 | 444.05 | –58.6 | –13.20 | 80 | 20 |
| 2004 | 385.45 | –5.15 | –1.34 | 100 | 30 |
| 2005 | 380.3 | 102 | 26.82 | 130 | 0 |
| 2006 | 482.3 | 452.5 | 93.82 | 130 | 25 |
| 2007 | 934.8 | –717.95 | –76.80 | 155 | 5 |
| 2008 | 216.85 | 400.75 | 184.81 | 160 | 0 |
| 2009 | 617.6 | 61.35 | 9.93 | 160 | –80 |
| 2010 | 678.95 | –343.7 | –50.62 | 80 | 40 |
| 2011 | 335.25 | 101.1 | 30.16 | 120 | 0 |
| 2012 | 436.35 | –436.35 | –100 | 120 | –120 |

http://economictimes.indiatimes.com/tata-steel-ltd/infocompanydividends/companyid-12902.cms

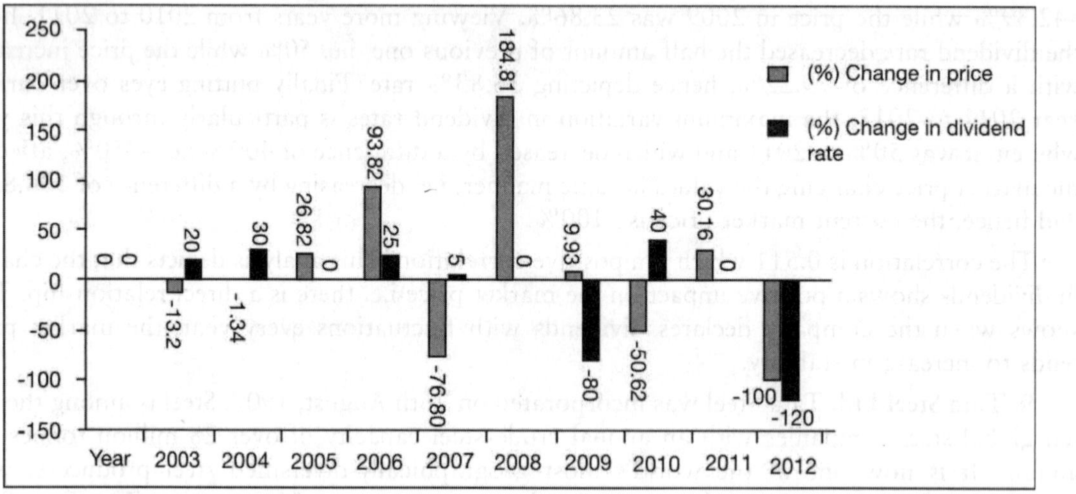


**Fig. 9:** Movement of closing price and dividend declared during 2003-2012.

As per Table 9 and graph (Fig. 9), it is seen that from years 2003 to 2004, the dividend rates have increased by 10%, i.e. earlier in 2003 it was 20% and in the upcoming year it came up to 30% while this affected the market price which also increased by 11.86% as earlier also it was negative only. While moving further to years 2004 to 2005, the dividend rate came down to zero level i.e. 0% while the market price came up from –1.34% to 26.82% due to no dividend rate. Seeing years 2005 to 2006, the dividend rates announced have been increased by a difference of 25% i.e. a rate of 25% itself that shows directly the change in price where in 2005 it was 26.82% and in 2006 it came up to 93.82%, here this description shows a direct relationship between the two, as in if one increases, the other one automatically rises. Moving further to years 2006 to 2007, it can be observed clearly from the table corresponding to it that the dividend rates were 25% which came down to 5% with a decrease of 20%. Through this observation, price came down from 93.82% to –76.8% with a decrease of 170.62%, the same situation as above. Putting emphasis on years 2007 to 2008, here, the dividend rate once again came down to zero level i.e. 0% changing the market price to 184.81% from –76.8% in 2007. In 2008 to 2009, dividend rates have decreased up to a difference of 80% claiming –80% as the particular rate, hence the price changed with a decrement of 174.88% i.e. value decreased from 184.81% in 2008 to 9.93% in 2009. Further observing back years 2009 to 2010, the dividend rate claimed is 40% with an increase in difference of 120% which highly affected the price indulging into a decreased rate of –50.62% while the price in 2009 was 9.93%. Focusing on years 2010 to 2011, the observation depicts that the dividend rate once again came down to zero level i.e. 0% which highly affected the market price into an increased rate of 30.16% due to the rising difference of 80.78%. Finally switching over current years 2011 to 2012, the dividend rate moved into the negative mode with a decreased difference of 120% placing –120% as the particular rate which affected the market price in the same manner, i.e. decreasing by a difference of 130.16% and hence, the current market price is –100%.

The correlation is 0.303 which is again a positive correlation. This analysis depicts that the change in dividends shows a positive impact on the market price i.e. there is a direct relationship. This shows when the company declares dividends with fluctuations every year, the market price tends to increase in stability.

**10. Wipro Ltd.** In the year of 1945, in pre-independent India, a vision was born, which would eventually stand out as a brand name synonymous with innovation and integrity. Starting off with consumer products business, Wipro then diversified into newer areas including IT hardware and IT services. Such has been the dynamic power of the organization that over the past 50 years, Wipro has evolved into a leading global IT company, a company which has pioneered many an innovation in the IT services, BPO and R&D services space. Wipro Global IT Business delivers winning business outcomes through its deep industry experience and a 360 degree view of "Business through Technology"—helping clients create successful and adaptive businesses. A company recognized globally for its comprehensive portfolio of services, a practitioner's approach to delivering innovation and an organization wide commitment to sustainability. Wipro Technologies has over 130,000 employees and clients across 54 countries.

**Table 10:** Movement of closing price and dividend declared during 2003-2012

| Year | Close price | Change in price | (%) Change in price | Dividend (%) | (%) Change in dividend rate |
|---|---|---|---|---|---|
| 2003 | 1,737.60 | –989.60 | –56.95 | 50 | 1400 |
| 2004 | 748 | –284.55 | –38.04 | 1450 | –1200 |
| 2005 | 463.45 | 141.10 | 30.45 | 250 | 0 |
| 2006 | 604.55 | –78.95 | –13.06 | 250 | –200 |
| 2007 | 525.6 | –292.05 | –55.57 | 50 | 150 |
| 2008 | 233.55 | 445.85 | 190.90 | 200 | 0 |
| 2009 | 679.4 | –189.15 | –27.84 | 200 | 100 |
| 2010 | 490.25 | –91.45 | –18.65 | 300 | –100 |
| 2011 | 398.8 | –24.60 | –6.17 | 200 | 0 |
| 2012 | 374.2 | –374.20 | –100 | 200 | –200 |

http://economictimes.indiatimes.com/wipro-ltd/infocompanydividends/companyid-12799.cms

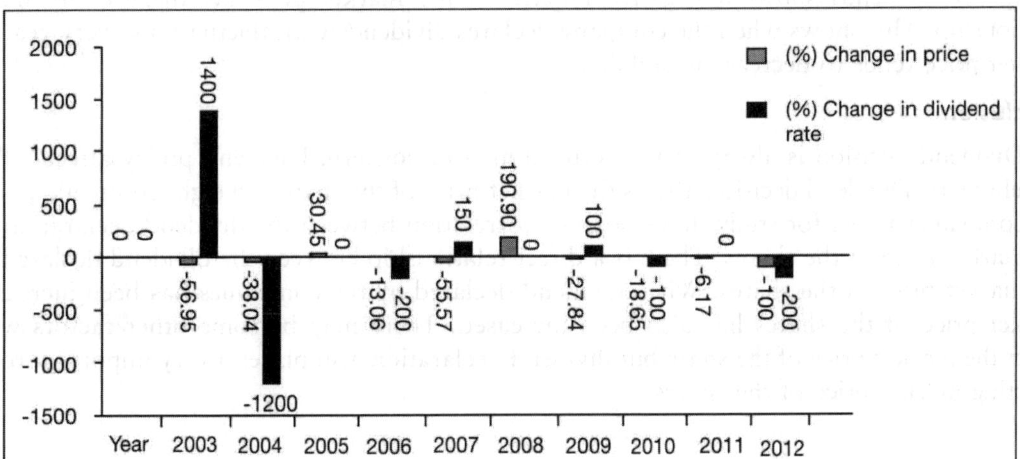


**Fig. 10:** Movement of closing price and dividend declared during 2003-2012.

As per Table 10 and graph (Fig. 10), it is seen that from years 2003 to 2004, the dividend rates have decreased by 2600% i.e. earlier in 2003 it was 1400% and in the upcoming year it came down to –1200% while this affected price indirectly as in the price came up to –38.04% from –56.95% in 2003 with an increased difference of 18.91%. Now, moving further to years 2004 to 2005, the dividend rate came down to zero level i.e. 0% while the market price came up from -38.04% to 30.45% due to no dividend rate for this particular year. Seeing years 2005 to 2006, the dividend rates announced have been decreased by a difference of 200% which came to –200% that directly shows the change in price where in 2005 it was 30.45% and in 2006 it came down to –13.06%, it is showing a direct relationship where the values would be shown downward to x-axis. Moving further to years 2006 to 2007, it can be clearly observed through this table that the dividend rates were –200% which came up to 150% with an increase of 350%. After focus on it, result says price came down from –13.06% to –55.57% with a decrease of 42.51%, this situation is opposite and hence, depicts indirect relationship and variation on putting up the values in any area (graph). Putting emphasis on years 2007 to 2008, here, the dividend rates again came down to zero level i.e. 0% changing the market price to 190.9% from –55.57% in 2007. In 2008 to 2009, dividend rates have increased up to a difference of 100 claiming 100% as the particular rate, hence the price changed with a decrement of 218.74% i.e. value decreased from 190.9% in 2008 to –27.84% in 2009. Further observing back years 2009 to 2010, the dividend rate claimed is –100% with a huge decrease in difference of 200% which affected the price indulging into an increased rate of –18.65% while the price in 2009 was –27.84%. Giving focus towards years 2010 to 2011, the dividend rate once again came down to zero level i.e. 0% while the market price came up from –18.65% in 2010 to –6.17% in 2011 with an increased difference of 12.48%. Finally, putting eyes over current year i.e. 2011 to 2012, the dividend rates came down in negative direction indicating –200% as particular rate which affected the market price same way, i.e. decreasing by a difference of 98.83% and claiming the current market price to be –100%.

The correlation is –0.04 which is a negative correlation. This analysis depicts that the change in dividends shows a negative impact on the market price i.e. there is an indirect relationship. This shows when the company declares dividends with fluctuations every year, the market price tends to decrease in stability.

## Conclusion

Dividend decision is always a very crucial area of concern. Dividend policy affects all the stakeholders. Dividend decision affects the market price of the shares. In eight companies, out of ten companies taken for study, have positive correlation between the dividend declaration and the market price of the shares. There is a direct relationship between the dividend declared and the market price of the shares. When dividend declared by the companies has been increasing, market price of the shares has also been increased. There may be some other factors which affect the market price of the share but dividend declaration also places a very important role in affecting market price of the shares.

## REFERENCES

Bhat, R. and I.M. Pandey, "Dividend decision: A Study of Managers' Perceptions", *Decision*, Vol. 21, pp. 67-86, January-June 1994.

Bhushan, R., "Firm characteristics and analyst following", *Journal of Accounting and Economics*, Vol. 4, pp. 255-74, 1989.

Chandra, P. "Dividend Policy: Practical Aspects" in *Financial Management: Theory and Practice*, Fourth Edition, Chapter 15, New Delhi: Tata McGraw Hill, 1997.

Chaturvedi, H.O. "Half Yearly Financial Results and Behavior of Share Prices in India", *Finance India*, Vol. 14, pp. 537-45, 2000.

Gupta, N.C. and Sharma, G.L., "Dividend Behaviour in Tea Industry in India: A Case Study of Selected Firms", *ASCI Journal of Management*, Vol. 20, No. 4, pp. 274-83.

Jayaraman, N., and K. Shastri. "The Valuation Impacts of Specially Designated Dividends." *Journal of Financial and Quantitative Analysis*, Vol. 23, pp. 301-12, 1988.

Raghunathan, V. and Prabina Dass, "Corporate Performance: Post Liberalization," *ICFAI Journal of Applied Finance*, Vol. 5(2), pp. 6-31, 1999.

# 10

# RECENT TRENDS IN REPORTING OF INTANGIBLE ASSETS IN SELECTED INDIAN COMPANIES

–*Shurveer S. Bhanawat* and *Nidhi Bhanawat*

## Introduction

Rise of 'Virtual' corporations and flourishing service industry has brought Intangible assets (IA) in sharp focus in recent years. For these businesses Intangible assets are more than ever the "Core assets" that drive business success in today's challenging business climate. The investment pattern of U.S. Corporate Sector in 1929 and 1990 had been compared by Prof. Baurch Lev in 2001. He concluded that in 1929 among U.S. companies approximately (70 per cent) of their investment were into tangible assets and (30 per cent) were into intangible assets. In contrast, in 1990 the trend was reversed, it was found that major part of investment went into intangibles (67 per cent) such as research and development, IT, Software, education, competencies and internet. Further, Lev compared that relationship between market and book value of shares. In 1970, it was 1:1 and in mid-1990 it has increased to an average of three times. This statistical information provided an insight into recognizing the importance of Intangible assets. Several studies in past shown that future growth is determined not only by historical financial accounts alone but factors such as management skills, innovation, capability, brands and collective Know-how of the workforce. So, an organization needs to identify Intangible assets from its countless assets knowledge based resources that can be helpful to achieve strategic objective and competitive advantage. Such Intangible assets should also be disclosed in annual report so that an investor or interested party knows about the strength of the company. This will affect the equity mobilization activities of Indian Corporate Sector. So, in this context, here an attempt has been made to analyze the recent practices adopted by selected Indian companies.

## Review of Literature

Intangible Assets (IA) disclosure and reporting is still an ongoing discussion topic in the accounting literature and in order to study reporting practices of Intangible assets adopted by selected sample companies an intensive review of existing literature has been done which having direct and indirect emphasis on the objective of present research paper.

Indra Abeysekara and Guthrie (2002) conducted study using data from 30 companies listed in Colombo Stock Exchange during year 1998-99. Companies were selected based on highest market capitalization to examine Intellectual Capital reporting practices on the basis of content analysis. 45 Intellectual capital items in the categories of internal, external and human capital were identified. The authors found that only small proportion of Intellectual capital reported was quantified and findings were different from developed countries. Further (2004) conducted another research study using method of content analysis to identify human capital disclosure patterns in Sri Lankan companies using method of content analysis and compared the differences in disclosure patterns of between Sri Lanka and developed nations. A.S. Kantawala (2006) examined how disclosure are made by few Indian companies namely, Patni Computers Ltd., Nicholas Piramal Ltd., Finolex Cables Ltd., Bombay Burmah Trading Corporation Ltd., Deepak Fertilizers Corporation Ltd. and Bharti-Tele Ventures Ltd. from financial year 2004-05. Convenience based sampling is used for the purpose of study. She concluded from her study that for better transparency of financial statement IC should be disclosed in annual reports of companies either as part of 'Management Discussion and Analysis Report' or as part of the Corporate Governance Report. Madan Bhasin (2007) analyzed the trend of Intellectual Capital reporting in Indian Corporate Sector. He found that only three Indian companies published their first Intellectual Capital Reports in 1997. These firms are Balrampur Chini Mills Ltd., Shree Cement Ltd. and Reliance Industries Ltd. However, he concluded that reports prepared by these companies do not focus on business models, values, and mission and Knowledge management issues. Ali Mohobbot (2008) examined 22 Bangladesh companies listed in Dhaka Stock Exchange to investigate the level of awareness of Bangladesh companies about Intellectual Capital and their disclosures in annual reports. The major findings revealed that companies do not have positive approach in reporting and interpreting the Intellectual capital and reporting is limited to qualitative form rather than in quantitative form. Bharthi Kamath (2008) study the extent of voluntary Intellectual Capital disclosures in India's emerging information, communication, technology sector and the relationship between size of the firm and extent of disclosures. Content analysis of the 30 technology, entertainment, communication and other knowledge "TECK" companies listed on Bombay Stock Exchange is carried out. A list of Intellectual Capital related terms is searched for its presence or absence within the annual reports of these forms for the financial year 2005-06. The list of term is determined on the extensive survey of literature on content analysis and Intellectual capital. The study undertaken found small extent of Intellectual capital disclosures in Indian firms. Information technology industries disclosures are more than any other sectors disclosures, closely followed by telecommunication industry. Entertainment industry show minimal disclosures. Tilak Chandana, (2008) described various voluntary and mandatory reporting practices adopted for measuring Intellectual Capital and highlighted on some recent trends in reporting of Intellectual Capital worldwide. He concluded that though the usefulness of voluntary reporting practices is unquestionable, the prevalent practices being followed have no common grammar, language, no third party verification, high transaction cost involved, no legal sanction, absence of universally accepted and recognized measurement principles. Thus reporting of IC in India is not adequate. Pradeep Kumar Singh (2009) explains the need and importance of intangible assets in Knowledge era, various ways of intangible assets reporting by Indian companies and the method for the valuation of intangible assets. The present study is based on both primary and secondary data related to 30 leading BSE Indian companies for five years from 2003 to 2007. Companies are further sub-grouped according to their nature and business as Information and Technology Industry, Pharmaceutical Industry, FMGC Industry, Automobile Industry and Infrastructure Industry and under each sub-group six leading units are included. For, IC reporting and disclosure practice, a comprehensive industry-wise analysis is made related to amortization method, duration and categories of intangible assets. He concluded from his article that highly innovative companies i.e. IT and Pharma sector are voluntary reporting information related to IC in their annual report but traditional companies are still behind the reporting and disclosure practices related to IC. P.K. Rathod and Sangita Prajapati (2010), made an attempt to study the reporting and disclosure practices of IC in selected IT companies in India. A study of annual reports (2008-09) of IT giant-Infosys Technologies Ltd. (Infosys), Tata Consultancy Services Ltd. (TCS), Wipro Ltd. (WIPRO), GTL Infrastructure (GTL), Cranes Software International Ltd. (CRANES) and Sonata Software Ltd. (SONATA) has been undertaken. The authors revealed from the study that only Infosys Ltd. has used popular method of human resource valuation model i.e. Lev and Schwartz to compute value of human resources and prepare balance sheet including Intangible assets comprised mainly of two type of assets—brand value and human resources while reporting of other IT companies were not found adequate.

## Objectives

1. To analyze the recent practices adopted in reporting of intangible assets by selected sample Indian companies.
2. To study the concept, accounting and disclosure of intangible assets by sample Indian companies.
3. To analyze item-wise and frequency-wise reporting practices of selected sample companies through content analysis.

## Research Methodology

This research study is based on secondary data related to 35 leading BSE Indian companies from years (2007-11). Most of the data collected from annual published reports available on official websites of sample companies. Related theoretical literature collected from various secondary sources i.e. leading journals, magazines and information available in official websites of selected companies. Further, for identification of intangible items content analysis technique has been used in present paper.

## Reporting Trends of Intangible Assets of Selected Indian Companies

The reporting of intangible assets by selected Indian companies has been discussed in following paragraphs:

- **Infosys Technologies Ltd.:** The Infosys is one of largest IT Company in India. Intangible assets are recorded at the consideration paid for acquisition and amortized over their respective individual estimated useful lives on straight line basis, commencing from the date the asset is available to the company for its use. The Infosys Ltd.

published Intangible asset score sheet using Karl Erik Sveiby model of intangible asset monitor as a base and classified intangible assets into following categories: (a) Human resources, (b) Intellectual property assets, (c) Internal assets, and (d) External assets. Beside this company also gives report on Brand valuation, EVA Statement, Current cost adjusted financial statement, risk management report and Human resource accounting statement by using Lev & Schwartz model.

- **WIPRO Technologies Ltd.:** The company disclose only that part of intangibles that is acquired either individually or as business combination. The total assets are further classified as marketing related intangibles, customer related intangibles and technology related intangibles. The annual report of company reported goodwill and human resources as an inseparable part of their growth, however, there is no exclusive measurement of the value of their human capital. Technical know-how, brands, patents, trademark and rights amortized over the determined useful life ranging between 20 to 25 years based on expected life, performance, market share and longevity of the brand.
- **SATYAM Computer Services Ltd.:** Satyam Ltd. has used Lev & Schwartz model for estimating human resource value and cost of application software for internal use are generally charged to revenue as incurred due to its estimated useful lives being relatively short usually less than one year. The annual report of company also include a statement of economic value added of the company over a period of time provided as additional information to investors to judge the true value of firm.
- **PATNI Computer Ltd.:** Computer software is mentioned along with other fixed assets. It is not even titled as intangible asset. No other information is given about intangible asset. Thus, the details given falls short of requirement of standard.
- **TCS Ltd.:** The company does not mention the value of its intangible assets as part of its overall balance sheet requirements. The report comprehensively report about the growth of its human resources, technology base and investment it makes in R&D and training development of resources. TCS Intellectual Property/Distribution rights amortized on the basis of straight line within 24-36 months. Software license are depreciated on straight line basis @ 20 per cent.
- **SONATA Software Ltd.:** There was no intangible asset reported either in the balance sheet or in the schedule of fixed assets and hence there was no disclosure related to intangible as per the AS-26.
- **CRANES Ltd.:** Computer software is vital intangible asset (93 per cent of fixed asset). Customised software/commercial rights amortized over their estimated useful life 3 years on straight line basis while other intangible asset amortized over their individual estimated life on straight line basis.
- **HCL Technologies Ltd.:** Estimated useful life of goodwill five years and carrying value of goodwill at the end of each accounting years is reviewed for impairment and software is amortized for 3 years.

- **LUPIN Ltd.:** The intangible assets are recorded at cost less accumulated amortization and accumulated impairment losses, if any intangible assets (including computer software) amortized within the period of 6 years.
- **RANBAXY Ltd.:** Intangible assets (patent, designs and licenses) are capitalized and amortized on straight line basis over period of 5 years. Computer software which is not an integral part of the related hardware is classified as an intangible asset and is being amortized over a period of 6 years. Non-compete fee is capitalized and amortized on a straight line basis over the term of the non-compete agreement. Product Development cost incurred for acquiring rights for product underdevelopment are recognized as intangible assets and amortized on a straight line basis over a period of 5 years from the date of regulatory approval. Further, subsequent expenditures on development of such products are also added to the cost of intangibles.
- **Dr. Reddy's Laboratories Ltd.:** Intangible assets are recorded at the acquisition and amortized over their estimated useful lives on straight line basis. The management estimate the useful lives of various intangible asset as follows: customer contracts 2 to 5 years, Technical know-how 10 years, Non compete fee 1.5 to 10 years, Patents, Trademark and designs (including marketing know-how) 3-10 years. The company disclosed intangible assets under the head "Significant Accounting Policies".
- **Nicholas Piramal India Limited:** The company intangible assets other than computer software comprise of brands, trademark, technical know-how and business intellectual property right and approvals acquired by the company over the years. No internally generated intangible assets have been recognized in the books of accounts. Computer software is being depreciated on SLM at rates specified XIV of Companies Act 1956. The company has provided extensive details of intangible assets, first in fixed asset schedule and second in the policy for recognition and lastly in detail reconciliation as required as per AS-26.
- **Glaxo Smith Kline Pharmaceuticals (India) Limited:** Capital expenditure on R&D is written off over useful lives of assets. Revenue expenses are recognized in the year in which they are incurred. The useful life of intangible assets used for amortization purpose, has not been disclosed in the annual report.
- **Merck Ltd.:** The company intangible assets are disclosed along with other Fixed asset, without separate titled as intangible assets. Trademark are amortized over expected benefit period of 5 years while software amortized over an estimated useful life of 3 years. Acquired intangible assets are recorded at cost and amortized on straight line basis over their useful life.
- **Pizfer Ltd.:** Intangible asset (Trademarks) are recorded at their acquisition cost and amortized over the lower of their estimated useful life and period of ownership on straight line basis i.e. over a period of 3 years. Cost of application software not exceeding US$ 1 million is being charged to the profit and loss account. Capital expenditure on research and development is capitalized as fixed assets and depreciated in accordance with the depreciation policy of the company.

- **HUL Ltd.:** Intangible assets are stated at cost of acquisition less accumulated amortization. Goodwill and other intangible assets (except computer software) are amortized over the asset useful life not exceeding 10 years. Computer software is amortized over a period of 5 years on straight line method. Goodwill arising on consolidation in accordance with AS-21 is amortized over 4 years at quarterly rests commencing from the quarter of recognition of goodwill.
- **Colgate Ltd.:** Goodwill and other intangible assets are amortized over useful life of the assets not exceeding 10 years.
- **Finolex Cables Ltd.:** The fixed asset schedule mention only "Intangible asset" and then in gross block depreciation and net block respectively details are given. The significant accounting policies mention that software costs of enterprise resource planning (ERP) system along with software, commercial right under agreements and other intangible resources controlled by the company and having future economic benefit are considered as intangible assets and amortized over the economic life of the respective assets. Thus, it does not give specific details about separate class of asset, amortization period, amortization method and reconciliation of intangible assets.
- **Hero Honda Motors Ltd.:** The Intangible assets information is disclosed in 'Significant accounting policies and notes to accounts' under head 'Depreciation and amortization' of annual report and disclosed model fee in Fixed asset schedule which is amortized on straight line basis method over period of 3 to 5 years respectively. The company assets costing up to ₹ 5000 each fully depreciated in the year of purchase and depreciation on revised unamortized depreciable amount is provided prospectively over the residual useful life of asset.
- **Eicher Ltd.:** Intangible assets comprising of product designs and prototypes either acquired or internally developed are amortized over a period of 10 years, the estimated minimum useful life of the related products. Cost of software is amortized over a period of 5 years or less depending on the estimated useful life of the asset. Goodwill purchased is amortized on a *pro rata* basis from the month of acquisition over a period of 3 years.
- **Gujarat Ambuja Cements Ltd.:** The company's Fixed asset schedule disclose water drawing right and computer software as intangible assets. Expenditure to acquire Water drawing right from government/Local authorities/other parties is amortized over period of right to use, the facilities ranging from 10-30 years while expenditure on computer software is amortized over the period of expected benefit not exceeding five years. The carrying amount of assets are reviewed at each balance sheet date as if there is any indication of impairment based on internal and external factors.
- **Tata Indicom Ltd.:** The Intangible asset information is disclosed along with other fixed assets. Computer software is amortized over useful life of 3 years, Technical know-how is amortized over useful life of underlying assets. Indefeasible Rights of use (IRU) amortized over period of 15-year based on technical estimate of useful life of assets or period of the agreement whichever is lower. Depreciation on License fees is provided for uniformly over the license period of 20 years.

- **Pantaloon Retail (India) Ltd.:** Intangible assets are disclosed under schedule of fixed assets but not separately titled as Intangible assets. Computer software and brand is mentioned along with other fixed assets. No, other information is given about Intangibles regarding class of assets, amortization period, method and reconciliation of intangible assets. Thus, the detail given fall short of requirement of standard.
- **Tata Chemicals Ltd.:** The Company is not disclosing Intangible assets. Although, Intangible assets like R&D has been recorded in P&L A/c but no disclosure has been made elsewhere in annual reports.
- **BHEL Ltd.:** The company intangible assets information is disclosed in 'Significant accounting policies' under heading of 'Intangible assets' and also in fixed assets schedule. The company capitalized intangible assets at cost only when following three conditions are satisfied: (i) If disclosure is probable that future economic benefits that are attributable to the assets will flow to the company, (ii) the company will have control over that assets, and (iii) the cost of these assets can be measured reliably and is more than ₹ 10,000. Software are amortized over their useful estimated lives not exceeding 3 years whereas in case of other intangibles amortized not exceeding 10 years on straight line pro rata monthly basis.
- **Bajaj Auto Limited:** Capital expenditure on R&D is shown as an addition to fixed assets while revenue expenses are charged to revenue account. The expense made to acquire technical know-how is amortized over a period of six years.
- **SAIL Ltd.:** The Company treat mining rights as intangible assets and all the related cost thereof are amortized over the lease period. Software which is not an integral part of related hardware, is treated as intangible asset and amortized over a period of five years or its license period, whichever is less.
- **Deepak Fertilizers & Corporation Ltd.:** Intangible assets are disclosed in fixed asset schedule by way of last line and amortized over a period not exceeding 60 months. The company does not give specific details about amortization method and reconciliation between opening and closing balance.
- **ITC Ltd.:** Intangible assets amortized over a period of ten years and all expenditure made on capital assets required for R&D work are included under fixed assets and depreciated accordingly. Further, all revenue expenses of the R&D department are written off through the P&L A/c.
- **Asian Paints Ltd.:** Capital expenditure on R&D is shown separately under respective heads of fixed assets while revenue expenses are charged to the revenue account for the year. Know-how related to plans, designs and drawings are capitalized under relevant heads and know-how developed related to manufacturing process is expensed in the year in which it is incurred.
- **BASF India Ltd.:** Capital expenditure on R&D is shown as an addition to fixed assets in the year in which it is incurred. Revenue expenses are charged to the P&L A/c. The company mainly imports know-how from its German parent.

- **Ceat Ltd.:** The company's revenue expenditure is recognized as an expense in the year in which it is incurred and capital expenditure on R&D is treated as an addition to fixed assets and is depreciated at applicable rates.
- **Reliance Industries Ltd.:** The company annual report focused on Intangible assets and addresses several key topics: the importance of IC report itself, IC and value creation, human capital, structural capital, customer capital and investor capital. However it does not address business model. It constitutes an independent document from the annual report with a total of 20 pages.
- **Hindustan Lever Ltd.:** The company's intangibles are written off in the year in which it is incurred and trademark acquired after 1-1-1998 are amortized over a period of four years. Capital expenditure on R&D is shown as an addition to fixed assets while revenue expenses are charged to Profit & Loss account of the year.
- **The Bombay Burmah Trading Corporation Ltd.:** "Intangible assets are recognized as per criteria specified in AS-26 issued by the ICAI and amortized as follows: (i) Technical know-how fees for new product development is amortized over period exceeding 10 years, of the agreement with the franchisor" this does not give the exact period of amortization however disclosure categorically conveys that the provision of the AS are not contravened. The reconciliation is also not given as required as per the standard.

**Analysis of Reporting of Intangible Assets Item of Selected Sample Units:** Out of 35 sample units selected total 21 Intangible items were identified from annual reports of selected sample units which reveals that out of total 21 intangible items maximum 5 items were disclosed by two companies that are Dr. Reddy, Laboratories Ltd. and Deepak Fertilizers & Corporation Ltd. throughout the study period and highest disclosure is made by Ranbaxy Ltd. i.e. 6 items were disclosed out of total 21 intangible items. whereas no item were disclosed by Tata Chemicals Ltd., Ceat Ltd., Sonata Software Ltd. & Glaxo Smithkline Ltd. Further, four sample units disclosed 4 items out of 21 items that are WIPRO, Lupin, Eicher & Nicholas Piramal Ltd. Further, frequency distribution of item no. 7 (Software) is highest as it disclosed by selected 13 companies. The disclosure of Intangible items and frequency-wise disclosure of selected sample units summarized in Table 1.

**Table 1:** Item-wise and Frequency-wise Disclosure of Sample Units

| S. No. | Item No. | Intangible Items | No. of Companies Disclosing Intangible items | per cent out of 35 sample unit |
|---|---|---|---|---|
| 1. | Item no. 1 | Human Resource Value | 3 | 8.57 |
| 2. | Item no. 2 | Brand Value | 8 | 22.85 |
| 3. | Item no. 3 | Goodwill | 9 | 25.71 |
| 4. | Item no. 4 | Technical Know-how | 10 | 28.57 |
| 5. | Item no. 5 | Patents | 4 | 11.42 |
| 6. | Item no. 6 | Trademarks | 9 | 25.71 |
| 7. | Item no. 7 | Software | 13 | 37.14 |
| 8. | Item no. 8 | Computer Software | 7 | 20.00 |
| 9. | Item no. 9 | License | 3 | 8.57 |

| | | | | |
|---|---|---|---|---|
| 10. | Item no. 10 | Non-Compete Fee | 2 | 5.71 |
| 11. | Item no. 11 | Customer Contract | 1 | 2.85 |
| 12. | Item no. 12 | Intellectual Property Right | 2 | 5.71 |
| 13. | Item no. 13 | Copyright | 1 | 2.85 |
| 14. | Item no. 14 | Model Fees | 1 | 2.85 |
| 15. | Item no. 15 | Product Design | 1 | 2.85 |
| 16. | Item no. 16 | Prototypes | 1 | 2.85 |
| 17. | Item no. 17 | Water Drawing Right | 1 | 2.85 |
| 18. | Item no. 18 | Indefeasible Right to use | 1 | 2.85 |
| 19. | Item no. 19 | Internally Developed Patent and Trade marks | 1 | 2.85 |
| 20. | Item no. 20 | Mining Rights | 1 | 2.85 |
| 21. | Item no. 21 | Designs | 1 | 2.85 |

The Table 2 discloses item wise intangible assets of selected sample units throughout the study period.

**Table 2:** Item-wise Disclosure of Intangible Assets of Selected Sample Units (2007-2011)

| S. No. | Name of Companies | Intangible Items | | | | | | | | | | | | | | | | | | | | | |
|---|---|---|---|---|---|---|---|---|---|---|---|---|---|---|---|---|---|---|---|---|---|---|---|
| | | 1 | 2 | 3 | 4 | 5 | 6 | 7 | 8 | 9 | 10 | 11 | 12 | 13 | 14 | 15 | 16 | 17 | 18 | 19 | 20 | 21 | Total |
| 1. | Infosys Ltd. | Y | Y | Y | N | N | N | N | N | N | N | N | N | N | N | N | N | N | N | N | N | N | 3 |
| 2. | WIPRO Ltd. | N | Y | N | Y | Y | Y | N | N | N | N | N | N | N | N | N | N | N | N | N | N | N | 4 |
| 3. | SATYAM Ltd. | Y | Y | N | N | N | N | Y | N | N | N | N | N | N | N | N | N | N | N | N | N | N | 3 |
| 4. | Patni Ltd. | N | N | N | N | N | N | N | Y | N | N | N | N | N | N | N | N | N | N | N | N | N | 1 |
| 5. | TCS Ltd. | N | Y | Y | N | N | N | Y | N | N | N | N | N | N | N | N | N | N | N | N | N | N | 3 |
| 6. | SONATA Ltd. | N | N | N | N | N | N | N | N | N | N | N | N | N | N | N | N | N | N | N | N | N | 0 |
| 7. | Cranes Ltd. | N | N | N | N | N | N | N | Y | N | N | N | N | N | N | N | N | N | N | N | N | N | 1 |
| 8. | HCL Ltd. | N | N | Y | N | N | N | Y | N | N | N | N | N | N | N | N | N | N | N | N | N | N | 2 |
| 9. | Lupin Ltd. | Y | Y | Y | N | N | N | Y | N | N | N | N | N | N | N | N | N | N | N | N | N | N | 4 |
| 10. | Ranbaxy Ltd. | N | N | N | N | Y | Y | Y | N | Y | Y | N | N | N | N | N | N | N | N | N | N | Y | 6 |
| 11. | Dr. Reddy's Ltd. | N | N | N | Y | Y | Y | N | N | N | Y | Y | N | N | N | N | N | N | N | N | N | N | 5 |
| 12. | Nicholas Ltd. | N | Y | N | Y | N | N | N | Y | N | N | N | Y | N | N | N | N | N | N | N | N | N | 4 |
| 13. | Glaxo Smith Ltd. | N | N | N | N | N | N | N | N | N | N | N | N | N | N | N | N | N | N | N | N | N | 0 |
| 14. | Merck Ltd. | N | N | N | N | N | Y | Y | N | N | N | N | N | N | N | N | N | N | N | N | N | N | 2 |
| 15. | Pizfer Ltd. | N | N | N | N | N | Y | Y | N | N | N | N | N | N | N | N | N | N | N | N | N | N | 2 |
| 16. | HUL Ltd. | N | N | Y | N | N | Y | Y | N | N | N | N | N | N | N | N | N | N | N | N | N | N | 3 |
| 17. | Colgate Ltd. | N | N | Y | Y | N | N | N | N | N | N | N | N | Y | N | N | N | N | N | N | N | N | 3 |
| 18. | Finolex Ltd. | N | N | N | N | N | N | Y | N | N | N | N | N | N | N | N | N | N | N | N | N | N | 1 |
| 19. | Hero Honda Ltd. | N | Y | Y | N | N | N | N | N | N | N | N | N | N | Y | N | N | N | N | N | N | N | 3 |
| 20. | Eicher Ltd. | N | N | Y | N | N | N | N | Y | N | N | N | N | N | N | Y | Y | N | N | N | N | N | 4 |
| 21. | Ambuja Cement | N | N | N | N | N | N | N | Y | N | N | N | N | N | N | N | N | Y | N | N | N | N | 2 |
| 22. | Tata Indicom | N | N | N | N | N | N | N | Y | Y | N | N | N | N | N | N | N | N | Y | N | N | N | 3 |
| 23. | Pantaloon Ltd. | N | Y | N | N | N | N | N | Y | N | N | N | N | N | N | N | N | N | N | N | N | N | 2 |
| 24. | Tata Chemicals | N | N | N | N | N | N | N | N | N | N | N | N | N | N | N | N | N | N | N | N | N | 0 |
| 25. | BHEL Ltd. | N | N | N | Y | N | N | Y | N | N | N | N | N | N | N | N | N | N | N | Y | N | N | 3 |
| 26. | Bajaj Auto Ltd. | N | N | N | Y | N | N | N | N | N | N | N | N | N | N | N | N | N | N | N | N | N | 1 |

| | | | | | | | | | | | | | | | | | | | | | | | |
|---|---|---|---|---|---|---|---|---|---|---|---|---|---|---|---|---|---|---|---|---|---|---|---|
| 27. | Hindusthan Lev. | N | N | N | N | N | Y | N | N | N | N | N | N | N | N | N | N | N | N | N | N | N | 1 |
| 28. | Bombay Burmah | N | N | N | Y | N | N | N | N | N | N | N | N | N | N | N | N | N | N | N | N | N | 1 |
| 29. | SAIL Ltd. | N | N | N | N | N | N | Y | N | N | N | N | N | N | N | N | N | N | N | | Y | N | 2 |
| 30. | Deepak Fertilizer | N | N | Y | N | Y | Y | Y | | Y | N | N | N | N | N | N | N | N | N | N | N | N | 5 |
| 31. | ITC Ltd. | N | N | N | N | N | Y | N | N | N | N | N | Y | N | N | N | N | N | N | N | N | N | 2 |
| 32. | Asian Paints Ltd. | N | N | N | Y | N | N | N | N | N | N | N | N | N | N | N | N | N | N | N | N | N | 1 |
| 33. | BASF Ltd. | N | N | N | Y | N | N | N | N | N | N | N | N | N | N | N | N | N | N | N | N | N | 1 |
| 34. | Ceat Ltd. | N | N | N | N | N | N | N | N | N | N | N | N | N | N | N | N | N | N | N | N | N | 0 |
| 35. | Reliance Industries Ltd. | N | N | N | Y | N | N | Y | N | N | N | N | N | N | N | N | N | N | N | N | N | | 2 |

Y = Yes N = No

## Conclusions

After examining the reporting practices of intangible assets in annual reports of selected 35 Indian companies, it has been found that some knowledge intensive, and service sector companies accept IA as useful part of their assets while other selected companies follows skipping policies in reporting of intangible assets. Most of the companies does not give specific details about separate class of asset, amortization method and reconciliation of intangible assets. Thus, the details given fall short of requirement of accounting standard. So, there is urgent need to create a standardized approach for reporting on intangible assets with end goal of creating a comprehensive IA accounting system that address all types of intangible assets whether developed or acquired by organization.

## REFERENCES


Abeysekara and Guthrie. (2002), Status of Intellectual Capital Reporting in Sri Lanka. A Research note presented at critical perspectives on Accounting conference, New York www.ssrn.com

Chandana, Tilak. (2008), "A Study on Intellectual Capital Reporting in India". *The Chartered Accountant*, pp. 1991-98.

Kamath, Bharthi. (2008), "Intellectual Capital Disclosure in India: Content Analysis of "TECK" firms". *Journal of Human Resource Costing and Accounting*, pp. 213-24.

——. (2008), "Content Analysis of IC Disclosure of IT firms in India". *Pacific Business Review: A Quarterly Journal of Management*, pp. 1-13.

Kantawala, A.S. (2006), "Some Aspects of Accounting for Knowledge Capital". *The Management Trends* (Vol. 3), pp. 7-13.

Lev, Baurch. (2001), *Intangibles: Measurement, Management and Reporting*, Brooking Institution, pp. 71-72.

Mohobbot, Ali. (2008), "Intellectual Capital Reporting Practices: A Study on Selected Companies in Bangladesh". *Journal of Business Studies*, Vol. 29(1), pp. 81-104.

Rathod, P.K. and Prajapati Sangita. (2010), "Reporting and Disclosure of Intangible Assets (IC) of Selected IT companies in India". *The Chartered Accountant*, pp. 1766-74.

Singh, Pradeep. (2009), "Intangible Assets Accounting and Reporting Practices in India". *The Indian Journal of Commerce*, Vol. 62(2), pp. 126-36.

www.emeraldinsight.com

# 11

# FAIR VALUE ACCOUNTING: THE CONTROVERSIAL ISSUE IN IFRS WITH SPECIAL REFERENCE TO PROPERTY, PLANT AND EQUIPMENT

–*Neha Varyani* and *G. Soral*

**Introduction**

We all know that every business concern, or any corporate entity whether listed or not is aimed at providing its shareholders true and fair financial position and proper valuation of the assets and liabilities. On the basis of which they can take wise investment decision. But whether that financial statement is true in its real sense?

The answer is NO.

Do you know why....

We all know the concept named as Historical Cost Concept, yes, in India we follow this method for considering and showing our Assets in our Balance sheet.

Can you imagine as a land purchased by a great grandfather of Mr. A of around 1 acre for ₹ 1000 in year 1960 will have the same value today?

No, today the valuation of that land may be of lacs of rupee.

Shareholders are kept in dark as the companies report the assets value at historical cost whereas shareholders are not interested in cost; they want to know the current value of assets and liabilities. Relevance and reliability are two key attributes of financial reports that are useful to readers.

The basic difference between IFRS and Indian GAAP is that in India the main emphasis is given on profit and loss statement whereas under IFRS balance sheet (valuation of assets and liabilities) is more emphasized. Also IFRS is a principle based model and Indian GAAP is a rule based model.

In India we are following Indian accounting standards complying with the Section 211(3) of the companies act 1956 (except few globalized companies which are reporting two sets of financial statements). But now measurement methodology and yardstick need to be changed in future as the entities adopt new norms converging with IFRS. The primary purpose of any corporate enterprise should be to create wealth legally and ethically.

Fair value accounting continues to be one of the most complex and controversial areas of accounting today and its impact on global economy is well documented. Also it has been the subject of intense scrutiny and debate in the uncertainty of the current economic times. As we have taken big steps towards globalization and many of our Indian companies are being listed in Stock exchanges world over, and are moving ahead with the winning strategy with high flag of triumph, we do have to widen our mindset and welcome the concept accepted and recognized internationally.

Proponents of marking to market argue that the market value of an asset or liability is more relevant than the historical cost at which it was purchased because the market value reflects the amount at which the asset or liability could be bought or sold in a current transaction between willing parties. Good corporate governance and fair value accounting are seen as two sides of the same coin.

Most investors and creditors have an image of accountants as professionally careful and conservative. Even recent accounting standards are viewed as an aberration that will be addressed by changes in law, oversight and penalties. The new theory assumes that the 412 year old "Accounting Model" is broken and must be replaced by an "economically satisfying" method for valuing assets and liabilities.

The balance sheet prepared using fair value as a basis of measurement gives better reflection of the actual worth of the company. Until and unless another better basis of accounting measurement can be identified, fair value accounting is the fairest option available.

### Financial Statements under IFRS

Generally in India we have the following as financial statements:

- Balance Sheet
- Profit & Loss Account
- Cash Flow
- Significant Accounting Policies and Notes to Accounts.

Under IFRS the financial statements would comprise:

- Statement of financial position as at end of the period
- Statement of comprehensive income for the period
- Statement of changes in equity for the period
- Statement of cash flow for the period
- Notes, comprising a summary of significant accounting policies and other explanatory information
- Statement of financial position as at the beginning of the earliest comparative period when an equity applies an accounting policy retrospectively or makes a retrospective restatement of items in its financial statements, or when it reclassifies items in its financial statement.

IFRS permits an entity to choose either the cost model or the revaluation model for accounting of one of the largest components of the balance sheet, namely, Property, Plant and

Equipment (PPE). This article discusses the salient features of IFRS for accounting and reporting of the application of the revaluation model for PPE, the implications and includes case studies to highlight the analytical implications of the revaluation exercise.

### IAS 16 (Property, Plant and Equipment)

Extracted from IAS 16 under IFRS

**Objective:** The objective of this standard is to prescribe the accounting treatment for PPE so that the users of financial statements can discern information about the entity's investment in its PPE and the changes in such investment.

**Principle issues in accounting for PPE:** The principle issues under IAS 16 are recognition of assets, determination of their carrying amounts, depreciation charges and impairment charges and disclosures.

**Exclusions:**

- PPE classified as held for sale
- Biological assets related to agricultural activity
- Exploration and evaluation assets
- Mineral rights and mineral reserves such as oil, natural gas and similar non-regenerative resources.

### Recognition Concepts

The cost of an item of PPE comprises:

- Its purchase price, including import duties and non refundable purchase taxes, after deducting trade discounts and rebates
- Any cost directly attributable to bringing the asset to its present location and condition
- The initial estimate of the costs of dismantling and removing the item and restoring the site on which it is located, the obligation for which an entity occurs
- Borrowing costs.

### Measurement after Recognition

- Measurement at initial recognition is always at cost.
- Measurement after initial recognition.
- Cost model
  After recognition as an asset, an item of PPE shall be carried at its cost less any accumulated depreciation and any accumulated impairment losses.
- Revaluation model
  An item of PPE whose fair value can be measured reliably shall be carried at a revalued amount.
- Deemed cost model
  A first time adopter of IFRS has an option to voluntarily account as per deemed cost model.

### Revaluation Model

**Fair value:** Fair value is the amount for which an asset could be exchanged between knowledgeable, willing parties in an arm's length transactions.

| Item of PPE | Determining the fair value |
|---|---|
| Land and buildings | Market based evidence based on appraisal undertaken by professionally qualified valuers. |
| Plant and equipment—Where there is a market for the same | Market value determined by appraisal. |
| Plant and equipment—Where there is no market for the same | Estimate fair value using an income or a depreciated replacement cost approach. |

### Other Comprehensive Income

While the profit or loss comprises of the post tax results of the financial performance of the period under report, the OCI comprises of items of income and expenses that are not recognized in the profit or loss statement. Examples of items that are reported under OCI are gains on revaluation of PPE, gains and losses on re-measurement of available-for-sale financial assets, etc. And these items form distinct components of equity and are accumulated and reported as separate components of the statement of stockholders equity. The reporting requirement is to isolate components that do not partake the character of retained earnings. These are in a sense 'not ready for distribution to shareholders'.

### Accounting Treatment

**I. Initial revaluation of items of PPE.** If an asset's carrying amount is increased as a result of revaluation, the increase shall be recognized in OCI and accumulated in equity under the heading—'Revaluation surplus'.

There are two acceptable alternatives to adjust the carrying amount of the revalued asset:

i. The first alternative is increase the gross cost and accumulated depreciation pro-rata to provide a net amount equivalent to the revalued amount.

ii. The other alternative is to net off the accumulated depreciation against the gross cost and then increase the value to the extent of the revaluation.

And if an asset's carrying amount is decreased as a result of revaluation, the decrease shall be recognized in profit or loss.

**II. Subsequent revaluation of items of PPE.** For assets that have been revalued in the past:

i. A subsequent revaluation increase shall be recognized in profit or loss to the extent that it reverses a revaluation decrease of the same asset previously recognized in profit or loss account.

ii. A subsequent revaluation decrease shall be recognized in OCI to the extent of any credit balance existing in the revaluation surplus in respect of that asset. The decrease recognized in OCI reduces the amount accumulated in equity under the heading of 'Revaluation surplus'.

### Presentation in Financial Statements

If for example the gain on property revaluation is ₹ 150,000, then in the following way we will represent it into income statement and statement of changes in equity.

**Income statement:**

| | | |
|---|---|---|
| Revenue | XXX | |
| Cost of sales | (XXX) | |
| Gross profit | XXX | |
| Other income | XXX | |
| Distribution costs | (XXX) | |
| Administrative exp. | (XXX) | |
| Other expenses | (XXX) | |
| Finance cost | (XXX) | |
| Profit for the year | | XXX |
| Other comprehensive income | XXX | |
| Gains on property revaluation | 150,000 | |
| Exchange differences on translating foreign operations | XXX | |
| Income tax relating to components of OCI | (XXX) | |
| TOTAL OCI | | XXX |
| Total comprehensive income for the year | | XXX |

**Statement of changes in equity:**

| | Share capital | Retained earnings | AFS Assets | Cash flow hedges | Revaluation surplus | TOTAL | Non-controlling interest | Total equity |
|---|---|---|---|---|---|---|---|---|
| Opening balance | XXX | XXX | XXX | XXX | XXX | XXX | XXX | XXX |
| Changes in equity | | | | | | | | |
| Issue of share capital | | | | | | | | |
| Dividends | | | | | | | | |
| TOTAL | | | | | | | | |
| Comprehensive income for the year | | | | | 150,000 | | | |
| Transfer to retained earnings | | | | | | | | |
| Closing balance | XXX | XXX | XXX | XXX | XXX | XXX | XXX | XXX |

### Depreciation

- Component accounting.
- If residual life and value of the asset differs in subsequent year end, the same will be a change in accounting estimate.

- The depreciable amount is determined after deducting its residual value.
- No prescribed depreciation method—method to be reviewed at every year end and any change is effected prospectively i.e. change in accounting estimate.
- Charge depreciation on revalued asset by depreciating the revalued carrying amount of the asset over its remaining useful life.

| | |
|---|---|
| Depreciation A/c | Dr |
| To Fixed assets | |
| Revaluation Reserve | Dr |
| To Retained earnings | |

***De-recognition***

The carrying amount of an item of property, plant, and equipment shall be derecognized on disposal or when no future economic benefit is expected from its use or disposal. Any gain on disposal is the difference between the net disposal proceeds and the carrying amount of the asset. Gains on disposal shall not be classified in the income statement as revenue.

***Disclosure requirements***

Para 77 of IAS 16 property, plant and equipment requires the entities that revalue assets to disclose the following:

(a) The effective date of revaluation,

(b) Whether an independent valuer was involved in the revaluation exercise,

(c) The methods and significant assumptions applied in estimating the items fair values,

(d) The extent to which the fair values of the items were determined directly by reference to observable prices in an active market or market transactions on arm's length terms or estimated using other valuation techniques,

(e) For each revalued class of PPE, the carrying amount of the assets if the assets were carried under the cost model,

(f) The revaluation surplus, indicating the change for the period and any restrictions on the distribution of the balance to the shareholders.

**Case Studies**

**1. Case study concerned with subsequent costs**

*Facts.* Road Truckers Inc. has acquired a heavy road transporter at a cost of ₹ 100,000 (with no breakdown of the component parts). The estimated useful life is 10 years. At the end of the sixth year, the power train requires replacement, as further maintenance is uneconomical due to the off-road time required. The remainder of the vehicle is perfectly roadworthy and is expected to last for the next four years. The cost of a new power train is ₹ 45,000.

*Required.* Can the cost of the new power train be recognized as an asset, and, if so, what treatment should be used?

***Solution:***

The new power train will produce economic benefits to Road Truckers Inc., and the cost is measurable. Hence the item should be recognized as an asset. The original invoice for the transporter did not specify the cost of the power train; however, the cost of the replacement—₹ 45,000—can be used as an indication (usually by discounting) of the likely cost, six years previously. If an appropriate discount rate is 5% per annum, ₹ 45,000 discounted back six years amounts to ₹ 33,500 [₹ 45,000 / (1.05)]$^6$, which would be written out of the asset records. The cost of the new power train, ₹ 45,000, would be added to the asset record, resulting in a new asset cost of ₹ 111,500 (₹ 100,000 – ₹ 33,500 + ₹ 45,000).

**2. Case study concerned with directly attributable costs**

***Facts.*** Extravagant Inc. is installing a new plant at its production facility. It has incurred these costs:

| | ₹ |
|---|---|
| 1. Cost of the plant (cost per supplier's invoice plus taxes) | 2,500,000 |
| 2. Initial delivery and handling costs | 200,000 |
| 3. Cost of site preparation | 600,000 |
| 4. Consultants used for advice on the acquisition of the plant | 700,000 |
| 5. Interest charges paid to supplier of plant for deferred credit | 200,000 |
| 6. Estimated dismantling costs to be incurred after 7 years | 300,000 |
| 7. Operating losses before commercial production | 400,000 |

***Required.*** Please advise Extravagant Inc. on the costs that can be capitalized in accordance with IAS 16.

***Solution:***

According to IAS 16, these costs can be capitalized:

| | ₹ |
|---|---|
| 1. Cost of the plant | 2,500,000 |
| 2. Initial delivery and handling costs | 200,000 |
| 3. Cost of site preparation | 600,000 |
| 4. Consultants' fees | 700,000 |
| 5. Estimated dismantling costs to be incurred after 7 years | 300,000 |
| | 4,300,000 |

Interest charges paid on "deferred credit terms" (see discussion under the "Measurement of Cost" section) to the supplier of the plant (not a qualifying asset) of ₹ 200,000 and operating losses before commercial production amounting to ₹ 400,000 are not regarded as directly attributable costs and thus cannot be capitalized. They should be written off to the income statement in the period they are incurred.

**3. Case study concerned with revaluation loss**

A building was purchased on the 1st January 2006 at a cost of ₹ 100 million. It is being depreciated over 50 years. The company decided to use the revaluation model for valuing buildings in 2011 and at the 31st December 2011, the building was valued at ₹ 80 million by a professional valuer.

***Solution:***

By the 31st December 2011, the asset has been depreciated for 6 years. This means that the accumulated depreciation is ₹ 12 million (₹ 100 million / 50 years × 6 years). Per IAS 16, this accumulated depreciation is netted against the cost; ₹ Cost 100 million less Accumulated Depreciation 12 million.

Carrying Value 88 million.

This carrying value of ₹ 88 million is compared against the revalued amount of ₹ 80 million and a revaluation loss of ₹ 8 million need to be accounted for.

**4. Case study concerned with revaluation gain**

A company revalued their land from ₹ 200,000 to ₹ 300,000. The profit for the year from normal day-to-day activities of the company is ₹ 350,000 and at the start of the year there was a revaluation surplus of ₹ 75,000. The retained earnings at the start of the year amounted to ₹ 120,000.

The ledger entry and the extracts from the SOCI and SOFP for this revaluation are shown below:

***Solution:***

| The ledger entry is as follows: | ₹ |
|---|---|
| Dr. PPE (SOFP) | 100,000 |
| Cr. OCI (SOCI) | 100,000 |
| *Extract from SOCI* | |
| Profit for the Year | 350,000 |
| *Other Comprehensive Income* | |
| Revaluation Gain from Land | 100,000 |
| Total Comprehensive Income for the Year | 450,000 |

*Extract from SOFP*

| Non-Current Assets: | ₹ |
|---|---|
| PPE | 300,000 |
| Total Non-Current Assets | 300,000 |

| *Equity* | | ₹ |
|---|---|---|
| Retained Earnings | (120,000 + 350,000) | 470,000 |
| Revaluation Surplus | (75,000 + 100,000) | 175,000 |
| Total Equity | | 645,000 |

**Note:** Total Comprehensive Income amount of ₹ 450,000 is taken to the Equity section of the SOFP but ₹ 350,000 of it goes to retained earnings and the ₹ 100,000 revaluation gain is added to the revaluation surplus.

**5. Case study of revaluation gain (Earlier revalued downwards)**

A company revalued their land from ₹ 200,000 to ₹ 300,000. Previously, the same land had been revalued downwards from ₹ 260,000 to ₹ 200,000 creating a revaluation loss of ₹ 60,000 which was taken to profit or loss as there was no revaluation surplus as this was the first time the asset had been revalued. The profit for this year from normal day to day activities of the company before revaluation is ₹ 300,000 and at the start of the year the retained earnings amounted to ₹ 150,000.

The ledger entry and the extracts from the SOCI and SOFP for this transaction are shown below:

***Solution:***

The ledger entry is as follows:

| | | ₹ |
|---|---|---|
| Dr. PPE (SOFP) | | 100,000 |
| Cr. Profit or Loss (SOCI) | | 60,000 |
| Cr. OCI (SOCI) | | 40,000 |
| *Extract from SOCI* | | |
| Profit for the Year | | 300,000 |
| Revaluation Gain | | 60,000 |
| Profit for the Year | | 360,000 |
| *Other Comprehensive Income* | | |
| Revaluation Gain from Land | | 40,000 |
| Total Comprehensive Income for the Year | | **400,000** |
| *Extract from SOFP* | | |
| Non-Current Assets: | | |
| PPE | | 300,000 |
| Total Non-Current Assets | | **300,000** |
| *Equity* | | |
| Retained Earnings | (150,000 + 360,000) | 510,000 |
| Revaluation Surplus | | 40,000 |
| Total Equity | | **550,000** |

**6. Case study concerned with revaluation loss (Earlier revalued upwards)**

A company revalued their land from ₹ 500,000 to ₹ 400,000. The profit for the year from normal day-to-day activities of the company is ₹ 300,000 and at the start of the year there was a revaluation surplus of ₹ 75,000. The retained earnings at the start of the year amounted to ₹ 180,000.

The ledger entry and the extracts from the SOCI and SOFP for this transaction follow:

***Solution:***

The ledger entry is as follows:

| | | ₹ |
|---|---|---|
| Dr. OCI (SOCI) | | 75,000 |
| Dr. Profit of Loss (SOCI) | | 25,000 |
| Cr. PPE (SOFP) | | 100,000 |
| *Extract from SOCI* | | |
| Profit for the Year | | 300,000 |
| Revaluation Loss | | (25,000) |
| Profit for the Year | | 275,000 |
| *Other Comprehensive Income* | | |
| Revaluation Loss | | (75,000) |
| Total Comprehensive Income for the Year | | **200,000** |
| *Extract from SOFP* | | |
| Non-Current Assets: | | |
| PPE | | 400,000 |
| Total Non-Current Assets | | **400,000** |
| *Equity* | | |
| Retained Earnings | (180,000 + 275,000) | 455,000 |
| Revaluation Surplus | (75,000 – 75,000) | 0 |
| Total Equity | | **455,000** |

**Note:** The Total Comprehensive Income amount of ₹ 200,000 is taken to the Equity section of the SOFP but ₹ 275,000 of it goes to retained earnings and the ₹ 75,000 revaluation loss is taken from the revaluation surplus brought forward.

**Reporting in Financial Statements**

*From the annual report 2012 of WIPRO Ltd.

**Property, plant and equipment**

**(a) Recognition and measurement**

Property, plant and equipment are measured at cost less accumulated depreciation and impairment losses, if any. Cost includes expenditures directly attributable to the acquisition of the asset. Borrowing costs directly attributable to the construction or production of a qualifying asset are capitalized as part of the cost.

**(b) Depreciation**

The Company depreciates property, plant and equipment over the estimated useful life on a straight-line basis from the date the assets are available for use. Assets acquired under finance lease and leasehold improvements are amortized over the shorter of estimated useful life of the asset or the related lease term. The estimated useful life of assets are reviewed and where appropriate are adjusted, annually. The estimated useful lives of assets for the current and comparative period are as follows:

| Category | Useful life |
|---|---|
| Buildings | 30 to 60 years |
| Plant and machinery | 2 to 21 years |
| Computer equipment and software | 2 to 6 years |
| Furniture, fixtures and equipment | 3 to 10 years |
| Vehicles | 4 years |

When parts of an item of property, plant and equipment have different useful lives, they are accounted for as separate items (major components) of property, plant and equipment. Subsequent expenditure relating to property, plant and equipment is capitalized only when it is probable that future economic benefits associated with these will flow to the company and the cost of the item can be measured reliably.

Deposits and advances paid towards the acquisition of property, plant and equipment outstanding as of each reporting date and the cost of property, plant and equipment not available for use before such date are disclosed under capital work-in-progress.

**Property, plant and equipment**

| | Land | Buildings | Plant | Furniture machinery* | Vehicles fixtures and equipment | Total |
|---|---|---|---|---|---|---|
| *Gross earning value*: | ₹ | ₹ | ₹ | ₹ | ₹ | ₹ |
| As at April 1, 2010 | 2,794 | 19,359 | 46,657 | 9,855 | 2,929 | 81,594 |
| Translation adjustment | 17 | 117 | 117 | 68 | 11 | 550 |
| Additions | 943 | 3,533 | 8,360 | 1,692 | 117 | 14,645 |
| Disposal/adjustments | – | (41) | (1,145) | (591) | (458) | (2,235) |
| As at March 31, 2011 | 3,754 | 22,968 | 54,209 | 11,024 | 2,599 | 94,554 |
| *Accumulated depreciation impairment*: | | | | | | |
| As at April 1, 2010 | – | 1,998 | 30,995 | 5,497 | 2,004 | 40,494 |
| Translation adjustment | – | 50 | 231 | 45 | 14 | 340 |
| Depreciation | – | 493 | 5,500 | 1,271 | 455 | 7,719 |
| Disposal adjustments | – | (39) | (1.077) | (375) | (354) | (1,845) |
| As at March 31, 2011 | – | 2,502 | 35,649 | 6,438 | 2,119 | 46,708 |
| Capital work-in-progress | | | | | | 7,248 |
| Net carrying value as at March 31, 2011 | | | | | | 55,094 |
| *Gross earning value*: | | | | | | |
| As at April 1, 2011 | 3,754 | 22,968 | 54,209 | 11,024 | 2,599 | 94,554 |
| Translation adjustment | 30 | 389 | 1,951 | 229 | 26 | 2,625 |
| Additions | 445 | 2,113 | 10,096 | 1,729 | 69 | 14,452 |

| | | | | | | |
|---|---|---|---|---|---|---|
| Acquisition through business combination | 58 | 15 | 279 | 51 | 9 | 412 |
| Disposal adjustments | (44) | (159) | (960) | (523) | (621) | (2.307) |
| As at March 31, 2012 | 4,243 | 25,326 | 65,575 | 12,510 | 2,082 | 109,736 |
| *Accumulated depreciation imp ailment*: | | | | | | |
| As at April 1, 2011 | – | 2,502 | 35,649 | 6,438 | 2,119 | 46,708 |
| Translation adjustment | – | 136 | 1,233 | 132 | 21 | 1,522 |
| Depreciation | – | 649 | 6,537 | 2,077 | 281 | 9,544 |
| Disposal/adjustments | – | (28) | (622) | (381) | (536) | (1,567) |
| As at March 31, 2012 | – | 3,259 | 42,797 | 8,266 | 1,885 | 56,207 |
| Capital work-in-progress | | | | | | 5,459 |
| Net carrying value as at March 31, 2012 | | | | | | 58,988 |

*Including computer equipment and software.

## Conclusion

The Fair value measurement says about valuation of assets as per the valuation done as against the historical cost concept that goes on the same value in the balance sheet. In nutshell the FVM is a logical practical and advanced model as against Historical model, gives more relevant and reliable information to the decision-makers i.e. Shareholders, government and outsiders. Also widening the mindset from the temporary to long-term and more sound approach that also targets towards the Balance sheet part and narrow approach to P&L.

There are essentially two broad areas where fair value and IFRS intersect: the preparation of your opening balance sheet, and the adoption of optional valuation models for ongoing accounting under IFRS. There are many factors to consider and implications to weigh before making these decisions and you must be aware of the positives, the negatives and the unknowns.

Also if one company uses fair value to achieve an initial bump in asset value, the other company's balance sheet may appear weak in comparison. So considering other companies could be the reason to consider using fair value.

## REFERENCES

CA Vinayak, Pai V. (2009), "Revaluation Model for Property, Plant and Equipment under IFRS—A Review".

CA Bhatia, Anand (11th Feb. 2011-Session 2), "Property, Plant and Equipment—IAS 16", UGC—National Level Seminar—IFRS.

Fair Value Measurements: Make your views count, Price Waterhouse Coopers (2007).

Gupta Varun, IFRS: A Fair Valuation Perspective, IFRS Summit—Roadmap to Convergence (Nov. 2010).

Haldeman Robert G., Jr (Nov. 2006), "Fact, Fiction and Fair value accounting at ENRON".

Mongiello Marco, *International Financial Reporting* (2009) Marco Mongiello & Ventus Publishing.

Muller Karl A., III, Riedl Edward J., and Sellhorn Thorsten, "Consequences of Voluntary and Mandatory Fair Value Accounting: Evidence Surrounding IFRS adoption in the EV Real Estate Industry, Harvard Business School, Working Paper—09-033.

Nissim Doron, Penman Stephen, (Aug. 2007), "Preliminary Draft of White Paper Number Two on the application of Fair Value Accounting", Columbia Business School (Centre for Excellence in Accounting and Security Analysis).

Swamynathan Shobana, Sindhu A.R., "Financial Statement effects on Convergence to IFRS—A case study in India", Zenith, *International Journal of Multidisciplinary Research*, Vol. 1, Issue 7, Nov. 2011.

**Websites**

www.wipro.com
www.ifrs.org
www.iasb.org
www.iasplus.com
www.ifrs.icai.org/imgs/ias_16.pdf
www.accounting-financial-tax.com/2009/05/accounting-for-property-plant-and-equipment-ias-16/

# 12

# FINANCIAL IRREGULARITIES IN COOPERATIVE BANKS IN MAHARASHTRA

–S.H. Indurwade

## Introduction

Cooperative banks have for long been the backbone of rural banking. Since their inception, they have been doing excellent work in the field of rural and cooperative banking. The recent scams in cooperative banks have been a jolt to cooperative banking system. Many analysts have suggested that cooperative banks should be brought under the complete control of RBI ending the dual control by the State governments and RBI-NABARD. According to N. Patel, Vice-Chairman of Gujarat Urban Cooperative Banks Federation, control by a single authority will ensure smooth governance of cooperative banks. Some analysts also feel that interference from the registrar of cooperatives should be minimized....

The Indian banks including the cooperative banks have shown a high incidence of frauds over a decade and the trend is likely to continue with the country's economy betraying signs of weakness. No banks whether public, private or foreign are able to buck the trend. All of them are equally affected by it. The prospects of an imminent slowdown in the economy are only expected to boost the incidence of financial crimes in the country. Asset size, lack of supervision by senior staff and complicated business scenario and business pressure as the main factors responsible for the growing incidence of frauds in the banks.

According to the RBI sources, the number of fraud cases rose up from 21,247 in 2007-08 to 24,797 in 2009-10. Most of the banks are yet to show enough preparedness to prevent the fraud cases.

Cooperative banks across the country face similar problems of poor management and political interference. Meant to be a primary financial support structure to farmers and small depositors, cooperative banks have been consistently criticised by the RBI for their weak performance. According to the RBI, collectively the banks have ₹ 5,500 crores of non-performing assets. Yet the central bank appears to be doing little to implement suggestions made by several committees. In 1999, the RBI appointed a high-power committee on urban cooperative banks to study the viability of this sector. The committee's recommendations included aligning the cooperative bank sector with other segments of the banking sector, removal of preferential treatment and "removing the irritants of the dual control regime".

The Monetary and Credit Policy for 2002-03 has sought to address directly the issues concerning cooperative banks. The report states: "The events of the last two years have made it abundantly clear that the present system of dual/triple regulatory and supervisory control is not conducive to efficient functioning...." Mincing no words, the policy document adds: "The managements and boards of several cooperative institutions continue to reflect political interests rather than genuine cooperative spirit." It recommends that a separate supervisory authority be set up with representatives from the Centre, the States and other interested parties.

With the surfacing of the co-operative banks scam, once again the financial sector and its markets fell victim to the regulator's failure to check malpractices within the system. Every time the new scam involving the co-operative sector points to a crying need to have a speedier and better co-ordinated process for dealing with financial frauds as well as an effective governance structure and settlement system for efficient functioning of financial institutions.

### Banking Cooperatives in Maharashtra

Maharashtra has more than 616 cooperative banks, the largest number for any State in the country. Most of them are completely controlled by politicians. It requires only ₹ 1 lakh to start a cooperative bank. The depositors are mainly farmers and local people. Some banks are offshoots of the sugar and dairy cooperative societies, which are also controlled by politicians.

A number of co-operative banks in Maharashtra are saddled with bad debts. Political interference seems to have silenced the banking regulator. It is high time the RBI, and the shareholders and depositors of these beleaguered entities woke up. Recent news reports suggest that there are nearly 28 co-operative banks in Maharashtra which are having large NPAs (non-performing assets) and negative net worth and are in a bad financial state. However, there is nothing new about this situation. A lot of such banks have collapsed in the recent past, and no doubt many more will in the future. The RBI (Reserve Bank of India) seems to be inactive instead of being proactive in making sure that these banks close down and are acquired by other banks to safeguard the interests of the depositors. There is a strange argument doing the rounds that if the RBI takes action (like declaring a moratorium on sick banks) there will be a run on most banks that are sick. If this happens, it will actually be a good thing. Instead of protecting weak banks for 'safeguarding' depositors, let the RBI merge them. The banking authorities ignore Vaidyanathan and Madhavan Committee recommendations. Most state governments have signed MoUs (memorandums of understanding) with the RBI and have given the regulator all powers for supervision of co-operative banks as far as banking regulations are concerned, though state governments still have powers over these banks as these banks are under the control of their respective Registrar of Co-operatives (ROCs).

### Cooperative Bank Fraud Cases in Maharashtra

There are some cases of frauds reported in Maharashtra. The numbers of fraud cases reported are many in Maharashtra with different avenues. Some cases are discussed below:

In 2002, Pune-based board of Rupee Co-operative Bank was dismissed. There was a run on this bank sometime and it was put under an Administrator. According to some banking professionals who were advising the administrators, they were appalled that no proper records were available and the bank was unable to prepare its financial statements. The bank needed to be put under moratorium at that time itself. After five years under the 'supervision' of these administrators, fresh elections were held for the board of directors and many who were responsible to get the bank into trouble in the first place were re-elected. However, as the RBI assured liquidity support and said there was no need to panic, the same depositors stood in long queues to re-deposit their money as the bank announced increased interest rates to lure the customers back. The simple rule in finance is a bad borrower is forced to pay an interest rate higher than the market rate as a reward for higher risk that an investor requires. However, most depositors do not even understand that when they put money in a bank; the bank is a borrower. It will be worthwhile to see what security the bank is holding against the accepted NPAs of ₹ 500 crores, and what is the value of these securities?

Cooperative Banks image was dashed when the chairman of the Pen Cooperative Bank, Shishir Dharkar, his wife and six others were arrested in connection with a ₹ 480-crore gold export fraud. Some exporters took an advance from MSTC Limited, a Government of India enterprise for export of gold, but allegedly usurped the amount and deposited the amount in the Pen Urban Cooperative Bank and later used some of it to buy property in and around Pen.

Bhandari Co-operative Bank, for their alleged involvement in a ₹ 19-crore fraud came into limelight. The bank had allegedly sanctioned loans for non-existent parties for 1,100 autorickshaw owners and a housing project in Thane despite knowing that the documents submitted in both the cases were bogus. The Bank had claimed to have constructed a building for 65 BEST workers. But, during investigation, it was found that the bank authorities had issued bogus loans for 1,100 autorickshaws in the city that do not even exist based on forged documents. The Bhandari Co-operative Bank officials had allegedly prepared all the forged documents, including the registration books that are issued by the regional transport offices (RTOs) and the applications, and they did not even submitted the documents at the local RTO office.

Maharashtra State Cooperative Bank used to be Asia's largest cooperative bank. But it now seems turned it into a family lending bank. The whole episode reeks of another major scam.

National Bank for Agriculture and Rural Development (Nabard) has found that Maharashtra state cooperative bank instead of working for the welfare of the low investment group for which Maharashtra state cooperative bank was actually formed, it has been helping high sector investments and sugar factory owners, many of which belong to political family in the state. NABARD report shows how this political family took huge loans from the bank and never repaid it. Some of the prominent loan defaulters include people related to the sugar factories in Maharashtra including spinning mill loan owes the bank ₹ 182 crores. A sugar factory controlled by the family has not repaid a loan of ₹ 175 crores. One sugar factory has not paid the bank nearly ₹ 100 crores and a factory has defaulted on a loan of ₹ 16 crores. Nabard also found that in blatant violation of the Nabard and RBI norms, the bank sanctioned ₹ 100 crores to the Maharashtra State housing finance corporation and ₹ 200 crores to the Maharashtra state electricity distribution company.

Chairman of Nagpur District Central Co-operative Bank (NDCCB) is also assumed to be a party to the scam. The scam came to light when an FIR was lodged with Nagpur police station against five brokerages, Home Trade, Gilt Edge securities, Century Dealers, Indramani Merchants and Syndicate services for non-delivery of government securities worth ₹ 125 crores. With interest this amount came to ₹ 150 crores. Soon many other Co-operative Banks informed that they had similar problems too. Even Seaman's Provident Fund, with about ₹ 430-crore savings, admits to having indulged in transactions of G-secs worth ₹ 100 crore without taking physical delivery. The scam operated through a simple mechanism, taking money from victims for the purchase of government securities and never delivering them. First of all, it must be understood that all urban cooperative banks have to invest in government securities to meet Statutory Liquidity Requirement (SLR) of 25 per cent. RBI allowed small entities like cooperative banks to transact physically in G-secs and all others take the demat route. When these cooperative banks pay money to their brokers for purchase of these securities, the brokers buy the securities and send them to RBI for transfer. RBI issues a receipt listing details of securities, the buyer and the seller. The broker hands over these receipts to the bank and walks away with his commission. The physical delivery by RBI to the bank takes 3-4 weeks. However, here banks paid money for the securities, but the broker would never buy them. Even if he buys them, he would pledge them as collateral with other banks and use the money. If the bank asked about the securities, they would be informed that their securities had been sent to RBI for delivery. Some banks did insist on some proof that the transaction had been completed. This proof often ended up being a receipt issued by one brokerage, which was part of the ring to another, which was merely a paper transaction. It is believed that the money was used for stock market transactions to earn higher returns that would enable payment to these banks. Whenever securities of some bank came to maturity, they could utilize this money or money borrowed from some other bank for repaying the amount. However, it seems that they were not able to make enough money so their checks started bouncing and the cooperative banks realized that they had been cheated and their money siphoned. In this case, chairman of NDCCB not only invested money of Co-operative bank through Home Trade; he even put it in touch with many other Co-operative Banks that wanted to invest in G-secs. As for the ₹ 125 crores that NDCCB spent on buying these securities, he did not even insist on a receipt from Agarwal or Sheth (broker). It is also interesting to note that regulations regarding Co-operative Banks are much lax when compared to commercial banks.

Home Trade Ltd., a broking firm, used government securities (G-Secs) to avail itself of money. The Nagpur District Central Co-operative Bank gave ₹ 124 crores to Home Trade on the assurance that the broking firm would deliver G-Secs worth the same amount to the bank within 30 days. But these securities were never delivered. An analysis reveals that the scams more or less followed the same pattern—The Ketan Parekh—Madhavpura Mercantile Co-operative Bank (MMCB) scam occurred in 2001 and is also an instance of diversion of funds from the banking sector to the stock market, like the 1992 securities scam.

The RBI found 25 urban co-operative banks—spread across Gujarat, Maharashtra and West Bengal—to be in violation of the RBI norms. Of these, eight co-operative banks have exposures to Home Trade. Among these, six banks are in Gujarat and the balance in Maharashtra. Four district central co-operative banks (rural) from Maharashtra also have exposure to Home Trade. In all, these 12 banks are suspected to have run up losses of around ₹ 500 crores. As more than one co-operative bank is involved, it is feared that this could be only the tip of the iceberg. In November 2001, the RBI found that these banks had flouted banking norms stipulated by it.

Delay in registering the First Information Report (FIR) with the police often proves advantageous for the culprits involved in the white-collared crimes as they get sufficient time to tamper with the evidence. Is the delay in registering the FIR about a ₹ 140 crores fraud in the Nagpur-based Samata Sahakari Bank Limited a deliberate one to shield the bigwigs involved? This is the question making rounds in the co-operative sector and investors. The concerned officials' two months to lodge the FIR in this regard. The audit was conducted as per the recommendation of the task force set up by State Government and Reserve Bank of India (RBI) a few months back.

The Reserve Bank of India (RBI) calls it 'corrective action'. With it, over ₹ 250 crores of hard earned money belonging to around 1,80,000 depositors of three prominent urban co-operative banks of the city has been locked up indefinitely, it was the turn of 60,000 customers of Parmatma Ek Sevak Bank to taste the RBI bitter pill. The customers of Nagpur Mahila Nagari Sahakari Bank and Samata Nagari Sahakari Bank already know the feeling. Each of these banks had close to 60,000 depositors. Now they await helplessly for things improve so they can get their money back. Which may never happen. And the banks' directors and defaulters, who brought the banks to this pass, haven't lost a stitch of their shirts. Bank depositors are shocked at a system that punishes the innocent while apparently rewarding the crook. They want to know whether it is time to take action against regulators who were either asleep at their watch or too indulgent of the crooks.

Why did the RBI not act when loans were given flouting all norms? Why the state cooperation department, that also monitors the banks, did nothing? Experts in co-operative banking say an early RBI action would have stemmed the rot.

Giving a new twist to the probe into multi-crore Samata Sahakari Bank Ltd. scam case, another fraud allegedly committed by the directors and officials of the bank has come to light. In this case, the directors and officials of the bank had disbursed loan worth over ₹ 1.58 crores to Ashoka Safe Deposit Vaults Company Ltd. by mortgaging its five-storeyed illegally constructed building in Sitabuldi without proper verification of the documents.

As the company did not repay the loan, the bank sold it to its own customer after seven years against his deposits worth ₹ 85 lakhs and diverted the entire amount to the loan account. The valuation of the mortgaged property (including the cost of the lockers) made at the time of sanctioning of loan by the bank valuers was over ₹ 2.33 crores. Even after selling the mortgaged assets, the total recovery to be made from Ashoka Safe Deposit Vaults Company was over ₹ 3.39 crores.

Apart from regular audits, even flying squads visit the banks. What did they do? It is surprising that the RBI or the co-operation did not take any action against any of the banks, said Kailashchandra Agrawal, a former member of the task force on co-operative urban banks (TAFCUB). Moreover, the move to stop deposits and loans in Parmatma Ek Sevak Bank, only worsened the situation. Probably, allowing it to function normally could have helped it survive, he said. A chartered accountants' firm conducts an yearly audit on behalf of the co-operation department. Apart from this, the RBI conducts a yearly inspection of a bank categorised as Grade 4 or Grade 3 institutions. All the three banks facing restrictions were of Grade 4. The grades are allotted on the basis of financial performance.

Till now not a single politician involved in above scams were punished though more than 10 years are passed. Will the small investors are going to get justice? Will they get their money back? Only future can answer.

## REFERENCES

Co-operative Movement in Maharashtra, *At a Glance*, 30 December 2004.

Deepak Shah (2007), Banking Sector Reforms and Co-operative Credit Institutions in Maharashtra: A Synthesis, *Agricultural Economics Research Review*.

RBI Bulletin (2001), 'Monetary and Credit Policy for the year 2001-2002', Mumbai.

RBI (2009), Report of Trend and Progress of Banking in India, Mumbai.

*Times of India*, Various issues.

13

# DISCLOSURE OF VALUATION PRINCIPLE OF WORK-IN-PROGRESS INVENTORY IN INDIAN CORPORATE SECTOR

–*Shurveer S. Bhanawat* and *Abhay Jaroli*

## Introduction

After examining the literature it is observed that research work which has been done on the disclosure of items in general in annual report but no specific research work has been done except Manaswee K. Samal regarding whether Indian manufacturing industry disclose the all aspect of work-in-progress in annual report which has been suggested in AS-2 entitled "Valuation of Inventory". The present study is concentrated with sector-wise disclosure of principal of work-in-progress only of fifty-three companies of ten sectors along with testing of the hypothesis. The critical operative part of the Accounting standard-2 (Revised) is that "inventories should be valued at the lower of (a) cost and (b) net realizable value". This standard requires an enterprise should disclose the accounting policies adopted in measuring or valuing inventories including the cost formula used and the total carrying amount of inventories and its classification appropriate to the enterprise. Common classifications of inventories are work in progresss and components, finished goods, stores and spares and loose tools. Here an attempt has been made to examine whether such disclosure is followed by sample units or not in relation to work-in-progress only. We were tried to point out the gap exists between theory and practice in many sectors of Indian manufacturing industry.

## Review of Literature

Bajpayee, H.S. and Srivastava, Anubha (2010) analyze the compliance of accounting standards practices in India by various companies. So far as mandatory accounting standards are concerned all the companies are complying with those all but in case of optional accounting standards there are some, which are disclosing full information regarding their compliance with the accounting standards, and on the other hand there are some companies which are clarifying the true picture. As a conclusion it could be said that that there must be uniformity in financial statement of companies in order to make inter-firm and intra-firm comparison easy.

Samal K. Manaswee (2005) states in his article that Inventory valuation plays a significant role in reporting operating results, as well as the state of affairs of a business entity. Empirical literature suggests that inventory valuation is one of the devices often resorted to smooth out a firm's operating results. The findings suggest that the disclosure of accounting policies regarding inventory valuation in listed Indian companies is more of a form than of substance, and there is ample scope for improvement in fixing the valuation norms.

Ole-Kristian Hope (2003) investigates that there is relation between the accuracy of analysts' earnings forecasts and the level of annual report disclose, and between forecast accuracy and the degree of enforcement of accounting standards. He documents that firm-level disclosures are positively related to forecast accuracy, suggesting that such disclosures provide useful information to analysts. He took sample from twenty-two countries.

Stephen L. Buzby (1974) explained that there have been several attempts to measure the relative importance and/or the extent of disclosure of selected types of financial and non-financial information an annual reports. For example, Copeland and Fredericks studied the extent to which changes in common stock outstanding were disclosed in annual reports. Singhvi and Desai developed an index of disclosure which was primarily based on work done by Cerf several years earlier. The index consisted of 34 items of information which were used as the basis for a composite measure of the extent of disclosure in annual reports for the items taken as a group. Carpenter, Francia, and Strawser surveyed four user groups in order to determine their perceptions of the importance of, and information deficiencies for, several problem areas in accounting.

Singhvi, Surendra S. and Desai, Harsha B. (1971) highlighted that the quality of corporate disclosure influences to a great extent the quality of investment decision made by investors. This study attempts to identify some of characteristics of corporations in the United States which are associated with, and the probable implications of the quality of corporate disclosure. In order to evaluate the quality of information disclosed in annual reports, an index of disclosure of 34 items was used.

Ronald M. Copeland and William Fredericks (1968) identified that theoretical solutions to accounting problems are tempered in practice by the concept of materiality and extent of disclosure. Unfortunately, practitioners do not have a precise definition of extent of disclosure. This paper attempts to develop a measure for its and to relate it to conventional measures of materiality.

**Objective Sample Design**

- To examine the disclosure pattern of valuation principle of work-in-progress inventory in different sectors of Indian manufacturing industry with special reference to Accounting Standard-2.

**Null Hypothesis**

- There is no significance difference among the different sectors of Indian manufacturing industry as regard to disclosure pattern of valuation principle of work-in-progress inventory according to Accounting Standard-2 entitled "Valuation of Inventory" issued by ICAI, New Delhi.

**Sample Collection and Source of Data:** A sample of fifty-three companies engaged in various manufacturing activities has been selected for the purpose of present study. Sample has been chosen according to stratified random sampling technique. For this purpose 10 strata has been identified in the Indian manufacturing industry. Thereafter sample units have been selected on the random basis in each strata. The selection of sample is not without reasons. It is partly to keep the study within manageable limits and resources. The required information on disclosure for sample units is collected from annual reports and websites of respective sample units. The number of companies varied (7.57 per cent to 13.20 per cent) among the industry groups. Table 1 provides Industry-wise strata of the sample units.

**Table 1:** Industry-wise Classification of the Sample Units

| S.No. | Sectors | No. of Units | per cent | Sample Units |
|---|---|---|---|---|
| 1. | Textiles | 5 | 10 | 1. Alok Industries |
| | | | | 2. Arvind Ltd. |
| | | | | 3. Bombay Dyeing |
| | | | | 4. Grasim Ltd. |
| | | | | 5. Raymond Ltd. |
| 2. | Pharmaceuticals | 6 | 11 | 6. Aventis Pharma |
| | | | | 7. Cipla Ltd. |
| | | | | 8. Dr. Reddy's Lab. |
| | | | | 9. Ranbaxy |
| | | | | 10. Twilight Litaka |
| | | | | 11. Orchid Chem & Pharma |
| 3. | Cement | 6 | 11 | 12. ACC Ltd. |
| | | | | 13. J.P. Associates |
| | | | | 14. India Cement |
| | | | | 15. J.K. Cement |
| | | | | 16. Shree Cement |
| | | | | 17. Ultratech |
| 4. | Automobiles | 5 | 10 | 18. Bajaj Auto |
| | | | | 19. Hero Honda |
| | | | | 20. Mahindra & Mahindra |
| | | | | 21. Maruti |
| | | | | 22. TVS |
| 5. | Sugar | 4 | 8 | 23. Bajaj Hindustan |
| | | | | 24. Balrampur Chinni |
| | | | | 25. Renuka Sugars |
| | | | | 26. Triveni Engg. & Inds. |

| | | | | |
|---|---|---|---|---|
| 6. | Fertilizers & Chemicals | 4 | 8 | 27. Nagarjuna Fertilizers<br>28. Gujarat State Fertilizers<br>29. Zuari Industries<br>30. Deepak Fertilizers |
| 7. | Consumer Goods & Durable | 7 | 13 | 31. BPL Ltd.<br>32. Colgate<br>33. Emami<br>34. HUL<br>35. ITC<br>36. Videocon Inds.<br>37. MIRC Electronics |
| 8. | Capital Goods (Heavy Electrical Equipments) | 5 | 9 | 38. BHEL<br>39. Siemens<br>40. ABB<br>41. Crompton Greaves<br>42. Thermax |
| 9. | Iron & Steel | 6 | 11 | 43. SAIL<br>44. Ispat Inds<br>45. Jindal Steel & Power<br>46. JSW Steel<br>47. Tata Steel<br>48. TISCO |
| 10. | Paper Industries | 5 | 9 | 49. Ballarpur (BILT)<br>50. Andhra Paper<br>51. J.K. Paper<br>52. Rainbow Paper<br>53. Tamil Nadu Newsprint (TNPL) |
| | Total | 53 | 100 | 53 |

**Techniques**

Statistical techniques like mean, standard deviation, coefficient of variation and chi-square test are used in the present research paper.

**Period**

A period of five years from 2001-02 to 2005-06 has been taken into account for the purpose of analyzing the disclosure pattern of valuation pattern of work-in-progress inventory in different sectors of manufacturing industry in India.

## Analysis and Discussion

Industry-wise disclosure of valuation principle of work-in-progress is discussed here in special reference to AS-2. On the observation of the annual reports of the sample units, it is found that the disclosure of valuation principle of work-in-progress may be done in two forms, viz., inventory of work-in-progress is valued either at cost or at NRV ($M_1$) and inventory is valued at cost or NRV whichever is less ($M_2$). This disclosure has been examined separately in relation to $M_1$ and $M_2$ for Textile, Pharmaceutical, Cement, Iron and Steel, Sugar, Electrical equipments, Automobile, Consumer Goods and Durables, Fertilizers and Chemicals and Paper industry. The cross mark "×" denotes that the company has not separately disclosed the cost formula in respect of that item of inventory.

The following abbreviations are used in the tables:

**Method: 1 ($M_1$):** Inventory is valued either at cost or at NRV.

**Method: 2 ($M_2$):** Inventory is valued at cost or NRV, whichever is less.

**Method: 3 (×):** Not separately disclosed (The cross mark "X" denotes that the company has not separately disclosed the cost formula in respect of that item of inventory). A frequency distribution table has been prepared in form of discrete series.

**Table 2:** Disclosure of valuation principle in case of work-in-progress

| Item of Inventory | Work-in-Progress | | | | |
|---|---|---|---|---|---|
| **Company/Year** | **2001-02** | **2002-03** | **2003-04** | **2004-05** | **2005-06** |
| **Textiles** | | | | | |
| Alok Industries | $M_1$ | $M_2$ | $M_2$ | $M_2$ | $M_2$ |
| Arvind Ltd. | $M_2$ | $M_2$ | $M_2$ | $M_2$ | $M_2$ |
| Bombay Dyeing | $M_1$ | $M_1$ | $M_1$ | $M_1$ | $M_1$ |
| Grasim | × | × | × | × | × |
| Raymond | $M_2$ | $M_2$ | $M_2$ | $M_2$ | $M_2$ |
| **Pharmaceuticals** | | | | | |
| Aventis Pharma | $M_2$ | $M_2$ | $M_2$ | $M_2$ | $M_2$ |
| Cipla | × | × | × | $M_2$ | $M_2$ |
| Dr. Reddy's Lab | $M_2$ | $M_2$ | $M_2$ | $M_2$ | $M_2$ |
| Orchid | $M_1$ | $M_1$ | $M_1$ | $M_1$ | $M_1$ |
| Ranbaxy | × | $M_1$ | $M_1$ | $M_1$ | $M_1$ |
| Twilight Litaka | × | × | × | × | $M_2$ |
| **Cement** | | | | | |
| ACC Ltd. | $M_2$ | $M_2$ | $M_2$ | $M_2$ | $M_2$ |
| J.P. Associates | $M_1$ | $M_1$ | $M_1$ | $M_1$ | $M_1$ |
| India Cement | $M_1$ | $M_1$ | $M_1$ | $M_1$ | $M_1$ |

| | | | | | |
|---|---|---|---|---|---|
| J.K. Cement | × | × | × | × | × |
| Shree Cement | $M_1$ | $M_1$ | $M_1$ | $M_1$ | $M_1$ |
| Ultratech | × | × | × | × | × |
| **Automobiles** | | | | | |
| Bajaj Auto | $M_2$ | $M_2$ | $M_2$ | $M_2$ | $M_2$ |
| Hero Honda | $M_2$ | $M_2$ | $M_2$ | $M_2$ | $M_2$ |
| Mahindra & Mahindra | × | × | × | × | × |
| Maruti | × | × | × | × | × |
| TVS | × | × | × | × | × |
| **Sugar** | | | | | |
| Bajaj Hindustan | $M_2$ | $M_2$ | $M_2$ | $M_2$ | $M_2$ |
| Balrampur Chinni | × | × | × | × | × |
| Renuka Sugar | $M_2$ | $M_2$ | $M_2$ | $M_2$ | $M_2$ |
| Triveni Engg. & Inds. | $M_2$ | $M_2$ | $M_2$ | $M_2$ | $M_2$ |
| **Fertilizers & Chemicals** | | | | | |
| Nagarjuna Fertilizers | $M_1$ | $M_1$ | $M_1$ | $M_1$ | $M_1$ |
| Gujarat State Fertilizers | $M_2$ | $M_2$ | $M_2$ | $M_2$ | $M_2$ |
| Zuari Industries | × | × | × | × | × |
| Deepak Fertilizers | × | × | × | × | × |
| **Consumer Goods & Durables** | | | | | |
| BPL Ltd. | $M_1$ | $M_1$ | $M_1$ | $M_1$ | $M_1$ |
| Colgate | $M_2$ | $M_2$ | $M_2$ | $M_2$ | $M_2$ |
| Emami | $M_2$ | $M_2$ | $M_2$ | $M_2$ | × |
| HUL | × | × | × | v | × |
| ITC | × | × | × | × | × |
| Videocon Inds. | × | × | × | × | × |
| MIRC Elec. Ltd. | $M_1$ | $M_1$ | $M_1$ | $M_1$ | $M_1$ |
| **Capital Goods (Heavy Electrical Equipments)** | | | | | |
| BHEL | $M_2$ | $M_2$ | $M_2$ | $M_2$ | $M_2$ |
| Siemens | $M_2$ | $M_2$ | $M_2$ | $M_2$ | $M_2$ |
| ABB | $M_2$ | $M_2$ | $M_2$ | $M_2$ | $M_2$ |
| Crompton Greaves | $M_1$ | $M_1$ | $M_1$ | $M_1$ | $M_1$ |
| Thermax | $M_2$ | $M_2$ | $M_2$ | $M_2$ | $M_2$ |

| | | | | | |
|---|---|---|---|---|---|
| **Iron & Steel** | | | | | |
| SAIL | × | $M_2$ | $M_2$ | $M_2$ | $M_2$ |
| Ispat Ind. | × | × | × | × | × |
| Jindal Steel & Power | $M_2$ | $M_2$ | $M_2$ | $M_2$ | $M_2$ |
| JSW Steel | $M_2$ | $M_2$ | $M_2$ | $M_2$ | $M_2$ |
| Tata Steel | $M_2$ | $M_2$ | $M_2$ | $M_2$ | $M_2$ |
| TISCO | $M_2$ | $M_2$ | $M_2$ | $M_2$ | $M_2$ |
| **Paper Industries** | | | | | |
| Ballarpur (BILT) | × | × | × | × | × |
| Andhra Paper | $M_1$ | $M_1$ | $M_1$ | $M_1$ | × |
| J.K. Paper | × | × | × | × | × |
| Tamil Nadu News | $M_1$ | $M_1$ | $M_1$ | $M_1$ | $M_1$ |
| Rainbow Paper Ltd. | $M_1$ | $M_1$ | $M_1$ | $M_1$ | $M_1$ |

On examining the above Table 2, it is found that all the sample units of capital goods (Heavy Electrical Equipments) have followed the AS-2 strictly throughout study period i.e. inventory of WIP is valued at cost or NRV WEL ($M_2$) except Crompton Greaves who followed $M_1$ method throughout study period. It clearly indicates that Greaves do not follow the principal of AS-2.

There is no good practice has been observed in automobile industry as regard to disclosure of valuation principal of WIP inventory. Only 40 per cent sample units (2 out 5) followed AS-2 strictly. These units (Bajaj Auto and Hero Honda) followed $M_2$ method of valuation throughout study period. The well known sample companies—Mahindra & Mahindra, Maruti and TVS do not disclose valuation principal of inventory of work-in-progress in their annual report.

In textile industry, only Raymond and Arvind Ltd. have reported $M_2$ method in annual report throughout the study period. Bombay Dyeing followed $M_1$ method during study period. The consistency has been maintained by all sample units of textile industry except Grasim Ltd. Grasim Ltd. did not disclose any method of valuation principle of work-in-progress inventory during the study period.

The sample units of pharmaceutical industry followed either $M_1$ or $M_2$ method during entire study period. Once they followed either $M_1$ or $M_2$ then consistency has been observed. Cipla Ltd. started to disclosed $M_2$ method from 2004-05 while Twilight Litaka Ltd. started from 2005-06. These companies did not disclose any method during initial period of study.

The sugar and iron & steel sectors followed a good practice of disclosure of valuation principle in case of work-in-progress. All sample units of these two sectors followed $M_2$ method during entire study period except Balrampur Chinni and Ispat Ltd. These two companies do not disclosure any method of valuation principle of work-in-progress during entire study period.

In fertilizers & chemicals and cement industries, the consistency has been observed. The sample units followed either $M_1$ or $M_2$ method throughout the present study period. While

Zuari Industry, Deepak Fertilizers, J.K. Cement and Ultratech Ltd. did not followed any method of disclosure regarding work-in-progress in their annual reports during the study period.

The sample units of paper industry followed only $M_1$ method during entire study period from 2001-02 to 2005-06. It clearly indicates that these sample units did not follow the valuation principles of work-in-progress as per norms of AS-2. The BILT and J.K. Paper failed to disclosure any methods of valuation principles of work-in-progress during study period. It clearly indicates the violation of principles mentioned in AS-2.

There are only two sample units i.e. Colgate and consumer goods, and durable sector which followed AS-2 strictly during entire study period as Colgate followed $M_2$ method during study period. However Emami Ltd. has unfavorably moved to non-disclosure of valuation principle of work-in-progress in 2005-06. All other sample units of this sector either followed $M_1$ method of disclosure or do not followed any method of disclosure during study period.

The consistency has been observed in all sample units (53) of various sectors regarding disclosure of either $M_1$ or $M_2$ throughout the study period except in case of Alok Industries. This is only sample unit out of 53 units who shifted from $M_1$ to $M_2$ method in 2002-03 then thereafter consistency has been maintained. As per AS-1 disclosure must include any change but no disclosure is found in the annual report of Alok Industries.

**Table 3:** Year-wise disclosure summary in respect of valuation principles of work-in-progress

| Year ⇒ | 2001-02 | | 2002-03 | | 2003-04 | | 2004-05 | | 2005-06 | | Average | |
|---|---|---|---|---|---|---|---|---|---|---|---|---|
| Method of Disclosers | No. | per cent | No. | per cent | No. | per cent | No. | per cent | No. | per cent | per cent | C.V. |
| $M_1$ | 13 | 24.53 | 13 | 24.53 | 13 | 24.53 | 13 | 24.53 | 12 | 22.64 | 23.02 | 3.49385 |
| $M_2$ | 21 | 39.62 | 23 | 43.40 | 23 | 43.40 | 24 | 45.28 | 24 | 45.28 | 43.40 | 5.32497 |
| Total | 34 | 64.15 | 36 | 67.93 | 36 | 67.93 | 37 | 69.81 | 36 | 67.92 | 66.42 | 3.05990 |
| Non-Disclosures | 19 | 35.85 | 17 | 32.07 | 17 | 32.07 | 16 | 30.19 | 17 | 32.08 | 33.58 | 6.36886 |
| Total | 53 | 100 | 53 | 100 | 53 | 100 | 53 | 100 | 53 | 100 | 100 | |

*Source*: Own Calculation.

On analyzing the Table 3 pertaining year-wise disclosure of valuation principle in case of work-in-progress, it is found that the highest degree of disclosure (69.81 per cent) has been noticed in the year 2004-05 whereas a lowest degree of disclosure (64.15 per cent) of valuation of principle has been observed in the base year 2001-02. It can be seen that on an average over the time series, 24.15 per cent of the sample unit are followed $M_1$ method of disclosure. In 43.40 per cent of the cases on an average over the period of study followed the disclosure of $M_2$ method as per norms of Accounting Standard-2. Again in respect of 32.45 per cent of cases on an average over the period of study no separate disclosure is made.

It is noticed that in the year 2001-02, 34 sample units out of 53 (64.15 per cent) disclosed the valuation principle separately. This mean 35.85 per cent of the sample units did not think it prudent to disclose it to stakeholders. In the year 2002-03, 2003-04 and 2005-06, 36 companies out of 53 (67.92 per cent) disclosed the valuation principle of WIP separately and 17 sample units (32.08 per cent) did not disclose it separately. In the year 2004-05, 37 companies (69.81 per cent) disclosed and 16 companies (30.19 per cent) did not disclose it separately.

So, on an average over the period of five years, 67.55 per cent of the sample units have disclosed the valuation principle separately whereas 32.45 per cent of the companies did not disclosed separately about the valuation principle of work-in-progress.

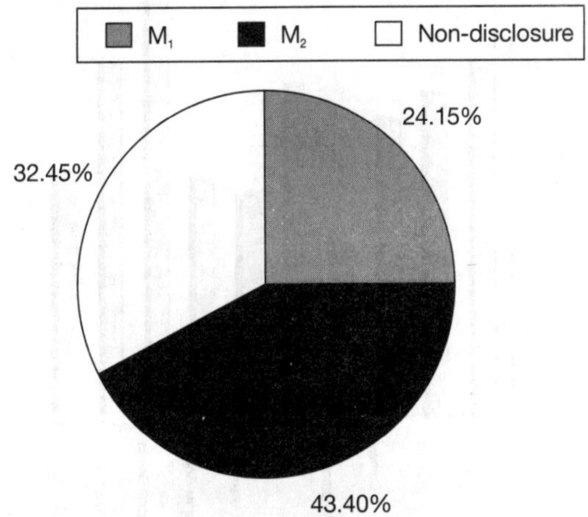


**Fig. 1:** Average disclosure of valuation principle of work-in-progress.

**Table 4:** Intra sector comparison of disclosing sample units in respect of valuation principle of work-in-progress

| Year ⇒ | 2001-02 | | 2002-03 | | 2003-04 | | 2004-05 | | 2005-06 | | Average |
|---|---|---|---|---|---|---|---|---|---|---|---|
| Industrial Sector | No. | per cent | No. | per cent | No. | per cent | No. | per cent | No. | per cent | per cent |
| Textiles | 4 | 80 | 4 | 80 | 4 | 80 | 4 | 80 | 4 | 80 | 80 |
| Pharmaceuticals | 3 | 50 | 4 | 67 | 4 | 67 | 5 | 83 | 6 | 100 | 73 |
| Cement | 4 | 67 | 4 | 67 | 4 | 67 | 4 | 67 | 4 | 67 | 67 |
| Automobiles | 2 | 40 | 2 | 40 | 2 | 40 | 2 | 40 | 2 | 40 | 40 |
| Sugar | 3 | 75 | 3 | 75 | 3 | 75 | 3 | 75 | 3 | 75 | 75 |
| Fertilizers and Chemicals | 2 | 50 | 2 | 50 | 2 | 50 | 2 | 50 | 2 | 50 | 50 |
| Consumer Goods and Durables | 4 | 57 | 4 | 57 | 4 | 57 | 4 | 57 | 3 | 43 | 54 |
| Capital Goods (Heavy Electrical Equipments) | 5 | 100 | 5 | 100 | 5 | 100 | 5 | 100 | 5 | 100 | 100 |
| Iron and Steel | 4 | 67 | 5 | 83 | 5 | 83 | 5 | 83 | 5 | 83 | 80 |
| Paper Industries | 3 | 60 | 3 | 60 | 3 | 60 | 3 | 60 | 2 | 40 | 56 |

Table 4 indicates the sector-wise disclosure pattern in different years in respect of valuation principle of work-in-progress. The 100 per cent disclosure of valuation principle has been noticed in the capital goods sector throughout the study period whereas a least disclosure has been observed in the automobiles sector. On an average only 40 per cent of sample unit of automobile industry disclosed the valuation principle of work-in-progress in the annual reports. An increasing trend in terms of percentage of sample unit have been noticed in case of pharmaceutical sector wherein only 50 per cent sample units disclosed the valuation principle in the initial year 2001-02 which has been increased to 100 per cent in 2005-06. Most of the sample units followed a consistent policy of disclosure over the period of study. However, on an average 14 per cent sample units of consumer goods and durable sector and 20 per cent sample units of paper industries have declined the item-wise disclosure in 2005-06.

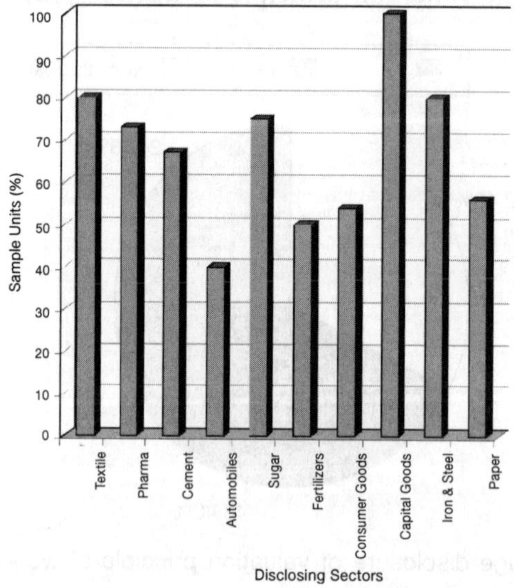


**Fig. 2:** Intra-sector comparison in respect of disclosure of valuation principle of work-in-progress.

## Testing the Hypothesis

In order to examine whether the difference between disclosure pattern of inventory of work-in-progress in form of $M_1$ or $M_2$ among different sectors of manufacturing industry are significant or only due to chance, chi-square test has been administered. The numbers of companies that disclosed either $M_1$ or $M_2$ and calculated value of chi-square are given below:

**Table 5:** No. of Sample units disclosed either $M_1$ or $M_2$

| Sector | Textile | Pharma | Cement | Automobile | Sugar | Fertilizers & chemicals | Consumer goods & durable | Heavy electrical | Iron & steel | Paper |
|---|---|---|---|---|---|---|---|---|---|---|
| Average No. of companies (In %) | 80 | 73 | 67 | 40 | 75 | 50 | 54 | 100 | 80 | 56 |

Calculated chi-square value = 58.4896

Table value of $\chi^2$ at 5 per cent level of significance at 9 d.f. = 16.919

At 5 per cent level of significance our null hypothesis that all ten sectors of manufacturing industry have same disclosure pattern regarding valuation principle of work-in-progress is rejected. Since calculated value of $\chi^2$ (58.4896) is much greater than table value i.e. 16.919. It clearly indicates that visible difference in the ratio of different sector is not only due to chance but due to major reasons. Hence, it is matter of further investigation to identify specific reasons.

## Concluding Remarks

After analyzing the fifty-three sample units of different sectors of Indian manufacturing Industry the following conclusions can be drawn:

1. It may be concluded that on an average two-third sample units (66 per cent) have been disclosed either $M_1$ or $M_2$ valuation principles of work-in-progress during entire study period. It means one third (34 per cent) of the sample units did not think it prudent to disclose it to stakeholders during study period.
2. Only capital goods and electrical equipment sector that has followed the AS-2 strictly. All the sample units disclosed $M_2$ method in their annual report except Crampton Greaves which has followed $M_1$ method during entire study period. It can be concluded that electrical sector disclosed that inventory of work-in-progress has been valued at cost or NRV, whichever is less.
3. A very poor disclosure has been identified in automobiles sectors of Indian manufacturing industry. The well known companies of automobile industry, viz. Mahindra and Mahindra, Maruti and TVS failed to disclose the valuation principle of work-in-progress in their annual reports. While other sample units of automobile industry, viz., Bajaj Auto and Hero Honda companies followed good practice of disclosure during entire study period.
4. There is a more inconsistency has been observed in case of $M_2$ as compared to $M_1$ during entire study period, it is evident by having higher C.V. (5.32497 per cent) of $M_2$. It indicates that there is uniformity of disclosure pattern of work-in-progress in $M_1$ during five years of period as compare to $M_2$.
5. At 5 per cent level of significance our null hypothesis that all ten sectors of manufacturing industry have same disclosure pattern regarding valuation principle of work-in-progress is rejected. Since calculated value of $\chi^2$ (58.4896) is much greater than table value i.e. 16.919.

## REFERENCES

Bajpayee, H.S. and Srivastava, Anubha, "An empirical study of disclosure practices of accounting standards in India". *Foundation for organisation research and education*, Jan., 2010, Vol. 28, No. 1.

Bhanawat, Shurveer S. (2010), "An analysis of raw material cost in Indian manufacturing industries". *IUP Journal of Accounting Research and Audit Practices*, Vol. IX, No. 3, July, pp. 65-80.

Copeland, Ronald M. and Frederick William. "Extent of disclosure". *Journal of Accounting Research* (Spring) 1968. pp. 106-13.

Ole-Kristian Hope. "Disclosure Practices, Enforcement of Accounting Standards, and Analysts' Forecast Accuracy: An International Study". *Journal of Accounting Research,* 2003, Vol. 41, issued 2, pp. 235-72.

Samal K. Manaswee. "An Empirical Study of Inventory Valuation and Disclosure Practices in Listed Indian Companies". *The ICFAI Journal of Accounting Research*. October 2005. pp. 7-35.

Singhvi, Surendra S. and Desai, Harsha B. "An empirical Analysis of the Quality of Corporate Financial Disclosure", JSTOR. *The Accounting Review*, 1971, Vol. 46, No. 1, Jan. pp. 129-38.

Stephen, I. Buzby. "Selected items of Information and Their Disclosure in Annual Reports". *The Accounting Review*, July 1974, Vol. XLIX, No. 3, pp. 423-35.

# 14

# NEW ISSUES IN ACCOUNTING–IFRS

*–Dharmendra Kumar*

## Introduction

International Financial Reporting Standards (IFRS) are standards, interpretations and the framework adopted by the international accounting standards board. Many of the standards forming part of IFRS are known by the older name of international accounting standards. IAS were issued between 1973 and 2001 by the board of the international accounting standards committee in 2000. IASC member bodies approved IASC's restructuring. On 1 April 2001 the new IASB took over from the IASC the responsibility for setting international accounting standards. During its first meeting the new board adopted existing IAS and SICs. The IASB has continued to develop standards calling the new standards IFRS. The objective is to develop a single set of high quality, understandable and enforceable global accounting standards that will form the platform for international accounting.

According to Securities and Exchange Commission as of August 2007, approximately 85 countries in the world mandate IFRS reporting for all domestic, listed companies. It is worthy to note that all listed EU companies have been required to use IFRS since 2005. The 12 Indian companies listed in New York Stock Exchange, Dr. Reddy's Laboratories Ltd. moved to IFRS with a transition date of April 1, 2007. Of the 3 Indian companies listed in NASDAQ Infosys Technologies Ltd. and SIFY Technologies Ltd. moved to IFRS with transition dates of April 1, 2007 and April 1, 2006 respectively the above action are regarded as a good corporate governance gesture since these companies are ahead of the game perfecting their financial reporting processes and are avoiding the US GAAP reconciliation process, which is time consuming and expensive. When these companies switched to IFRS, a great deal of scrutiny on their internal controls were also done after implementing the top-down risk management approach as envisaged by the Section 404 of the Sarbanes Oxley act.

Though Indian accounting standards are framed based on standards issued by the IASB, there are certain differences due to the legal and regulatory environment prevailing in the country. Conceptual issues and the economic environment in 2007, the ICAI decided that India should converge towards IFRS in a definite time frame in the wake of developments taking place in other major jurisdictions which had set up time schedules for migrating towards IFRS.

IFRS in India would cover the following public interest entities in its first wave:

1. Listed companies
2. Bank, insurance companies, mutual funds, and financial institutions
3. Entities having turnover in preceding year exceeding ₹ 1 billion
4. Entities having borrowing in preceding year exceeding ₹ 250 million
5. Holding or subsidiary companies of the above.

Adopting IFRS by Indian corporate is going to be very challenging but at the same time could also be rewarding. Indian corporate is likely reap significant benefits from adopting IFRS. The correct adoption of IFRS will bring more transparency and a higher degree of comparability, both of which promises many benefits for the organizations, including investor confidence, greater consistency and transparency of financial reporting as well as the ability to compare financial information from companies around the world. The European Union's experience highlights many perceived benefits as a result of adopting IFRS. Overall most Investors financial statement preparers and auditors were in agreement that IFRS improved the quality of financial and that IFRS implementation was a positive development for EU financial reporting.

The present paper identifies the opportunities and challenges of IFRS.

### Objective of the study

- To know the benefits of implementing IFRS.
- To analyze the challenges faced by the companies while implementing IFRS.

### Methodology

The study is conducted to assess and analyze the benefits and problems in implementing IFRS. Descriptive study is conducted and the primary and secondary data is used for the study.

### Opportunities

A financial reporting system supported by strong governance. High quality standards and firm regulatory framework is the key to economic development. Indeed sound financial reporting standards underline the trust that investors place in financial reporting information and thus, play an important role in contributing to the economic development of a country. Needless to mention, internationally accepted accounting standards play a major role in this entire process.

Converging to global accounting standards i.e. IFRS facilitates comparability between enterprises operating in different jurisdiction. Thus, global accounting standards would remove a frictional element to capital flows and lead to wider and deeper investment in markets. Convergence with IFRS is also in the interest of the industry since compliance with them would be able to create greater confidence in the mind of investors and reduce the cost of raising foreign capital. It is also burdensome and costly for enterprises operating across several countries to comply with a multitude of national accounting standards and convert them to a single standard for group reporting purposes. Convergence would thus help reduce both the cost of capital and cost of compliance for industry.

There are several areas that IASB has not yet developed standards or in which IFRS allows options to be applied, including:

1. Common control merger, recapitalization transaction, reorganizations, acquisitions of minority shares not resulting in a change of control and similar transactions as to which there is an absence of specific standards or interpretations on accounting treatment.
2. Income statements, as to which there is an absence of specific conventions as to the form and content.
3. Insurance contracts and extractive activities, as to which differing accounting treatment exists. SEC has indicated that it expects companies to provide transparent disclosure in the financial statements and operating and financial review and prospects disclosure about the accounting policies selected and the effects of those on the IFRS financial statements.
4. The adoption of IFRS is expected to result in better quality of financial reporting due to consistent application of accounting principles and thus, improvement in reliabilities of financial statements. This, in turn, will lead to increased trust and reliance placed by investors, analysts and other stakeholders in a company's financial statements.
5. An IFRS balance sheet will be closer to economic value. Historical value will be substituted by fair values for several balance sheet items, which will enable a corporate to know its true worth. For example, intangible assets acquired in business combinations will be recorded at separately at fair values, and all financial instruments and investment properties will be reflected at fair values, thereby reflecting a better view of net assets of the entity.
6. With the knowledge of IFRS, the Indian chartered accountants would be globally acceptable. It would bring new opportunities for them.
7. IFRS financial can also result in more accurate risk evaluation by international lenders and lower risk premium for international debt offerings.
8. Even companies raising capital and listed on the local stock exchanges would be able to better attract international investors and reduce risk premium by providing financial statement that is more transparent and understandable for the international investor's community.
9. The transparent and more comparable financial information would result in more cross border transaction. IFRS reporting provides an impetus to cross border acquisitions, enables partnerships and alliances with foreign entities, and lower the costs of integration in post acquisition periods.
10. IFRS would eliminate multiple reporting. Currently, different entities within the group that resides in different jurisdictions may be required to prepare multiple set of financial statements; one for each countries in which these entities have operations.

Thus, convergence with the IFRS and to a globally accepted standard will result in growth in international business, higher cross boarder transactions and capital flows and will provide an impetus to economic growth.

### Challenges

The Indian accounting standards (IAS) have conceptual differences with IFRS, keeping the extent of difference between existing IAS and the corresponding IFRS's, conversion process would need careful handling, by introducing a new company law, the Indian government has initiated the process to amend the legal and regulatory framework, much needed to adopt IFRS. The actual conversion would involve impact assessment, revisiting accounting policies and thereafter changing the accounting and operational systems (including ERP) in order to be fully compliant with IFRS.

The institute of chartered accountants of India is laying down the strategy for IFRS convergence and adoption. The adoption date is indicated as April 1, 2011, however, it is worthwhile to note that IFRS requires that previous year's comparatives are presented alongside. Therefore, when an entity follows IFRS for the first time in its financial statements for the year ending March 31, 2012, it will need to provide the previous year's comparative i.e., for the financial year ending March 31, 2011.

The important key challenges which is faced by the Indian companies are given below:

- Adjustment in policy and data analyzing
- Training and development
- Cost
- Supervision
- Project planning

1. Switching to IFRS is a strategic move for all companies adopting IFRS since it requires an effective management of stakeholder expectations, including ample budgeting and managing investor relations. This accounting exercise requires monetary sponsorship and strong support from senior management in terms of resource sourcing and commitment for the enterprise wide accounting revamp. Careful pre-planning and efforts to obtain buy-in across the organization are critical, as are related efforts to limit disruption to business and ongoing operations. Companies must unlearn many of their current finance knowledge and relearn new IFRS standards when adopting IFRS. They need a finance function that knows to expect an increased use of judgment in IFRS reporting.

2. This is a fundamental shift in the thought process for many accounting personnel who have been trained to operate in an environment where more application and industry guidance exists. Companies will likely have to hire finance consultants and auditors who have the requisite IFRS reporting knowledge and experience, presumably within the same industry group. Companies will also have to upgrade and adapt new accounting information systems across the enterprise that is line with the changed standards.

3. Conversion to IFRS will mandate the need to renegotiate current business contracts and debt agreements under IFRS instead of U.S. GAAP. Companies also need to budget for advisory/consulting cost.

4. Convergence also entails maintaining consistency with legal and regulatory requirements prevalent in the country. Towards this end amendments need to be made to existing laws and

regulation, notably the Companies Act, 1956 provisions and schedules that detail the requirements of financial statements need to be harmonized with IFRS requirements and converged Indian Accounting Standards need to be notified under Section 211(3C) of the said Act. Additionally, there are also issues relating to taxation under an IFRS-converged environment.

5. There is also a need to improve awareness in general and build technical competence for the accounting and auditing profession on IFRS. The ICAI has already included a comparative study of Indian Accounting Standards with international standards in its syllabus for CA final Advanced Accountancy and is also offering course and seminars for its members to update them in the fields.

6. In respect of banks and NBFC's, in view of the special issues involved (finalization of IFRS 9 expected in the middle of 2011), a separate roadmap was prepared in March 2010 for convergence with IFRS for the banking industry and NBFC's. The convergence process would be from period beginning April 1, 2013, with a phased approach for urban banks and NBFC's. This gives the banking system some time to adapt to the standards in a smooth and non-disruptive manner.

7. It has to be noted, however, that banks will be significantly affected by the IAS 39 replacement project and number of other accounting developments including those relating to financial instruments, fair value measurement, financial statement presentation and consolidation. Some of the major changes pertain to certain critical areas such as classification and measurement of financial assets, Classification and valuation of liabilities, impairment provisions and fair value measurement. One area of concern has been the drawback of the incurred loss model of IAS 39 and the need to introduce more forward-looking provisioning.

8. The IFRS convergence process will involve significant challenges for the banking system in general. Banks would need to upgrade their infrastructure, including IT and human resources, to face the complicities and challenges of IFRS.

9. Finally, if 2011 is the year when we would be totally aligned to IFRS, then what would happen to inter period comparisons because the accounts that would emerge after convergence to IFRS would be based on different accounting principles than those based on Indian GAPP.

### Conclusion

The study reveals that the implementation of IFRS will more benefited to the corporate world and the accounting professionals, but the same time the Indian companies and the accounting professional want to face some key challenges in their convergence process. It also comes to know that the auditors having the awareness regarding the implementation of IFRS. Transition to IFRS will not be a swift and painless process all parties concerned with financial reporting also need to share the responsibility of international harmonization and convergence.

The system of financial reporting is a function of the economic, legal, and political environment of a business entity. The financial reporting changes with the changes in these environment. There have been major changes in worlds as well as Indian economics environment in last two decades. Substantial increase in cross border flow of capital and goods and services has been recorded. A number of transnational companies have emerged on the scene. The acceptance of global standards like IFRS is result of all these changes.

## REFERENCES

IFRS: A Guide on Transition to IFRS: CII.

IFRS: The impact on Indian corporate: Richard Rekhy.

IFRS: The way Forward: CA Dolphy D'souza.

India and IFRS: Can we bridge the GAAP: Sirjjan Preet.

International Financial Reporting Standards: K.S. Muthupandian.

www.icai.org

www.journalofaccountancy.com

www.ifrs.org

www.articlesbase.com

www.ifrs.co

# 15

# CORPORATE GOVERNANCE PRACTICES IN INFORMATION TECHNOLOGY INDUSTRY IN INDIA: A COMPARATIVE ANALYSIS

*–Swati Patel*

## Introduction

Corporate governance refers to the structures and processes for the direction and control of companies. Corporate governance matters because it improves investee companies' performance and helps develop capital markets. Sound corporate governance reduces risk, adds value to investments, and avoids reputation risks for investors. Given the strong links between good corporate governance and sustainable economic development, improving corporate governance practices has become an important element of the development mission of financial institutions.

Good corporate governance practices are a "sine qua non"—indispensable for sustainable business that aims at generating long-term value to all its shareholders and other stakeholders. Some aspects of corporate governance have been enshrined in the law that is administered by the Ministry of Corporate Affairs, SEBI and other sectoral regulators. However, a transparent, ethical and responsible corporate governance framework essentially emanates from the intrinsic will and passion for good governance ingrained in the business entity. The global financial crisis during the recent past, along with some of the large format corporate failures and frauds have convincingly revealed that while the corporate governance superstructure in India is fairly durable, there are certain weaknesses that may have their roots in the ethos of individual business entities.

SEBI Committee on Corporate Governance defines corporate governance as the "acceptance by management of the inalienable rights of shareholders as the true owners of the corporation and of their own role as trustees on behalf of the shareholders. It is about commitment to values, about ethical business conduct and about making a distinction between personal and corporate funds in the management of a company." On the basis of guidelines of OECD principles published and respective norms of corporate governance, combined with the strategic importance of role of Indian IT sector this research paper tries to understand the corporate governance practices in different IT companies in India.

**Literature Review**

Dilek Demirbas, Andrey Yukhanaev (2011) examined the role of the board of directors in Russia with specific attention to their independence, employee relations and ability of successful adaptation of the international standards. The authors used a survey questionnaire to provide an empirical example from a transition economy to the corporate governance literature by exploring the attitudes of the 55 board directors from 30 listed companies on the Russian Trading System (RTS) Stock Exchange. Authors concluded that the board of directors as an important instrument of efficient and good corporate governance practice. More surprisingly, they are also in favour of employee representatives on the board of directors and agree that board size and composition should be enhanced by employee representatives on the board.

Yiming Hu, Siqi Li, Thomas W. Lin, Shilei Xie (2011) attempted to examine whether Chinese banks exercise effective monitoring over borrowers in two lending decisions, including loan interest rates and loan renewals. The author used a sample of Chinese public industrial firms from 2000 to 2005, and performed multivariate regression analysis to investigate whether banks adjust their loan interest rates and consider loan renewal decisions in response to borrowers financial performance. The authors also examined these bank lending decisions before and after 2003, when the major banking reforms started to take place in China. A negative relation was found between the loan interest rate spread and the financial performance of borrowers. However, a negative relation was found between loan renewals and the financial performance of borrowers, consistent with firms in financial difficulties being in need of more funding and hence more likely to get its bank loans renewed. Additionally, it was found that the factors banks consider when making loan decisions vary before and after 2003.

Sungho Choi, Iftekhar Hasan, Maya Waisman (2009) investigated the impact of corporate governance on the risk and return of Korean banks during the 10 years that followed the financial crisis era. In particular, they investigated the ownership structure of banks, the extent of involvement of foreign institutions and investors in ownership and board membership of Korean banks, and the heterogeneity of board structure on bank performance. The authors found front research that foreign ownership, the extent of external board involvement, and the presence of foreign directors on the board are associated with significantly higher bank returns. Although foreign ownership and the number of outside board directors are associated with lower risk, the involvement of foreign board members is positively associated with risk.

Racha Ghayad (2008) aimed to study the operation of Islamic banks and the elements which determine their performance. This paper supposes that corporate governance of Islamic banks imposes an important constraint on Islamic banks operations. The author found from the paper that the performance of an Islamic bank—as a company based on principles of Islam—is affected not only by the internal variables of quantitative nature (for example financial ratios) but also by the internal qualitative variables like the managerial variables. Moreover, the performance of an Islamic bank and a conventional bank should not be measured in the same way because of their divergence on the level of the objectives. The Shari'a member must have a qualification in finance and commerce to ensure better quality of supervision and consultation.

Anne Abraham, Hemant Deo, Helen Irvine (2008) aimed to focus on a number of unexpected disclosures by major Australian banks, to highlight the subjectivity of financial reports and their failure to present an accurate portrayal of the underlying realities, and proposed that corporate governance disclosures are required to provide reassurance that financial reports are trustworthy. The author found that disclosures about corporate governance practices play a strong legitimizing role, enhancing perceptions that financial reports correspond with organizational realities.

Morrison Handley-Schachler, Linda Juleff, Colin Paton (2007) attempted to overview the goals of corporate governance in the financial services sector from a theoretical perspective. The broad parameters of corporate governance are discussed, from a theoretical perspective. The main attention of this paper is banks and a key issue like the typical structure of their balance-sheets—high leverage, and a mismatch in their assets and liabilities, mean that it is imperative that they keep lenders' confidence, and imply a wider duty of care for bank directors. From survey the authors concluded that External regulators (FSA) and auditors have vital oversight functions, which should encourage sound governance practices.

Andy Mullineux (2006) considered the implications of the banks fiduciary duty to their depositors (as well as the shareholders) and the government's fiscal duty to taxpayers (in the presence of deposit insurance) for the corporate governance (CG) of banks. The author outlined recent contributions to the literature and assessed in the context of the asymmetric information literature relating to banking. From survey the authors found that the good CG of banks requires regulation to balance the interests of depositors and taxpayers with those of the shareholders.

### Research Objective

To study the adherence of governance norms by major IT Companies of India by analyzing major difference between corporate governance practices within the sector. It leads to the understanding of the weightage given to particular parameters by different companies to the mandatory and non-mandatory corporate governance norms.

### Research Methodology

Parameters based Score card method has been adopted for comparative analysis, on the basis of Clause 49 under listing agreement norms set by SEBI and Kumar Mangalam Birla Committee Recommendations. Annual reports of 4 major companies have been analyzed and selection of the companies are based on its market capitalization as on financial year ending 2012 to ascertain its level of governance mechanism. Scorecard method has been adopted to analyze the level and percentage of norms adherence by different company.

### Originality/Value

This paper makes a valuable contribution given the fact that there are only a limited number of comprehensive studies dealing with the assessment corporate governance issues in Indian IT sector based scorecard method. The paper should be quite useful to fundamental analyst and investment advisors apart from stakeholders of the said companies for better understanding of the companies status and corporate governance issues.

### Data Analysis

As discussed earlier, specified norms or score parameters are important and should be complied by the listed companies. These are statutory requirements as prescribed by SEBI through Clause 49 of the Listing Agreement and its respective amendments in the Companies Act, 1956 serves as a guideline for the formation of scorecard.

### Analysis of Corporate Governance Status of Information Technology Industry

Table 1: Average Corporate Governance Scorecard for Year 2008 to 2011

| No. | Governance Parameters | Scores Assigned | TCS | Infosys | Tech Mahindra | Wipro |
|---|---|---|---|---|---|---|
| 1. | Statement of Company's philosophy on code of governance | 2 | 2 | 2 | 2 | 2 |
| 2. | Structure and Strength of board | 2 | 2 | 2 | 2 | 2 |
| 3. | Chairman & CEO Duality | 5 | 5 | 3 | 4 | 5 |
| 4. | Disclosure of Tenure and Age limit of directors | 2 | 0 | 2 | 1 | 0 |
| 5. | Disclosure of definition of Independent Director and Financial Expert and also selection Criteria of Board of Directors including independent directors | 3 | 0 | 3 | 1 | 1 |
| 6. | Post Board meeting follow up system and compliance of the board procedures | 2 | 0 | 2 | 0 | 2 |
| 7. | Appointment of lead independent director | 2 | 0 | 2 | 0 | 0 |
| 8. | Disclosure of other provision as to the boards and committees | 1 | 1 | 1 | 0 | 0 |
| 9. | Disclosure of Remuneration Policy and Remuneration of Directors | 2 | 2 | 2 | 1 | 2 |
| 10. | Code of Conduct | 2 | 2 | 2 | 2 | 2 |
| 11. | Board Committee | 25 | 15 | 21 | 17 | 11 |
| 12. | Disclosure and Transparency | 25 | 12 | 25 | 9 | 14 |
| 13. | General Body Meetings | 3 | 2 | 2 | 3 | 3 |
| 14. | Means of Communication and General shareholder information | 2 | 2 | 2 | 2 | 1 |
| 15. | CEO/CFO Certification | 2 | 0 | 2 | 2 | 1 |
| 16. | Compliance of corporate governance and auditor's certificate | 10 | 10 | 10 | 10 | 10 |
| 17. | Disclosure of Stakeholders' interests | 10 | 4 | 9 | 8 | 5 |
| | **TOTAL** | **100** | **59** | **92** | **64** | **61** |
| | | | 4 | 1 | 2 | 3 |

Scorecard model: Das S.C. (2007), Corporate Governance Standards and Practices Information Technology Industry in India, *The Management Accountant*, 111-13, Clause 49.

### Interpretation

**1. Statement of Company's philosophy on code of governance:** In the IT industry there are 4 companies, while looking to the Corporate Governance, the first score point was statement of Company's philosophy on Corporate Governance and thus the point was assigned a weightage of 2 on a scale of 100. All 4 companies get the expected score of 2. All companies have sufficient disclosure of the statement of Company's philosophy on code of governance. However, Infosys have better described Company's philosophy on code of governance.

**2. Structure and Strength of board:** In the Corporate Governance score, the second score point was about the Structure and Strength of the board. The point was assigned a weightage of 2 on a scale of 100. All 4 companies get the expected score of 2. All companies have sufficiently disclosed the composition of the Board of Directors.

**3. Chairman & CEO duality:** The appointment of Chairman of the board carries of critical importance. The third point describes about the duality of Chairman and CEO. The point assigned a weightage of total 5 points, which are assigned on the following basis. TCS and Wipro among this companies has assigned a score of 5. Whereas Infosys scored 3 points and Tech Mahindra scored of 4.

**4. Disclosure of Tenure and Age limit of directors:** In the Corporate Governance score, the fourth point was about Disclosure of Tenure and Age limit of directors. The point was assigned a weightage of 2 on a scale of 100. The disclosures about the tenure and age limit of directors are sufficiently available in the annual report of the Infosys and Tech Mahindra whereas it is not sufficiently available in TCS and Wipro.

**5. Disclosure of definition and selection criteria for (Independent) directors:** In the Corporate Governance score, the fifth point was about the definition of 'Independent Director' and 'Financial Expert' and selection criteria for board members (including independent director). The point was assigned a weightage of 3 on a scale of 100. Only Infosys have disclosed definition of 'Financial Expert' and selection criteria for board members (including independent director). However, the definition of 'Independent Director' is available in the annual report of Wipro and Tech Mahindra hence it is assigned a score of 1 point. TCS does not score here.

**6. Post Board meeting follow up system and compliance of the board procedures:** In the Corporate Governance score, the sixth point was about disclosure of Post Board meeting follow up system and compliance of the board procedures. The point was assigned a weightage of 2 on a scale of 100. The systematic disclosures about the Post Board meeting follow up system are sufficiently available in the annual report of the Infosys and Wipro whereas it is not sufficiently available in TCS and Tech Mahindra. Hence, 2 companies did not get any point in this section and 2 companies get 2 points in this section.

**7. The appointment of lead independent director:** The point was assigned a weightage of 2 on a scale of 100. Among the companies, only Infosys have formally appointed lead independent director and the rest of the companies have not appointed lead independent director. Hence, only Infosys get 2 points and rest of the companies did not get any point in this section.

**8. Disclosure of other provision as to the boards and committees:** In the Corporate Governance score, the eighth point was about the disclosure of other provision as to the boards and committees. The point was assigned a weightage of 1 on a scale of 100. It is observed that 3 companies have sufficiently disclosed about the various committees and sub-committees of the board except Wipro. Hence, the two companies, i.e. TCS and Infosys get expected score of 1 whereas Tech Mahindra and Wipro did not get any points.

**9. Disclosure of Remuneration Policy & Remuneration of directors:** In the Corporate Governance score, the ninth point was about the disclosure of Remuneration Policy & Remuneration of Directors. The point was assigned a weight age of 2 on a scale of 100. The point was further equally divided into two points, (i) Disclosure of remuneration policy and (ii) Disclosure of remuneration to directors. All companies have sufficiently disclosed about remuneration to directors except Tech Mahindra. Hence, the 3 companies gets 2 points and Tech Mahindra gets 1 point.

**10. Code of Conduct:** In the Corporate Governance score, the tenth point was about the code of conduct. The point was assigned a weightage of 2 on a scale of 100. The point was further equally divided into two points, (i) Information on Code of Conduct and (ii) Affirmation regarding compliance for code of conduct. It is observed that all the companies have sufficiently disclosed about both the above points. Hence, all 4 companies get expected score of 2.

**11. Board Committees:** In the Corporate Governance score, the eleventh point is about the various Committees of the board. The point carries a weightage of 25 on a scale of 100. The sub-classification of the point is as under: (i) Audit Committee 8, (ii) Remuneration Committee 6, (iii) Shareholders'/Investors Grievance Committee 5, (iv) Nomination Committee 2, (v) Other Committees 4. Total 25.

(i) **Audit Committee:** The Audit Committee is assigned a weightage of 8. It is observed that all companies have made sufficient disclosure about the audit committee. All companies have sufficiently disclosed committee charter and terms of reference. However, none of the companies, have scored completely and none have published Audit Committee Report in the annual report. Their scores remain different and top score is of Infosys while lowest is Wipro.

(ii) **Remuneration/Compensation Committee**: The Remuneration/Compensation Committee is assigned a weightage of 6. It is observed that all companies have formed the committee. They have also made sufficient disclosure. None of the companies have published Remuneration Committee Report in the annual report except Infosys, scoring 6. Rest of the companies are scoring 4.

(iii) **Shareholders'/Investors Grievance Committee**: The Shareholders'/Investors' Grievance Committee is assigned a weightage of 5. It is observed that all the sample companies have formed the committee. However, none of the companies have published information about the investors'/shareholders' survey (if conducted). The Report of this committee is also not published by any of the companies (except Infosys). Hence, again Infosys scores maximum available points and Wipro is last on the list scoring 3.

(iv) **Nomination Committee:** The Nomination Committee was assigned a weightage of 2. It is observed that two of the sample companies (Infosys and TCS) have formed this committee, however other sample companies have not formed the committee. Hence, Infosys scores 2, TCS and Wipro gets a score of 1, whereas Tech Mahindra gets no score.

(v) **Other Committees:** The formation of other committees is assigned a weightage of 4. Its classification is already mentioned earlier. It is observed that following committees are not formed by any of the sample companies. (a) Health, Safety and Environment and (b) Investment Committee. Infosys have made HSE Committee in 2008-09 but then after they have removed, Ethics-Compliance Committee is formed by TCS & Wipro, who score 1 each. Share Transfer Committee is formed by Tech Mahindra so it scores 2 whereas surprisingly Infosys is yet to score.

**12. Disclosure and Transparency:** In the Corporate Governance score, the twelfth point is about the various disclosure and transparency shown by the company in the annual report. The point is assigned a weightage of 25 on a scale of 100. The classification of the point is as under. Significant related party transactions having potential conflicts with the interest of the company scores 2, Non Compliance related to capital market matters during last three years scores 2, Accounting Treatment score 2, Board Disclosure—Risk Management scores 3, Management Discussion and Analysis provides for score 2, Shareholders' Information 4, Shareholder Rights 2, Audit Qualification 2, Training of Board Members 2, Evaluation of Non-Executive Directors 2, Whistle Blower Policy 2, Totalizing 25 score points.

It is observed that (i) All sample companies have sufficiently disclosed about significant related party transactions. (ii) All sample companies have adequately disclosed about Non Compliance related to capital market matters during last three years. (iii) All sample companies have clearly mentioned about the accounting treatments and significant changes in their accounting policy. (iv) All sample companies have given sufficient information about risk management and policies of the board. However, no sample company (Except ITL & WIL) has published risk management report. (v) All sample companies have published the Management Discussion and Analysis as a part of the annual report. (vi) All sample companies have sufficiently disclosed the shareholders' information. (vii) All sample companies have published rights of the shareholders as a part of their annual report. (viii) All sample companies (Except PCS) are clear from any audit qualification. (ix) ITL and WIL have given information about the training to board members. However, it is not given by other sample companies. (x) ITL and WIL have systematically informed about evaluation of Non-Executive Director, whereas other companies have not disclosed about it. (xi) ITL, PCS, TCS and WIL have given information about the Whistle Blower Policy. However, it is not given by other sample companies. Hence, Infosys gets a highest score of 25, Tech Mahindra gets a score of 17 followed by TCS at 15 and Wipro stands at 11.

**13. General Body Meetings:** This point was about the General Body Meetings, carrying a weightage of 3. All companies have sufficiently disclosed about the various points related to General body meetings in the annual report. Hence, all sample companies get the expected score of 3. This point is further equally divided into the disclosure regarding the following:

(i) Location and time of general meetings held in last three years.

(ii) Details of Special Resolution passed in last three AGMs/EGMs.

(iii) Details of resolution passed last year through postal ballot including conducting official and voting process. All 4 companies have sufficiently disclosed about the above points in the annual report. Infosys and TCS get the expected score of 2. Wipro and Tech Mahindra get 3 points.

**14. Means of Communication and General shareholder information:** The Fourteenth score point was disclosure about the means of communication and general shareholder information and carries weightage of 2. All companies have sufficiently disclosed about the point in the annual report. Hence, all companies get the expected score of 2, except Wipro which scores 1.

**15. CEO/CFO Certification:** The Fifteenth score point was about the certification of CEO/CFO, carrying a weightage of 2. It is observed that TCS has not disclosed this certification whereas Tech Mahindra and Infosys have disclosed this certificate. Hence, Tech Mahindra and Infosys get the expected score of 2 and Wipro gets 1.

**16. Compliance of Corporate Governance and Auditors' Certificate:** The Sixteenth score point was about the compliance of Corporate Governance Guidelines issued by SEBI and Auditor's Certificate, carrying a weightage of 10. It is observed that all sample companies have clean certificate from Auditor. Hence, all companies get the expected score of 10.

**17. Disclosure of Stakeholders' interests:** The Seventeenth score point was about the disclosure of the stakeholders' interest and was assigned a weightage of 10. This point is divided equally to the following:

(i) Environment, Health & Safety Measures (EHS)

(ii) Human Resource Development Initiative (HRD)

(iii) Corporate Social Responsibility (CSR)

(iv) Industrial Relation (IR)

(v) Disclosure of policies on EHS, HRD, CSR & IR

It is observed that most of the companies have provided information about above mentioned points in various forms. EHS, HRD, CSR & IR policies are not disclosed adequately in the report of any sample companies. Most of all sample companies have sufficiently provided details about HRD and CSR. Therefore, Infosys scores 9, Tech Mahindra gets the score of 8 whereas Wipro gets a score of 5, and TCS get a score of 4.

### Future Research Directions

There is possibility of further research on each parameters under Clause 49 of listing agreement issued by SEBI from India's perspective as an developing countries current and prospective scenario, with changing laws as well as policy matters of government for better governance and transparency.

### Managerial Implications

Number of research papers and guidelines of renowned organizations emphasis on fund inflows from the perspective of investments and advances is correlated with corporate governance policy of different sectors and companies. The study makes an efforts to understand role of governance norms in strategic operations of the company and its impact on companies performance and future prospects.

## Conclusion

After analysis of governance structure, process and disclosures made on corporate governance, the question comes to mind is what is the standard and quality of governance that has been achieved by various companies?

**Table 2:** Company Ranks as per Score Range

| Score Range | Rank | Name of the Company |
|---|---|---|
| 86 – 100 | Excellent | INFOSYS |
| 71 – 85 | Very Good | |
| 56 – 70 | Good | TCS, WIPRO, TECH MAHINDRA |
| 41 – 55 | Average | |
| Below 41 | Poor | |

From the above analysis and criteria given in the table, Corporate governance performance of its industry is given below. Infosys has got the 1st rank and it is in excellent category while Tech Mahindra secures 2nd rank, Wipro 3rd whereas TCS gets 4th rank and they all are in good category as per the corporate governance criteria.

Literature review and overall study envisages the possibility of enhancing the corporate governance capabilities through mandatory and non mandatory governance norms leading to vigilant and transparent system. As a suggestion authors provide for further analysis on shifting major parameters of non mandatory clauses to mandatory norm or law as to increase the transparency and better corporate governance and disclosure norms for the benefit of all stakeholders.

## REFERENCES

Anne Abraham, Hemant Deo, Helen Irvine (2008), "What lies beneath? Financial reporting and corporate governance in Australian banks", *Asian Review of Accounting*, Vol. 16, Iss: 1, pp. 4-20.

Andy, Mullineux (2006), "The corporate governance of banks", *Journal of Financial Regulation and Compliance*, Corporate Governance Development Framework "a framework for integrating corporate governance into investment operations", 'International Financial Corporation' annual meeting agenda report 2011.

Das, S.C. (2007), "Corporate Governance Standards and Practices Information Technology Industry in India", *The Management Accountant*, 111-13 Clause 49.

Dilek Demirbas, Andrey Yukhanaev (2011), "Independence of board of directors, employee relation and harmonisation of corporate governance: Empirical evidence from Russian listed companies", *Employee Relations*, Vol. 33, Iss: 4, pp. 444-71.

Morrison Handley-Schachler, Linda Juleff, Colin Paton (2007), "Corporate governance in the financial services sector", *Corporate Governance*, Vol. 7, Iss: 5, pp. 623-34.

Racha Ghayad (2008), "Corporate governance and the global performance of Islamic banks", *Humanomics*, Vol. 24, Iss: 3, pp. 207-16.

Sungho Choi, Iftekhar Hasan, Maya Waisman (2009), "Does corporate governance matter? Korean banks in the postfinancial crisis era", in Mark Hirschey, Kose John, Anil K. Makhija (ed.), *Corporate Governance and Firm Performance* (Advances in Financial Economics, Volume 13), Emerald Group Publishing Limited, pp. 217-41.

Yiming Hu, Siqi Li, Thomas W. Lin, Shilei Xie (2011), "Large creditors and corporate governance: the case of Chinese banks", *Review of Accounting and Finance*, Vol. 10, Iss: 4, pp. 332-67.

### Web Sources

Annual Report of Infosys Ltd, available at http://www.infosys.com/investors/pages/index.aspx

Annual Report of TCS, available at http://www.tcs.com/investors/Pages/default.aspx

Annual Report of Tech Mahindra, available at http://www.techmahindra.com/Pages/Default.aspx

Annual Report of Wipro Ltd available at http://www.wipro.com/investors

Corporate governance voluntary guidelines 2009 available at http://www.mca.gov.in

# 16

# XBRL: EXPLORING ADOPTION IN INDIA

–*Vivek Sharma* and *G. Soral*

## Introduction

As the result of globalization MNCs required globally comparative accounting and business information. Now companies have to provide different type of accounting and business information to management, investors, Govt. authorities, bankers, stock exchange and SEBI. It takes a lot of time and money with complexities. A common language for the electronic communication is needed to avoid these problems which led to born of XBRL. It is an open standard, free of license fees. It is already being put to practical use in a number of countries and implementations of XBRL are growing rapidly around the world. In India XBRL is facilitating by the Institute of Chartered Accountants of India (ICAI). XBRL India is governed by a steering committee. The members of the committee includes regulators such as RBI, IRDA, SEBI, MCA, NSE, BSE and some private sector companies.

XBRL stands for eXtensible Business Reporting Language. It is a language for the electronic communication of business and financial data which is revolutionising business reporting around the world. It is one of a family of "XML" languages which is becoming a standard means of communicating information between businesses and on the internet. The idea behind XBRL is simple. Instead of treating financial information as a block of text—as in a standard internet page or a printed document that provides an identifying tag for each individual item of data that is computer readable.

The Extensible Business Reporting Language (XBRL) is an open standard that supports information modeling and the expression of semantics commonly required in business reporting. XBRL uses the XML syntax and related XML technologies, such as XML Schema, XLink, XPath, XML namespaces, etc., to articulate this reporting semantics in the form of an information model. Most people focus too much on the XBRL syntax but miss the part about expression of semantics.

XBRL can handle data in different languages and accounting standard. It can flexibly be adapted to meet different requirements and uses. Data can be transformed into XBRL by suitable mapping tools or it can be generated in XBRL by appropriate software.

## Background of XBRL

Beginning of XBRL can be traced to the initial efforts of Charles Hoffman, a certified public accountant from Tacoma, Washington. The American Institute of Certified Public Accountants (AICPA) was also instrumental in pulling together what eventually became XBRL International. XBRL is being developed by an international non-profit consortium of over 600 major companies, organizations and government agencies.

The purpose of XBRL is to provide a format that enables users to exchange and validate business information that is self-descriptive (based on the XML specification), that is a non-proprietary and open source standard (XBRL is a public domain specification), that supports an "open" user community (one can use/repurpose any XBRL formatted information). To support these requirements, the language follows the model of separating:

- What constitutes a valid business report (structure and constraints—also called the "metadata" for a report) and
- The actual information communicated in the report.

In the case of XBRL, there two different types of documents are to be used Taxonomy document and Instance document. The taxonomy document defines the metadata for a report, and the instance document, provides the information of the business report. Since the instance document references the taxonomy document on which it is based, an application can validate the provided information against the structure and constraints set forward in the metadata. This also means that if the sender and receiver have access to the taxonomy document, the only thing to transmit is the actual business report information. The receiver can validate the received information using a local copy of the taxonomy. The sender can—before actually submitting the report—validate that all information is correct by validating the information against their local copy. By separating the content and metadata, the transmitted information can be very concise, while at the same time ensuring full validation of submitted information at the source. This is one of the crucial benefits that enable high-value business process improvements.

### *Taxonomies*

Taxonomies are the reporting area specific hierarchical dictionaries used by the XBRL community. Different taxonomies will be required for different business reporting purposes. Some national jurisdictions may need their own reporting taxonomies to reflect local accounting and other reporting regulations. Many different organizations, including regulators, specific industries or even companies, may require taxonomies or taxonomy extensions to cover their own specific business reporting needs.

An XBRL Taxonomy is a collection of taxonomy schemas and linkbases. A taxonomy schema is an XML schema document (file). Linkbases are XML documents (file) which follow the XLink specification.

### *Schemas*

Taxonomy schemas define Item and Tuple "concepts". Concepts provide names for the fact and indicate whether or not it's a tuple or an item, the data type (such as monetary, numeric, fractional, or textual), and potentially more metadata. Items and Tuples can be regarded as "implementations" of concepts, or specific instances of a concept. A good analogy for those familiar with object oriented programming would be that concepts are the classes, and Items and Tuples are Object instances of those classes. This is the source of the use of the "XBRL instance" terminology. In addition to defining concepts, taxonomy schemas reference linkbase documents.

*Linkbases*

Linkbases are a collection of links, which themselves are a collection of locators, arcs, and potentially resources. Locators are elements that essentially reference a concept and provide an arbitrary label for it. In turn, arcs are elements indicating that a concept links to another concept by referencing the labels defined by the locators. Some arcs link concepts to other concepts. Other arcs link concepts to resources, the most common of which are human-readable labels for the concepts.

There are five linkbases which are following:

**Label Linkbase:** This linkbase provides human readable strings for concepts. Using the label linkbase, multiple languages can be supported, as well as multiple strings within each language.

**Reference Linkbase:** This linkbase associates concepts with citations of some body of authoritative literature. Financial concepts appearing on business reports more often than not stem from regulatory documents issued by authorities.

**Calculation Linkbase:** This linkbase associates concepts with other concepts so that values appearing in an instance document may be checked for consistency.

**Definition Linkbase:** This linkbase associates concepts with other concepts using a variety of arc roles to express relations such as is-a, whole-part, etc.

The definition linkbase provides taxonomy creators with the opportunity to define different kinds of relations between elements. There are four standard types of relationships supported by the definition linkbase.

**Presentation Linkbase:** This linkbase associates concepts with other concepts so that the resulting relations can guide the creation of a user interface, rendering, or visualization.

*Tagging*

An identifying tag is provided to each individual item of data. This is computer readable. For example: Sales, Net Profit, Operating cost will be given unique tags for identification. Tagging will enable automated data processing by computer software. Cost and time wasted in manual data re-entry will be saved. Computer can treat XBRL data intelligently. Information in a XBRL document can be identified, selected, analyzed, stored, retrieved, exchanged, and presented in a variety of ways for multiple uses/users. Speed of handling data will be very high with high level of accuracy.

*XBRL Modules*

XBRL International has assured stability of the core XBRL 2.1 specification. It further continues the work on development of several new XBRL modules to define new compatible functionally. It has come out with the following modules:

1. XBRL Dimension 1.0: This supports the use of XBRL taxonomies to define additional, structured contextual information of Business facts. Each piece of such information is called a "Dimension".
2. XBRL Formula: It supports the creation of expressions using X path that can be applied to XBRL instances to validate its information or to compute new XBRL facts in a new instance.
3. XBRL Rendering: The rendering linkbase is intended to add the metadata that the balance sheet runs with the labels in order of presentation with comparative data of current and preceding period. It is rendered in defined and structured order T form or statement form.
4. XBRL Versioning: This module will support the creation of a standard versioning report with differences between two versions of the same taxonomy. This takes care of revised law, regulation and standards of reporting.

*Extensibility*

XBRL is designed to be extended. Additions of new elements and relation semantics when done in compliance with the XBRL Specification can still be read by XBRL processors. Thus, it provides a model of language extensibility that is not supported in the regular XML situation using XML Schema. It is the usage of XBRL Specification compliant (extension) taxonomies containing the elements and relations that make XBRL unique and extensible. There are many applications within business reporting where this extensibility is highly desirable. XBRL is extensible and that extensibility is a very useful feature. XBRL is extensible in a "predictable way" or it should be. The goal is to provide support for building meaningful extensions that can be consumed by any XBRL specification compliant application and to interpret what the extension is communicating, not to break software applications.

XBRL International supports several methods of continued expansion of shared XBRL functionally. These are as follows:

- **Link Role Registry:** This is hosted at www.xbr.org. It provides link roles and arc roles registration to facilitate re-use across taxonomies.
- **Functions Registry:** This collect X path functions for re-use in formula link bases.
- **Format Registry:** This collects common numeric formats for re-use in Inline XBRL applications.
- **Best Practice RFC's:** This will help XBRL users to improve interpretability of design through sharing of common best practices.

*Process for filing financial statements in XBRL form in MCA 21 system*

After the circular issued by MCA it is mandatory for certain class of companies to file financial statement in XBRL format in MCA 21 system accompany can file financial statement in XBRL format by following steps:

**Step 1 – Creation of XBRL instance document:** For creation of XBRL instance document a company have to map each financial statement element to a corresponding element in published taxonomy:

For this work each and every element in the Financial Statement of the company should be converted into a corresponding element in the Business Taxonomy. To get this done, the companies have to do tagging (classification) of the XBRL taxonomy elements with the corresponding accounting heads in the Financial Statements. This mapping of taxonomy elements will help to convert the accounting related information into XBRL format.

Having passed the mapping and classification stage, an instance document is to be created for the financial statements. An instance document is a XML file that contains business reporting information and represents a collection of financial facts and report-specific information using tags from the XBRL taxonomy. Separate instance documents need to be created for the Stand Alone Balance sheet of the company, Stand Alone Profit and Loss Account of the company and Consolidated Balance sheet and Consolidated Profit and Loss Account of the company.

After preparing of instance document it needs to be ensured that the instance document is a valid instance document and all the information has been correctly captured in the instance document.

**Step 2 – Download XBRL validation tool from MCA portal:** Validating the instance document is a pre-requisite before filing the balance sheet and profit & loss account on MCA portal. A validation tool is to be downloaded from MCA portal to validate the instance document. The validation should be done according the business taxonomy available on the MCA portal.

**Step 3 - Perform pre-scrutiny of the validated instance document through the tool:** Once the instance document is successfully validated from the tool, the next step is to pre-scrutinize the validated instance document with the help of the same tool. This can be easily done by connecting to internet.

**Step 4 - Attach instance document to the Form 23AC and Form 23ACA:** There shall be a separate set of Form 23AC and Form 23ACA available on the MCA portal for filing in XBRL form. After filing the form on MCA portal a validated and pre-scrutinized instance document is to be attached for balance sheet, Profit & Loss A/c and Consolidated financial statements.

**Step 5 - Submitting the Form 23ACA and Form 23ACA on the MCA portal:** Once the instance documents are validated and pre-scrutinize, e-form can be uploaded easily on the MCA portal.

**Step 6 - Viewing of balance sheet and profit and loss submitted in XBRL form on MCA portal:** The XBRL instance documents submitted along with Form 23AC and 23ACA are in machine readable format. Therefore, for viewing the same in a human readable format, these shall be converted into human readable format by the MCA21 system. For viewing the same on MCA21 portal and for taking certified copies of the same, these converted documents shall be made available.

## Review of Literature

The primary contribution of this research is to provide evidence as to the future of XBRL's use in accounting, corporate reporting and regulation. This study provides support for some of the common concepts of XBRL impacts, but tempers expectations on other impacts.

As per Circular No. 09/2011 dated on 31st March 2011 issued by Ministry of Corporate Affaires (MCA) it is mandatory for certain class of company to file Balance sheet and Profit & Loss A/c for the year 2010-11 onwards by using XBRL taxonomy.

As such, following class of companies is required to file their Balance Sheet and Profit and Loss Account in XBRL Format:

1. Listed Companies and their subsidiaries;
2. Companies having paid up capital of ₹ 5 crores and above;
3. Companies having turnover of ₹ 100 crores and above.

As per XBRL consulting partner LLC and UBmatrics (2008) practices of building XBRL taxonomies increase costs for software developers, forcing them to continually implement new and often obscure features because someone creating a taxonomy figures out a creative or clever way to make XML Schema do something interesting, when other approaches for achieving the same result may already exist. Businesses are then forced to incur consulting fees and additional development costs in order to convert information created in XBRL, from one system's implementation of XBRL (dialect) to another system's implementation of XBRL (dialect). This is unnecessary because there is a better way.

Amelia A. Baldwin and Brad S. Trinkle (2010) described potential impacts of XBRL that were considered to be of greatest interest to investors, corporations, and regulatory bodies were divided into a number of categories: (1) corporate and compliance, (2) financial reporting, (3) users of financial reports, and (4) auditing in their research.

According to Rikki George the implementation of XBRL is a step in the right direction towards transparency, timeliness & relevance of financial reporting information. The changes come too soon, with regards to convergence of IFRS with US GAAP. There is enough evidence to support that companies have difficulties with XBRL.

The Best Practices Board (BPB) is exploring interest in the formation of a Taxonomy Architecture Guidance task force to oversee the development and dissemination of a Taxonomy Architecture Guidance document (TAG). The changing face of business reporting and the fast moving adoption of XBRL mandates the need for a comprehensive guideline document for taxonomy architecture that can defines the various taxonomies have been built catering to various domains, common and key principles and the impacts of adopting a specific structure of taxonomy.

Taxonomies which have been officially recognized by XBRL International are listed under "Recognized Taxonomies". The Financial Reporting Taxonomies Architecture (FRTA) document guides the creation of taxonomies under version 2.1 of the Specification. It sets out recommended design architecture and establishes rules and conventions which help make taxonomies more usable and efficient. The FRTA has been approved as a Recommendation by the XBRL International Steering Committee. India Banking GAAP Taxonomy 2010 is example of acknowledged financial reporting taxonomy as per specification 2.1.

## Research Methodology

The aspects related with research methodology adopted in the paper are as follows:

**1. Objectives:** The objectives of research paper are:

i. To present an overview of XBRL in context of financial reporting.

ii. To explore opinion of professionals regarding implementation of XBRL in India.

**2. Data collection:** In order to present an overview of XBRL and various aspects related with its implementation relevant websites and publications have been gone through. An opinion survey was conducted on the basis of mailed questionnaire (Appendix 1). The respondent included practicing Chartered Accountants, Cost Accountants and Company Secretaries. Despite rigorous follow up, response rate in this survey has not been high. In all, 12 respondents respond properly to the questionnaire. This is worth being mentioned here that the principal reason of poor response rate has been lack of exposure about XBRL among the potential respondents.

**3. Analysis:** The response to the closed-ended questions has been analyzed by aggregating the response and calculating Averages. The ranks have been presented in ascending order which is actually the declining order of importance.

## Data Analysis and Discussion

An opinion survey has been conducted from respondent and discussed which is being analyzed follows:

**1. XBRL Benefits (Vide Q. No. 1 in Appendix 1)**

| Benefits | Average |
|---|---|
| Automatic checking | 1.75 |
| | 3.25 |
| Validation of data | 3.25 |
| High speed in handling of data | 4.00 |
| Accuracy | 3.50 |
| No chance of manual error | 6.50 |
| Interchangeability of data | 4.25 |
| Paperless business reporting | 5.25 |
| Cost cutting | 7.50 |

In addition XBRL increases the efficiency of financial reporting process and decreases the occurrence of errors in financial statements. It facilitates continues reporting and enhances the availability of financial reports. Interactive data will enable investors and other external users to make more productive decisions. It increases the ability of financial analysts to perform cross sectional analysis within industries.

**2. XBRL Challenges (Vide Q. No. 2 in Appendix 1)**

| Challenges | Average |
|---|---|
| Insufficient training resources | 7.00 |
| Hiding complexities | 2.75 |

| | |
|---|---|
| High cost of development of software | 5.25 |
| Heavy consulting fees | 6.25 |
| Different approaches negatively affect the comparability and extensibility | 3.25 |
| Risk of hacking & corrupting data | 2.75 |
| May be the error in taxonomies | 4.25 |
| XBRL can't ensure compatibility & comparability when customization is needed | 4.50 |

In to connection this, additional difficulties are adoption of XBRL—There are many number of "dialects" are increasing and each having a taxonomy created using a different approach or architecture. This is not cost effective for the business that has to report to all these different entities. XBRL runs the risk of fragmenting into a number of different dialects. While they will likely remain interoperable—because they are all structured information, but just structured differently but it will come at a high cost of consulting and development fees to achieve this interoperability in order to convert one dialect or architecture to another. There are three technical solutions or approaches to represent the same metadata within a taxonomy these are following:

- Item-based approach: This is the approach used to create the new version of the IFRS-GP taxonomy.
- Tuple-based approach: This is the approach taken by the old US GAAP taxonomy and the old IFRS-GP taxonomy.
- Dimensions-based approach: This is the approach taken by the current US GAAP Taxonomy and the COREP taxonomy.

These are three fundamentally different technical approaches (syntax) for expressing the same information (semantics). Clearly, using three different approaches must negatively affect the comparability, the extensibility, and interoperability of these different taxonomies and clearly, this cannot be beneficial for the business community. It will only increase TCO (total cost of ownership) of the XBRL based solutions and negatively affect the acceptance of XBRL.

**3. Type of taxonomy is used (Vide Q. No. 3 in Appendix 1)**

Generally the Global Ledger Taxonomy is used because it has been designed to support collation of data and internal reporting within organization. But in India taxonomy issued by Ministry of Corporate Affaires (MCA) is used.

**4. Challenges can be overcome (Vide Q. No. 4 in Appendix 1)**

For this work in India the government is regularly updating the taxonomy with ICAI, but still need of more support of IT professional and Accounting profession.

**5. Experience of error while assigning tags (Vide Q. No. 5 in Appendix 1)**

Sometimes there are few problems while assigning tags when users are unable to find eject head.

**6. Errors in tagging can be avoided (Vide Q. No. 6 in Appendix 1)**

If there will be appropriate head to describe the item of balance sheet.

**7. Future of XBRL as a business reporting language in India (Vide Q. No. 7 in Appendix 1)**

XBRL can handle data in different languages and accounting standards. It can flexibly be adapted to meet different requirements and uses. But due to lack of practical knowledge and training programs still there will be more difficulty as its scope will increase. Till now only selected companies are needed to follow that. Problems will increase when all companies will be included under this purview.

### Conclusion

On the basis of this case study we can say that there is no doubt about utility of XBRL. However, a few barriers or limitations may dent in its popularity. The benefits are seen in automation, cost saving, faster, more reliable and more accurate handling of data, improved analysis and in better quality of information and decision-making. Interactive data will enable investors and other external users to make more productive decisions. It increases the ability of financial analysts to perform cross sectional analysis within industries.

Auditors can detect errors in tagging financial data with the help of available application software. XBRL reduces financial statements audit cost through continuous auditing. It leads to improvement in internal controls.

### Suggestions

It is technology-oriented product so a complete training is essential for its users. Mere awareness will not lead to usage in their case. Auditors should ensure that errors in tagging process are not committed. The academic and professional educators and trainers are suggested to integrate XBRL in their curriculum on accounting and business information system and prepare standard reading materials and case studies.

## APPENDIX 1

## XBRL QUESTIONNAIRE

Q.1. XBRL results various benefits such as follows. Please rank them in highest (1) to lower order of your preferences:

| Benefits | Rank |
|---|---|
| 1. Automatic checking | |
| 2. Validation of data | |
| 3. High speed in handling of data | |
| 4. Accuracy | |
| 5. No chance of manual error | |
| 6. Interchangeability of data | |
| 7. Paperless business reporting | |
| 8. Cost cutting | |

Q.2. We have to face various challenges such as follows: please rank them in highest (1) to lower order of your preference:

| Challenges | Rank |
|---|---|
| 1. Insufficient training resources | |
| 2. Hiding complexities | |
| 3. High cost of development of software | |
| 4. Heavy consulting fees | |
| 5. Different approaches negatively affect the comparability and extensibility | |
| 6. Risk of hacking and corrupting data | |
| 7. May be the error in taxonomies | |
| 8. XBRL can't ensure compatibility & comparability when customization is needed | |

Q.3. Which type of taxonomy is used generally & why?

Q.4. How can the challenges be overcome? Suggest.

Q.5. How often have you experience of error while assigning tags?

Q.6. How can the errors in tagging be avoided?

Q.7. How does visualize the future of XBRL as a business reporting language in India?

## APPENDIX 2

**Abbreviations:**

| | |
|---|---|
| XML | eXtensible Markup Language |
| XBRL | eXtensible Business Reporting Language |
| HTML | Hyper Text Markup Language |
| MNCs | Multinational Companies |
| FRTA | Financial Reporting Taxonomies Architecture |
| AICPA | American Institute of Certified Public Accountants |
| TAG | Taxonomy Architecture Guidance document |

## REFERENCES

Baldwin, Amelia A. and Trinkle, Brad S. (2010), "The Impact of XBRL: A Delphi Investigation", *The International Journal of Digital Accounting Research*, Vol. 11, 2011, pp. 1-24, quoted in *www.uhu.es*, Visited on August 16, 2012.

Deshpande, Pankaj (2010), "eXtensible Business Reporting Language", *The Chartered Accountant Students' Journal,* Vol. 2.

Egmond, Raynier A. Van and Hoffman, Charles (2008), "How A Simpler XBRL can Make a Better XBRL", *XBRL Consulting partners LLC. and UBmatrix*.xbr, pp. 1-29.

George Rikki, "The Impact of XBRL on Financial Reporting", quoted in *www.financialexecutive.org*, Visited on August 16, 2012.

*www.deloitte.com*, Visited on August 19, 2012.

*www.mca.gov.in*, Visited on August 12, 2012.

*www.pwc.com*, Visited on August 19, 2012.

*www.xbrl.org*, Visited on August 5, 2012.

*www.xbrlwiki.info*, Visited on March 28, 2012.

# 17

# ACCOUNTING ISSUES OF CARBON CREDIT TRADING

–*O.P. Jain* and *Ravi Mandot*

## Introduction

Carbon accounting (also called GHG accounting) does assess the carbon footprint to help organizations adopt strategies aimed at fighting climate change. As with financial accounting and reporting, generally accepted carbon accounting principles are intended to underpin and guide carbon accounting and reporting to ensure that the reported information represents a faithful, true, and fair account of a company's carbon emissions.

Business community in India has started seeing value in undertaking carbon accounting and reporting it in public forums. Such forums include Carbon Disclosure Project (CDP) and company's Sustainable Development Reports. The number of companies which responded the CDP's information request on climate change strategy, risk and opportunities assessment and carbon accounting was answered by 37 companies in 2007. The number increased to 51 in 2008 and dropped marginally to 44 in 2009, partially explained by the global financial crisis.

There is still long way to go for Indian businesses on the path of carbon accounting and disclosures. Even in the top 200 firms in India (by market capitalization), the response rate in last few years has steadily increased and reached 20 per cent, compared to developed markets.

There are a few sectors like the software and services which are clear leaders in being carbon-aware, accounting carbon emissions from their emissions, taking efforts in reducing it and communicating it to the stakeholders. Part of this can be explained given the fact that these companies are most export dependent and draw majority of their revenues from markets of US and EU.

Very few companies in these sectors have responded to the CDP information request and have accounted for their carbon emissions.

## Accounting System

Determination of each Party's compliance with its commitment depends on the accurate accounting of each Party's emissions and assigned amount prior to, during and at the end of the commitment period. In order to ensure accurate accounting, emissions and the tracking of assigned amount by Parties at the national level. It also incorporates and strengthens the Convention's reporting requirements and review procedures. Together, these components, and the underlying data systems that support them, comprise the Kyoto Protocol accounting system. Finally, the Kyoto Protocol establishes a Compliance Committee to consider and determine cases of non-compliance.

The Kyoto Protocol accounting system is centred on two parallel information streams—GHG inventories and assigned amount information.

- Accounting of emissions and assigned amount starts at the national level. Each developed country is required to establish and maintain a national system for the preparation of its national GHG inventory. On the assigned amount side, each developed country is required to establish a national registry for tracking its holdings of and transactions of Kyoto units;
- GHG inventory data and assigned amount information are compiled in national reports, etc.
- National reports and are subject to review and compliance procedures. These procedures verify the countries level of emissions and assigned amount, and its eligibility to participate in the Kyoto mechanisms;
- Each countries emissions and assigned amount information are recorded as official only after the information has been reviewed and any questions of implementation have been resolved through the compliance procedures.

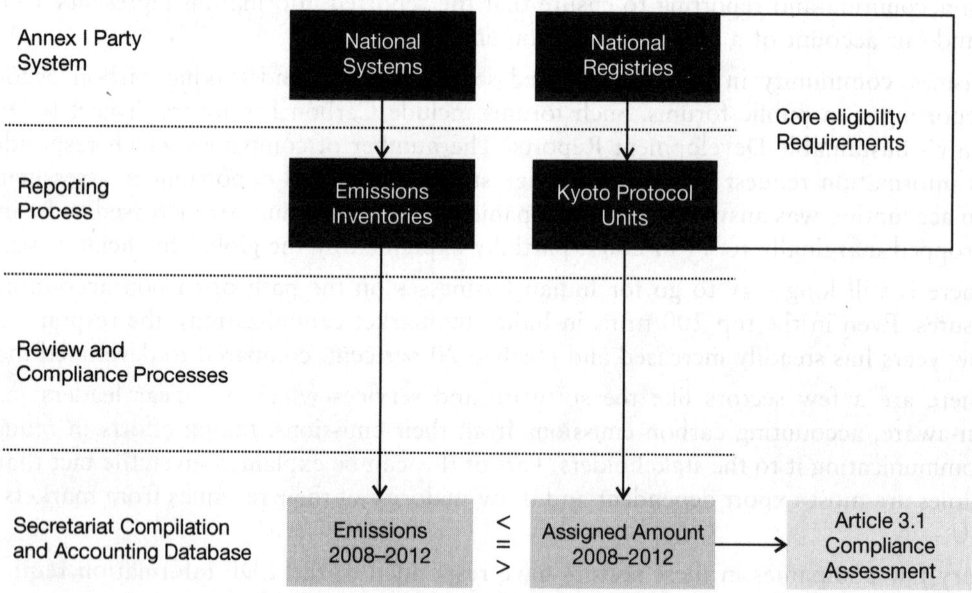


**Accounting system**

## Accounting Issues

There is continuing debate amongst academician, accountants, etc. on how to record carbon credit in the books of accounts. At present there is no authoritative accounting guideline is secondary available under genrally accepted accounting principles of India or US or international financial reporting standards. Carbon Credit Accounting is new concept, accounting of carbon credit in the books of companies from developed countries involve two issues:

A. Recognition of value of carbon they are allowed to emit.

B. Cost incurred to meet emission reduction commitments.

The following accounting issues are arising on accounting treatment of carbon credit:

- How to identify cost involved in CDM projects?
- Accounting and expenditure on CDM projects.
- How to account for self generated CERs?
- How to treat additional expenditure incurred on required training, research and development?
- How to recognize the effect of carbon credit and its trading on conventional accounting practice and framing accounting policies accordingly?
- Recognition of credits to be accounted,
- When these should be recognized in books of accounts and at what value, and
- Accounting for sale consideration of CERs and its disclosure in books and notes.
- What should be the code of good corporate governance in carbon trading?

Generation and trading in carbon credits has gained a lot of momentum but there remains lot of ambiguity for the accounting treatment to be rendered. Questions on accounting for expenditure on the CDM projects, accounting for self-generated CERs, accounting for sale consideration and so on. The answers are to be sought in the existing accounting standards as there are no separate accounting standards for accounting, measurement and disclosures of carbon credits.

Right now there is no need to issue separate accounting standard for carbon trading. A little change in accounting standard no. 2, 6, 11, 12, 17, 26, and 9 can help to bring out correct accounting of carbon credit. The existing standards are available for accounting of depreciation on capital investment (AS-6 and AS-9). Income reorganization can be used to record income from sale of CERs. A separate segment may be created for carbon project under AS-17 segment reporting. AS-11 accounting for foreign exchange may also be attracted.

Some of the countries suggest recognition of carbon credits as government grant (AS-12); however this approach would be inappropriate as government grants are received by an organization on concessional or nominal rates or free of cost, wherein government would grant or allocate some concessional benefit to an entity. In case of CERs, it is not any benefit that is provided by government or any affiliated authority, it is an incentive provided to entities for doing well to the environment.

Some experts, having admitted that there are presently no guidelines/standards for accounting of Carbon Credits, have suggested that they be accounted as Government Grant. Their logic is based on the definition of the term AS-12, which reads: "Government refers to government, government agencies and similar bodies, whether local, national or international." The logic forwarded appears to be misplaced, as in case of financial transactions arising out of carbon credit, monetary consideration will not flow from any government or government agency. UNFCC CDM registry acts as a DEMAT banker recognizing CER credits and keeping an account of it. There is no grant at all from any agency. Further, as soon as Carbon Credits are accounted as Government Grants.

Accounting Standard-9 (revenue recognition), CER credits are goods, their sales proceeds have to be recognized in financial accounts. The following conditions are self-explanatory:

"In a transaction involving the sale of goods, performance should be regarded as being achieved when the following condition have been fulfilled:

(i) The seller of goods has transferred to the buyer the property in the goods for a price or all significant risks and reward of ownership have been transferred to the buyer and the seller retains no effective control of the goods transferred to a degree usually associated with ownership; and

(ii) No significant uncertainty exists regarding the amount of the consideration that will be derived from sale of the goods."

To resolve the accounting issues, International Accounting Standards Board (IASB) had issued an interpretation IFRIC 3 (international financial reporting interpretation committee) on Emission Rights but had later withdrawn the same, continuing to debate on the appropriate treatment for CERs. The Accounting Standard Board of the Institute of Chartered Accountants of India (ICAI) has also issued an Exposure Draft of the Guidance Note on Accounting for Self-generated Certified Emission Reductions in 2009 enumerating the accounting principles for CERs generated by an entity. The exposure draft provides for accounting principles relating to recognition, measurement and disclosures of CERs generated under the Clean Development Mechanism.

### ICAI Exposure Draft

Accounting treatment for CERs taking in consideration the exposure draft issued by ICAI should be done in the following manner:

- **Expenses in the research and development phase:** While undertaking the project for reduction in carbon emission, any cost incurred on development should be accounted for as enumerated in AS-26 for intangible assets. Cost incurred on receiving the CER is measured with certainty at the time of incurring those expenses whereas revenue recognition will happen only at the time of sale of CERs. So there is a mismatch of in accounting for expenses and revenue.
- **CERs held with the CDM Executive Board:** The exposure draft on guidance note on accounting for carbon credits states that when the CERs are in the approval stage, these should be accounted for as per the provisions of AS-29 as Contingent Assets and once approved should be recorded in the books as an intangible asset. However, once the CER are approved by the Board, these should be recorded as intangible assets under AS-26.
- **CERs held for sale:** In case an enterprise possess CER which are to be traded in the ordinary course of business, i.e., the enterprise holds the asset as 'available for sale' then, these should be accounted for as Inventory under provisions of AS-2. Further,

intent of the entity would determine whether these credits should be recorded as intangible assets or as inventory. There are further questions on CERs cost at which CERs be recorded in the books, as huge amount of expenditure is incurred in terms of initializing the project, emission of reduction, approval and acceptance of CERs, etc.

The exposure draft of the guidance note clearly indicates that in case intangible asset is generated, expenses are to be capitalized as per AS-26, whereas in case CERs treated as inventory, costs relating to consultant fees, levies imposed by UNFCCC for approving of CERs are to be inventorized and are to be recorded as lower or cost or net realizable value as per the standard.

The cost incurred by the generating entity and the accounting treatment has been explained in the below Table 1:

**Table 1:** Accounting treatment

| Cost | Accounting treatments |
|---|---|
| Research cost arising from exploring alternative ways to reduce emissions<br>Cost incurred in developing the selected alternative as a process/ device to reduce emissions. | Research and development costs are pre-implementation costs of CDM projects. Such costs should be capitalised as intangible asset when they bring into existence any patent of a process to reduce carbon emissions (as per AS-26, intangible assets). |
| Cost incurred to prepare the Project Design Documents.<br>Fees paid to DOE for validation and verification and to the National Authority for approval.<br>Fees for registering with the UNFCCC.<br>Costs incurred for monitoring and reduction of emissions. | These costs do not result in CERs coming into existence, and therefore, these costs need to be expensed as incurred. |
| Cost incurred for certification of CERs. | These costs bring CERs into existence by way of credit of the same by the UNFCCC to the generating entity and therefore, these costs are treated as part of the inventory. |

**How can CERS be Valued?**

The two possible accounting value methods for initial recognition of carbon credits are "cost and fair value".

Assets acquired through purchase are commonly recorded at cost, but for carbon credits a direct cost recording is complicated by the facts that many entities have some credits that were allocated at no cost and some that were separately purchased.

The varieties in the way allowance can be acquired also complicate a market based fair value approach. It is rare that assets with a verifiable market value are required free, but it is possible to support such an approach with a concomitant recognition of an off-setting government grants. Such a grant recognized as revenue.

The "cost" and "fair value" question has the potential to result in very different financial reporting comparability issues, as the "inventory" vs. "intangible" questions. The two widely used methods might result on differing impact of financial statements in the following areas, in addition to disclosure requirements:

- Cash flow statement classification of both purchases and sales of emission.
- The frequency and mechanics of subsequent carrying value adjustments (lower of cost or market vs. impairment).
- Potential recapture of previous cost basis reduction under IFRS.
- Certain transaction resulting in exchange of one emission credits for another.

**Accounting Consideration–IFRS:**

In December 2004, the International Financial Reporting Interpretations Committee (IFRIC) released IFRIC 3, *Emission Rights*, in an attempt to address how participants should account for cap and trade emission trading schemes.

IFRIC 3 concluded that emission allowances, whether issued by government or purchased in the market, are intangible assets to be accounted for in accordance with IAS 38, Intangible Assets, as follows:

- On initial recognition, allowances issued for less than their fair value should be measured at fair value, with the difference between the amount paid and fair value reported as a government grant, in accordance with IAS 20, Accounting for Government Grants and Disclosure of Government Assistance. This grant should be recognized as deferred income and subsequently recognized as income, on a systematic basis over the compliance period for which the associated allowances are issued, regardless of whether those allowances continue to be held or are sold. An entity may subsequently choose to measure them under either the cost or revaluation model in IAS 38.
- As the entity actually emits greenhouse gases or carbon-equivalents, a liability should be recognized for the obligation to deliver allowances equal to those actual emissions. This liability is a provision within the scope of IAS 37, Provisions, Contingent Liabilities and Contingent Assets, and is required to be measured at the best estimate of the expenditure required to settle the present obligation at the balance sheet date. This should usually be the present market price of the number of allowances required to cover emissions made up to the balance sheet date. Reservations were expressed by companies due to different bases for measuring and presenting changes in the component assets and liabilities of the proposed accounting model. The main area of concern was around the fact that under IAS 38, changes in the market value of intangibles (i.e., emissions allowances held) are recognized in equity. However, the change in the value of the emissions obligation is recognized through profit and loss. Consequently, at its June 2005 meeting, the International Accounting Standards Board (IASB) withdrew IFRIC 3 to address the underlying accounting in a more comprehensive manner than originally envisaged by the IFRIC.

The IASB and the Financial Accounting Standards Board (FASB) have launched a joint project on carbon emission accounting models but have not yet published a conclusion.

### Possible Accounting of CERs

| S.No. | Issues | Relevant accounting standard |
|---|---|---|
| 1. | If CER held for inventory | IAS-2 "Inventories", AS-2 "Valuation of inventories". While CERs treated as inventory are measured at lower of cost and net realizable value at subsequent reporting date. |
| 2. | If CERs identifiable as non-monetary assets without physical substance | CERs should be treated as intangible assets. AS-26 will apply. If however, the CERs are classified as intangibles they should meet the definition of an intangible asset under AS-26. Those treated as intangibles are carried at cost less any amortization and impairment. |
| 3. | When revenue should be recognized? | CERs should be recognized once there is reasonable assurance that the conditions attaching to attribution of the CER are met—these condition may be met as the entity produces the "green product" (i.e., upon generation) or may require fulfilment of other condition attached to receiving the CERs. |
| 4. | Measurement | The CERs should be measured at either: Nominal amount—production cost should be allocated on rational and consistent basis between production cost of the "green product" if relevant and cost of production of the CERs; or<br>Fair value—CERs should be recognized at a fair value and a government grant recognized for the difference between nominal amount and fair value. |

### Reporting of CERs

The Kyoto Protocol maintains and extends the two regular, ongoing reporting requirements for developed country established under the Convention—an annual report and a periodic national communication. For each reporting requirement, Parties are expected to submit the information elements as required by the Convention and to include supplementary information related to the implementation of the Kyoto Protocol. In this way, submission of the annual report and the national communication under the Kyoto Protocol also fulfills the Party's reporting obligation under the Convention.

### Annual Reports

For the annual report, each developed country is required to submit an annual national GHG emission inventory by 15 April of each year, as required by the Convention, plus supplementary information on its implementation of the Kyoto Protocol. This supplementary information covers:

- The Party's holdings of and transactions of Kyoto units for the previous calendar year, reported in the standard electronic format for reporting Kyoto units;
- Emissions and removals from LULUCF activities and calculations of the amount to be added to and subtracted from the assigned amount;
- Changes in the Party's national system;
- Changes in the Party's national registry; and
- Information on the Party's implementation of policies and measures that minimize adverse social, environmental and economic impacts on developing country Parties.

### National Communications

Each Party must also provide the following supplementary information on its implementation of the Kyoto Protocol in its periodic national communications:

- A description of the national system;
- A description of the national registry;
- An explanation of how the Party's use of the Kyoto mechanisms is supplementary to domestic action;
- Information on the Party's implementation of policies and measures;
- A description of the Party's legislative, enforcement and administrative arrangements;
- A description of technology transfer, capacity-building and activities; and
- Information on the provision of financial resources to developing country Parties for the implementation of activities.

The parts of the national communication that are directly relevant to the accounting of the Party's assigned amount and its eligibility to participate in the Kyoto mechanisms are the sections on the national system and the national registry.

### Initial Report

In addition to the annual report and national communication, the Kyoto Protocol establishes two special reports to facilitate the accounting of emissions and assigned amount: the initial report and the true-up period report. The initial report is required to facilitate the calculation of the Party's initial assigned amount and to demonstrate its capacity to account for its emissions and assigned amount. Initial reports must be submitted by Parties by 31 December 2006 or one year after the entry into force of the Kyoto Protocol for the Party, whichever is later, and must contain the following information:

- A complete GHG inventory time series from the base year to the latest year available;
- The identification of the selected base year for hydro fluorocarbons (HFCs), per fluorocarbons (PFCs) and sulphur hexafluoride ($SF_6$);
- The Party's calculation of its assigned amount;

- The identification of the parameters related to the accounting of LULUCF activities (minimum value for tree crown cover, land area and tree height);
- The identification of the accounting period for each activity;
- A description of the Party's national system; and
- A description of the Party's national registry.

The first annual report under the Kyoto Protocol is due on 15 April 2010, 2010 being the year of submission of national inventories for the first year of the commitment period. At this time, submission of the annual report containing the national GHG inventory, and the supplementary information required by the Kyoto Protocol becomes mandatory. However, because the provision of certain information is required to maintain eligibility to participate in the Kyoto mechanisms, the Kyoto Protocol recognizes that Parties may voluntarily submit annual reports in advance of the formal 2010 submission date.

### Disclosure of CERs

- Disclosure is required in notes on accounts that procedure adopted for measurement and recognition of profit or loss either through P&L account or through revaluation reserve account.
- Disclosure is similarly required for measurement and profit or loss recognition of acquired/purchased CERs.
- Disclosure is required in notes on accounts for restriction if any imposed on trading of CERs by some authority.

## REFERENCES

Adukia, R. (2009), *Clean Development Mechanism and Carbon Credits.* Professional Development Committee, ICAI, Sahitya Bhawan Publication, Agra, p. 39.

Agrawal, S.K. (2006), "Accounting and taxation aspects of carbon trading". *The Chartered Accountant Journal of ICAI*, October, pp. 511-12.

Balkrishnan, N. (2010), "Accounting for carbon credit/CER". *KPMG in India*, p. 6.

Bhanawat, Shurveer S. (2011), Carbon Credit Trading: Taxation Issues, *34th All India Accounting Conference Proceeding*, Jaipur.

——. (2012), "Carbon Credit Trading: Accounting Issues", *Rajasthan Economic Journal*, Vol. 35, No. 1 & 2, January and July, pp. 79-87.

Chouhan, V. (2011), Carbon credit accounting: Unravelling accounting and taxation issues, 34th *India Accounting Conference Proceeding*, Jaipur.

Exposure draft on accounting for self-generated CERs. *Accounting Standard Board, ICAI.*

J. Ganatra. (2010), Carbon credit. *Accounting and Auditing Update*, KPMG in India, May, pp. 10-11.

Jones, J.G. (2008), Accounting for carbon: The impact of carbon trading on financial statement. *KPMG LLP* (U.K.), p. 3.

Maheswari, M.C. (2010), "Carbon credits: A Hot business opportunity in global warming". *The Chartered Accountant Student—Students Journal of ICAI*, February, p. 19.

Retrieved from www.slideshare.net/ramesh-sankhel/carbon-credit-direct-tax-issue. (2011).

(2008, October 16). Retrieved from www.hindubusinessline.com.

# 18

# CARBON CREDIT IN INDIA

–*Veerta Tantia* and *Kavitha Jayakumara*

## Introduction

The term Carbon Credit has been coined in response to the concern of global warming and climate change. One of the major reasons for global warming is the failure of ozone layer to protect the earth's atmosphere from ultra-violet rays. This failure is because of industrial pollution and some substances being emitted in the atmosphere by virtue of human activities. This global warming cause many changes in the climatic conditions that will make our earth unfit for living. To address the issue of global warming, the United Nations Framework Convention on Climate Change (UNFCCC) was adopted in 1992, with the objective of limiting the concentration of Green House Gases (GHG) in the atmosphere. Subsequently the Kyoto Protocol came into force in February 2005, which sets limits to the maximum amount of mission of GHG by countries. The Kyoto Protocol at present commits 41 developed countries (known as Annex I countries) to reduce their GHG emissions by at least 5% below their 1990 baseline emission by the period of 2008-12. As per the Kyoto Protocol developing and least-developed countries are not bound by the amount of GHG emissions. With large number of entities in India generating carbon credits and the carbon credits being a relatively new area, a need is required to provide important aspects of carbon credit.

## Objective

The development of carbon markets worldwide has created a host of challenges for companies. As carbon markets is evolving and incorporating new elements, additional accounting challenges will continue to emerge. Our scope of study will consider the following:

1. Carbon Credit Mechanism
2. Accounting concept
3. Taxation laws
4. Initiatives towards to low carbon

## Research Methodology

Looking into requirements of the objectives of the study the research design employed for the study is of descriptive type. Keeping in view of the set objectives, this research design was adopted to have greater accuracy and in-depth analysis of the research study. Available secondary data was extensively used for the study. Different news articles, books, journals and web were used.

## Carbon Credit Mechanism

Kyoto Protocol provides three market-based mechanisms:

- **Joint Implementation (JI):** Under JI, a developed country with a relatively high cost of domestic GHG reduction can set up a project in another developed country that has a relatively low cost and earn carbon credits that may be applied to their emission targets.
- **Clean Development Mechanism (CDM):** Under CDM, a developed country can take up a GHG reduction project activity in a developing country where the cost of GHG reduction is usually much lower and the developed country would be given carbon credits for meeting its emission reduction targets. In case of CDM, entities in developing/least developed countries can set up a GHG reduction project, get it approved by UNFCCC and earn carbon credits. Such carbon credits generated can be bought by entities of developed countries with emission reduction targets. The unit associated with CDM is Certified Emission Reduction (CER) where one CER is equal to one metric tonne of carbon dioxide equivalent.
- **International Emission Trading (IET):** Under IET, developed countries with emission reduction targets can simply trade in the international carbon credit market. This mechanism of buying and selling carbon credits is known as carbon trading.

Carbon credits are measured and traded in units of Certified Emission Reductions (CER). Each CER is equivalent to one tonne of carbon dioxide reduction. CER are in the form of certificates, just like a stock. A CER is given by the CDM Executive Board to projects in developing countries to certify that they have reduced greenhouse gas emissions by one tonne of carbon dioxide per year. To be eligible for CDM benefits, the proposed project must have the feature of additionality, i.e., the CDM project must provide reductions in emissions that are additional to that would occur in the absence of the project. An entity undertaking a CDM project activity to earn revenue needs to go through several stages. These are described below:

(i) **Registration/Accreditation of the Project.** An entity needs to get the project registered with the CDM Executive Board of the UNFCCC. To do so, it needs to develop a Project Design Document (PDD) which contains the description of the proposed CDM project. The entity also needs an approval from the Designated National Authority (DNA). India's DNA is the National CDM Authority (NCDMA). Once approved by the DNA, the proposed project is required to be validated by a Designated Operational Entity (DOE). DOE submits the validation report and all the other necessary documents to the CDM Executive Board. If within 8 weeks no request for review of the proposed CDM project is received by UNFCCC, the project is automatically registered.

(ii) **Monitoring, Verification and Issuance of CER.** The performance of the CDM project is monitored and verified periodically to determine whether emission reductions have taken place before the CDM Executive Board can issue CER. After successful verification, the DOE (DOE which is different from the one involved in the first stage) submits the verification report and other relevant documents to the Executive Board and requests for issuance of CER. UNFCCC issuses CER are certified and issued to the entity.

(iii) **Sale/Trade.** The CER obtained by the entity may be sold to those who need it.

### Accounting Concept

Institute of Chartered Accountants of India (ICAI) has issued guidance note on accounting for Self-generated CER which are:

### Recognition

- While undertaking the project for reduction in carbon emission, cost incurred on research and development should be accounted for as enumerated in AS 26 for intangible assets. Cost incurred on receiving CER is measured with certainty at the time of incurring those expenses whereas revenue recognition will happen only at the time of sale of CER.
- When the CER are in the approval stage, these should be accounted for as per the provisions of AS 29 as Contingent Assets, and once approved, should be recorded in the books as an intangible asset.
- In case an enterprise possess CER to be traded in the ordinary course of business, i.e., the enterprise would hold the asset as 'available for sale', the same should be accounted for as Inventory under provisions of AS 2.

### Measurement

- As stated above, CER are inventories for an entity the valuation principles will be followed as prescribed in AS 2. As per AS 2, inventories should be valued at the lower of cost and net realisable value.
- For the generation of CER, the generating entity may create certain intangible and tangible assets. Insofar as expenditure on research and development is concerned, the entity should apply AS 26, Intangible Assets.
- In some cases, an entity may use a tangible asset to reduce emissions. In respect of such equipments/devices, the provisions of the AS 10, (Revised) Tangible Fixed Assets will be applied.

### Disclosure

An entity should disclose the following information relating to certified emission rights in the financial statements:

(a) No. of CER held as inventory and the basis of valuation.

(b) No. of CER under certification.

(c) Depreciation and operating and maintenance costs of Emission Reduction equipment expensed during the year.

An entity should apply this Guidance Note for accounting periods beginning on or after April 01, 2012.

### Taxation on Carbon Credit

Income from sale of CER should be accounted for under the head 'Business and Profession'. However, in case of sale of intangible, it would be taxable under the head 'Capital Gains' though most companies in India are recording earnings from carbon credit trading as Income from 'Other Sources' currently. Claims for concessional rate of taxation should also be made if credit is held for more than 36 months immediately preceding the date of transfer. This gives an opportunity to take a decision about timings of sale of such credits, keeping a balance between cash flow needs, interest factor and difference in rate of tax between long-term and short-term holdings. As there would be no cost of acquisition for self-generated CER credits, Section 55(2) of the Income Tax Act will come into operation, and total sale consideration will be liable for Capital Gains Tax (long-term/short-term) according to the period of holding Trading in CER is carried out either in spot market or in futures. Service tax could be applicable on account of dealing in CER on the exchange platform, and in case of contracts resulting in delivery, VAT could be applicable. Typically, carbon credits in India are sold to overseas buyers; hence, there would be no VAT applicable on these goods. Thus, sale of CER to overseas buyers should qualify as exports. However, there is no explicit mention made in this regard by the revenue authorities. Further, in light of India undergoing a revolutionary amendment from regulatory perspective, like the proposed Direct Taxes Code, 2010, Goods and Service Tax, IFRS, etc., the position and treatment of carbon credits would have to be commented accordingly.

### Initiatives towards to Low Carbon

To support global climate change efforts in 2008, India announced a National Action Plan on Climate Change (NAPCC). The plan prioritizes energy efficiency gains and an increased substitution of conventional fuels with renewable energy as key milestones to achieving sustainable economic growth and climate change co-benefits. Two market-based mechanisms were introduced to address these goals: Renewable Energy Certificate (REC) schemes and the Perform Achieve and Trade (PAT).

In March 2011, India's REC mechanism was introduced to support the country's Renewable Purchase Obligations (RPOs) targets under the NAPCC. The RPOs require that 5 per cent of the nationwide share of electricity be sourced from renewable energy in 2010, increasing at 1 per cent per year for ten years. In addition to taking actions, to meet the targets eligible participants may buy or trade RECs. RECs are issued to eligible renewable energy operators and purchased at monthly auctions by any obligated entity not reaching its RPO requirements. The India Energy Exchange (IEX) and Power Exchange India Ltd. (PXIL) provide the auction platforms. As of December 31, 2011, 341 renewable energy generation projects had been accredited by State Nodal Agencies across India. This represents a combined 1,890 MW or 9.4 per cent of the country's total renewable energy generation installed capacity, according to data from the Central Electricity Regulatory Commission (CERC).

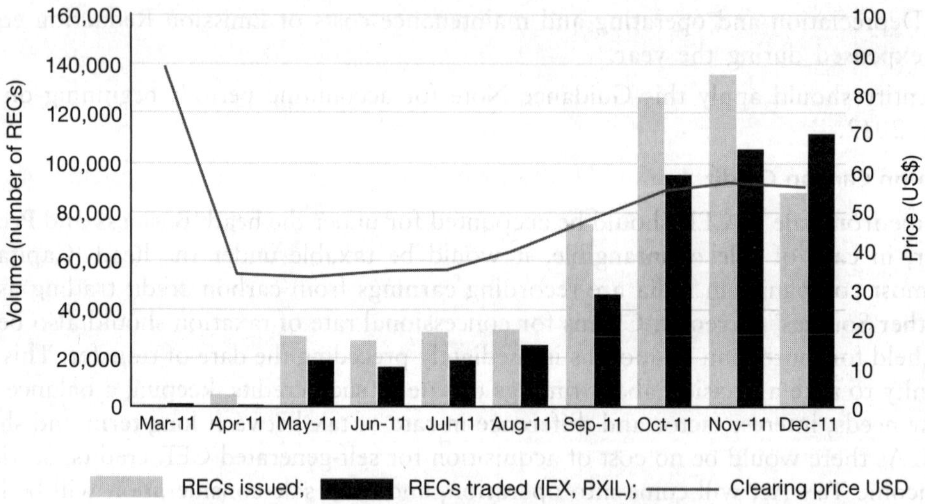


**Fig. 1:** Renewable Energy Certificates—traded volumes and clearing prices.

*Source*: World Bank, data from IEX, PXIL, and India REC Registry.

As shown in Fig. 1,546,808 RECs were issued in India's registry in 2011, and 438,249 were purchased on exchanges and subsequently retired for compliance. The resulting 2011 market value was US$22.6 million. Since April 2012, the CERC has fixed new floor and ceiling prices for non-solar and solar RECs which will remain valid for a period of five years. The floor and ceiling prices are intended to provide market participants with longer-term visibility and a competitive alternative to the Clean Development Mechanism (CDM) given current weak prices.

On April 1, 2012, the PAT was introduced, covering eight industrial sectors identified in the NAPCC's National Mission on Enhanced Energy Efficiency (NNEEE). The scheme mandates specific energy consumption reduction targets to designated consumers (DCs) that collectively account for 25 per cent of national GDP and about 45 per cent of its commercial energy use. Those DCs that over-achieve on their benchmarks are issued Energy Efficiency Certificates (ESCerts) to be traded bilaterally or through the two national power exchanges. The Bureau of Energy Efficiency at India's Power Ministry has issued the rules and procedures pertaining to measuring, reporting, and verification (MRV). The PAT is projected to avoid 19,000 MW of additional generation capacity, save 6.6 million tons oil equivalent (toe), and reduce GHG emissions by 26.21 MtCO2e by the end of the first compliance period (March 31, 2015). Using support provided through the World Bank's Partnership for Market Readiness, India has plans to expand the PAT by deepening the scope of coverage in existing sectors and extending it to new sectors.

## Conclusion

Environmental restrictions and activities have been imposed on businesses through regulation. Many are uneasy with this approach to managing emissions. In the meantime, there are numerous companies currently impacted by carbon emissions (and likely many more in the near future). The recent times have witnessed a rise in the number of transactions involving carbon trading. With India being an important partner in such transactions, the Accounting Standards Board of Institute of Chartered Accountants of India (ICAI) has formulated this Guidance Note on Accounting for Self-generated Certified Emission Reductions (CER) to provide guidance on the accounting issues involved in such transactions. Carbon accounting does assess the carbon footprint to help organizations adopt strategies aimed at fighting climate change. Attention to accounting and taxation policy regarding carbon credits can provide positive contribution the societal discourse about environmental degradation and also provide us platform to take steps for achieving sustainable economic growth and climate change co-benefits.

## REFERENCES

Accounting for carbon, IETA.

Bothra Nidhi, "Carbon Credits—Unravelling Regulatory, Taxation & Accounting Issues".

Kerr Stephen G., Bradley University, USA, "Accounting Policy and Carbon Credits", *Journal of Business & Economics Research*—August 2008 Volume 6.

Murray, E.V., "The emerging market for carbon trading: a new business opportunity for banks", Cab calling Oct-Dec, 2007.

PROTOCOL, 16th October 2008.

The Chartered Accountant October 2006.

http://carbonukcredit.blogspot.com/carbon accounting and disclosure in India, May 17, 2011.

http://carbonukcredit.blogspot.com/May 6, 2011.

http://en.wikipedia.org/wiki/Carbon_credit

http://siteresources.worldbank.org/INTCARBONFINANCE/ResourcesState_and_Trends_2012_Web_Optimized_19035_Cvr&Txt_LR.pdf

http://sivanesh.com/?p=294

http://www.articles.timesofindia.indiatimes.com-Accounting norms on C-credit from July 1, Namrata Singh, TNN, June 13, 2009.

http://www.deloitte.com/energysolutions

http://www.epcandi.com/Default.aspx,Shailendra Sharma, Sept. 2011.

http://www.globaladvisors.in/carboncredits.htm

http://www.ijrcm.org.in

http://www.itatonline.org/info/?dl_id=791

http://www.scribd.com (Presentation by J.K. Dadoo, Secretary (Environment)-cum-Chairman (DPCC), Govt. of NCT of Delhi, CARBON CREDITS AND KYOTO.

http://www.wikipedia.com

19

# CARBON CREDIT TRADING (SPECIAL REFERENCE TO SALE OF CARBON CREDIT)

*–Ravi Mandot* and *Gaurav Mandot*

**Introduction**

Day-to-day the cycle of climate on earth is warming and led to season shifting, changing landscape, rising sea levels, increased risk of drought and flood, stronger storms, increase in health related illness and disease all over world. This warming is largely due to emission of carbon dioxide and other greenhouse gases from human activities including industrial processes, fossil fuel combustion and deforestation, etc.

The protections of environment become a big issue now-a-days. This issue have gained paramount importance in the political, industrial and social circles globally. The though process of protection of environment started two decades back and more than 2500 scientists made a joint research in nineties and found that the average temperature of earth may be increased by 6.5 degree Fahrenheit by 2100.

Burning of fossil fuel is a major source of industrial greenhouse gas emission, especially for power, cement, steel, textile, fertilizer and many other industries which relay fossil fuel. Some GHGs (hydro fluorocarbon, methane and nitrous oxide) are adversely affecting the ozone layer, leading to global warming. The simplest way to control the GHGs is to stop using fossil fuels. But this is neither practically feasible nor commercially viable. A common viable plan has thus been devised to systematically reduce the emission of GHGs. This process is known as carbon trading.

Carbon credit trading is a key constituent of national and international emission trading norms that have been implemented to ease global warming. Carbon credit is like sanction that allows an entity to emit a specified quantity of GHGs. Credit can be exchanged between businesses and traded in international market at a prevailing market price.

Carbon credit trading is a initial idea about tradable right to control pollution was coined by Canadian economist John Dales in 1968 later implementation of Kyoto Protocol from 15th February 2005, had constructed a ground for Clean Development Mechanism (CDM) to mitigate the climate change.

In March, 2006. The Kyoto Protocol's CDM was implemented by forwarding the CERs to the holding account of a project participants by CDM registry administrator of United Nations. Hence, it is construed that first carbon trading took place in March, 2006.

The concepts of carbon credit serve dual purpose of protection of nature and as a source of revenue generation for a developing and underdeveloped countries. Carbon credits are measured in unit of certified emission reduction (CER).

Carbon credit trading creates a market for reducing greenhouse gases emission by giving monetary value to the cost of polluting the air. Carbon credits are reductions of emissions of greenhouse gases caused by a project or a product utilized by anybody which directly or indirectly reduces greenhouse gases. Currently this reduction is measured in terms of carbon-dioxide reduced.

1 Carbon Credit = 1 Ton of Carbon Dioxide Reduction

The concept of carbon credits came into existence as a result of increasing awareness of the need for pollution control. They provide a way to reduce greenhouse emissions on an industrial scale by reducing total annual emissions and letting the market assign a monetary value to any shortfall through trading. Credits can be used to finance carbon reduction schemes between trading partners and around the world. It was formalized in the Kyoto Protocol, an international agreement between 169 countries. Carbon credits are certificates awarded to countries that are successful in reducing emissions of greenhouse gases.

### Kyoto Protocol—The Birth of Carban Credit Trading

The Kyoto Protocol is an amendment to the international treaty of United Nations Framework Convention on Climate Changes (UNFCCC) which is a legally binding agreement under which more than 169 industrialized countries have agreed to reduce greenhouse gas emissions. The Kyoto Protocol was adopted in Kyoto; Japan on December 10, 1997 with the objective of tackling climate change by reducing greenhouse gas emission which were identified to be responsible for global warming. The treaty was opened for signature on March 16, 1998, and closed on March 15, 1999. The agreement came into force on February 16, 2005, following ratification by Russia on November 18, 2004. Under which the industrialised countries will reduce their collective emissions of greenhouse gases by 5.2 per cent over the 2008 to 2012 period relative to their 1990 levels. This is the first phase target. The target for second phase is yet to be decided.

Protocol highlights:

- As of November 2007, 175 parties have ratified the protocol.
- India acceded to the Kyoto Protocol on 26th August 2002.
- As of December 2007, U.S. and Kazakhstan are the only signatory nations not to have ratified the protocol.

(US did not ratify the protocol because the developing countries were exempted from the emission norms even when China is the 3rd largest emitter of carbon dioxide. Other economic analysis, however, prepared by the Congressional Budget Office and the Department of Energy Info Administration, demonstrated a potentially large loss to GDP from implementing the Protocol of up to 4.2 per cent).

The protocol aim is to lower overall emissions of six greenhouse gases. Table 1 lists the gases and their relative strength to carbon.

Table 1: Kyoto Protocol greenhouse gasses, chemical composition and Global Warming Potential*

| Gas | Chemical composition | Global warming potential |
|---|---|---|
| Carbon dioxide | ($CO_2$) | 1 |
| Methane | ($CH_4$) | 21 |
| Nitrous oxide | ($N_2O$) | 310 |
| Hydrofluoric carbons | (HFCs) | 11,700 |
| Perfluoro carbons | (PFCs) | 6500 – 9200 |
| Sulphur hexafluoride | ($SF_6$) | 23900 |

* A factor describing the radioactive forcing impact (degree of harm to the atmosphere) of one unit of a given GHG relative to one unit of $CO_2$.

Under Kyoto Protocol, Members countries are divided into two categories:

1. Developed countries who have accepted GHG emission reduction obligations and must submit annual greenhouse gas inventory account. (Annex 1 countries)
2. Developing countries who have no GHG emission reduction obligation but may participate in the clean development mechanism. (Non-Annex 1 countries)

### Kyoto Mechanism (How to Reduce Greenhouse Gases?)

The Kyoto Protocol provides for three mechanisms that enable developed countries with quantified emission limitation and reduction commitments to acquire greenhouse gas reduction credits. The following three mechanisms are available to developed countries to reduce greenhouse gases at target level:

- Joint Implementation (JI)
- Clean Development Mechanism (CDM)
- International Emission Trading (IET)

### Joint Implementation

Under JI, a developed country with relatively higher cost of domestic greenhouse reduction would set up a project in another developed country, which has relatively low cost. Hence, under joint implementation, project is implemented by a developed country in another developed country to meet out their emission reduction targets. The credit generated out of JI is called as Emission Reduction Unit (ERU).

The two procedures to implement JI Projects:

- When developed country meet all the eligibility and reporting requirement under the Kyoto Protocol. It can issue ERUs to a project, which can then transfer them to the investing entity.

- When developed country is not in compliance with all the requirements, ERUs generated by a project must be verified by an external body under a procedure. The other developed country must meet several requirements relating to the establishment of its assigned amount and national registry before it can issue and transfer ERUs.

**Clean Development Mechanism (CDM)**

Under CDM, a developed country which has specific obligation to reduce GHG emission reduction can take up a greenhouse gas reduction project activity in a developing country where the cost of GHG reduction project activities is usually much lower. The developed country would be given Credit (Carbon credit) for meeting its emission reduction targets, while the developing country would receive the capital and clean technology to implement the project.

These two countries entities may enter into an agreement for the CDM project in the developing country for the reduction of gas emission. The credit in CDM project is termed as Certified Emission Reduction (CERs). Such emission reduction has to be certified by an appropriate authority under the protocol and then the CERs are transferred ton investing country to meet their commitment of gas emission under Kyoto Protocol. Developed countries have to spend nearly $300-500 for every tonne reduction in carbon dioxide, against $10-25 to be spent by developing countries.

**International Emission Trading (IET)**

The developed nations can reduce their emission as per Kyoto agreements through international emission trading mechanism. The developing countries can receive certificate for reducing their emission for greenhouse gases. The surplus carbon credit can be sold to developed nations who fail to reduce their emission as per Kyoto agreement. Countries can trade in the international carbon credit market. Countries with surplus credit can sell the same to countries with qualified emission limitation and reduction commitment under Kyoto Protocol.

These three mechanisms are designed to help developed countries cut the cost of meeting their emissions targets by taking advantage of opportunities to reduce emissions, or increase greenhouse gas removals, that cost less in other countries than at home. To participate in the mechanisms, developed countries must meet the following eligibility requirements:

- They must have ratified the Kyoto Protocol.
- They must have calculated their assigned amount, as referred to the Protocol in terms of tonnes of $CO_2$ equivalent emissions.
- They must have in place a national system for estimating emissions and removals of greenhouse gases within their territory.
- They must have in place a national registry to record and track the creation and movement of ERUs, CERs, AAUs and RMUs and must annually report such information to the secretariat.
- They must annually report information on emissions and removals to the secretariat.

**Objective of Study**

The main objective of this research is to study the various sectors/companies which can benefits from carbon credits and explain concept and meaning of carbon credits.

## Scope of the Study

The scope of carbon credit trading is broad. Many Indian companies follow carbon credit trading through CDM projects. In research study, I considered four companies which earn revenue from carbon credits. These companies are:

- RSMML (Rajasthan state mines and minerals limited)
- Shree Cement Limited
- Jaiprakash Power Venture Limited
- Sesa Goa Limited.

## Methodology

Data's were collected both primary and secondary sources, Annual reports and Interviews were the main source of collection of data which were provided both the financial and quantitative information about the company and views about the income from sale of CERs from the respondents.

To carry out the objective of this study, various tools and techniques like Mean, Coefficient of variance, Geometric Mean and 't' test, would be used.

## Hypothesis

The following hypothesis are formulate for this study:

$H_0$ = There is no significant difference among share of sale of CERs to total revenue of different sample units.

## Data Analysis and Interpretation

**1. Rajasthan State Mines and Minerals Limited (RSMML):** The RSMML earn income from sale of carbon credits or CERs for last five years. The individual year income has been showed in following Table 1.

**Table 1:** Income from CERs

(in Crores)

| Year | Income from sale of CERs | Total income | Percentage (%) |
|---|---|---|---|
| 2006-2007 | 3.50 | 565.44 | .619 |
| 2007-2008 | 4.17 | 643.37 | .648 |
| 2008-2009 | 4.37 | 975.43 | .448 |
| 2009-2010 | 0.85 | 951.29 | .089 |
| 2010-2011 | 2.82 | 1125.00 | .251 |

**Mean** $(\overline{X})$ = 3.14

**C.V.** = 40.44%

**Geometric Mean** = 0.3314

The RSMML generated average income of CERs worth ₹ 3.14 crore during five years and the annual average growth rate (G.M.) has been noticed .3314 during the present study period. The variation in income from sale of CERs has been noticed 40.44 per cent during five years.

**2. Jaiprakash Power Venture Limited:** The Jaiprakash Power Venture Limited earns income from sale of carbon credits or VERs for last three years. The individual year income has been showed in following Table 2.

**Table 2:** Income from VERs

(in Crores)

| Year | Income from sale of VERs | Total income | Percentage (%) |
|---|---|---|---|
| 2008-2009 | 7.79 | 319.91 | 2.45 |
| 2009-2010 | 41.12 | 717.79 | 5.73 |
| 2010-2011 | 38.21 | 840.74 | 4.54 |

**Mean** $(\overline{X})$ = 29.04

**C.V.** = 51.90%

**Geometric Mean** = 3.994

The Jaiprakash Power Venture Limited generated average income of VERs worth ₹ 29.04 crore during three years and the annual average growth rate (G.M.) has been noticed 3.994 during the present study period. The variation in income from sale of VERs has been noticed 51.90 per cent during three years.

**3. Shree Cement Limited:** The Shree Cement Limited earns income from sale of carbon credits or CERs for last four years. The individual year income has been showed in following Table 3.

**Table 3:** Income from CERs

(in Crores)

| Year | Income from sale of CERs | Total income | Percentage (%) |
|---|---|---|---|
| 2007-2008 | 16.02 | 2139.13 | .749 |
| 2008-2009 | 17.84 | 2797.92 | .637 |
| 2009-2010 | 8.62 | 3707.96 | .232 |
| 2010-2011 | Nil | – | – |

**Mean** $(\overline{X})$ = 14.16

**C.V.** = 28.18%

**Geometric Mean** = 0.4801

The Shree Cement Limited generated average income of CERs worth ₹ 14.16 crore during three years and the annual average growth rate (G.M.) has been noticed 0.4801 during the present study period. The variation in income from sale of CERs has been noticed 28.18 per cent during three years.

**4. Sesa Goa Limited:** The Sesa Goa Limited earns income from sale of carbon credits or CERs for last three years. The individual year income has been showed in following Table 4.

**Table 4: Income from CERs**

(in Crores)

| Year | Income from sale of CERs | Total income | Percentage (%) |
|---|---|---|---|
| 2008-2009 | 2.76 | 4996.23 | .055 |
| 2009-2010 | Nil | – | – |
| 2010-2011 | 4.44 | 8008.28 | .055 |

Mean ($\overline{X}$) = 3.6

C.V. = 23.33%

Geometric Mean = 0.055

The Sesa Goa Limited generated average income of CERs worth ₹ 3.6 crore during two years and the annual average growth rate (G.M.) has been noticed 0.055 during the present study period. The variation in income from sale of CERs has been noticed 23.33 per cent during two years.

**'T' test on different sample units mean**

| S.N. | Name of company | Mean ($\overline{X}$) | μ | 't' value | Critical value | $H_0$ |
|---|---|---|---|---|---|---|
| 1. | RSMML | 3.14 | 12.485 | 14.73 | 2.776 | Rejected |
| 2. | Jaiprakash Power Venture Ltd. | 29.04 | 12.485 | 1.553 | 4.303 | Accepted |
| 3. | Shree Cement Ltd. | 14.16 | 12.485 | 0.593 | 4.303 | Accepted |
| 4. | Sesa Goa Ltd. | 3.6 | 12.485 | 10.57 | 12.706 | Accepted |

## Conclusion and Finding

**Mean and co-efficient of variation of different sample units**

| S.N. | Name of company | Mean | Co-efficient of variation |
|---|---|---|---|
| 1. | RSMML | 3.14 | 40.44% |
| 2. | Jaiprakash Power Venture Limited | 29.04 | 51.90% |
| 3. | Shree Cement Limited | 14.16 | 28.18% |
| 4. | Sesa Goa Limited | 3.6 | 23.33% |

The above Table expressed average amount of income generated from sale of CERs/VERs and co-efficient of variation from different sample units.

The Jaiprakash Power Venture Limited reported highest average income of CERs/VERs while Sesa Goa Limited lowest average income of CERs/VERs.

As far as range of Mean income from sale of CERs/VERs is concerned, it is ₹ 25.44 (29.04–3.6).

The highest variation in income from sale of CERs/VERs has been noticed in Jaiprakash Power Venture Limited as it is evident by highest C.V. that is 51.90 per cent, it is clearly indicates that there is very much fluctuation in generating CERs income as compared to other sample units.

**According to analysis of 't' test:** In the RSMML, the $H_0$ is rejected because calculated value of 't' (14.73) is greater than the table value (2.776) at 5 per cent level of significance, it indicates that visible difference between mean value of revenue from sale of CERs of RSMML and parameter is due to major reasons, not due to sampling fluctuation. It implies that the RSMML generated significant revenue from sale of CERs as compared to other units of selected samples.

In Jaiprakash Power Venture Limited, Shree Cement Ltd. and Sesa Goa Ltd., the $H_0$ is accepted because calculated value of 't' is less than the table value at 5 per cent level of significance, it indicates that visible difference between mean value of revenue from sale of CERs and parameter is due to sampling fluctuation, not due to major reasons. It implies that the companies generated significant revenue from sale of CERs as compared to other units of selected samples.

## REFERENCES

Adukia, R. (2009). *Clean Development Mechanism and Carbon Credits*. Professional Development Committee ICAI, Sahitya Bhawan Publication, Agra, pp. 3-4.

Bhanawat, Shurveer S. (2011). Carbon credit trading: Taxation issues. *34th All India Accounting Conference Proceeding*, Jaipur.

Chakraborty, D. (2008). "Clean development mechanism and carbon credit: A new challenge for Indian industries". *The Chartered Accountant Journal of ICAI,* October, pp. 650-52.

Raveendran, K. (2008). Carbon trading: Minting money out of clean air. *ICFAI Reader*, ICFAI University Press, August, pp. 52-53.

www.indiainfoline.com.

20

# HUMAN RESOURCES ACCOUNTING—EVOLVING CONCEPTS AND MEASURING VALUE OF EMPLOYEES

–*Bharti Pandya* and *N.K. Pandya*

**Introduction**

Researches have proved time and time again that animate resources (human resources) have always activated inanimate resources (physical resources). The efficiency and effectiveness of inanimate resources depends mainly on quality, creative abilities, innovative thinking, intuition, imagination, knowledge, experience, skills, caliber, perception and character of human resources, as physical resources cannot act on their own. This necessitates treatment of human resources as assets like physical and financial assets because animate resources are the real assets for a firm. It has become vital to value human resources.

Human Resource Accounting is comparatively a new concept for HR and Accounting professionals and it can be better understood through following definitions:

American Accounting Association (1973)—"Human Resource Accounting is the process of identifying and measuring data about human resources and communicating this information to interested parties."

Woodruff Jr., Vice President of R.G. Batty Corporation—"Human Resource Accounting is an attempt to identify and report investments made in human resources of an organization that are presently not accounted for in conventional accounting practice. Basically it is information system that tells the management what changes over time are occurring to the human resources of the business."

Flamholtz and Lace (1981)—"Human resource accounting may be defined as the measurement and reporting of the cost and value of people as organizational resources. It involves accounting for investment in people and their replacement costs, as well as accounting for the economic values of people to an organization."

Basically, human resource accounting attempts to identify, quantify, measure, record and disclose human resources in the financial statements of the business. Human resource accounting makes decision-making more efficient and effective as it helps in employment, utilizing human resources, transfers, promotion, training, retrenchment, human resource planning, cost-benefit analysis of training, analyze labor turnover and to evaluate long-term employee's investment.

Human Resource accounting is mainly done to collect cost information related to acquisition, allocation, development and maintenance of human resources. It facilitates human resources valuation and presentation of the same in corporate financial statements. It makes decisions for recruitment, manpower utilization, reallocation, budget controls more effective.

**Review of Literature**

The concept of human capital is not a recent discovery. Its origin dates back to the late seventeenth century when the economists, Sir William Petty first attempted to estimate the monetary value of population of England in 1681. He considered labor as the father of wealth and stressed that it should be included in the estimate of the total national wealth. The credit for recognizing the value of human resources as an asset goes to Paton (1962). When he commented, "in a business a well-organized and loyal personnel may be a more important asset than a stock of merchandise". The fact remains; however, that it was Likert (1967), Social Psychologist, The institute for Social Research, University of Michigan, who first use the term 'human asset' a term since replaced by human resources. Therefore, he originally developed it. Different techniques have been developed to measure the value of human resources. The original cost model of Brummet et al. (1968) suggested to capitalize the firm's expenditure on recruitment, selection, training and development of human resources, amortizing such costs over a period and hence reporting the net investment in human resources in the Balance Sheet under the heading Human Assets. R.G. Barry corporation of U.S.A. during 1968-74 implemented this method for valuation of human resources and reported this information externally. Replacement cost approach was developed by Likert and Flamholtz in 1973. The cost of alternative use of employee is value of human resources as per this approach. Hekimian and Jones (1967) gives an Opportunity Cost Approach based on the principle that human assets will be valued while it is scarce. Hermanson (1964) proposed an adjusted present value model to quantify the value of human capital of a company. He suggested that the amount of future wages payable represents a liability while human resources as an asset in the Balance Sheet. Lev and Schwartz (1971) valued human capital as the present value of future earnings of employee till retirement. Flamholtz (1971) developed Stochastic Rewards Valuation model and determined the value of human assets by aggregating the present value of expected future services of employees. Jaggi and Lau (1974) model considers groups for valuation rather than individuals. As per Giles and Robinsons (1972) Human Asset Multiplier Model the capitalized value of the company calculated on the basis of price earnings ratio minus net assets are the human resources. Morse (1973) in his net benefit method considers that human resources value is equal to the present value of the gross value of services to be rendered by human beings minus present value of the future payments to human beings. Ogan's (1976) suggested a model known as "Certainty Equivalent Net Benefit Model" that is the extension of net benefit model of Morse. Certainty with which the net benefit in future will accrue to the organization is the value of human resources. Chakraborty (1976) suggested a model for valuation of human resources known as Aggregate Payment Approach. The value of human resources is calculated by multiplying the average salary with the average tenure of the employee. Dasgupta (1978) also gives his total cost concept to value the human resources. Likert (1967), Flamholtz (1972), Myer's and Flowers (1974), suggested the non-monetary approaches for assessing the economic value of human resources that measures the human resources not in dollar or money terms rather they rely on various indices or ratings and rankings. Different studies have been conducted time to time. Elias (1972) conducted the first published research concerning the effect of human resource outlay data on stock investment decisions. For this, he selected two hypothetical companies ABC and XYZ operating in the same industry. Two different sets of financial statements were prepared and supplied to the Chartered Financial Analysts, certified Public Accountants and accounting students asking them to choose the company for their investment based on the analysis of the given financial statements. The choice decision of the respondents varied when the HRA information along with the traditional information was supplied. This shows the importance of providing HRA data in addition to conventional data. Gambling (1974) suggested a system dynamics approach to human resource accounting considering an organization as a dynamic system with feedbacks. Flamholtz (1976) carried out an experimental study of the impact of human resource valuation on managerial decision-making. He found significant differences in decisions taken by those who used traditional trait evaluations relative to those who used two types of HRA data. Schwan (1976) studied the effects of human resource cost measures on banker making decision-making. For the purpose of his study, the participants were managers and analysts employed in investment, credit and trust departments of large banks. Schwan found that the inclusion of HRA data in published statements resulted in significantly different ratings of management's preparedness to meet the future challenges and opportunities and statistically different predictions of a firms 'net income'. Tomassini (1977) in his study concluded that HRA cost estimates caused different managerial preferences in the personnel lay off decision context. Gul (1984) attempted to study the usefulness of human resources turnover cost information for the labor turnover decision-making in a sample of Australian Accounting firms. The results of the study concluded that human resource turnover cost information significantly reduced accountant's level of uncertainty and increased their level of relevance and sufficiency. All these studies showed the relevance of HRA information in various decisions. Gupta (1990), Bhatia and Singh (1992), Rao (1993), Batra and Bhatia (1994), Prakash (1997), Verma (1999), Patra and Khalik (2003), Sonara and Patel (2009) conducted a study to know the current status of human resource accounting in Indian Context. All these studies were conducted to find out the current practices followed by the Indian organizations for HRA. The studies concluded that very few companies come forward for reporting HRA as it is not compulsory for them to disclose human resources information in their annual reports. The present paper is an attempt to critically review the HRA practices of selected organization with a step forward to rank the organizations based on their extent of disclosure of HRA information. An attempt also been made to rank the items that companies disclosed more and the relevance of such disclosure.

## Methodology

All the information are obtained and compiled mostly from internet, overseas magazines, accounting journals, reference books, publications, scholarly articles and companies' annual reports. This paper is solely based on secondary data. In the present study, the purposive sampling technique has been used for the selection of companies. All the four companies are selected from state owned heavy industries. These organizations are considered as giant corporations on India. These companies are known to value their human resources and present these values in their annual reports. The audited annual reports from the year 2006-07 to 2010-11 were extracted from the corporate websites. Three main factors were extracted from these reports, viz., turnover, number of employees and value added.

### Results/Analysis

#### *Measurement of Human Resources*

There are several methods developed over a period of time for individuals, groups and for valuation of expense centre groups.

**Table 1:** Methods to measure Human Resources

| For Individuals Value | For Group Value | For Expense Centre Group |
|---|---|---|
| <u>Cost Methods</u><br>• Historical Cost method<br>• Replacement Cost method<br>• Opportunity Cost method<br>• Standard Cost method<br><u>Economic Value Approach</u><br>• Flamholtz's model of determinants of individual value of formal organizations<br>• Flamholtz's stochastic rewards valuation model<br>• Lev & Schwartz model<br>• Hekimian & Jones Competitive bidding model<br>• Skills inventory<br>• Performance evaluation<br>• Assessment of potential<br>• Attitude measurements | • The Likert & Bowers Model<br>• Brummet, Flamholtz, & Pyle's economic value model<br>• Hermanson's unpurchased goodwill model<br>• Human organizational dimensions method | • Capitalization of Compensation<br>• Replacement Cost Valuation<br>• Original Cost Valuation |

### Value and Strength of Human Resources—A Comparative Analysis

#### *Bharat Heavy Electricals Limited (BHEL)*

BHEL is an integrated power plant equipment manufacturer and one of the largest engineering and manufacturing companies in India in terms of turnover. It was established in 1964, ushering in the indigenous Heavy Electrical Equipment industry in India—a dream that has been more than realized with a well-recognized track record of performance. The company has been earning profits continuously since 1971-72 and paying dividends since 1976-77. It is engaged in the design, engineering, manufacture, construction, testing, commissioning and servicing of a wide range of products and services for the core sectors of the economy, viz.

Power, Transmission, Industry, Transportation, Renewable Energy, Oil & Gas and Defence. It has 15 manufacturing divisions, two repair units, four regional offices, eight service centres, eight overseas offices and 15 regional centres and currently operate at more than 150 project sites across India and abroad. Its greatest strength is its highly skilled and committed workforce of over 49,000 employees. Every employee is given an equal opportunity to develop himself and grow in his career. Continuous training and retraining, career planning, a positive work culture and participative style of management—all these have engendered development of a committed and motivated workforce setting new benchmarks in terms of productivity, quality and responsiveness.

Table 2: Value and Strength of HR in BHEL

| Year | Value of Turnover (in cr. ₹) | No. of Employees | Value per Employee (in ₹) | Value Added (in cr. ₹) |
|---|---|---|---|---|
| 2006-07 | 18,739 | 42,124 | 0.44 | 7,182 |
| 2007-08 | 21,401 | 43,636 | 0.49 | 8,323 |
| 2008-09 | 28,033 | 45,666 | 0.61 | 9,894 |
| 2009-10 | 34,154 | 46,274 | 0.74 | 13,171 |
| 2010-11 | 43,337 | 46,748 | 0.93 | 18,476 |

From Table 2, data depicts that value of turnover is increasing from year 2006-07 to 2010-11. In last five years the turnover has increased by more than 250%. We can clearly analyze that number of employees also has increased from 42,124 in 2006-07 to 46,748 in 2010-11. It is also observed that there has been continuous increase in value added. It has increased by more than two folds, ₹ 7,182 crore in year 2006-07 to ₹ 18,476 crore in year 2010-11.

### *Cement Corporation of India (CCI)*

CCI was incorporated as a Company wholly owned by Government of India on 18th January 1965 with the principal objective of achieving self-sufficiency in cement production. CCI is a multi-unit organization at present having ten units spread over eight states. In line with the advancement in cement technology CCI had been adopting the latest one with one million tonne plants at Tandur and Nayagaon. CCI manufactures various types of cements like Portland Pozzolana Cement (PPC), Portland Slag Cement (PSC) and Ordinary Portland Cement (OPC) of varying grades, viz. 33, 43, 53 and 53S (special grade cement for manufacture of sleepers for Indian Railways) grades under strict quality control with the brand name of CCI Cement. CCI with a strong workforce of 988 employees (as on 31-03-2011) has always encouraged balanced regional growth with most of its factories located in underdeveloped/backward areas.

Table 3: Value and Strength of HR in CCI

| Year | Value of Turnover (in cr. ₹) | No. of Employees | Value per employee (in ₹) | Value Added (in cr. ₹) |
|---|---|---|---|---|
| 2006-07 | 326 | 1523 | 0.21 | 201 |
| 2007-08 | 343 | 1460 | 0.23 | 203 |

| | | | | |
|---|---|---|---|---|
| 2008-09 | 367 | 1159 | 0.32 | 219 |
| 2009-10 | 363 | 1078 | 0.34 | 222 |
| 2010-11 | 333 | 988 | 0.34 | 189 |

From Table 3, data depicts that value of turnover is increasing from year 2006-07 (₹ 326 crore) to 2008-09 (₹ 367 crore). But then it has started declining reaching to ₹ 333 crore in year 2010-11. We can clearly analyze that number of employees also has decreased from 1523 in 2006-07 to 988 in 2010-11. It is also observed that there has been fluctuation in value added. It was ₹ 201 cr. in 2006-07; ₹ 203 cr. in 2007-08; ₹ 219 cr. in 2008-09; ₹ 222 cr. in 2009-10 and decreased to ₹ 189 cr. in 2010-11.

***Steel Authority of India Limited (SAIL)***

SAIL is the leading steel-making company in India. It is a fully integrated iron and steel maker, producing both basic and special steels for domestic construction, engineering, power, railway, automotive and defense industries and for sale in export markets. SAIL is also among the five Maharatnas of the country's Central Public Sector Enterprises. SAIL manufactures and sells a broad range of steel products, including hot and cold rolled sheets and coils, galvanized sheets, electrical sheets, structurals, railway products, plates, bars and rods, stainless steel and other alloy steels. SAIL produces iron and steel at five integrated plants and three special steel plants, located principally in the eastern and central regions of India and situated close to domestic sources of raw materials, including the Company's iron ore, limestone and dolomite mines. With technical and managerial expertise and know-how in steel making gained over four decades, SAIL's Consultancy Division (SAILCON) at New Delhi offers services and consultancy to clients worldwide. SAIL has its own in-house Centre for Engineering and Technology (CET), Management Training Institute (MTI) and Safety Organization at Ranchi.

**Table 4:** Value and Strength of HR in SAIL

| Year | Value of Turnover (in cr. ₹) | No. of Employees | Value per employee (in ₹) | Value Added (in cr. ₹) |
|---|---|---|---|---|
| 2006-07 | 39,189 | 132,973 | 0.29 | 17,973 |
| 2007-08 | 45,555 | 128,804 | 0.35 | 20,874 |
| 2008-09 | 48,738 | 121,295 | 0.40 | 19,407 |
| 2009-10 | 43,935 | 116,950 | 0.38 | 17,289 |
| 2010-11 | 47,041 | 110,794 | 0.42 | 16,742 |

From Table 4, data depicts that value of turnover is fluctuating in SAIL. It has increased from ₹ 39,189 cr. (2006-07) to ₹ 48,738 cr. (2008-09), then it was decreased in year 2009-10 and then increased again in 2010-11. We can clearly analyze that number of employees decreased from 132,973 in year 2006-07 to 110,794 in year 2010-11. The main reason for this decline is reorganization.

***Hindustan Copper Limited (HCL)***

HCL, a public sector undertaking under the administrative control of the Ministry of Mines, was incorporated on 9th November 1967. It has the distinction of being the nation's only vertically integrated copper producing company as it manufactures copper right from the stage of mining to beneficiation, smelting, refining and casting of refined copper metal into downstream saleable products. The Company markets copper cathodes, copper wire bar, continuous cast copper rod and by-products, such as anode slime (containing gold, silver, etc.), copper sulphate and sulphuric acid. HCL's mines and plants are spread across four operating Units, one each in the States of Rajasthan, Madhya Pradesh, Jharkhand and Maharashtra.

Table 5: Value and Strength of HR in HCL

| Year | Value of Turnover (in cr. ₹) | No. of Employees | Value per Employee (in ₹) | Value Added (in cr. ₹) |
|---|---|---|---|---|
| 2006-07 | 1800 | 5451 | 0.33 | 781 |
| 2007-08 | 1840 | 5405 | 0.34 | 726 |
| 2008-09 | 1349 | 5440 | 0.25 | 402 |
| 2009-10 | 1430 | 5300 | 0.27 | 702 |
| 2010-11 | 1258 | 5100 | 0.25 | 969 |

From Table 5, data depicts that value of turnover has been fluctuating from year 2006-07 to 2010-11. We can also analyze that number of employees also has decreased from 5451 in 2006-07 to 5405 in 2007-08, then increased to 5440 in 2008-09 and it started decreasing to 5100 in 2010-11. It is also observed value added was ₹ 781 cr. in 2006-07 and ultimately increased to ₹ 969 cr. in 2010-11.

From the above table, data depicts that value of turnover is increasing from year 2006-07 (₹ 326 crore) to 2008-09 (₹ 367 crore). But then it has started declining reaching to ₹ 333 crore in year 2010-11. We can clearly analyze that number of employees also has decreased from 1523 in 2006-07 to 988 in 2010-11. It is also observed that there has been fluctuation in value added. It was ₹ 201 cr. in 2006-07; ₹ 203 cr. in 2007-08; ₹ 219 cr. in 2008-09; ₹ 222 cr. in 2009-10 and decreased to ₹ 189 cr. in 2010-11.

### Value Per Employee—A Comparison

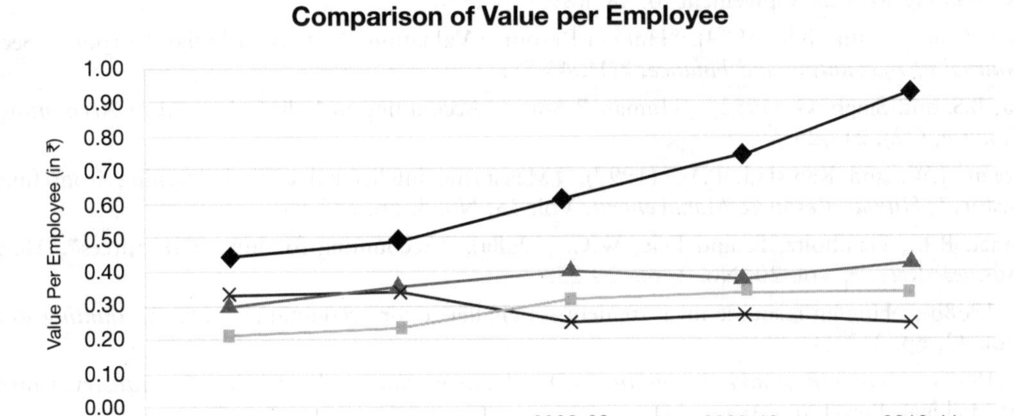


| | 2006-07 | 2007-08 | 2008-09 | 2009-10 | 2010-11 |
|---|---|---|---|---|---|
| BHEL | 0.44 | 0.49 | 0.61 | 0.74 | 0.93 |
| CCI | 0.21 | 0.23 | 0.32 | 0.34 | 0.34 |
| SAIL | 0.29 | 0.35 | 0.40 | 0.38 | 0.42 |
| HCL | 0.33 | 0.34 | 0.25 | 0.27 | 0.25 |

From the chart above, the company that has highest levels of Value per employee is BHEL. It has increased from 0.44 in 2006-07 to 0.93 in 2010-11. The next company with high value per employee after BHEL is SAIL, but it has been observed that in has increased from 0.29 in 2006-07 to 0.40 in 2008-09 and decreased to 0.38 in 2009-10, shooting back to 0.42 in 2010-11. While observing data of CCI, we can analyze that value per employee has increased from 0.21 in 2006-07 to 0.34 in 2009-10 and then remained same in 2010-2011. The value per employee in HCL was 0.33 in 2006-07, 0.34 in 2007-08, 0.25 in 2008-09, 0.27 in 2009-10 and 0.25 in 2010-11.

### Conclusion

The value that a company creates results from the way human resources apply their skills, abilities, initiatives, energies, and expertise to the physical resources of the company. It is high time to recognize this through demanding a rigorous and credible approach to both valuing this most important asset, and reflecting the same in corporate financial statements showing the benefits to stakeholders. Through literature review, we can see that the concept of Human Resources Accounting is developing, with several empirical studies and establishment of Human Resource measurement models. Though Human resources accounting has been widely accepted in western countries, but India is standing at par. With companies like BHEL, CCI, SAIL, HCL, Infosys measuring human resources is a step forward not only for the progression of HR profession but for Accounting professionals to account human resources which was considered as immeasurable three decades ago.

## REFERENCES

AAA Committee (1973), "Report of the AAA Committee on Accounting for Human Resources". *The Accounting Review*, Supplement to, 48, 189.

Batra, G.S. and Bhatia, B.S. (1994), "Human Resource Valuation: A Study of Indian Corporate Sector". *Journal of Accounting and Finance*, 8(1), 43-57.

Bhatia, B.S. and Singh, G. (1992), "Human Resource Accounting in India". *Journal of Accounting and Finance*, 6(2), 217-25.

Boudreau, J.W. and Ramstad, P.M. (1997), "Measuring intellectual capital: learning from financial history", *Human Resource Management*, Vol. 36, No. 3, pp. 343-56.

Brummet, R.L., Flamholtz, E. and Pyle, W.C. (1968a), "Accounting for human resources", *Michigan Business Review*, Vol. 20, No. 2, pp. 20-25.

——. (1968b), "Human resource measurement—a challenge for accountants", *The Accounting Review*, Vol. 43, pp. 217-24.

——. (1969a), *Human Resource Accounting—Development and Implementation in Industry*, University of Michigan Press, Ann Arbor, MI.

Brummet, R.L., Flamholtz, E., Pyle, W.C. and Likert, R. (1975), "Human Resource Accounting: Development and Implementation in Industry", *Foundation on Human Behavior*, Ann Arbor, MI.

Cascio, W.F. (2000), *Costing Human Resources: The Financial Impact of Behavior in Organizations*, 4th ed., South-Western College Publishing, Cincinnati, OH.

Chakraborty, S.K. (1976), *Human Asset Accounting: The Indian Context in Topics in Accounting and Finance*. Oxford University Press.

Dasgupta, N.D. (1978), *Human Resource Accounting*. Sultan Chand and Sons, New Delhi.

Edvinsson, L. and Malone, M.S. (1997), *Intellectual Capital: Realizing Your Company's True Value by Finding its Hidden Brainpower*, HarperBusiness, New York, NY.

Elias, N. (1972), "The Effects of Human Asset Statement on Investment Decision: An Empirical Research in Accounting". *Journal of Accounting Research* (Supplement Empirical Research in Accounting Selected Studies), 10, 215-33.

Flamholtz Eric G., "Human Resource Accounting: A Review of Theory and Research". *The Journal of Management Studies*, Feb., 1974.

Flamholtz, E.G. and Likert, E. (1973), "HRA: Measuring positional replacement costs". *Human Resource Management* 12(Spring), 8-16.

Flamholtz, E.G. (1971), "A Model for Human Resource Valuation: A Stochastic Process with Services Rewards". *Accounting Review*, 46(2), 253-67.

——. (1972), "Towards a Theory of Human Resource Value in Formal Organizations". *The Accounting Review*, 48(4), 666-78.

——. (1976), "The Impact of Human Resource Valuation on Management Decision: A Laboratory Experiment". *Accounting, Organization and Society*, 1, 153-65.

——. (1999), *Human Resource Accounting—Advances in Concepts, Methods and Applications*. Kluwer Academic, Boston, MA.

Gambling, T.E. (1974), "A System Dynamic Approach to Human Resource Accounting". *The Accounting Review*, 49(3), 538-46.

Giles, W.J. and Robinson, D.F. (1972), *Human Asset Accountants*. Institute of Personnel Management and Institute of Cost and Management Accountants, London.

Lev, B. and Schwartz, A. (1971), "On the use of the Economic Concept of Human Capital in Financial Statements". *Accounting Review*, 46(1), 103-12.

Likert, R. (1967), *The Human Organization: In Management and Value*. McGraw Hill Book Co, New York, 83-84.

Mayo, A. (2004), "Measuring human capital", *Worldwide Link*, Vol. 14, No. 2, p. 3.

Morse, W.J. (1973), "A Note on the Relationship between Human Asset and Capital". *The Accounting Review*, 37(3), 589-93.

Ogan, P.A. (1976), "Human Resource Value Model for Professional Service Organizations". *The Accounting Review*, 51(2), 306.

Olsson, B. (1999), "Editorial: the construction of transparency through accounting for intellectual capital (IC)", *Journal of Human Resource Costing & Accounting*, Vol. 4, No. 1, pp. 7-9.

——. (2003), "Editorial: the annual report is more than a report on the results from the last operating year in the company", *Journal of Human Resource Costing & Accounting*, Vol. 7, Nos. 1/2, pp. 5-7.

Patra, R. and Khatik, S.K. (2003). "HRA Policies and Practices: A Case Study of BHEL Limited, Bhopal, India". *International Journal of HRD and Management*, 3(4), 285-96.

Pfeffer, J. (1997), "Pitfalls on the road to measurement: the dangerous liaison of human resources with the ideas of accounting and finance", *Human Resource Management*, Vol. 36, pp. 357-65.

Prakash, O. (1997), "Human Resource Accounting Practices in Bharat Heavy Electricals Limited". *Finance India*, 11(1), 92-94.

Rao, D.P. (1993), "Human Asset Accounting: An Evaluation of the Indian Practices". *ASCI Journal of Management*, 22, 37-42.

Scarpello, V. and Theeke, H.A. (1989), "Human resource accounting: a measured critique". *Journal of Accounting Literature*, Vol. 8, pp. 265-80.

Schwan, E.S. (1976), "The Effects of Human Resource Accounting Data on Financial Decisions: An Empirical Test". *Accounting, Organization and Society*, 1(2), 219-37.

Sonara, C.K. and Patel, A. (2009), "Valuation and Reporting Practices of Human Resource Accounting in India". *The Management Accountant*, 44, 16-19.

Tomassini, L.A. (1977), "Assessing the Impact of Human Resource Accounting: An Experimental Study of Managerial Decision Preferences". *The Accounting Review*, 52(4), 904-14.

Verma, S.B. (1999), "HRA Practices in Public Sector Undertakings in India". *The Management Accountant*, 34(8), 575-82.

Websites: www.shrm.com

Websites:www.bhel.com

Websites:www.cementcorporation.co.in

Websites:www.hindustancopper.com

Websites:www.sail.co.in

Journal of Social and Development Sciences, Vol. 3, No. 2, pp. 69-76, Feb. 2012.

# 21

# INVESTMENT OPTIONS DURING RECESSION IN BIKANER CITY

*–Alka Swami*

## Introduction

Economy can be said in recession only when GDP falls for two consecutive year. It was observed by the whole of the globe during 2007-08. The impact of the subprime crisis along with a slowdown in mortgages has led to a significant lowering of growth estimates in USA and later on its effect spread to the rest of the world. Although India's growth is driven by the domestic production and consumption and there is no direct link with US banking sectors.

For India, it could mean a further appreciation in the rupee *vis-à-vis* the US dollar and a darkening of business outlook for sectors dependent on US companies. The overall impact of a US slowdown on India would, however, be minimal as the factors driving growth here are more local in nature. Unlike the rest of Asia, India is a strong domestic demand story, so any slowing in the US is likely to have a more muted impact on India. Strong growth in domestic consumption and significant spending on infrastructure are the two pillars of India's growth story. No sector has a dominant influence on earnings growth and risks to our estimate are limited. Corporate India is also learning to master the art of efficient capital management, reduction in costs and delivery of value-added services to sustain profit margins. Further, interest rates are expected to be stable primarily due to control over inflation and proactive measures undertaken by the RBI.

## Research Methodology

For the conduction of this exploratory research, questionnaire was prepared for the collection of primary data from 100 respondents from different professions on the basis of Random sampling. About 50 per cent of the respondents are having income in range of ₹ 2.5 lakh to 5 lakh, followed by 38 per cent respondents having income 1 lakh to 2.5 lakh. Rest 6 per cent respondents each had income in range of lakh and more than 5 lakh. Out of the total 81 per cent were taxpayers and remaining 19 per cent were non-taxpayer.

## Result

About 56 per cent of the respondents have annual savings more than 25 per cent of the total income and 44 per cent have 10 to 25 per cent savings. This shows that people in small cities still believe a lot on savings which is one of the major reasons of less impact of recession.

When asked about the investment, all respondents invest in some instrument. Majority 69 per cent of the respondents invest 20 per cent of their total income whereas 19 per cent didn't disclose and 13 per cent invest about 16 to 20 per cent of the total income. The main objective of the investment for 50 per cent respondents were to secure future whereas 44 per cent invest to generate regular income and 6 per cent, i.e. government servants invest for tax benefits.

**Table 1:** Prioritization of the reason for investment

| Reasons of investments | Rank |
|---|---|
| Saving for future | 2 |
| Tax incentives | 3 |
| Returns | 1 |
| Future outlook | 5 |
| Brand value | 6 |
| Risk covering | 4 |

When asked about the reason for investment, returns on investment were the main reason on the basis of which investments is being made. Second was saving for future, whereas third was tax benefits, fourth was risk covering, fifth was future outlook and lastly for brand value. When asked about the expected returns on investments, 56 per cent expect a return of atleast 20 per cent whereas 44 per cent is happy with even 16 to 20 per cent returns. Seventy-five per cent respondents preferred the income schemes whereas 25 per cent preferred growth schemes.

**Table 2:** Investment instruments

| Type of investment | Respondents (%) |
|---|---|
| Post office schemes | 13 |
| Insurance | 6 |
| Bank | 38 |
| Gold | 13 |
| Mutual fund | 6 |
| Govt. securities | 19 |

When asked about the major investment instruments 38 per cent were happy with banks whereas 19 per cent believe in govt. securities, 13 per cent of respondents were investing in post office, gold, and share market each. Six per cent were investing in insurance and mutual funds each.

**Table 3:** Change in investment option after recession

| Change in investment | Respondents (%) |
|---|---|
| Yes | 88 |
| No | 12 |

When asked about the change in investment option after recession, 88 per cent has changed their options in some way or other whereas 13 per cent had not changed anything.

**Table 4:** Change of investment option after recession

| Change in investment | Respondents (%) |
|---|---|
| Yes | 31 |
| No | 69 |

When asked that whether they have changed investment options after recession, 69 per cent agreed whereas 31 per cent have not changed the options.

**Table 5:** Percentage decrease on return after recession

| Decrease (%) | Respondents (%) |
|---|---|
| Between 5-10 | 13 |
| 10-25 | 25 |
| Above 25 | 44 |
| None | 19 |

When asked about the percentage decrease after recession 44 per cent said that they faced a decrease of more than 25 per cent, whereas 25 per cent said that they realized a less of 10 to 25 per cent and 19 per cent said that they did not observed any decrease. Thirteen per cent observed a minimization of 5 to 10 per cent in returns.

**Table 6:** Better investment option during recession period

| Better investment option | Respondents (%) |
|---|---|
| Post office scheme | 13 |
| Insurance | 6 |
| Banks | 31 |
| Gold | 25 |
| Govt securities | 13 |
| Mutual fund | 13 |

When asked about the best option of invest during recession then 31 per cent said bank, 25 per cent said gold, 13 per cent were agree with govt. securities, post office and mutual funds each. Six per cent found insurance as good option.

## Conclusion

Majority of the respondents agreed that they save a significant amount of their income, which is the main reason for their future securities. This shows that people in small cities still believe a lot on savings which is one of the major reasons of less impact of recession.

When asked about the reason for investment, returns on investment were the main reason on the basis of which investments is being made. Second was saving for future, whereas third was tax benefits, fourth was risk covering, fifth was future outlook and lastly for brand value. This shows that most of them are aware about the returns offered by different instruments.

People expect a decent amount of returns on their investment, most of them are happy with 20 per cent returns that's why they are not looking towards high return investment which are risky. Majority of the respondents do not want to take risks.

It was found that during recession most of the respondents have changed their options, more faith was shown on the traditional instruments like banks, gold, government securities, etc.

## REFERENCES

### Websites

www.\recession\America's recession officially over.mhtion\10 Myths About The Subprime Crisis.mht

www.\recession\Article More investment in infrastructure sector to fight recession_PTI-The Press Trust of India Ltd_HighBeam Research-FREE trial.mht

www.\recession\automobile.mht

www.\recession\Bank of America Joins China as Buyer of Treasuries (Update 2)-Bloomberg_com.mht

www.\recession\bar.htm

www.\recession\bar.htm2.htm

www\recession\BBC NEWS  Business  Bush claims no recession for US.mht

# 22

# ACTIVITY-BASED COSTING: RELOADED

–*Vineet Chouhan, G. Soral* and *Shagufta Khan*

## Introduction

*Competition is the name of the game.* This theory is now old and a new theory which came to replace this is "*Cost competition and activities are the name of the game*". In the present era of globalization, liberalization and global competitive environment, computation of correct cost of product/services is of upmost importance. Over the time traditional cost accounting system has proven itself difficult for reaching the goal of getting appropriate cost information. Therefore a drastic change has been taken place in the business environment, financial market, financial instrument and products. The structural changes and emerging trends associated with the new regime have rendered the traditional costing measures. A radical departure from the traditional cost accounting system with the passage of time and new innovations, represents by Activity based Costing (ABC).

## Historical Perspective and Development

The ABC method is most well-known management accounting innovation in last 20 years (Gregory Wegmann, 2009). It is a method of charging the indirect cost to the product and services. The changes in the traditional cost behavior and present cost behavior are increase in the share of overhead in total cost and variability of product (which increases). It shows need to maintain cost of overheads. The ABC method was designed in the US during the 1980 (Cooper and Kaplan, 1988) though General Electric experimented with a kind of ABC during 1960 and prepares a base for using ABC (Bouquin, 2006). However, by underlining the limitations of traditional costing systems in overheads cost allocation in a situation of product diversity in terms of volume and complexity Cooper (1988a) demonstrated the necessity for activity-based costing system. Further in (1988b) he found that the firms facing high level of competition and having diverse product mix are more likely to benefit from precise cost information and the introduction of activity-based cost systems with an added caution that the activity-based costing system introduction initiative itself should be cost effective.

The history of ABC development is presented under Table 1.

Table 1: Synthesis of ABC development

| Techniques | Main Feature |
|---|---|
| **First stage:** | |
| Customer Driven ABC | Special widening of the cost perimeter Customer, |
| Market Driven ABC | market, consumer, society, etc. |
| Benchmarking-driven ABC | |
| Environment-driven ABC | |
| Inter-organizational Cost Management | |
| **Second Stage:** | |
| ABB | Temporal widening of the cost perimeter: |
| ABC and Life Cycle Costing | Analysis of future cost. |
| Target ABC Accounting | |
| Feature Costing | |
| **Third Stage:** | |
| RCA: Resource Consumption | Determination of relevant level to analyse the |
| Process Costing and Lean Accounting | cost: |
| Time-driven ABC and other equivalent | Relevant level: resource pool |
| methods | Relevant level: the process |
| | The level of analysis depends on the cases (department, activities, or tasks) |

*Source*: Wegmann, G., 2009, The activity-based costing method: development and applications, the ICFAI *University Journal of Accounting Research*, VIII(1), pp. 7-22.

## Methodology

Activity-based costing system consolidated in the later part of the last century from a business process perspective and it is now a very important feature of current generation cost accounting system. Activity-Based Costing (ABC) is a method of costing which recognizes the activities which consume resources as a key element in Cost Management, as against the traditional Cost Accounting which is in existence in most of the industries. This approach helps indirectly identifying value adding and non-value adding activities which are of immense help to the management in controlling costs (Raman, 2005).

Kaplan (1988) observed that many companies used single cost system to meet their three diverse needs, namely inventory valuation and financial reporting, product/service/customer costing and providing 'operational feedback to frontline employees' in the plant. He concluded that, in a complex manufacturing environment with 'product and process diversities', and 'concern for excellence', 'single cost system' for all the three needs might not be enough.

ABC is a method which firstly treats activities as cost object and thereafter the costs pooled in activities are assigned to products (Horngren, 2005). It is a system that focuses on activities as fundamental cost object and utilized the cost of these activities as building blocks or compiling the cost of other cost object (Horngren, 2005). ABC is a method of collection of overhead according to activity for the purpose of their allocation to cost object (Turny, 1995). Under this the cost are first traced to activities and then to the product (Jawahar Lal). According to American institutes of management accountants (IMA, 1992), ABC is defined as a methodology that measures the cost and performance of activities, resources and cost object based on their use, and recognizes the causal relationship of cost drivers to activities. It is important to quote Michael Porter here, who revealed that, "Cost is generated by performing activities and cost advantages arise from performing particular activities more efficiently than that of competitors. Differentiation arises from both the choice of activities and how they are performed. Activities are thus basic unit of competitive advantages." Hence we can say that under ABC the cost of each activity is calculated and the vase of cost distribution is consumption of activities by the product. Thus activity becomes an important strategic basis for competition and competitive advantage.

**Practical Use**

Diverse product portfolio and with high proportion of overheads cost when they have adopted activity-based costing along with other strategic initiatives such as JIT and TQM, it resulted in substantial improvement in their return on investments (Cagwin and Bouwman; 2002).

Kennedy and Affleck-Graves (2001) examined the link between activity-based costing implementation and creation of shareholder value found that choice of management accounting system such as activity-based costing for a sample of UK firms had a significant impact on firm value. Hubbell (1996) also argued in favour of integrating activity-based cost management systems with the measures of shareholder value such as economic value added.

Ittner et al. (2002) examined the association between the extensive use of activity-based costing and plant level operational and financial performance indicators such as cycle time, quality, manufacturing cost improvements and return on assets.

Bromwich and Bhimani (1989) observed that though activity-based costing corrects the product-cost distortions but no such study has been done to demonstrate that it increases the profitability of the firm (Shim and Stagliano 1997). Groth and Kinney (1994) observed that success at cost management could have substantial impact on the firm value.

The major motivations for introduction of activity-based costing are performance measurement/improvement, accurate cost information for product/service pricing and profits analysis, improved insight into cost drivers, accurate customer profitability analysis, cost reduction, process improvements, product-mix strategy, performance measurement and improvement, customer profitability; inventory valuation; value chain analysis; supply chain analysis, and cost modeling. The inventory valuation use had the lowest adoption rate amongst ABC users (Armitage and Nicholson, 1993; APQC/CAM-I, 1995; Innes and Mitchell, 1995; Clarke, 1996; and Clarke and Mullins, 2001). Similarly these are also most commonly used areas for activity-based costing.

## Need of Reloading ABC

During the last 2-3 decade the ABC became popular and it has also lost its relevance (Cooper & Kaplan, 2005)and it shows that is at a declining stage (Acharya, 1996), and it is because of few limitation included in it. Those are to be taken as reasons for reloading the ABC which are as under:

1. The first and main reason is the amount of time and efforts needed to interview people to collect the data (Doyal, 2001). This problem can be bargain with the help of other effective measure like strategic cost management technique and life cycle techniques.
2. ABC is told to be too complicated for small and medium sized business (Acharya, 1996). But the main problem of these businesses is to get more accurate cost information which is needed to improve their size from small business to MNC's.
3. ABC is not the panacea for all the difficulties in the traditional financial and management reporting (Bishop et al., 2001). So with the help of resource consumption accounting and time driven ABC we can try to improve the nature and the accuracy of information which reduces the deficiencies of cost accounting system.
4. Product costing is frequently not the main benefit derived from adopting ABC/M (Kennedy, 1999). The main benefit of any system of cost accounting is to provide the better product cost information, with the use of life cycle costing and integrated target costing better cost information can be generated (Cokins, 2002).
5. ABC itself is unable to produce the change (Sikdar et al., 2002). It can give the better cost information but some time the results got unrealistic and contribution approach might lead current way (Wilson et al., 1996). So at the time of taking decision other measures like contribution approach, contribution based activity (Cleland, 1997) approaches are required to improve the decision of change.

In the previous article (Chouhan, 2008) it was mentioned that ABC is a new stream of cost and management accounting which will improve the product cost information and the quality of decision improves with the use of ABC (Chouhan, 2009). The refinement which is suggested by ABC will be more adequate and useful if other techniques are also correlate with it. So the other techniques are evaluated in a way that it improves the quality of decision by fulfilling the need of the ABC.

## Reloading with ABM

ABM is a discipline that focuses on the management of activities as the route to continuously improving the value received by the customer and the profit achieved by providing this value (Turney, 2001). This discipline provides information for managing activities using ABC data and other tools to achieve continuous improvement (Jain, 1998). ABM includes cost driver analysis, activity analysis and performance analysis (Turney, 2001). ABM is focused on using this information to manage activities. Improving business based on the information obtained from ABC is called as ABM. ABM is a management analysis that brings the full benefits of ABC to an organization.

ABM draws on ABC to provide management reporting and decision-making. ABM supports business excellence by providing information to facilitate long-term strategic decisions about such things as product-mix and sourcing. It allows product designers to understand the impact of different designs on cost and flexibility and then to modify their designs accordingly. ABM also supports the quest for continuous improvement by allowing management to gain new insights into activity performance by focusing attention on the sources of demand for activities and by permitting management to create behavioral incentives to improve one or more aspects of the business.

Clarity and understanding between value-added and non-value-added activities are achieved when people understand and accept the reasons why an activity is classified as non-value-added or value-added (Miller, 1996). Making non-value-added cost visible is one of the major benefits of ABM, but also the most difficult to achieve (David and Robert, 1995).

ABM should focus on the activities, not on the people who perform the activities. ABM system, performance measures include both Financial and non-Financial measures, and are designed to influence the behavior of cost management. A fundamental issue is that a single performance measure will not reflect all the aspects of a company. Managers may require multiple performance measures even from individuals (Innes et al., 1994). ABM refers to the use of ABC information to understand and to make beneficial changes in the way institutions do their business in an environment of limited resources and increasing demands (Khalid, A., 2005).

### Reloading with Strategic Management Accounting

ABM enables the organization to accomplish its outcomes with fewer demands on organizational resources; that is, the organization achieves the same outcomes at a lower total cost. ABM accomplishes its objective through two complementary applications: *operational* and *strategic* ABM.

Operational ABM—doing things right—works to enhance efficiency, lower costs, and enhance asset utilization. Operational ABM can increase the capacity of resources (equipment and people) by reducing machine downtime, improving, or even eliminating entirely, faulty activities and processes, and increasing the efficiency of the organization's resources.

Operational ABM takes the demand for resources as given and attempts to either increase capacity or lower spending (i.e., reduce the cost driver rates of activities), so that fewer physical, human, and working capital resources are required to generate revenues. The benefits from operational ABM can be measured by reduced costs, higher revenues (through better resource utilization), and cost avoidance (the expanded capacity of existing resources obviates the need for additional investments in capital and people).

Strategic ABM—doing the right things—attempts to alter the demand for activities to increase profitability while assuming, as a first approximation, that activity efficiency remains constant. For example, the organization may be operating at a point where the revenues earned from a particular product, service, or customer are less than the cost of generating those revenues. Strategic ABM encompasses shifting the mix of demand for activities away from such unprofitable applications by reducing the cost driver quantities demanded by unprofitable activities. The ABC model signals when individual products, services, and customers appear to be highly profitable. This information can be used by marketing and sales experts to explore whether demand for those highly profitable products, services, and customers can be expanded to generate incremental revenues that exceed their incremental costs. Managers can then shift the activity mix toward more profitable uses. They can also use ABC information to choose suppliers that are low-cost, not just low-price.

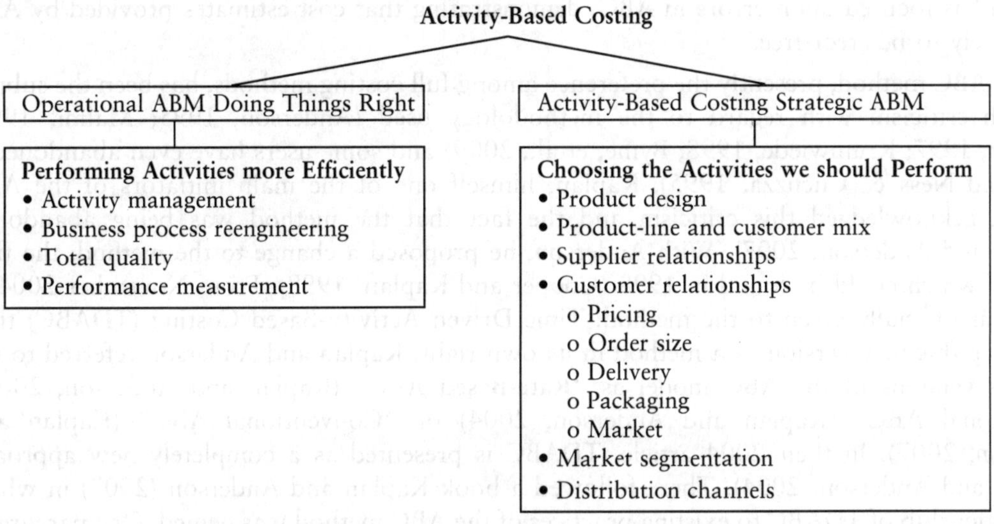


**Fig. 1:** Using ABM for Operational Improvements and Strategic Decisions.

The Table 1 presents a synthesis of the ABC uses dimensions. This typology is a result of a state of the art review (academic and professional)

| ABC uses dimensions | Tools examples |
|---|---|
| 1st dimension: The stakeholders (Freeman, 1984), Spatial widening of the cost perimeter: to the customers, suppliers and other stakeholders (Horngran, 2005) | Customer-Driven ABC, Benchmarking-Driven ABC, Inter-organizational Cost Management, Target Activity-Based Costing |
| 2nd dimension: Temporal widening of the cost perimeter: (Antos and Brimson, 1999; Howvath, 1998; Cokins, 2002) analyze of future costs on a life cycle, on a project,... | Planning and Activity-Based Budgeting, Beyond Budgeting, Project Management Accounting, Target Activity-Based Costing |
| 3rd dimension: Complexifying of the analysis model Refined resources allocation stage diversified cost drivers rationalization of the model | Feature Costing, Resource Consumption Accounting statistical methods to correlate the costs, Time-Driven Activity-Based Costing |
| 4th dimension: Simplifying of the analysis model (Merwe, 2002), Simplified resources allocation stage reduced number of cost drivers and activities | Direct costing, Time-Driven ABC and other equivalence methods, Lean Accounting (Maskell and Bagaley, 2003), Process Costing |

## Reloading with Time Driven ABC

In the 1980s, activity-based costing (ABC) was introduced as a response to increasing product diversity, which had changed the nature of cost drivers so that traditional, volume based costing systems was no longer sufficient. However, due to high maintenance costs in dynamic environments, many ABC systems were not updated, have become outdated and were finally abandoned. Moreover, in the management accounting literature, a substantial body of research has focused upon errors in ABC, demonstrating that cost estimates provided by ABC are unlikely to be error-free.

The ABC method, presently the preference among full costing methods, has been the subject of much criticism with regard to the methodology used (Anderson, 1995; Malmi, 1997; Gosselin, 1997; Krumwiede, 1998; Byme, et al., 2009) and some users have even abandoned it (Ness and Ness & Cucuzza, 1995). Kaplan, himself one of the main initiators of the ABC method, acknowledged this criticism and the fact that the method was being abandoned (Kaplan and Anderson, 2007). With Anderson, he proposed a change to the method, the first traces of which could be found in 1998 (Cooper and Kaplan, 1998). From November 2004, a name was officially given to the method: Time Driven Activity-Based Costing (TDABC) thus presenting this new version as a method in its own right. Kaplan and Anderson referred to the previous versions of the ABC model as "Rate-Based ABC" (Kaplan and Anderson, 2003), "Traditional ABC" (Kaplan and Anderson, 2004) or "Conventional ABC" (Kaplan and Anderson, 2007). In their 2004 article, TDABC is presented as a completely new approach (Kaplan and Anderson, 2004). There followed a book Kaplan and Anderson (2007) in which any relationship of TDABC to existing practices of the ABC method was denied. One paragraph entitled "Time-Driven ABC: Old Wine in New Bottles?" (Kaplan and Anderson, 2007) is even devoted to denying any relation with ABC in the use of time drivers. The authors justify the difference.

To overcome the difficulties associated with traditional ABC in dynamic environments and to better capture the full complexity of activities, Kaplan and Anderson (2004) developed a new approach for ABC, called time-driven ABC. With this new approach, the time required to perform a certain activity plays a pivotal role in allocating resources to cost objects and time equations are used to incorporate multiple cost drivers per activity.

**Reloading with Activity-Based Budgeting (ABB)**

Developing budgets and planned levels of costs; and measuring variances of actual (and subsequently assigned) costs against those budgeted targets.

There are a variety of issues related to determining budgeted and planned targets (e.g. ideal, theoretical, average, or standard cost) but, in the end, there has historically been an interest in knowing how an organization performs relative to its spending plan. The aim of activity based management is to meet the demands of customers by creating value (Currie, 1998: 28) and to manage the relationship and interaction between production processes and product performance (Senyshen, 1998: 3). Activity based budgeting as a part of activity based management is a budgeting methodology determining the forecasted costs of activities required for the production of a specific product and/or service.

The usage of activity-based costing in budgeting process enables the managers to transform the fixed costs into variable costs and to think about the costs more objectively (Cooper and Kaplan, 1998: 114). Activity-based budgeting is a powerful cost planning and controlling instrument increasing cost efficiency by eliminating the activities that do not create value added (Hansen and Mowen, 1999). Consequently, activity-based budgeting is a part of activity-based costing and management and ensures to analyze costs and profitability possibilities easier and more accurate. It also provides information about production process improvement, pricing and customer profitability analyses. Activity-based budgeting instead of volume based budgeting will generate any difference in target costing practices.

### Reloading with Benchmarking

We lack clear empirical or analytical evidence directly linking cost system accuracy to corporate profitability (e.g. Dedrick et al., 2003). One possible explanation for the mixed results is the mitigating effect of feedback on cost information inaccuracy (e.g. Briers et al., 1999; Waller et al., 1999 and Callahan et al., 2009). The sparse studies that examine this issue show feedback allows managers to partially overcome the effects of an inaccurate system.

All activities should be compared with similar activities in another company or within the organization which performs the best in class. Benchmarking should be carried out for both value-added and non-value-added activities. Comparing an activity with a benchmarked of good practice helps to determine the scope for further improvement. The activities should be measured based on factors, e.g. quality, lead-time, flexibility, cost and customer satisfaction. Then, each activity should be rated against an identified best practice (Coburn et al., 1995).

A company with a number of different departments can improve the efficiency and effectiveness of each activity by comparing similar activities of different departments. Obtaining information from other companies is quite difficult. Therefore, benchmarking within the company or with the best practice is mostly used in real-life situations. For example, on-time delivery of customer orders is an essential activity and it can be performed manually. The best practice, however, uses electronic data interchange (EDI) that costs less per transaction, has a lower error rate and provides a faster service. This clearly shows that there is room for improvement over manual order taking (Turney, 1992).

Benchmarking provides a systematic approach to identify the activities with the greatest room for improvement. For example, the marketing resource group of US WEST, the telephone company performed an ABC analysis of the activities carried out in the accounting department. Managers computed the activity rates for the activities of the accounting department and then compared these rates to the costs of carrying out the same activities in other companies. Two benchmarks were used:

1. A sample of fortune 100 companies, which are the largest 100 companies in the United States.
2. A sample of world class companies that had been identified by a consultant as having the best accounting practices in the world. These comparisons are as follows:

| Activity | Activity Measure | US WEST Cost | Fortune 100 Benchmark | World-Class Benchmark |
|---|---|---|---|---|
| Processing accounts receivables | Number of invoices process | $3.80 per invoice | $15.00 per invoice | $4.60 per invoice |

| | | | | |
|---|---|---|---|---|
| Processing accounts payables | Number of invoices processed | $8.90 per invoice | $7.00 per invoice | $1.80 per invoice |
| Processing payroll checks | Number of checks processed | $7.30 per check | $5.00 per check | $1.72 per check |
| Managing customer credits | Number of customer accounts | $12.00 per account | $16 per account | $5.60 per account |

*Source:* http://www.accountingformanagement.com/targeting_process_improvements.htm

It is clear from this analysis that US WEST does a good job of processing accounts receivable. Its average cost per invoice is $3.80, where the cost in other companies that are considered world-class is even higher—$4.60 per invoice. On the other hand, the cost of processing payroll checks is significantly higher at US WEST that at benchmark companies. The cost per payroll check at US WEST is $7.30 versus $5.00 at Fortune 100 companies and $1.72 at world-class companies. This suggests that it may be possible to wring some waste out of this activity using total quality management, process reengineering, or some other method.

In general, benchmarking can be viewed as an external focus on internal activities, functions, or operations in order to achieve continuous improvement (McNair and Leibfried, 1992). It is also argued that benchmarking is an ongoing search for best practices that produce superior performance when adopted and implemented in one's own organization (Bogan and English, 1994).

Benchmarking is a new concept developed on a broad basis of industrial utilization, without a strong theoretical foundation, making it very result oriented (Godfrey, 1993; Watson, 1993). The concept of quality cost measurement was introduced in the early 1950s based on the theories of Juran (1951) and Feigenbaum (1956), and has not developed adequately with changing business environments.

The final stage of the benchmarking study will give new updated information back to the poor quality cost model and close the loop. This stage enables the company to verify the effects of the benchmarking study and document the financial savings due to the improvement efforts.

The success of benchmarking feedback depends on the cooperation of the benchmarking partners (Delpachitra, 2008). Panagiotou (2007) found that firms from the same strategic group use results from benchmarking to adjust their firms' competitive strategies to reflect the groups' strategic behavior. Firms with similar cost structures in highly competitive markets may wish to cooperate at an earlier stage, such as the product cost system design stage, in order to create later-stage perceived cost asymmetries so that total profit to the oligopolies is maximized (Lapan and Hennessy, 2006). As Alles and Datar (1998) observe, product costs are known to the firm only as its information gathering technology allows. Consequently, through studies of benchmark feedback, firms may be able to identify similarities and differences in their product cost systems and those of their competitors. Through industry knowledge and best practices benchmarking feedback, it is plausible that firms could revise their product cost systems so that the errors between the product costs systems are correlated which would induce reported cost asymmetries. This knowledge could be used to coordinate production decisions, a conjecture we formally model in this study.

### Reloading with Target Costing

Target costing, firstly emerged in Japan in 1970s, has been derived from Japanese words "Genka Kikaku" (Hiromoto, 1989: 330; Horvath et al., 1993: 13; Hasegewa, 1994: 5) and/or "Kokukyou Genkakaizen" (Yıldırım, 2000: 6). Then, especially after 1980s, target costing concept has gained a greater popularity in England and Germany (Saitoh, 1978; Hiromoto, 1989; Seidenschwarz, 1991: 198; Niemand, 1996: 27) and various studies have been done regarding the concept. In German literature, target costing concept may sometimes be referred as "Zielkosten Management", meant as "Cost Management" (Seidenschwarz, 1993).

Target costing (TC) is a market-driven strategy. Under this scheme, a firm's product is priced based on the levels that give it the best competitive advantage. Target costs are derived from the target prices. Then a certain amount of desired profit is subtracted from the prices. The resulting target costs are often well below the currently achievable costs, which are based on the standards established by product/process engineers. The target costs thus become both the benchmarks and the driving force for the company's (cost) improvement activities. For cost reduction be incorporated with and/or supported by activity-based costing (ABC). For ABC to work well, the activities, the costs, and the relationships between the two must be identified. CEA does just that. It helps identify cost drivers—the activities that cause the incurred costs.

The importance about the combination between activity-based costing and target costing is underlined and it is firmly put emphasis on using the mentioned methodologies together (Buggert and Wielpütz, 1995: 129). While target costing methodology informs managers about market demand and target costs; activity-based costing shows the effects of alternative production styles on indirect cost centers (Horvath, 1993; Koons, 1994: 11). In activity-based costing, the cost drivers are better and more correct to be determined in order to achieve the aim of reaching the target costs related with products and/or services and this enables companies to adapt their cost management plans according with the market demand (Cervellini, 1994: 70).

### Reloading with Life Cycle Costing

Much effort has been made in the modeling, analysis and application of LCC. Fabrycky and Blanchard presented a sophisticated life cycle cost model to address detailed cost analysis of all the costs associated with the product entire life cycle (Bras et al., 1996). It decomposes LCC into four categories: research and development costs, production and construction costs, operation and maintenance costs, and retirement and disposal costs.

Activity-Based Costing (ABC) model focuses on calculating the costs incurred on performing the activities to manufacture a product (Adnan Niazi et al., 2006). It is proved useful in highlighting high-cost elements because the inclusion of uncertainty and the use of Monte Carlo simulation in conjunction with the process steps. Four cost related activities are considered: unit-level, batch-level, product-sustaining, and facility-sustaining activities (Takakuwa, 1997). The ABC model can be applied when the activities are described in detail. It is proved as a good alternative to traditional estimation techniques since it provided more accurate product manufacturing cost estimates (Andrade et al., 1999). It can also be utilized to analyze other aspects of cost, such as overhead cost (Fixson, 2004).

Woodward's Life Cycle Cost Analysis (LCCA) model aims specially to optimize the value of money in physical assets ownership, by identifying and quantifying the trade-offs between different costs relating to the assets during their operational life. This model has the best potential for effective cost assessment in life cycle design (Woodward, 1997).

Design for cost (DTC) model presents a methodology to integrate cost modeling into Quality Function Deployment (QFD) for making trade-off decisions between quality and cost at the early stages of product design (Eversheim, 1998).

"The life cycle cost of an item is the sum of all funds expended in support of the item from its conception and fabrication through its operation to the end of its useful life" (White and Ostwald, 1976). Such life cycle costs of a product can be many times the initial purchase or investment costs (Woodward, 1997), and according to several sources 70-90% of these total life cycle costs become defined already in the design phase (Bescherer, 2005; Dowlatshahi, 1992; Lindholm and Suomala, 2005).

Like most technologies, ABC's life cycle is marked by changing attitudes and increasing diffusion into the marketplace over time. Intense interest at the beginning of its life gave way to criticism and lowered visibility, followed by a longer, unpublicized period of steady growth in adoption rates and functionality. It has now reached maturity and acceptance in the marketplace for management ideas and methods.

### Reloading with Resource Consumption Accounting (RCA)

Resources Consumption Accounting (RCA) is a management accounting approach focusing on creating reliable information to minimize costs and maximize revenues to enhance the productive capability of the business, aiming greater success in a highly competitive market. RCA combines German management accounting methods known as "Grenzplankostenrechnung" or GPK which means "flexible cost planning and control" and strict form of Activity-Based Costing (ABC) for detailed process insights.

With the RCA systems, we try to provide decision-makers with more granular information about the operations. With the third dimension of the Table 1, we put together techniques which propose to determine the relevant level to analyse the costs, depending on the features (strategic and organizational) of a firm. In some cases, the processes and strategy complexity is great. The ABC method is not sufficient so we need another approach to allocate the resources. The Resource Consumption Accounting method (RCA, Keys and van der Merwe, 2002a and b) complete the ABC with a deeper analysis of resources.

Within complex organizations, the variety of resources is great so that we need to multiply the number of resources drivers and allocations. Thanks to the RCA method, resources originated from different departments of an organization are classified in several resources pools. In this way, it becomes easier to allocate the resources to the activities.

We could think that ABC instruments of this category are less strategically oriented. But a tool like RCA enables a better identification of the allocation processes so that managers could have a better understanding of the consequences of their strategic decisions.

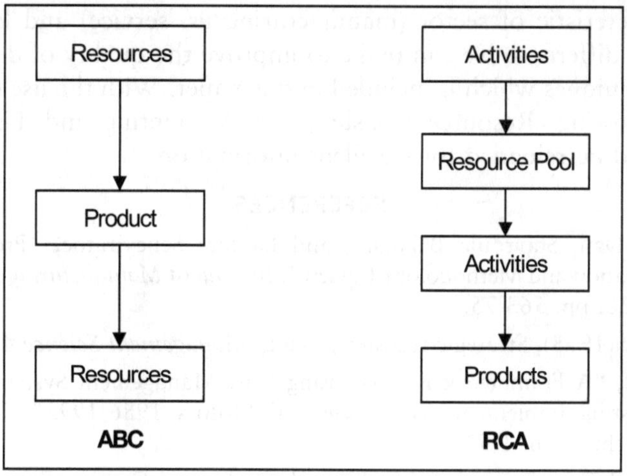


**Fig. 2:** Activity-Based Costing and RCA.

Conversely, some scholars explain that the resources allocation question represents a problem and must be examined strategically. In some circumstances, the activity is an excessive level of detail (standard processes, just-in-time approaches, specific sectors like the chemical industry,...) and the ABC can lead to a useless and non-relevant analysis. It is why the Process Costing and the Lean Accounting supporters suggest bringing together the activities in processes, value chains or "value streams". These techniques belong to the fourth dimension of the Table 1. When the processes complexity is low, the standard ABC method is too detailed. So, we need a simplified ABC, bringing together several activities to set up a "metaactivity" or a process with a single cost driver. This is the general principle of the Process Costing (Horngren et al., 2005: 594) and the Lean Accounting methods. We also have the Time-Driven ABC (Kaplan and Anderson, 2007) which is an "equivalence method". It is the most recent ABC development. It is clearly a simplification of the ABC. With this technique, the activity cutting can be more simple (like with the Process Costing and Lean Accounting). But it can also be more refined (like with RCA).

## Conclusions

Management practices and methods have been changed over the last decade, and organizations are moving from managing vertically to manage horizontally. Activity-based costing and activity-based management provide cost and operating information that mirror the horizontal view. ABC provides accurate cost information and ABM uses this information to initiate improvements. ABC systems produce a large amount of information that is used by the ABM. The analysis of activities is done to identify value-added and non-value-added activities and benchmark activities at the activity level for direct improvement efforts.

In this paper, an attempt has been made to study the application of activity-based costing with other techniques to improve the cost information, which has resulted in changes in various management decision areas, prominent among them, being focus on profitable customers, pricing strategies, and sourcing decisions. However, the quantum of change observed is not found to be a characteristic of sector (manufacturing *vs.* service) and level or stage of ABC implementation. The difference we can make to improve the quality of decision is with the use of other effective techniques which is included in this paper. With the use of Life Cycle Costing, Integrated Target Costing, Resource Consumption Accounting and Time Driven ABC, the current system should be reloaded for excellent information.

## REFERENCES


Adnan Niazi, Jian S. Dail, Stavroula Balabani, and Lakmal Seneviratne, "Product Cost Estimation: Technique Classification and Methodology Review". *Journal of Manufacturing Science and Engineering*, May 2006, Vol. 128, pp. 563-75.

Alles, M., and S. Datar (1998), Strategic transfer pricing. *Management Science* 44(4): 451-61.

Anderson, S.W. (1995), "A Framework For Assessing Cost Management System Changes: The Case of Activity-Based Costing Implementation at General Motors 1986-1993", Journal of Management Accounting Research, 7: pp. 1-51.

Andrade, M.C., Filho, R.C.P., Espozel, A.M., Maia, L.O. A.; and Qassim, R.Y., Activity-Based Costing for Production Learning. *Int. J. Prod. Econ.*, 62(3), 1999, pp. 175-80.

APQC/CAM-I (1995), *Activity-Based Management Consortium Study*, American Productivity & Quality Center/CAM–I.

Armitage, H.M. and R. Nicholson (1993), *Activity-Based Costing: A Survey of Canadian Practices*, Issue Paper no. 3, Mississauga, Ontario, Canada: Society of Management Accountants of Canada.

B. Bras, J. Emblemsvag, "Designing for the Life Cycle: Activity Based Costing and Uncertainty". In *Design for X, Concurrent Imperatives*, Chapman & Hall, UK, 1996.

Bescherer, F. (2005), *Established life cycle concepts in the business environment—Introduction and terminology*, Helsinki University of Technology, Laboratory of Industrial Management report series, Report 1/2005, available at: http://www.tuta.hut.fi/library/raportit/teta_reportreport%20 Bescherer%20final1.pdf

Bogan, C.E. and English, M.J. (1994), *Benchmarking for Best Practices: Winning Through Innovative Adoption*, McGraw-Hill, New York.

Bromwich, M. and A. Bhimani (1989), *Management Accounting: Evolution not Revolution*, London, UK, Chartered Institute of Management Accountants.

Cagwin, Douglass and Marinus J. Bouwman (2002), "The association between activity-based costing and improvement in financial performance", *Management and Accounting Research*, Vol. 13, pp. 1-39.

Clarke, P. (1996), "A survey of activity-based costing in large manufacturing firms in Ireland", *Working Paper*, University College, Dublin, Ireland.

Clarke, P. and T. Mullins (2001), "Activity-based costing in non-manufacturing sector in Ireland", *Working Paper*, University College, Dublin, Ireland.

Cooper, R. (1988a), "The rise of activity-based costing—Part one: What is an activity-based cost system?" *Journal of Cost Management*, Vol. 2, Summer, pp. 45-54.

——. (1988b), "The rise of activity-based costing—Part two: when do I need an activity-based cost systems?", *Journal of Cost Management*, Vol. 2, Fall, pp. 41-48.

Cooper, R., and Kaplan, R.S. (1998), Cost & Effect; Using Integrated Cost Systems to Drive Profitability and Performance, Harvard Business School Press, Boston.

D.G. Woodward, "Life Cycle Costing—Theory, Information Acquisition and Application". *International Journal of Project Management* 15(6), 1997, 335.

David, E.K., and Robert, J.L. (1995), "Departmental activity based management". *Management Accounting*, January, 27-30.

Denschwarz, W. (1991), "Target Costing—Ein Japanischer Ansatz für das Kostenmanagement", *Controlling*, 4(3): 198-203.

Dowlatshahi, S. (1992), "Product design in a concurrent engineering environment: an optimization approach", *Journal of Production Research*, Vol. 30, No. 8, pp. 1803-18.

Feigenbaum, Armand V. (1956). Total Quality Control. *Harvard Business Review*. Vol. 34, Nov-Dec, pp. 93-101.

Godfrey, Blanton A. (1993), "Ten Areas for Future Research in Total Quality Management", *Quality Management Journal*, October, pp. 47-65.

Gosselin, M. (1997), "The Effect of Strategy and Organizational Structure on the Adoption and Implementation of Activity-Based Costing", *Accounting, Organizations and Society*, 22(2): pp. 105-22.

Groth, John C. and Michael, R. Kinney (1994), "Cost management and value creation", *Management Decision*, Vol. 32(4), pp. 52-57.

Hasegewa, T. (1994), "Entwicklung des Management Accounting Systems und der Management Organisation in Japanischen Unternehmungen", *Controlling*, 1(6): 4-11.

Hiromoto, T. (1989), "Management Accounting in Japan-Eine Vergleich Zwischen Japanischen und Westlichen Systemen Des Management Accounting", *Controlling*, 6(1): 316-22.

Horngren, C.T. et al. (2005), *Cost Accounting—A Managerial Emphasis*. 12th edition, Upper Saddle River, New Jersey: Pearson Education.

Horvath, P.T. Tani and S. von Wagenheim (1996), "Genka Kikaku und Marktorientiertes Zielkosten management—Deutschjapanischer Systemvergleich zu Entwicklungsstand und Verbreitung", *Controlling*, 2: 80-89.

Hubbell, William W. (1996), "A case study in economic value added and activity-based management," *Journal of Cost Management*, Summer, pp. 21-29.

Innes, J., Mitchell, F., and Yoshikawa, T. (1994), *Activity Costing For Engineers* (Chichester, UK: Wiley).

Innes, John, and Falconer Mitchell (1995), "A survey of activity-based costing in the UK's largest companies," *Management Accounting Research*, Vol. 6(2), pp. 137-53.

Ittner, Christopher D.; William, N. Lanen; and David, F. Larcker (2002), "The association between activity-based costing and manufacturing performance", *Journal of Accounting Research*, Vol. 40(3), June, pp. 711-26.

Jaeil Park, Timothy W. Simpson, "Production cost modeling to support Product family design optimization". *Proceedings of DETC '03*, Chicago, September 2-6, 2003.

Juran, Joseph M. (1951), *Quality Control Handbook*. McGraw-Hill, Inc., USA.

Kaplan, R.S. and Anderson, S.R. (2007), *Time-Driven Activity-Based Costing*. Boston: Harvard Business School Press.

Kaplan, R.S. and Anderson, S.R. (2004), "Time-Driven Activity Based Costing." *Harvard Business Review*, 82(11): pp. 131-38.

——. (2003), "Time-Driven Activity-Based Costing", White Paper presented at the First European Summit on Time-Driven Activity-Based Costing.

Kennedy, Tom and John Affleck-Graves (2001), "The impact of activity-based costing techniques on firm performance", *Journal of Management Accounting Research*, Vol. 13, pp. 19-45.

Keys, D.E. and van der Merwe, A. (2002a). "The Case for Resource Consumption Accounting". *Strategic Finance,* 83(10), 30-36.

——. (2002b). "The Case for Resource Consumption Accounting". *Strategic Finance,* 83(11), 41-47.

Khalid, A. (2005), "Activity-based costing in Saudi Arabia's largest 100 firms in 2003", *Journal of American Academy of Business*, Vol. 6, No. 2, pp. 285-92.

Krumwiede, K.R. (1998), "The Implementation Stages of Activity-Based Costing and the Impact of Contextual and Organizational Factors", *Journal of Management Accounting Research*, 10: pp. 239-50.

Kwang-Kyu Seo, Beum Jun Ahn, "A learning algorithm based estimation method for maintenance cost of product concepts". *Computers & Industrial Engineering* 50 (2006), 66-75.

Lapan, H.E. and D.A. Hennessy (2006), "A note on cost arrangement and market performance in a multi-product Cournot oligopoly". *International Journal of Industrial Organization* 24: 583-91.

Lindholm, A. and Suomala, P. (2005), "Learning by Costing: Sharpening Cost Image through Life Cycle Costing?", *The 7th Manufacturing Accounting Research Conference*, Tampere, Finland, May 30-June 1, 2005.

Malmi, T. (1997), "Towards Explaining Activity-Based Costing failure: Accounting and control in a decentralized organization", *Management Accounting Research*, 8: pp. 459-80.

McNair, C.J. and Leibfried, K.H.J. (1992), *Benchmarking*, Harper Collins, New York.

Miller, J.A. (1996), *Activity Based Management in Daily Operation* (Chichester, UK: Wiley).

Ness, J.A. and Cucuzza, T.G. (1995), "Tapping the Full Potential of ABC", *Harvard Business Review*, 73(4): pp. 130-38.

Niemand, S. (1996), "Target Costing für Industrielle Dienstleistungen", Controlling Praxis, Verlag Vahlen, München.

Saitoh, J. (1978), "The Net Profit of Eighty Million Yen Earned Through The Introduction of Target Costing", *Factory Management*, December.

Sebastian, K. Fixson, Assessing Production Architecture Costing: Production Life Cycles, Allocation Rules, and Cost Models. *Proceedings of DETC'04*, Salt Lake City, September 28 October 2, 2004.

Shim, E. and A.J. Stagliano (1997). "A survey of US manufacturers on implementation of ABC", *Journal of Cost Management,* March/April, pp. 39-41.

Takakuwa, S. (1997), "The Use of Simulation in Activity-Based Costing for flexible Manufacturing Systems". *Proceeding of the 1997 Winter Simulation Conference*, pp. 793-800.

Turney, B.B.P. (1992), "Activity-Based Management". *Management Accounting*, January, 20-25.

——. (1996), *Activity-Based Costing: The Performance Breakthrough* (London: CLA).

Turney, B.B.P. and Stratton, A.J. (1992), "Using ABC to support continuous improvement". *Management Accounting*, Sept., 46-50.

W. Eversheim, J. Neuhausen, M. Seaterhenn, "Design to Cost for Production Systems". *Annual of the CIRP* 47, 1998, 357.

W.J. Fabrycky, B.S. Blanchard, "Life Cycle Cost and Economics Analysis". *Prentice Hall, Englewood Cliffs*, NJ, 1991.

Watson, Gregory H. (1993), *Strategic Benchmarking: How to Rate Your Company's Performance against the World's best*, John Wiley & Sons, New York, USA.

White, G.E., and Ostwald, P.F. (1976), "The life cycle cost of an item is the sum of all funds expended in support of the item from its conception and fabrication through its operation to the end of its useful life", *Management Accounting*, Vol. 57, No. 7, p. 39.

Woodward, D. (1997), "Life cycle costing—theory, information acquisition and application", *International Journal of Project Management*, Vol. 15, No. 6, pp. 335-44.

# 23

# JUST-IN-TIME PRODUCTION SYSTEM (JITPS) IN DEVELOPING COUNTRIES: THE INDIAN EXPERIENCE

–*Bhupesh Lohar* and *G. Soral*

## Introduction

Just-in-Time (JIT), as the name implies, is to produce goods just-in-time for use or sale. It as a Japanese management technique developed in the 1970's which had its motivation in the Japanese urge to develop better and effective methods capable of rebuilding their economy. But still concept is just beginning to be understood and used by many industrial enterprises throughout the world today. Many researchers have reported that JIT has potential of reducing lead-time, decreasing inventory-carrying cost.

Despite the immense advantages of the Just-in-Time Production system (JITPS), its adoption in the third world manufacturing is quite limited. Manufacturing systems are still run on the basis of old production systems that included so many activities that add little value to the final production process. Production processes are therefore slow, wasteful and characterized by avoidable complexities. This research paper examines the extent of JITPS in a typical third world country—India, with a view to identifying the extent of adoption as well as the hindrances on the part of adopting the technique. Structured On-line questionnaire were sent to companies to indicate whether or not they were adopting the technique. The findings include that fairly larger companies adopt JIT method more while relatively smaller ones are still not aware of the existence of the technique. The paper also identifies structural hindrances to the adoption of JITPS; solutions were also suggested to overcome some of these problems.

## Literature Review

A few papers are available on JIT practices which highlight the positive impact of JIT on Indian industries. Sharma and Singhvi (2009) conducted a case study on two Indian agricultural equipment manufacturing companies, which have implemented JIT. In one case the profits of the company were found to have increased by 10 per cent. While in the second case the company was successful in reducing the level of inventory by over 20 per cent and reduction of waste up to 5 per cent. The lead-time was also reduced to over 20 per cent.

Yasin and Small (2006) conducted on the basis of investigation of 86 organization of US public sector, that JIT is a form of "managerialism", has the potential to increase the operational efficiency, service quality and organizational effectiveness of public sector organizations.

Garg, Deshmukh and Kaul (1998) have conducted a survey of 31 Indian industries to analyze the importance of the attributes pertaining to JIT purchasing and supplier evaluation criteria. The surveyed companies has given great importance to some attributes such as high quality, mutual trust, cooperated relationship, on time deliveries, supplier evaluation, stable production schedule, reliable network of suppliers, reduced delivery time, long-term contract and continuous improvement. The study has also indicated the scope of JIT as 70 on scale (0-100), which is predicted better compared to earlier studies.

Chandra and Kodali (1997) have developed a multi-attribute decision model using analytical hierarchy process (AHP) for justification of JIT manufacturing system in Indian industries. The selection of important JIT attributes and sub-attributes were then used in AHP to achieve the related benefits. The results of the study have quantified the JIT benefits in descending order: increased profit margin, improved competitive position, quality improvement and reduction in inventory.

Deshmukh (1996) has attempted review on the state of the art of JIT and its possible ramifications in the purchasing and manufacturing systems. It has been pointed out that JIT from a system perspective requires that suppliers and manufacturing functions must be in relation with design, planning and control. JIT must be viewed as a binding force coupling all the activities from incoming raw material to the finished goods.

Garg and Gupta (1996) have conducted a case study in JIT implementation of an Indian tractor assembly industry. Records of company have indicated that significant benefits are achieved by improvement in quality and productivity and reduction in inventory, material movement, space, manpower, work-in-process and lead-time. The key elements in JIT implementation were extensive training of employee on pull concepts; identification of key performance parameters; new layout based on U-shaped cells, visual control and multi-skill training.

Garg, Kaul and Deshmukh (1994) has explored the specific cultural required in JIT implementation and also reported their presence in Indian industries. They have stated that trust, locality, responsibility, development, motivation, authority, long-term relationship, and respect for human beings mark work culture required in JIT environment. It is critical for industries to make conscious efforts to change the work culture for successful implementation of JIT. These changes require top management commitment and worker participation in decision-making and massive education and training to the people concerned.

Vrat, Mittal and Tyagi (1993) have conducted a Delphi study to assess the applicability of implementing JIT elements in Indian context. The results have shown that quality circles and good communication are not very difficult to implement having a rating 30 and above on a 40 point scale. Top management attitude, multifunctional workers, long-term relationship with supplier and support from worker have high rating, which indicates that JIT implementation in

India is not an impossible task. The study has also stressed on focusing more on error prevention, reduced set up time, Kanban system and quality of incoming material.

## Objectives

Despite the advantages of JIT and efforts and exhortation of Indian companies to overhaul the manufacturing sector, there are indications that there are fewer manufacturing companies in the country that are adopting JIT. Thus, this study had been conducted with the following objectives:

1. To identify the benefits of a JITPS in companies currently adopting the techniques in India.
2. To identify the factors that hinders the adoption of the techniques among companies not applying it.

### *Just-in-Time Production Technique: The Indian Experience*

Since, the Indian government, industries, scholars, all has strongly been sensitized on the need for productivity improvement in both public and private sectors of the economy. Efforts have been directed towards mobilizing local initiatives at reducing inefficiency and unproductive time in the production process so as to improve the process and the quality of the process or service.

Since improving productivity has been a matter of interest to government and scholars, the task that lies ahead for Indian manufacturers to promote the concept of JIT more widely, get more manufacturing industries to implement it and expand the concept to departments other than manufacturing. Experts have been involved to conduct workshop and practice-oriented seminars on JIT. This is expected to assist the country to sustain her productivity growth and enable the more effective use of capital.

## Research Methodology Applied

The first step was to carry out a survey of companies in the country to determine whether the companies were using JIT or not. Some of the JIT companies that did not respond to the first mailing were sent reminders so as to encourage the filing up of the On-line questionnaire and to render any further assistance it required within 3 months, response were received from 53 JIT and 33 non-JIT companies.

One detailed questionnaire is prepared for 126 companies. The questionnaire was first pre-tested on two JIT consultant and two academicians. Based on our discussions, with some local JIT consultants and practitioners, the local Hindustan Zinc Limited is the most popular area of JIT application.

Consequently, the On-line questionnaires were mailed to about 126 companies which were sourced from ASSOCHAM, ACMA, and social networking sites like Linkedin also used to get target respondents.

The data collected from 96 companies were analyzed using comparative percentage.

Table 1 show that most of the respondents come from large sized companies. Inman and Mehta (1990) found that many small companies cannot afford JIT due to cost of training preventative maintenance and cost of consultants. However, it appears that large size alone is not the only factors that decide whether a company adopts JIT or not.

**Table 1:** Size of Respondents Companies in Terms of Sales

| Annual Sales | JIT companies | Non-JIT companies |
|---|---|---|
| Between 1m to 5m | 10 | 5 |
| Between 5m to 10m | 15 | 11 |
| More than 5m | 30 | 25 |
| | 55 | 41 |

### Benefits of JIT Application in India

Table 2 shows that a number of benefits have been realized in implementing JIT companies in India. 57 per cent of the JIT companies' adopters experienced a significant reduction in inventory cost. Apparently despite Indian manufacturers being heavily reliant on importers for raw materials and inputs, a JITPS can still allow most of the firms to enjoy some of these benefits.

Nearly 50 per cent of the respondents benefited from large-space savings. Such savings are suspected to have resulted from

- Better factory layout thereby reducing travelling distance.
- Better quality of service which reduces the need to keep inventory.
- Reduction in set up time.
- Produce inventory as and when required.

Besides these JIT also allows for flexibility in the local environment. 60 per cent of the respondents agreed that the increase in flexibility enable a faster response to change in the environment and the subsequent developments of a competitive advantage. 57 per cent of the respondents also felt that there is improved in competitive position, such a benefit is possible with a JITPS in use. 70 per cent of the respondents also enjoyed a reduction in lead time after implementing JIT. One company managed to shorten lead-time by 69 per cent after having implemented JITPS for 4 years. The survey also revealed that 58 per cent of the JIT applicants experienced productivity improvements.

Another advantage brought up by a small percentage of the respondents is that a JITPS enable better visual control as the shop floor becomes neater. In a JIT environment, the rapid detection of machine or human errors is enabled by the greater visibility afforded by the small lot sizes in the system.

On the whole the survey findings seem to be consistent with the empirical research. Thus, a JITPS can offer a range of benefits to the local firms and the three most important and commonly experienced benefits are reduction in inventory carrying cost, large space savings and increase in flexibility.

**Table 2:** Expected Benefits of JIT Implementation as Perceived by Respondents

| S.No. | Expected Benefits | Degree of difficulty Low 1 | 2 | → 3 | 4 | High 5 | No Response | Mean Score | t-value Calculated | Result Let$H_0$=3 |
|---|---|---|---|---|---|---|---|---|---|---|
| 1. | Improved competition position | 0 | 3 | 0 | 16 | 13 | 1 | 4.091 | 5.554* | $H_0$= Rejected |
| 2. | Increased inventory turn | 0 | 4 | 0 | 20 | 7 | 2 | 3.737 | 3.260* | $H_0$= Rejected |
| 3. | Increased productivity | 0 | 3 | 2 | 14 | 8 | 6 | 3.273 | 0.883* | $H_0$= Accepted |
| 4. | Increased profit margin | 0 | 0 | 2 | 15 | 12 | 4 | 3.818 | 3.032* | $H_0$= Rejected<br>$H_1$= Accepted |
| 5. | Low scrap rate | 0 | 7 | 2 | 17 | 2 | 5 | 2.969 | -0.112* | $H_0$= Accepted |
| 6. | Reduced Inventories | 0 | 3 | 1 | 15 | 11 | 3 | 3.757 | 5.013* | $H_0$= Rejected<br>$H_1$= Accepted |
| 7. | Reduced production lead time | 0 | 3 | 4 | 18 | 5 | 3 | 3.485 | 2.029* | $H_0$= Accepted |
| 8. | Reduced purchase lot size | 0 | 3 | 0 | 22 | 7 | 1 | 3.909 | 5.013* | $H_0$= Rejected<br>$H_1$= Accepted |
| 9. | Reduced raw material/parts | 0 | 3 | 2 | 15 | 10 | 3 | 3.696 | 2.727* | $H_0$= Rejected<br>$H_1$= Accepted |
| 10. | Reduced work-in-process | 0 | 2 | 0 | 19 | 9 | 3 | 3.787 | 3.212* | $H_0$= Rejected |

## Factors Hindering JIT Applications

Despite the relentless effort, research has shown that the promotion of JITPS among small Indian companies has not been very effective in terms of implementation. Hence, this research paper places more emphasis on factors that hinders the JIT implementations. To facilitate analysis, the factors hindering JIT applications will be analyzed in terms of 5 categories, namely supplier factors, personnel factors, product factors, production factors and others.

**Supplier factors:** The lack of control of timing of overseas supplies, shipment is the most serious problem faced by the companies. The respondents quoted that this factor as being most important. Although the current JIT literature deems this as an excuse for not applying JIT, the importance given to it by the JIT manufacturers indicate that it should be given serious consideration, as many companies has to rely on the overseas suppliers; to overcome this hindrances, a JIT applicant indicated that they employed JIT on partial basis i.e. buffer inventory for raw materials from overseas is still being stored. Reducing such inventory level can also be kept to a minimum by better materials planning and providing the overseas suppliers with real time production plans so that the overseas suppliers would be able to produce and deliver the goods timely to its local customers.

The second most important hindrances are the lack of reliable suppliers (in terms of quantity and cost). The JIT respondents indicated that company's serious problem faced by their companies because if a supplier delivers a bad batch, the whole production line will have to stop. A JIT applicant indicated that a solution lies in a setting up a strict qualification for suppliers. Another solution is to work closely with suppliers. A fair price must also be provided so that suppliers are motivated to enhance their quality and delivery times.

In addition, companies may resort to having outgoing quality inspection at the suppliers place rather than have the incoming quality inspection so that poor quality products may be detected and corrected earlier.

Many respondents noted that the unpredictability of supply quantity for each shipment creates a problem for their implementation of a JITPS. There is need to ensure that the quantity supplies are exactly what the company has ordered, in order for the production line to run smoothly.

**Personnel factors:** The lack of commitment by management is the most serious factor with JIT and non-JIT respondents agreed on this problem. The successful implementation of a JITPS requires amongst others, redesigning the factory layout and educating the employees on the concept value-adding activities which will requires the use of the company's scarce resources. As such top management must not only indicate the process of change but must also be fully committed to such changes.

The lack of commitment and experience by management may be attributed to relative newness of the JIT concept in India and this might be a reason why few companies have implemented JIT. Steps must therefore be taken to educate top management on the benefits of JIT and ways to successfully implement JIT. The inter-departmental conflict of interest is the second most important factor. This means that coordination among departments is a must before JIT can be implemented. Team efforts are utmost importance. To reduce inter-departmental conflicts one JIT applicant suggested a restructuring of the organizations so that lines of communications, cooperation and responsibility can be clearly drawn out.

Some of the JIT companies found resistance to change by workers a problem as compared with only 10 per cent of the non-JIT companies. Further, with a greater emphasis on education and upgrading of skills, the current generation is probably better educated and skilled as compared with the older generation.

**Product factors:** For the two factors of high product mix and irregularity of demand, responses from JIT and non-JIT companies are controversial. 47 per cent of the respondents of the JIT group considered product mix as a more serious problem. While 53 per cent of the non-JIT respondents indicated that irregularity of demand is a more important factor to overcome the product mix problem, one JIT respondent resorted to the standardization of parts so that the standard part could be used interchangeably between various products. Another solution was to adopt Flexible Manufacturing System (FMS) so that a greater variety of products can be produced.

**Production factors:** A low production volume is the most commonly quoted problem by both type of respondent as indicated by the comparative chart of production factors by one applicant is to adopt FMS and cellular manufacturing systems which allows for a shorter production schedule.

The responses between JIT and non-JIT groups regarding a batch-oriented production process are different. The JIT companies reckon the redesigning of factory layout as a more formidable problem then having a batch-oriented production process; while the Non-JIT respondents viewed the batch orientation is a main hindrance to JIT application.

Layout is a serious problem. Only 10 per cent of the Non-JIT respondents had the same viewpoints.

**Other factors:** Other hindrances indicated by respondents which the questionnaire did not specifically cover were also received. One of the factors is priorities. Due to a tight project schedule, the possibility of implementing JITPS is shelved.

Secondly, before a JITPS can be implemented successfully, the Pre-JIT production system must give a consistent yield and output rate. An inconsistent yield might be the result of quality problems. Therefore, unless quality problems are solved, implementation of JIT will be fraught with problems.

The third problem is whether the company is manufacturing custom-made products.

### Ways the Successful JIT Applicants Overcome the Other Implementation Problems

Besides the resolutions of technical problems are mentioned earlier, 60 per cent respondents were surveyed again, to determine how they overcome the other hurdles and difficulties in implementing JITPS. Most of the respondents claimed that the key to success is to overcome the human problem i.e. the personnel factor. Firstly, the management must be fully committed. As literature indicated, JIT philosophy requires nothing less than a new way of thinking. It is a cultural change that must be led by management.

Some of the applicants of JIT are subsidiaries of MNCs whose parent companies have already applied JIT in their own countries. Some respondents feel that JIT education an important key to successful implementation of a JITPS. JIT education was carried out by visiting a JITPS, using a JIT consultant, conducting, watching video tapes as well as having on-job-training. The JIT companies also conducted preliminary studies to help in smoothen the implementation process. The objectives of the JIT project team were to analyze the philosophy of JIT, its benefits and limitations and whether the system can be adopted by the company. Generally many companies have spent about 5-8 months to research on the feasibility about applying JITPS in their companies.

The respondents also claimed that employee involvement is just as critical as management commitment in ensuring the successful implementation of a JITPS. In addition, the normal kind of change management such as counseling and job assurance are also required.

### JIT Purchasing: Analyzing Survey Results

Implementation of JIT purchasing is a multi-phased process that embraces both JIT purchasing characteristics and JIT inventory management principles. The implementation strategy should involve top management commitment to establish JIT purchasing as a top priority. Also, the system should be changed to subordinate everything toward the goals of this system. Once the new role of the JIT purchaser is established, suppliers that can support a JIT operation must be selected. When a supplier or group of suppliers is selected, JIT purchasing requires a continuous effort for improving the relationship between the purchaser and supplier.

According to Hahn, Pinto, and Bragg, the utilization of JIT purchasing usually leads to reduced lot sizes, frequent and reliable supplies, higher quality of incoming materials, and reduced lead-times. Ansari and Modarress report that the potential tangible benefits of JIT purchasing are generally divided into several groups. The most important benefits that the companies achieve are higher material turnover, reduced lead times, and satisfaction of the delivery promises. Raia specifies improved quality, reduced paperwork, and improved supplier-purchaser relationships as benefits of this progressive system in purchasing. A survey of plant managers of automotive, electronic, and machinery firms, performed by Norris, Swanson, and Chu, reveals that 98 per cent of the managers interviewed reported a reduction of work-in-process (WIP) inventory, 96 per cent indicated an improvement in inventory turnover, and 88 per cent realized an improvement in their inventory records. These improvements led to lower manufacturing costs, higher production quality, and significantly higher customer satisfaction. Although JIT purchasing produces a number of impressive results, problems associated with the implementation and usage of this system still exist. A survey conducted by Ansari found the following seven problems to be most significant:

1. Poor support from suppliers;
2. Lack of top management commitment;
3. Poor product quality;
4. Lack of employee readiness and support;
5. Poor engineering support;
6. Lack of communication; and
7. Inadequate support from carrier companies.

Some experts believe that the greatest problem with JIT purchasing is the lack of flexibility available to meet unexpected demand. Since planning, purchasing, and scheduling are performed right before production and safety stocks are minimized, last minute situations are difficult to react to. Another problem is the dependency that companies develop on suppliers. If an unanticipated incident occurs—such as a supplier's crew going on strike or a factory burning down—goods may arrive late or not at all. According to Raia, increased transportation costs—associated with frequent deliveries—are another disadvantage.

Besides the differences in evaluating problems in JIT purchasing, we found few industry surveys that related to JIT purchasing. The available surveys proved an unevenness of results and problems associated with JIT purchasing. We decided to conduct a new survey concerning benefits and pitfalls of JIT purchasing. This article describes the results of the survey we conducted among various manufacturing, distribution, and service companies. Using a regression analysis based on the survey data, we identified the leading predictors that most strongly influence the utilization of JIT purchasing.

### *Survey Data*

The survey was performed over a period of fifteen months and was fairly extensive.

The survey questionnaire consisted of 18 questions that were both qualitative and quantitative in nature. The qualitative questions asked managers about their perception of JIT purchasing, how it worked in their companies, reasons for switching to a JIT system, benefits and difficulties that the companies encountered, and implications of the new purchasing systems. The majority of the qualitative questions contained a set of possible answers, one or more of which could be marked by the respondents as applicable to their situation. A value of 1 was assigned to each possible answer if the answer was marked and 0, otherwise. The quantitative questions focused on numeric results of JIT purchasing. They assessed the new JIT system with respect to inventory and production costs, numbers of years JIT purchasing has been in use, quality of incoming materials, and proportion of materials purchased according to JIT purchasing.

***Results of the Survey***

Table 3: Critical Elements of JIT Purchasing

| Questions | Frequency of Response (per cent) |
|---|---|
| Relationships with suppliers | 51.5 |
| Management commitment | 31.8 |
| Proper scheduling | 30.3 |
| Coordination among departments | 25.8 |
| Quality of incoming materials | 19.7 |
| Long-term contact agreement | 16.7 |
| Type of material purchased | 13.6 |
| Special policies and regulations | 10.6 |

The results of the survey, including qualitative and quantitative data, are presented in Table 3. The survey shows that, on average, more than 54 per cent of all incoming materials are purchased using JIT. The majority of the managers specified several advantages of JIT purchasing including significant reduction of inventory (65.1 per cent), higher supplier reliability (41.9 per cent), improved quality of incoming materials (39.5 per cent), and reduction in scrap costs (32.6 per cent). Almost 45 per cent of the managers stated that utilization of JIT purchasing helped their company's free additional space for production processes. More than a third of the managers specified that JIT purchasing has improved delivery times and customer service.

Table 4: Problems Solved by JIT Purchasing

| Questions | Frequency of Response (per cent) |
|---|---|
| Space reduction | 44.8 |
| Cost reduction | 34.5 |
| Improved customer service | 34.5 |
| On-time delivery | 34.5 |
| Stock out problem | 17.2 |
| Improved cash flow | 17.2 |
| Lead-time reduction | 10.3 |

Table 5: JIT Effect on Production Process

| Questions | Frequency of Response (per cent) |
|---|---|
| Reduction of in-plant inventory | 65.1 |
| Improved suppliers' reliability | 41.9 |

| | |
|---|---|
| Reduction of in-transit inventory | 39.5 |
| Improved quality of incoming materials | 39.5 |
| Reduction in scrap costs | 32.6 |
| Reduced paperwork | 23.3 |

Table 6: Difficulties in Using JIT Purchasing

| Questions | Frequency of Response (per cent) |
|---|---|
| Lack of suppliers' support | 23.6 |
| Poor coordination between departments | 20.0 |
| Lack of incentives for suppliers | 18.2 |
| Types of materials purchased | 16.4 |
| Poor quality of incoming materials | 12.7 |
| Special policies and regulations | 7.10 |

Table 7: Problems with Suppliers in JIT Purchasing

| Questions | Frequency of Response (per cent) |
|---|---|
| Hard to find good suppliers | 35.6 |
| Unreliable suppliers | 31.1 |
| Remote suppliers | 26.7 |
| Too many suppliers | 24.4 |
| Suppliers avoid frequent deliveries | 17.8 |

Table 8: Quantitative Data

| Data | Number |
|---|---|
| Number of years JIT has been in use | 4.0 years |
| Percentage of materials purchased according to JIT | 54.3 per cent |
| Average reduction in inventory costs | 30.7 per cent |
| Average reduction in total production costs | 18.2 per cent |
| Average frequency of supplies | 1.7 times/unit time |

Our analysis of the survey results reveals that many issues, described previously as the most critical, do not currently represent the critical elements in JIT purchasing. For example, almost 70 per cent of the managers did not specify lack of top level management's commitment as a factor preventing a successful implementation of JIT purchasing. This proves that top management is becoming more and more supportive in implementing and using JIT because of an increasing pressure from competitors and a growing perception of the benefits. Also, almost 75 per cent of the managers were reluctant to conclude that the quality of incoming materials was a major problem in JIT purchasing. Some of the managers stated that the improved quality of incoming materials was due to the vast implementation of total quality management (TQM) and, particularly, statistical quality control (SQC) on the supplier's side.

The survey results show (Table 3) that the main concern of the companies that used JIT purchasing was a lack of suppliers' support (23.6 per cent). They specified the following problems in dealing with suppliers:

1. Hard to find "good" suppliers that will utilize JIT delivery (35.6 per cent);
2. Supplier reliability (31.1 per cent);
3. Proximity of suppliers (26.7 per cent); and
4. Too many suppliers for a company (24.4 per cent).

According to the survey results, the second main problem was the low level of coordination between different departments with respect to JIT purchasing (20.0 per cent). Managers pointed out that they experienced poor cooperation and understanding between purchasing and engineering, and purchasing and accounting departments in subordinating their efforts towards the goals of the JIT purchasing system. More than 18 per cent of the managers specified the lack of supplier incentives as a problem in using JIT purchasing (the third major problem). Also, more than 16 per cent of the managers pointed out that they could not fully install the JIT system because of the specific conditions of delivery imposed on some type of materials purchased (the fourth major problem).

The results of the survey serve as a starting point for improving the utilization of JIT purchasing. Some qualitative insights derived from survey responses make it possible to speak more specifically about which actions by management are most likely to be productive.

### Conclusion

Using JIT purchasing philosophy yields a number of positive results with respect to the manufacturing and service organizations. The primary areas of improvement, according to the survey, include inventory reduction, increased quality, and an overall reduction of the total production and inventory costs.

An analysis of the survey results reduced the importance of previously recognized problems in JIT purchasing, such as the lack of management commitment and poor quality of incoming materials. From the interviews we conducted, several common elements of JIT purchasing were viewed as important to each of the individual companies. Of these similarities, the topic of relationships with suppliers and their support surfaced as a major focal point in running an efficient JIT purchasing system. The coordination between departments inside the company was identified as another major problem in JIT purchasing. The lack of incentives appeared to be the third major problem in using JIT purchasing.

The survey results allowed us to formulate several possible directions that companies should follow for the successful utilization of JIT purchasing:

1. Improve relationships with suppliers by providing special incentives for the employees in the supply companies—sharing with them the results of JIT purchasing with respect to the reduction of inventory production costs;

2. Organize and control the relationships between departments by installing, for each department involved, special measures to estimate the results and effectiveness of JIT purchasing; and
3. Create a measurement system to evaluate the results of JIT purchasing and its influence on other business functions inside an organization.

These logical conclusions are based on a qualitative analysis of the survey's responses.

## REFERENCES

Chandra, S. and Kodali, R. (1997), "Implementation of JIT manufacturing system: An overview". *Journal of Productivity,* 38, 312-21.

Chandra, S. and Kodali, R. (1997), "Justification of Just-In-Time Manufacturing systems for Indian Industries". *Production and Inventory Management,* 9(5), 126-30.

Deshmukh (1996), "Productivity measurement and the relationship between plant performance and JIT intensity". *International Journal of Operation and Production Management,* 11(3), 277-301.

Garg, D., Deshmukh, S.G. and Koul, O.N. (1996), "Attributes for JIT purchasing and supplier evaluation". *Journal of Productivity,* 38, 322-26.

Garg, D., Deshmukh, S. and Kaul, O.N. (1996), "Critical analysis in JIT purchasing in Indian Context". *Journal of Productivity,* 37, 271-77.

Garg, D. and Gupta, A. (1996), "JIT in Service Sector". *Productivity,* 43(4), 45-46.

Garg, D., Kaul, O.N. and Deshmukh, S.G. (1994), "JIT Implementation: A Case Study". *Production Inventory Management,* 22, 92-96.

Sharma and Singhvi (1999), "JIT concept and relevance in Indian Context". *Industrial Engineering Journal,* 28(1), 14-18.

Vrat, P., Mittal, S. and Tyagi, K. (1993), "Implementation of JIT in Indian Environment: A Delhi Study". *Productivity,* 34, 19-24.

Yasin, M.M. and Small, M.A. (1994), "An empirical examination of factors influencing JIT success". *International Journal of Operations and Production Management,* 16(1), 23-24.

24

# DIRECT TAX CODE: BOON OR BANE FOR NON-PROFIT ORGANIZATIONS

*–Priyabrata Pandam, Sovan Mishra* and *Kishore Kumar Das*

## Introduction

The age old Income Tax Act, 1961 has faced radical amendments since its inception. Surprisingly more than 5000 amendments have been made in this Act. The IT Act has become very complex to understand, administer and execute. Moreover different exemptions and reliefs in the present law have significantly eroded the tax base. The changing world economic conditions in general and Indian economic condition in particular paves the way to make a major amendment or abolish of the present IT Act, 1961. In this context the Direct Tax Code (hereforth referred as 'the code') is the blue print for Indian direct tax regime. The then finance minister Mr. Mukharjee released the draft direct tax code on 12th August 2009. The objective of the new code is to simplify the existing tax law, widening the tax base and intensifying the tax-gdp ratio. The new tax code also aims at equity and non-discrimination, removal of ambiguity to encourage voluntary compliance and stability in the new tax regime.

## The Code and NPOs

The code will bring both pains and gains for different assesses in different conditions. But the provisions of the new code seem to be stony-faced for Non-Profit Organizations (hereafter known as NPOs) and Trusts. It may lead to a gloomy future for such organizations. No NPO or Trust can easily accept the code as this gives minimum and marginal support to them. However the features of the new code in regard to NPOs and Trusts are as follows:

- Replacement of charitable purpose by charitable activity.
- Depreciation will be disallowed once the code becomes law.
- NPOs have to pay tax @ 15 per cent on the aggregate of the surplus.
- NPOs have to follow cash basis of accounting except Sec. 25 companies.
- No re-registration required.
- All receipts except loan or corpus donations are part of income.

- No compulsory welfare activity on annual basis results in cease of NPO for that particular year.
- It allows a 50 per cent deduction for donors who contribute to registered charities.
- 100 per cent application of income to get rid from the tax net.
- Anonymous donations to be taxed.

## Research Methodology

Research methodology gives the ways and means to carry the research work. It makes simple the total job. It gives the roadmap to execute the plan. Research Methods for the current study includes following steps:

1. Analytical or Descriptive research includes detail analysis of different provisions of the code from the point of view of NPOs. Information already available is being used for such purpose. An attempt is made to get a summary to give a suggestion out of the phenomenon already happened.
2. Exploratory research to examine the provisions of the code and to find out the pains and gains for NPOs and trusts.
3. Hypothesis testing research is to test hypothesis between expected and observed frequency.

The current study is both analytical and exploratory in nature.

### *Collection of Data*

Collection of data includes: (i) Collection of primary data, and (ii) Collection of secondary data.

**(i) Collection of Primary Data:** Only personal interview method of data collection is followed in the process of collecting the primary data. No questionnaire is made for this purpose. Few pre-structured questions are asked to professional practitioners and owners of NPOs regarding the code. Their views are well observed for this purpose.

**(ii) Collection of Secondary Data:** Secondary data is collected from different committee reports on the code, various publications of central, state and local government, different government and private websites, technical and trade journals, journals of ICAI, ICSI, and other bodies, books, magazines and newspapers, research articles already published.

While collecting the secondary data, reliability, suitability and adequacy of data is taken into consideration.

### *Sampling Plan*

Professionals like chartered accountants, company secretaries and NPO owners are taken as sampling unit. Two samples are drawn for the study, viz. Professionals and NPO proprietors. Sampling size is thirty for NPOs owners and thirty five for professionals. Purposive sampling technique is used to select persons who know about the provisions of the new code and provisions of existing law.

### Objectives of the Study

Research work is carried on with following objectives:

- To diagnose the provisions of the code for NPOs and Trusts and to find out the pains and gains for the concern organizations.
- To study the basic taxation structure and clarity of present scenario of taxation for NPOs.
- To compare between the provisions of IT Act, 1961 and DTC.
- To know about the probable and expected effects of DTC on NPOs and Trusts.
- To make a suggestion after the study.

### Hypothesis

In order to test the findings of the study the following hypothesis have been formulated:

- Null hypothesis (Ho) = Direct Tax Code has significant impact on NPOs and Trusts.
- Alternative hypothesis ($H_1$) = Direct Tax Code has no significant impact on NPOs and Trusts.

### Testing of Hypothesis

Two samples are purposively drawn for this study. Their reaction for the code and IT Act, 1961 is shown in the Table 1.

Table 1: Reaction of Sample Unit Towards the Code and Present Law

| | NPOs | Professionals | Total |
|---|---|---|---|
| Present Law | 19 | 20 | 39 |
| Proposed Code | 11 | 15 | 26 |
| Total | 30 | 35 | 65 |

*Source*: Field Survey.

In the above table out of thirty NPOs nineteen has supported present law and rest has supported the code stating they are providing service to the society not misusing the fund. They want stringent rules for NPOs as more NPOs are enjoying the benefit of loopholes of law. Out of thirty professionals twenty are supporting the existing rules and fifteen welcomes the change. They argued in favour of them. Out of total sixty-five sample units thirty-nine has opined in support of existing rules and twenty-six has in favour of the code. The data collected above is used as observed frequency to calculate expected frequency.

Table 2: Expected Frequency

| | NPOs | Professionals | Total |
|---|---|---|---|
| Present Law | 18 | 21 | 39 |
| Proposed Code | 12 | 14 | 26 |
| Total | 30 | 35 | 65 |

*Source*: Calculated values.

The above expected frequencies are calculated by using the formula $= \frac{CT \times RT}{N}$

**Table 3: Calculation Chi Square**

| Observed Frequency (O) | Expected Frequency (E) | $(O-E)^2/E$ |
|---|---|---|
| 19 | 18 | 0.05 |
| 11 | 12 | 0.08 |
| 20 | 21 | 0.04 |
| 15 | 14 | 0.07 |
| | | $\Sigma(O-E)^2/E = 0.25$ |

*Source*: Calculated values

v = (r–1) (c–1) = (2–1) (2–1) = 1

v = 1 chi square at 0.05 = 3.84

Here the table value is higher than the computed value. Hence the hypothesis is accepted. That means that code has greater impact on Non Profit Organizations.

### Review of Related Literature

Ashoka (2011) tried to make a comparison between existing provision and the provision of the Code in regard to NPOs. Several issues like replacement of charitable activity with charitable purpose, difference between application and accumulation of income in both the laws, confusion regarding treatment of all receipts as income, etc. are analyzed by him and concluding remarks are made.

Dr. A Panda and S. Dey (2011) clarified the Revised Discussion Paper (RDP) on NPOs and commented accordingly. Their interpretation about tax treatment of NPOs, including public religious trusts and partly charitable and partly religious trusts is noteworthy. They studied the practical difficulty of application of entire fund for purely religious purpose. Moreover they studied the ground application of RDP proposals.

M. Fogla (2010) opined for amendments and deletion of several sections of the proposed Code. He justified that Section 72 and the 16th schedule must be amended to give 100 per cent deduction to Donors. He suggested for both cash and accrual basis of accounting by amending Section 88(2). Moreover he focused on 85 per cent application and 15 per cent accumulation.

S. Ambedkar (2010) highlighted that the revised Direct Tax Code has emphasised on various marginal and smaller issues without touching the key and primary issues affecting the NPOs. It has provided negligible relief and becomes hard and strict for NPOs. Since 1922 till 2008, profit generated by the NPO sector was not a problem since it was being used for purposes that the NPOs were engaged in. Many of the NPOs are surviving due to this activity. Apart from this there are other harsh measures regarding the accumulation of surplus, which can be done only for three years and creates problems for NPOs during the time of inflation.

S. Patra (2010) commented on certain provisions of the proposed Code. He proposed not to disallow depreciation. It is totally unfair to disallow depreciation for NPOs where other types of organizations are getting such benefit. He also made a summary of all provisions of proposed Code regarding NPOs.

**Analysis of Provisions of Direct Tax Code for NPOs in Comparison with Existing Law**

**1. Charitable purpose replaced by charitable activity.** The Code has substituted the word 'charitable purpose' with 'charitable activity' which seems to be narrower in scope thereby increasing the ambiguity in the law. It gives an exhaustive meaning of permitted welfare activity u/s 96(2).

According to Section 2(15) of Income Tax Act, 1961 "charitable purpose" includes relief of the poor, education, medical relief, preservation of environment (including watersheds, forests and wildlife) and preservation of monuments or places or objects of artistic or historic interest and the advancement of any other object of general public utility.

**2. Constraints on application and accumulation of Income.** In the proposed code 100 per cent application of income is required to remain out of tax net. Provision of 15 per cent accumulation is withdrawn in the proposed code.

In the existing law it is required to apply 85 per cent of the income in charitable purposes. If this income is not applied then it shall be accumulated for a period of 5 years to be applied for specified charitable purposes provided the same is invested in specified modes of investment. The remaining 15 per cent of gross receipts is to be accumulated for an indefinite period without any condition related to application of the same.

**3. Disallow of Depreciation.** The proposed code has completely deleted the provision of treating depreciation as expenditure while other types of organizations are enjoying this benefit. The code only allows cash expenditure.

In the other side presently depreciation is totally allowed as expenditure.

**4. Payment of Tax.** The tax liability of a non-profit organization shall be 15 per cent of the aggregate of the amount of surplus generated from the permitted welfare activities; and the amount of capital gains arising on transfer of an investment asset, being a financial asset. The amount of surplus generated from the permitted welfare activities shall be the "gross receipts" as reduced by the amount of 'outgoing'.

In the IT Act, 1961 NPOs has not to pay any tax subject to the fulfilment of condition of Section 11/12.

**5. Exclusion of Religious trust.** In the proposed code exemption is applicable only for religious institutions established under any law of the Central, State or Provincial Government.

In the present Act exemption is applicable to income derived from property held under trust wholly for charitable or religious purpose.

**6. Compulsory activity on an annual basis.** In the current law no provision is there for compulsory activity each year.

But in the code if there will be no compulsory welfare activity on annual basis the NPO will be ceased to be a NPO for that particular year. In addition tax @ 30 per cent on net worth can be levied on the NPO ceased as NPO in that financial year and any two financial years out of any four financial years immediately preceding such financial year.

**7. Conversion into business organization.** The Code prescribes two situations for conversion of NPOs to profit making organizations. First, if there will be a merger between the NPO and a profit making organization. Second, if the NPO fails to transfer all its assets to another NPO within 3 months from its dissolution.

There is no such provision in the IT Act, 1961 for conversion of a NPO in to business organization.

**8. Insufficient incentives for donors.** 35AC of the Income Tax Act, 1961 allows Donors a deduction of 100 per cent for eligible projects or schemes.

The above provision is removed in the code. The DTC only allows a 50 per cent deduction for donors who contribute to registered charities.

**9. Method of Accounting.** Existing provision allows both cash and accrual basis of accounting for computation of income.

But the code allows only on cash basis of accounting for NPOs except Section 25 companies.

## Findings

- Now the code has focused on "activity" rather than on purpose or intent. The scope of charitable purpose is narrowed down to specified activities.
- Genuine charitable organizations may lose tax benefits in the additional income earning from incidental activities (in the interest of sustainability because of the ambiguities in the definition of 'incidental business' and 'charitable activity'. These words can be understood in more than one way.
- If present 15 per cent accumulation is withdrawn then NPOs can deprive of such limited benefit. They cannot create reserve for future sustainability out of this accumulation.
- Disallowing depreciation will result in erosion of corpus and net worth of NPOs. This provision is harassing for NPOs because depreciation provision is allowed to other assessees. In toto other non-cash expenditures are not been considered since the code only accounts cash inflow and cash outflow.
- Once the code becomes law exclusion of religious trust may result in needless confusion amongst these trusts as to their status and taxability. Moreover donations to such establishments will not enjoy any deduction in the hands of the donor.
- In case of cease of NPO, tax @ 30 per cent is applicable in two out of four financial years immediately preceding the financial year of cease. It will lead to double taxation to the extent it consists of surplus which has been taxed earlier.
- As the provision of Section 35AC removed and deduction for Donors reduced to 50 per cent, the Donors may hesitate to free their hand; as a result NPOs may lose significant contribution.
- The Code explains that a NPO should not be established for the benefit of any particular caste. The question that arises is whether a non-profit organization that works for manual scavengers, that tend to be dalits, would be excluded from the definition or not. This provision creates unnecessary litigation and confusion.

- The general anti-avoidance rules proposed in the code empowered the Commissioner of Income Tax to deny any deduction/incentive or impose tax if he is of the view that the arrangements are abusive or are not backed by any commercial substance. This provision results in loss of tax benefits for genuine NPOs as well as Donors.

**Recommendations**

1. **Large public trust and small organizations should not be treated equally.** The Code keeps large public trusts like Ports, Religious, Public Schools, and Corporate Hospitals and small organizations in one basket. It's not fare to treat both large and small organizations alike. Moreover the Code is applicable to all organizations operating as non-profit entities, which can range from foundations, NGOs research and advocacy organizations, charity hospitals, etc. Whether they are providing health or livelihood related services to marginalize in remote villages, or conducting research based advocacy, printing popular publications for public awareness, charging nominal user fee to provide sustainability to community initiative.

2. **All receipts should not be treated as income.** The proposed code should not treat all receipts as income. It should exclude those receipts, which cannot be considered as income, even under the mandate of the proposed code. For example, it should exclude legal obligations and restricted grants, receipts towards share capital, life membership fees, etc.

3. **Not to disallow depreciation.** The Code should not disallow depreciation for NPOs where it is allowed to all other assessees. Allowing depreciation as expenditure helps the NPOs to protect the erosion in the net worth. Not only depreciation but all other legitimate expenditures whether cash or non cash must be allowed.

4. **Not to withdraw 15 per cent accumulation.** It is unfair to withdraw 15 per cent indefinite accumulation of income by the code. This is a tough step for NPOs. This provision of the code has serious impact on the future survival and growth. In this regard Supreme Court's judgement must be considered. The apex court has held that it is reasonable to have up to 15 per cent of surplus in a year for future and expansion in the case of P.A. Inamdar & Ors. Vs. State of Maharashtra & Ors. *[2005] AIR 3226 SC, [2005] SCC 537 SC*. Therefore, the withdrawal of 15 per cent indefinite accumulation should be amended by Government and the existing provision must be retained.

5. **100 per cent application of income is not justified.** The new Code provides application of 100 per cent income during the year solely for charitable purposes. Practically such application is not possible. It will create some problems for NPOs receiving funds (i) towards the end of the year, (ii) for 2-3 years together. Moreover 100 per cent application means no reserve or saving for contingencies. In view of this Government should retain the existing provision of applying 85 per cent of the income for sustainability and to negate inflation.

6. **Compulsory activity every year.** The code prescribed NPOs to carry compulsory activity every year. It is not possible to carry compulsory activities in the year of no income. Moreover if the NPOs will receive donations or funds at the end of the year it will not be possible to carry out compulsory activities every year.

7. **Amendment of Section 77—100 per cent deductions to Donors.** The new code reduced deduction to 50 per cent for donors. This provision can slow down the flow of donations for

NPOs. Its worthless to state that NPOs are largely depends upon the external donations. Therefore the existing provision of 100 per cent deductions must be maintained.

**8. Amendment of Section 88(2).** Section 88(2) of the code states that cash basis of accounting must be followed by NPOs. This provision is contradictory to the guidelines issued by Institute of Chartered Accountants of India (ICAI) which prescribes accrual system of accounting. It may create accounting issues. Hence Section 88(2) must be amended and NPOs can be given freedom to choose their method of accounting.

### Concluding Remark

From the above discussion and observation it can easily be concluded that provisos of the code is baneful for Non-Profit Organizations. Government might have realized about the misuse of funds provided for such organizations. Moreover the international transparency report raises question on utilizations of funds by such organizations. Hence government is making strict and stringent provisions for NPOs. On the other hand, NPOs argued that the codes will significantly interrupt in discharging their basic objectives. The tough provisions of the code will create lot of problems in present survibility and sustainability in future of such organizations.

Thus Government should make some amendments in the proposed code in one hand and check tax avoidance in other hand. There should be a balance between incentivizing socially relevant work and preventing tax avoidance.

## REFERENCES

Ahuja, Girish. *Systematic Approach to Income Tax*, Bharat Law House Pvt Ltd., New Delhi, 2009.

Chandra, Mahesh and Shukla, D.C., *Income Tax Law and Practice*, Pragati Publications, New Delhi, 2009.

Fogla, Manoj and Patra, Sunil (2010), "NPO-Major Issues Not Addressed in Direct Tax Code". *Standard and Norms*, Vol. III, Issue 5, June 2010.

——. (2010), "Direct Tax Code for NPOs". *Standards and Norms*, Vol. III, Issue 9, September 2010.

Gupta, Sunil and Arrora, Madhu (2011), "Impact of Direct Tax Code on Individual". *International Journal of Research in Economics & Social Sciences*, Volume-1, Issue-1, October 2011.

Rao, M., Rao, G. and Rao, K.R. (2009), "Direct Taxes Code: Need for Greater Reflection". *Economic & Political Weekly*, XLIV (37) September.

Shetty, S.L. (2010), "Mare Tax Concessions for More Inequality". *Economic & Political Weekly*, 2010 XLV (11), March.

Singhania, Monica. *Student Guide to Income Tax*. Taxmann Publication Private Limited, 2009.

### URL Visited

http://finmin.nic.in/DTCode/index.Asp

http://www.pankajbatra.com/india/new-direct-tax-code-dtc-highlights/

http://www.deccanherald.com/content/19934/decoding-direct-tax-code.html

http://www.ndtv.com/article/business/new-direct-tax-code-pay-less-in-taxes-from-april-2011-47396

http://www.etaxindia.org/2010/08/direct-tax-code-2011.html

http://www.moneycontrol.com/.../proposed-direct-tax-code_481425.htm

# CONTRIBUTORS

**Abhay Jaroli,** 4, Jyoti Nagar, Sector 4, Udaipur-313001.

**Alka Swami,** Assistant Professor, Department of Management Studies, College of Eng. and Technology, Bikaner.

**Amitha Singhvi,** Daroli House, Sunderwas, Udaipur.

**Anil Kothari,** Associate Prof., Faculty of Management Studies, MLSU, Udaipur.

**Ashu Khanna,** Asst. Prof. IIT Roorkee-247001, Uttarakhand.

**B.L. Heda,** Associate Professor, Department of Accountancy and Statistics, CCMS, Udaipur.

**Bharti Pandya,** Gayatri Bhawan, Pandya Clinic, 3 K 65, Prabhat Nagar, Sec-5, Udaipur-313001.

**Bhupesh Lohar,** Faculty, College of Commerce and Management Studies, Udaipur.

**Dharmendra Kumar,** Research Scholar, Faculty of Commerce, BHU University, Varanasi.

**G. Soral,** Shree Kriti 14, Tripuati, Annexe, Badgaon, Udaipur-313001.

**Gourav Mandot,** c/o Shantilal Nandlal, 41-neem-ka-chowk, Maldas Street, Udaipur-313001.

**Hanuman Prasad,** Associate Prof. Faculty of Management Studies, MLSU, Udaipur-313001.

**Kamlesh Pritwani,** Lecturer, Government College, Kherwara, Udaipur.

**Kavitha Jayakumara,** c/o Krishnaveni Alur, 151, 3rd Cross, 14th Main, Koramangala 4th Block, Bangalore-560034.

**Kishore Kumar Das,** Plot No. 617, Mahanadi Vihar, Cuttack, Odisha-756121.

**N.K. Pandya,** Gayatri Bhawan, Pandya Clinic, 3 K 65, Prabhat Nagar, Sec-5, Udaipur-313001.

**Naveen Kumar Sharma,** Asst. Prof., Dept. of Management and Technology, Govt. Engineering College, Bikaner-334001.

**Neha Varyani,** 4, New Shakti Nagar, Udaipur-313001.

**Nidhi Bhanawat,** 17, Savina Kheda Road, Sector-12, Udaipur-313001.

**Nidhi Nalwaya,** Assistant Professor, Pacific Business School, Pacific University, Udaipur.

**O.P. Jain,** Assistant Professor, Department of Accountancy and Statistics, CCMS, Udaipur.

**Pallavi Kudal,** Research Scholar, Faculty of Management Studies, MLSU, Udaipur.

**Priyabrata Pandam,** Sankhula, P.O. Naami, Dist. Bhadrak, Odisha-756121.

**Rahul Vyas,** Faculty, College of Commerce and Management Studies, Udaipur.

**Ravi Mandot,** c/o Shantilal Nandlal, 41-neem-ka-chowk, Maldas Street, Udaipur-313001.

**Renu Choudhary,** Associate Prof., Xcellon Institute, Ahmedabad.

**Rohit Bansal,** Research Scholar, IIT Roorkee-247001, Uttarakhand.

**S.H. Indurwade,** Plot No. 17, Anand Nagar, Attrey Layout, Nagpur-440022.

**Shagufta Khan,** Research Scholar, School of Management, Sir Padampat Singhania University, Bhatewar, Udaipur-313601.

**Shilpa Lodha,** 153/10, Ashok Nagar, Udaipur-313001.

**Shurveer S. Bhanawat,** 26, Arvind Nagar, North Sunderwas, Near Jain Temple, Udaipur.

**Sovan Mishra,** c/o Late Damodar Mishra, Jhanjiri Mangla, Tala Telanga Bazar, Cuttack.

**Swati Patel,** Assistant Prof., National Institute of Cooperative Management, Gandhinagar-382007.

**Varsha Maheshwari,** Research Scholar, Faculty of Management Studies, MLSU, Udaipur-313001.

**Veerta Tantia,** c/o Krishnaveni Alur, 151, 3rd Cross, 14th Main, Koramangala 4th Block, Bangalore-560034.

**Vineet Chouhan,** Asst. Prof., School of Management, Sir Padampat Singhania University, Bhatewar, Udaipur-313601.

**Vivek Sharma,** Lal Singh Colony, Radhakishanpura, Ward No. 38, Sikar-332001.

